Formative Spirituality

Volume Six

TRANSCENDENT FORMATION

Formative Spirituality

Volume Six

TRANSCENDENT FORMATION

• ADRIAN VAN KAAM •

CROSSROAD • NEW YORK

BV
4501.2
.V353
1995

1995

The Crossroad Publishing Company
370 Lexington Avenue, New York, NY 10017

Printed in the United States of America

Library of Congress Cataloging-in-Publication Data

Van Kaam, Adrian L., 1920–
    Transcendent formation / Adrian van Kaam.
       p.   cm. — (Formative spirituality ; v. 6)
    Includes bibliographical references and index.
    ISBN 0-8245-1511-0
    1. Spiritual formation.   2. Man (Christian theology).
3. Philosophical anthropology.   4. Spiritual formation—Catholic
Church.   5. Catholic Church—doctrines.   I. Title.   II. Series: Van
Kaam, Adrian L., 1920–   Formative spirituality ; v. 6.
BV4501.2.V35   1995
248–dc20   95-19662
                                                         CIP

Contents

Acknowledgments

I t is my pleasure and duty to express my gratefulness to those who assisted me in the production of this sixth volume of my series. Dr. Susan Muto, herself a highly respected author in the field of Christian letters as one of the sources of my formation theology, coedited this volume with me. Through our discussion and her astute suggestions, the book is much closer to what I envisioned it could be.

I also thank Dr. Marie Baird, at that time an assistant professor in formation science, who read the manuscript and suggested improvements of language that heightened the quality of the text.

Earlier drafts of the tentative chapters were typed and retyped with infinite patience by Carol Pritchard, the then superb administrative secretary of the Institute of Formative Spirituality. I am deeply grateful for her dedication to the production of this volume as a whole. Then, too, the administrative assistant of the Epiphany Association, Marilyn Russell, with the invaluable assistance of Mary Lou Perez, deserves my thanks for putting the finishing touches on the manuscript and seeing it through to the end of production. Last but not least, I must thank Michael Leach and the Crossroad Publishing Company for their belief in this project and its seminal contribution to a transcendent understanding of character and personality formation in the world of science and religion.

Preface

This volume on transcendent formation originated in my dream of bringing people of various faith and formation traditions together spiritually. A yearning for transcendence was born in many suffering people in Europe at the time of World War II. It resulted in my simultaneous initiation of an incipient formation theology with its auxiliary pretheological formation science, its pre-scientific formation anthropology, and its postscientific application. My later work in the Dutch Life Schools for Young Adults in Holland included a further elaboration and more detailed integration of my new insights into traditional transcendent formation.

Further enhancement of this work came with the development of a graduate Institute of Formative Spirituality at Duquesne University in Pittsburgh. All of these works resulted in the cofounding of the Epiphany Association with Dr. Susan Muto, a professor and colleague at Duquesne from 1966 to 1988. This association maintains in Pittsburgh a publication, education, consultation, and archival resource center whose purpose is to protect the consistent unfolding and teaching of the basic original purpose and identity of formation theology and its auxiliary pretheological formation science, both of which I initiated in a more-systematic way over fifty years ago. At present and in the light of the end of the institute phase, the Epiphany Association is at the center of the research, writing, teaching, and speaking activities that assure the continuity of this formational approach.

In Hiding during the Hunger Winter

In 1944, during my summer vacation from the seminary with my family in the west of Holland, the Allied troops liberated the southern part of the country but lost the crucial Battle of Arnhem. That meant that the inhabitants of the northern and western parts of The Netherlands would have to endure German occupation until the end of the war.

The densely populated western regions where I was stranded were in dire straits. Food was scarce. So was fuel for heating during what was to prove to be a particularly cruel winter, the so-called Hunger Winter of 1944–45. Men were deported indiscriminately to work for the enemy in Germany. Families were split apart.

I was caught in this predicament a year before I was to have finished my theological studies. I found myself in hiding with many other distraught people, separated from family and friends. They were thrown intimately together by circumstances beyond their control. Many had nothing in common; they represented a diversity of ideological and religious traditions. Some had lost dear ones in the concentration camps. All were suffering in one way or another. I became known gradually to them as a theology student. Many came to me for spiritual encouragement. These were dark, seemingly hopeless days, and people were in peril of their lives.

Catapulted unexpectedly from the relative safety and security of seminary life into this utterly dissonant situation, I had to find a way to reach everyone on a deeper level of unity. This way could not be exclusively connected to any one religion, for example, to Catholicism, because many belonged to other Christian denominations; still others were Jewish, agnostic, Marxist, and so on.

Luckily for me, in my seminary, as in all those that were Roman Catholic, students were not allowed to study theology before they had followed an intense two-year program in philosophy.

The aim of philosophy was to make the students familiar with what people can know about their transcendent-immanent life by means of human reason. This pretheological approach made it possible for them to communicate about the basics of a spiritual life all people potentially share. In other words, I received at an early age an inkling of how to connect people who normally thought of themselves as disconnected.

Emergence of a New Approach

I soon found out that despite all its benefits the philosophical approach was not enough. It seems no longer effective by itself for the establishment of spiritual bonds between people of various backgrounds. People today are not as familiar with philosophical discourse as educated people may have been in ages past.

What often seems to influence people are the insights and findings of the clinical, human, and social sciences. Most appealing to many are the psychological and educational disciplines popularized in the media, which claim to address their immediate concerns.

I soon realized that a new approach was needed. For long hours, I would ponder the genius of Thomas Aquinas, who showed the need for a pretheological philosophy prior to the formal study of theology. His work had substantially influenced me thus far in my studies. Aquinas, however, could not have developed in detail a systematic empirical-experiential way of thought. What he could and did elaborate was a speculative-philosophical approach. In the thirteenth century, he did not have available, as we do today, social, psychological, clinical, educational, and other empirical-experiential disciplines. Today, these influence everyone either directly, as in therapy, counseling, high school and college courses, or indirectly, as in newspaper columns, novels, movies, plays, radio and television talk shows.

I soon concluded that I could foster spiritual ties among the people hiding with me by appealing to their empirical-experiential mind-set. I decided that it was time to complement the pretheological study of philosophy with pretheological studies in experiential life formation. My approach should be critical toward, yet appreciative of, empirical-experiential thinkers. It would parallel in some way Aquinas's approach to the philosophical thinkers of his time.

In other words, Aquinas's pretheological philosophy had to be complemented by a pretheological experiential science of formation. Thus was born in all its richness and diversity the approach I would later call "formative spirituality," which consisted of formation theology and its auxiliary pretheological formation science.

I found time in my hiding place—a small attic above the stable of a farm in the countryside—to lay the groundwork for these disciplines and to discuss them at length with some university students hiding with me. I often recount those days in books and articles and, of course, in my classes. What happened then continues to unfold in some way every day in my life's work of research, writing, and teaching. My systematic approach had also been prepared for by my presystematic attempt to address similar problems from 1935 onward. It was then that I started with my soul friend, Rinus Scholtes, the prototype Epiphany Association in The Hague.

Time for Lecturing

After the war and a year after my ordination, I was appointed a professor of philosophy in my Dutch seminary. There I was able to convince the faculty that they should add to the courses in philosophy a course in the social sciences in which the students could critique the findings and theories of these disciplines. My hope was that they would be able to distinguish what was compatible or incompatible with their own faith and formation tradition. They would badly need this expertise, for it would be part of their calling to make people in the pews aware of what to accept and what to reject in popularized psychology and education if they were to remain faithful to their own basic beliefs.

This lecturing gave me a chance to work out in more detail my formation science, its underlying anthropology, and my theory of personality. From the beginning, I strove to make my teaching compatible with the Christian faith and formation tradition. I followed in my pretheological formation science the example of Thomas Aquinas in his pretheological philosophy. He criticized and then integrated the compatible concepts of pagan thinkers, such as Aristotle and Plato, in order to use them for the systematization of his theology.

Life School Project

Soon thereafter another opportunity for formation practice presented itself. This proved to be an excellent occasion for the field-testing of my ideas. During the war, a state supervisor of education in Belgium, Ms. Maria Schouwenaars, started a so-called Life School in her country for a small group of young women. Almost miraculously, it escaped the scrutiny of the Nazi regime.

Because of its success, this extensive fall and winter program, often conducted in mills, factories, and company offices and running for three consecutive years, spread widely in The Netherlands. In the town of Gemert, where I taught at the seminary, a similar program was established. It came as no surprise, given my interest in formation, that I was invited to teach one of the two core courses in the program devoted to form-traditional Christian development as applicable to young adults. I based my teaching on my incipient formation theology and its pretheological formation science.

The teaching was so well received that the staff in charge of the Life Schools asked me to outline further how my findings could apply to the aims of these state- and company-supported schools, spreading in so many places in the nation. I also took on the responsibility of establishing in Gemert the first Life School for young men, which was soon followed by similar schools in other towns and cities.

As this work grew, it came to the attention of Monsignor Giovanni Baptista Montini, the then–secretary of state in the Vatican and later Pope Paul VI. Montini called the Papal Nuncio in The Hague asking him to request that my provincial superior make me available full-time for as long as it would take to develop a formation theory behind the Dutch Life Schools.

Schouwenaars and I were critical opponents of psychologism (not psychology), existentialism (not of what is "existential" as different from "essential" in Aquinas's thought). We wanted all psychological and existential thought carefully scrutinized in the light of my incipient formation theology and its pretheological formation science. This led to some division in the Dutch church between extremely psychological and existentialistically oriented people and those who followed us in our more critical stance. The Secretary of State of the Vatican did not deem it wise to exacerbate the division by making his implicit intervention public. Therefore, my provincial, the Nuncio, and I myself had to keep silent at that time about the source of my sudden change of appointment. Understandably, this upset the faculty and administration of the seminary, who in such a case of high-level confidentiality could not be consulted.

Core Courses on Formation

The original intuition of Ms. Schouwenaars was similar to my own during the wartime. We both saw that the basis of practical formation courses taught in the Life Schools had to be two core courses that would be seen as equally important. Together they would inspire and guide the style and content of the practical life formation courses.

One core course had to be about distinctively human formation—a popular version of the pretheological formation science I had conceived during my time of hiding. The other core course had to be about how to live this formation wisdom in terms of a person's own specific faith and formation tradition and their implied formation theology. Both courses were critical of insufficiently appraised psychologism and existentialistic leanings not illuminated by Aquinas's concept of existence.

Ms. Schouwenaars was so interested in this connection and its further development that she came regularly from Belgium to Gemert to teach the core course on distinctively human formation. In dialogue with her, I taught the other course in catechetical formation theology.

Practical Implementation

Courses about more practical formation issues were given around these core courses. They enabled students to implement the formation wisdom gathered in their core courses in the various dimensions of their daily life. They connected well with the spheres of the interformation field paradigm I had developed during the war.

For example, experts in the sociohistorical dimension of life formation gave courses on how people could profit from knowing the history of their culture when it came to creating attractive homes and pleasant surroundings. Experts in law would focus on legal developments that might affect directly or indirectly the formation of one's family life and of one's career in the workplace.

In regard to the vital physical dimension of life, medical doctors and nurses taught young workers how they could implement the principles they were learning in the two core courses in good health care and in relation to human sexuality. Courses in healthy and tasty meal preparation served the unfolding of the vital dimensions in one's family.

The functional dimension of life was served by praxis-oriented courses: how to cook well, how to be effective house managers; how to make repairs; how to dress well and to decorate homes on the basis of the spiritual formation motivation discussed in the two core courses.

All of these courses were seen as a way to give transcendent form to one's life and surroundings. Always the integrating theme was formation, both received and given. This was the thread that would tie together a wide variety of interests and responsibilities.

In regard to the transcendent dimension—the main topic of this volume—the young laborers learned how to go beyond self-preoccupation in genuine care and concern for others, especially their future husbands, wives, and children.

The girls, for example, would take courses in spiritually motivated concern for their makeup, not using cosmetics as a source of excessive self-interest but as an expression of how their love for others inspired them to appear in a gracious and pleasant manner so as to enhance their everyday formative interaction with their husband, children, and other people.

Respect for One's True Vocation

It was also important in the Life Schools to put people in touch with their vocation as one of the basic expressions of their life call. Thus marriage was never praised without giving commendation to the single or to the religious life and vice versa. Respect was shown for the way in which the formation mystery speaks to us in everydayness and in relation to our unique-communal calling as entailing one or the other vocation or vocations over a lifetime.

Call to Connect

From this brief history, I hope it is clear that the development of the Life Schools in Holland and Belgium was linked intrinsically with the unfolding of my formation theory of personality. This theory of mine and its many practical implementations are now being taught in many colleges, universities, seminaries, and other institutes in various countries. To safeguard its original identity and consistent unfolding, the archival, research, consultation, education, and publication center of the Epiphany Association was founded. Deviations from the original theory are understandable and probable with such a great variety of countries and cultures, to say nothing of overloaded teachers with little time for research and reflection due to the burden of school bureaucracies and ever-changing administrations. The Epiphany research and publication center is always available for those who want to return to the original source or update their knowledge about the latest faithful unfolding of the original paradigm, be it in the theology of formation or in pretheological formation science.

I see more and more that this is a theory cognizant of the connections that exist between us and the formation mystery, between us and other people, and between all the spheres and dimensions of our formation field. Briefly, it is basically interformational.

The program of the Life Schools fostered the integration of all aspects of the personality with persons near and far and with the world at large. It helped students and teachers to find peace both during and after the war that had destroyed so much they held dear.

It is my firm hope that this volume, *Transcendent Formation*, will acquaint students and readers with the transcendent path to personal and world peace that was disclosed to us during the terrible winter of starvation, death, and deportation. Our hunger for food may have passed, but our hunger for transcendent peace grows stronger and more poignant with the passing of time.

Part One

TRANSCENDENT FORMATION ANTHROPOLOGY

CHAPTER 1

Transcendent Formation Anthropology

Transcendent Formation

What happens when we try to give form to our life in a transcendent way? What is transcendent formation?

Transcendent formation is the distinctively human approach to the art and discipline of living the good life. It is our unique response to a hidden longing deep within us, a longing I call the transcendence dynamic. The transcendence dynamic is the salt of life; it impels us to receive form and to give form in our character and personality and through them in our world. The transcendence dynamic does this in such a way that we create space for our distinctively human transcendent dispositions.

We cannot at once reach the transcendent peak of human personality. We can only approach it by going through various formation phases. What is distinctively human may only be fully disclosed to us in the final phase of our journey when the transforming mystery elevates us to a state of transcendence unique for each of us.

We are preformed by the mystery of formation as transcendent persons. We are called to give form to our social, vital, and functional ways of life and at the same time to rise above them. The power of transcendence is at the heart of each human existence. How well we allow the formation mystery to actualize this potency in our core form, as, respectively, our centering core, heart, and its matching character, is the ultimate measure of our humanness.

The very ground of transcendent personhood is the unique-communal form of life each one of us is called to disclose over a lifetime. This call is the dynamic impetus to overcome the recurrent paralysis of a human existence tempted time and again to close itself in on itself. The transcendence dynamic, rooted in our will to love, is always forming us; it prepares us for transformation, at least implicitly, even when we deny or ignore it.

Response to Our Transcendence Dynamic

How do we feel when we respond out of our will to love to transcendent inspiration? We may experience awe about being called to so much more by a mystery that surpasses us infinitely. We sense that this mystery is the source of our destiny, thought, movement, and being. The more our character is rooted in transcendent love, the more we experience our personality as flowing from this source.

At times we may feel irresistibly attracted to this love of the mystery in which our call and our love-will originate continuously. At such moments we are not preoccupied with our everyday plans and projects. For a while we forget about controlling people and situations or the management of nature. Such engagements are suspended during a transcendent experience, but not for long. Soon we come down from the mountain top to the valley of daily existence, to the full context of our field of life. This is not to say that we betray our transcendence dynamic and its sustaining love-will. To be sure, we are not yet elevated to the *state* of transcendence. That may happen only in the last phases of our formation journey. Most of the time we are still living and acting on the pretranscendent level. Still we experience instances of transcendent presence. In between such episodes of light, our transcendence dynamic uplifts our everyday living in ways we may not even notice or suspect. It prepares us constantly for our ascendance on the ladder of transcendence. It incorporates the web of everydayness into our spiritual journey.

We learn that transcendence in daily life does not mean running away from the everyday world and its problems. It is not a trancelike openness to a nebulous whole nowhere to be found.

The transcendence dynamic moves all people when they allow themselves to become human in the deepest sense. The degree of transcendence, the horizons disclosed, the spiritual or mystical (not mystifying) experiences that may or may not accompany it, differ in people. Much depends on each one's unique-communal preformation, culture, form tradition, personal history, and form potencies but, also—as we shall see in this volume—on the phase of transcendence in which one finds oneself.

Transcendent experience is a normal human event, yet its acknowledgment may not be as common in our culture today as it was in former times and still is in some other cultures. Mass media, education, public information, popular literature, and the social sciences do not foster the acknowledgment of transcendent experience. They spotlight mainly our socio-vital-functional life.

Many people may become aware occasionally of the transcendent meaning of life. It may happen to them in special circumstances, such as death in the family, a serious illness or hardship, a celebration of marriage, the birth of a child. Fewer persons allow transcendence to blossom beyond that; its fragrance does not permeate the spheres and dimensions of their personality. Their character is not social, vital, and functional in a distinctively human way. It deteriorates instead into a set of socialistic, vitalistic, and functionalistic dispositions and attitudes. Although their life may be filled with fun, it is devoid of deeper peace and joy. Vitalism and functionalism threaten the atmosphere of trust, appreciation, and spontaneity in society and community.

Transcendent Formation and Acceptance of Limits

Transcendent formation sensitizes us to our limits. It inspires us to accept them, to appreciate their role in our pilgrimage to full humanness. Rising above our accepted limits does not happen at once. As we shall see, we have to pass through many preparatory phases. For most of us, it will only be during the later stretches of our journey that we may feel drawn by the mystery of formation to a state of transcendence. This mystery enabled us during many preparatory phases to distance ourselves from anxious preoccupations with our limits. We begin to realize that our limits are not the whole of human personhood.

Transcending our limits does not mean that we deny them. We disclose them and face them. We try to make the best of them. We count them among the signposts pointing us to our personal-communal life call. Affirming them as inspiring disclosures, we no longer feel imprisoned by them. Briefly, rising above our limits means to face, accept, and make the best of them in the light of classical formation traditions.

Transcendent formation reveals to us that we are endowed with potencies that can steer us beyond our socio-vital-functional confines. These borders will no longer dominate our consciousness. Transcendent formation discloses in us a power of peaceful strength rooted in our inmost being, a quiet confidence that lets us face life in equanimity. Transcendent formation is a source of gentle realism, of solidity and earthiness, of fidelity, of appreciative abandonment and courageous commitment. Transcendent formation creates inner spaciousness: we see more clearly what is happening in our life and its surroundings.

Transcendent vision is not of our own making. It flows from our participation in the power of the all-forming mystery, the animating and transforming source of universe, humanity, history, and personality.

Transcendent Formation as Respectful, Gentle, and Firm

A transcendent person is involved wholeheartedly in everyday endeavors while at the same time rising above them. Our embodied transcendent presence to self, others, and the world is beyond all things; yet it situates us in the midst of them, passionately, wisely, and effectively. It puts us in touch with the deepest meaning of cosmos, nature, the environment, events, and things as manifestations of the Most High. It makes us walk the earth in wonder and admiration; it transforms us into poets of transcendence. No longer do we look at others in anxious comparison and competition, which breed defensiveness, anger, envy, jealousy, rage, and violence. These dissonant feelings sap our energy and vitality. Tensions like these can aggravate our mental and physical weaknesses. If we do not overcome our angry dispositions, they may turn inward against our own life or against other people or populations.

Pretranscendent therapies may help us to find a compromise that makes life livable. Because they are pretranscendent, they do not create sufficient space for transcendent formation. Good pretranscendent compromises can keep symptoms of dissonance within manageable proportions. Yet we remain vulnerable as long as we cannot face the deepest root of our deformations. Pretranscendent formation may encapsulate us in a myopic view of life and world, whose ultimate splendor escapes us.

If pressures on our life become too much to bear, violence may again erupt. It may betray itself in subtle forms such as the clever manipulation of self and others. Violent rage can turn inward in self-rejection, self-hate, depression, dissonant guilt, shame, and self-punishment. Excessive tension may explode in discrimination against others who differ from us because of their race, creed, color, status, wealth or poverty, class, or form traditions.

Transcendent formation is a spring of progress, creativity, and consonance. When the power of transcendent formation in love unfolds, rage mellows; reverence, respect, and gentle love take its place. Transcendent formation is a slumbering power of the "will-to-love" deep within each one of us. We cannot compel its awakening. We can only promote or hinder its course, foster favorable conditions or allow unfavorable ones to delay its flight to the heights of humanness. Transcendent formation is a unique human manifestation of an ultimate mystery of all-embracing love.

Walking the Path

To talk about the transcendent life meaningfully, we must first of all follow its path ourselves. Turn to a classical formation tradition. Look at the way it presents the art and discipline of transformation. Do not only study it. Bring it into practice in your own life. At the same time always keep in mind that no discipline in and by itself alone can ever bring us to transcendence. It is only the mystery of transformation that can do that. Stay with the disciplines of the formation tradition you have chosen (as distinguished from, yet sustained by, your faith tradition) as long as they work for you. If possible, go to a person who has walked the path for a long time, who has learned from the masters of the tradition how to sustain others on the right road. Only by walking the way do we get some inkling of what it is all about. Without going through our own journey in the light of a classical tradition, we may not get a true sense of the path of spiritual formation. Personal experience makes us aware of the plots and tricks of our pride form, of the danger of being caught in the subtle spiritual arrogance of gnosticism, or of the many other ways of twisting the life of the spirit.

My formation science, theory, and practice aim at deepening such insights. In my initiation and development of this science, I drew, first of all, on classical formation traditions. I wanted to bring out certain basics of transcendent living which many of these traditions have in common. This makes it possible to talk with people from such traditions about certain basic things we all need to do to grow spiritually. Getting in touch with each other in this spiritual way makes it easier for us to look at one another with love and respect. It also helps us to imbibe other directives of spiritual living that we can share. Often such a breakthrough of new insight attracts us to kindred directives in some of the masters of formation in our own tradition. Few people realize how rich and deep their own formation tradition is, yet experts tell us that the treasures to be found in many classical formation traditions seem inexhaustible. Each symbol of a tradition is a gold mine of numerous possible meanings, interpretations, and explanations in the light of our personal and shared life situations and of our character and personality formation.

Transcendence, Formation Science, and Other Disciplines

In my formation science I try to give an across-the-board, anthropological overview of the basics of all transcendent formation (part one of this book). I do this to make people sensitive to similar findings in other disciplines. These are not necessarily the same as the insights that came to us from our own masters of formation. Usually, these new insights strike us as different from and yet somehow as related to what the masters have said so far.

I want people to realize that other disciplines about life can address the same human experiences they cherish. They will look at what happens to us in their own way. They may confine themselves, for example, to a psychological, psychiatric, educational, developmental, or sociological point of view, or some combination of these. None may look upon experience as formation scientists or practitioners would. Each discipline may bring up one or the other aspect of the same basic experience all these disciplines may somehow touch upon. They do not, however, put their entire interest in the particular aspect of the same experience that concerns me in my science.

The aspect of experience that sets my science apart from other disciplines is service. My concern, posed in the form of a question, is this: How does this new science serve the transcendent formation of our character and personality in the light of consonant traditions? All sciences can shed some light on the same overall experience. They may also touch, in a roundabout way, on the facet of the experience I myself as the initiator of formation science and formation theology hold in the center of my attention. But they will not be so thoroughly, intentionally, and systematically concerned with this peak or summit of personality fulfillment. My development of these new disciplines from 1944 to date, as well as their presystematic development since the initiation of the prototype Epiphany Association in 1935, has occupied my thinking for over fifty years.

Rejection of Kantian
and Husserlian Concepts of Transcendence

Keep in mind that the way in which I use the word transcendence is by no means the same as the way in which Emmanuel Kant and many other philosophers do. Kant holds that the transcendent self goes beyond cognition and the categories of the mind. He states that it belongs to the very essence of the transcendent self to be not only unknowable but also that it cannot be experienced in any way. I do not agree with this premise. It is true, we cannot know our transcendent life directly in a logical, analytical way; it can be known, however, by higher intuitive reason but never exhaustively; it shares in the hiddenness of the mystery of love that makes it be. It surely breaks into the experience of those who have been empowered by the mystery to make enough headway on their voyage of transcendent love. Numerous masters of transformation have written at length about these experiences. They give accounts that strike us as basically quite the same, even if these masters did not know each other, coming as they did from a variety of traditions, cultures, languages, and generations.

Neither should one mistake my own idea of the transcendent "I" for the absolutized subjectivity-concept of Edmund Husserl. The transcendent "I" of my science and its anthropology is linked to the mystery of formation and with the world to which it gives form. We converse with that world through our mind and senses. Going beyond the world does not mean that we leave it behind. Our transcendent "I" can take the world up in its own flight. Guided by the human spirit, it transforms the world; it makes known to us its deepest secret and sacred meaning. Therefore, I make the basis of my anthropology not the highest "I" in and by itself. Nor do I mistake my subjective self as the maker of my world. Therefore, I do not write about the world as merely a field of consciousness. In my science I call it a field of forms, a formation field that is also, but not merely, a creation of our own consciousness.

My idea of this field in all its objective and subjective forms, in all its spheres, dimensions, regions, ranges, and traditions, is the base and starting point of my formation science. I put it in the place of a field of mere consciousness with its subjectivistic connotations. In other words, the transcendent "I" of my science is at the same time immanent. I observed that this "I" interforms in and with the field of life, which shows me its own objective forms. The same mystery that makes me be—independent of my subjectivity—gives objective form to my field of life. I hold that the mystery of all formation allows each human person to unfold uniquely and communally in providential fields of life. These fields enable us to disclose, first of all, the objective forms and meanings they contain. They also make it possible for us to create consonant subjective and symbolic as well as epiphanic forms with which we endow these objective forms. We are called to interform with these fields of objective and subjective forms that are assigned to us as formation opportunities. The mystery keeps calling us to become coformers of these fields and their horizons. By working in, at, and with these unfolding fields, with their formative evolutions and histories, by following their manifestations of the forming love-will of the mystery, we are formed ourselves.

In the seminal period of my more systematic formation science and formation theology, during the Hunger Winter in Holland, I gave the inner "I"-information the name of intraformation or intrasphere (*innerlijke vorming*). This reminder of our inner formation helped me to show my fellow defenders of peace and justice that our resistance to abuse, our stand for social rights and for the famined population, should not make us neglect our inner life. Shaking up people "out there" should also be a shaking up of our sleepy inner life, pulling it out of its complacency. Giving new form to an unjust world implies giving form to ourselves. When we do so in and with the forming mystery, our resistance to the forces of evil in ourselves and others turns into a way of transcendence.

Pretranscendent "I" of the Social, Clinical, and Educational Disciplines

The mystery may grant us a breakthrough to transcendence. The transcendent "I" that I introduced into my science and theology shows us forms of a different kind from those that the clinical, social, and educational disciplines put before us. The forms and structures they bring out in our pretranscendent developmental life carry great weight. They truly matter. They will always be with us. They make us understand our pretranscendent "I," its dynamics and crises. They help us to turn that "I" into an effective tool of what I inaugurated as the concept of our higher "I." Naturally the disciplines that study the pretranscendent life will draw on their knowledge of the structures and forms of the lower "I" when they try to make sense of the transcendent experiences we all have.

I experienced soon that many theorists and practitioners in these fields felt leery and began to hold back when I claimed boldly that the transcendent dimension of the human personality shows us other structures and forms. I wanted to assure them that these forms do not deny or destroy the laws and structures of the pretranscendent life they studied so well. My emphasis on these transcendent structures complements and elevates the pretranscendent structures and their pretranscendent dynamics. I knew I had to follow my call to initiate a new science of transcendent formation that would round off and fill out the disciplines of pretranscendent human development. These two types of disciplines do not stand over against each other; they should enhance and enrich each other. They can only do so if each of them remains loyal to its own focus of inquiry.

Autonomy of Formation Science, Critical Consultation
of Other Disciplines

My formation science on the one hand and the sciences and disciplines about pretranscendent development on the other should keep to their own field of study and practice. The disciplines of pretranscendent development study the psychological, psychiatric, neurological, biochemical, sociological, anthropological, developmental, educational, and other aspects of experience, if they study experience at all. Some of their studies touch on the same experiences that my science looks at from the viewpoint of transcendent formation in the light of classical traditions of transcendent character and personality unfolding. I take their studies into account. The problem comes when pretranscendent disciplines impose their categories on truly transcendent experiences and dynamics as their only full explanation. They may put any spiritual search or experience down as only some kind of compensation or as a case of psychopathology. To explain transcendent experiences, they may reduce them to pretranscendent causes, such as symbiotic union, oceanic feeling, unconscious infantile fantasies, infantile omnipotence, repossession of the early gratifying mother, gratification of infantile sexuality, symbiotic togetherness of prenatal existence, symbiotic reunion or merger with the mother. I do not deny that such distortions of pretranscendent development occur. In my science I protest only against the suggestion that genuine transcendent experiences can be fully explained in such a manner.

We know a lot about such experiences from the observations of numerous experts in spiritual formation spanning more than six thousand years. I do not rule out that some of these historical reports, too, mistake a pretranscendent distortion for a truly spiritual experience. I hold in my science that we can look at all these reports critically, comparing them diligently. We can catch in them a sufficient number of reports by and about people over the centuries who experience and think alike in this matter. They show what true transcendent experiences look like. In their light I look at the same kind of experiences today and come to similar conclusions about them and their aftermath in our everyday life. Personality distortions disclosed by the clinical, social, and educational disciplines today sharpen my perception. They help me to separate fake or imaginary manifestations of transcendence from its true appearances.

Phasic Formation

Once we understand the basic anthropology of the distinctively human transcendence dynamic, rooted in the will to love and appreciate, we can see that our transcendent formation has to progress through successive formation phases (part two of this book). Each phase serves the actualization of a specific innate potency for giving form to a particular dimension of our life. Transcendent formation uses each dimension as a preparation for a well-balanced life that takes into account all the dimensions and spheres of our field of presence and action. The overall dimensional structure of our life may become temporarily unbalanced when a new phase emerges and the familiar flow of the already-established dimensions is discontinued. Our transcendence dynamic, in collaboration with the other dynamics of formation, restores that equilibrium.

The phasic nature of transcendent formation spawns moments of transition between one periodic life form and another. Such moments may trigger a transcendence crisis. This crisis can occur when we feel anxious about leaving behind the familiar supremacy of a previous form of life and venture out into a new, unfamiliar, and unknown form. Each of these current forms temporarily dominates our character and personality formation. What I began to distinguish and name as the periodic life form is a special type of current life form. The emergence of the periodic life form is related to biogenetic changes that take place in us around a certain age.

I distinguish from such periodic phases of life other kinds of current life forms. Our transcendence dynamic utilizes them, too, once we accept them as formation opportunities. These types of current variations in our life are the result of situational changes that are not biogenetic in origin. Take, for example, a change of job or country, the decision to stay single or to marry, the conditions of war and peace, or a change of form-traditional affiliation. Such changes are not necessarily linked biogenetically with our phasic age periods.

My science of formation as well as my formation theology uses the term *phasic formation* mainly when transcendent formation transitions are age-related and linked, at least implicitly, with biogenetic changes. We share such changes with others in our society who respond to similar biogenetic developments around the same age.

I make a distinction, therefore, between phasic and situational current life forms. Both play an important role in our transcendent formation.

The transition process from any current life form to another implies some mourning for the loss of the familiar supremacy of a previous form of life. I postulated that the transcendence dynamic led at the same time to a search for a new way of presence. In my science it is the transcendence dynamic, inspired by our inherent will and longing to grow in love, that elevates this developmental process to a transcendent one. It transforms it into a part of our growth in detachment and abandonment. It enhances our sensitivity to the disclosures of our unique-communal life call in relation to this crossing over process from one current life form to another.

Transcendent Formation and Tradition
My observations brought me to the insight that crises of transcendent formation can happen at any moment of our journey from lower to higher forms

of spiritual life. I noticed how their occurrence can be denied, delayed, facilitated, or precipitated. The war that was the birthplace of my science showed me how a shocking change of life situation can precipitate a transcendence crisis that otherwise would have come later in life. The diary of Anne Frank shows a situational transcendence crisis triggered by her hiding in the annex in Amsterdam from her Jewish family's Nazi persecutors. Such a crisis is not common to girls her age living in a Dutch society under less-extreme circumstances.

I also watched in the people hiding with me how their formation tradition may favor transcendent formation or reduce it to merely pretranscendent development. I saw how a climate of transcendence diminishes the discontinuity of a transcendence crisis without taking it totally away. Such crises within a transcendent environment begin earlier in life, are less striking, and succeed one another more gradually and smoothly.

By contrast, people living by less-transcendent traditions have little time, energy, or space left for formational reflection. In the first half of life, transcendent formation is less facilitated in these traditions than are human development, pretranscendent education, and training in practical skills. All of these are necessary, but often they are not sufficiently linked to the process of transcendent formation. I began to observe, however, how in mid-life, a number of people are compelled by suffering, disappointments, and failures to acknowledge the limits of their social, vital, and functional possibilities. This has led in pretranscendent traditions to the emergence of a new phenomenon called the mid-life crisis. It made me introduce the new idea that the neglect earlier in life of significant transcendent formation can lead to a mid-life crisis. This crisis shows a special intensity and a host of mental and emotional complications less obvious in similar crises in people who live by transcendent traditions. In pretranscendent traditions people in my observation are simply not prepared experientially and affectively for this painful breakthrough of a first experience of finitude and contingency.

The resulting panic in a number of people has turned this crisis—for the first time in history—into an object of study even for sciences and disciplines other than my formation science and formation theology. I also found that a mainly informational and functional adherence to one's transcendent tradition does not lessen the emotional complications of one's mid-life crisis.

Transcendent Formation and the Transcendence Crisis

Many of us experience a transcendence crisis when our social and vital powers and our functional effectiveness are waning. We sense that our life has to find a form that goes beyond our past outlook and attitudes. We are reminded of our mortality and finitude. We do not feel as fit, as keen, or as effective as we used to. We ask ourselves, What is life all about? To find the answer we have to go into a region of our personality where many of us do not feel very much at home. We must turn inwardly to its distinctively human or transcendent dimension. My transcendent-formation science wants to guide people in this inward adventure. It opens them to the possibility of a more inward, peaceful style of living, one that is richer and more rewarding than anything they felt before.

Countless people preceded us in the search for a transcendent life. Many of them described the path they had taken. Some of them did that so well that not only their own contemporaries but also generations after them agreed that their description of the way had general value and could be helpful for all. Their books and formation traditions became classics. In volume 5 of this series, I discussed traditional formation generally. In some of the following chapters, I will take this topic up again, only now even more explicitly in relation to transcendent formation. If one is committed to a classical religious or ideological tradition of transcendence, one should learn from its wisdom as much as one can. Even if we are not able to adhere to any such traditions, it is advisable to consult their deposit of knowledge to profit from the experience and wisdom of generations who sought the way before us.

In a transcendence crisis, life seems to lose its flavor. The daily round becomes oppressive. Weariness takes over. In winter months we cannot see how beneath the cold frosty earth and deep in the leafless trees growth is happening in hiddenness, yet new life is being prepared to burst forth in dazzling splendor when spring arrives again. Similarly, the mystery of transcendent formation is affecting an inner growth in us, no matter how bleak and dead our life in crisis seems to be. The mystery of transformation will shed the darkness of "what we feel" for the light of who we are called to be.

We may discover that we unwittingly keep ourselves in darkness by an overly functional life, by "doing" in preference to "being," by interior noise rather than quiet. If we candidly appraise ourselves, we may be granted the insight that the darkness hides the light of a transcendence dynamic ready to awaken us to the spring of transcendence.

CHAPTER 2

A Unifying Anthropological Vision of Distinctively Human Formation

The mystery of life-in-transcendence can be approached in its fullness by an anthropology that points to my transcendent-immanent assumptions about human life formation. These are basic and universal. Therefore, they cannot be understood by particular empirical observations alone. We need a formation anthropology. In the same vein as a medical, cultural, psychological, psychiatric, or sociological anthropology, so formation anthropology is not primarily a philosophical anthropology.

Many tenets of my formation anthropology can be found in the five preceding volumes of this series. Others are expressed directly or indirectly in the many glossaries I published in the journal *Studies in Formative Spirituality* (1980–1990) and now reformulated in my soon-to-be-completed volumes of a *Dictionary of Formation Science and Formation Theology* (Pittsburgh, PA: Epiphany Books, 1995-1998). This anthropology also comes to light in other books and articles of mine and in those of my colleagues and students, who strive to communicate my ideas to wider or particular audiences. Also, their dissertations and papers written about my work may be helpful in this regard.

The formation anthropology I will unfold in this and the following chapters is not meant to be an exhaustive treatment of my former work. My concern in this chapter is mainly to review my anthropology from the viewpoint of transcendent transformation, the specific topic of this volume.

Loss of a Unified Vision of Life and World

One of the first obstacles facing me when I tried to evolve in my country of birth a coherent formation anthropology was the loss of a unified vision of life and world. This was not always the case. The medieval image of the world, for instance, was marked by a vision of the unity of creation. Human life and its formation-in-dialogue-with-the-world was seen as a self-evident unity. The emergence of many separate, highly specialized empirical sciences interrupted this integral vision.

Each modern science and discipline explores one specific aspect of life and world. What we see happening today is the accelerated development of this trend. More and more specialized sciences and disciplines appear on the scene daily. Each of them focuses on an ever-smaller, particular facet of reality. Each realm of a science proliferates new specialties with their own particular focus of research, metalanguage, and methodology.

In the area of the social and human sciences, arts, and disciplines, one finds, to name a few, education, cultural anthropology, sociology, political science, business and administration, psychology, psychiatry, neurology, semiotics, ethnology, and so on. Each of these already highly specialized fields of study gives rise in turn to numerous new schools and disciplines. These, too, develop their own particular approach. All of them insist on their own autonomy. The same holds for the new science of formation outlined in this and my previous five volumes, the difference being, however, that from the beginning it is designed to be both universal-theoretical and integrational in regard to the whole of transcendent-immanent human formation.

Relative Autonomy

The autonomy of a science should not be absolutized. The reason is obvious. A highly specialized science can abstract only one main facet from the whole of reality or, in this case, from the whole of human formation. It selects such an aspect for highly specialized investigation and subsequent theorizing. Each science should maintain its autonomy and authority within its area of competence. A science violates this principle if it tries to stretch its authority beyond its own field of competence. No science can claim that its partial truth explains all facets of the whole of reality from which it has only taken one particular aspect for exploration. If a science were to claim ultimate autonomy, autocratic authority, or complete self-sufficiency, also in relation to other disciplines, it would make its own autonomy absolute. Such arrogance would imply that the science in question deny that it has only a limited, albeit significant, relationship to the whole from which it has split off its own limited focus of research and theorizing.

Making the autonomy and authority of a particular science absolute leads to a loss of integral vision of the whole of reality or, in our case, of the nuanced totality of human formation. Such denial makes it difficult, if not impossible, for one to see the complementary relationships between the discoveries of the sciences, arts, and disciplines. People who study the intricacies of human formation would no longer realize, for example, what political science or ecology has to do with situational formation; business and administration with ethical formation; art appreciation with aesthetic formation; psychoanalysis with transcendent formation or deformation; pretranscendent education with transcendent formation, yet they all may be striving wittingly or unwittingly after some transcendent form of life within a wide variety of formation fields and traditions.

Specialization and Reintegration

I am deeply convinced that postmedieval sciences should establish their own relative autonomy and authority. I applaud their unique mission. They are called to foster the effective formation of our life and world by exploring and explaining particular aspects of reality in their own right. I believe equally strongly, however, that this marvelous pursuit should be complemented, in this case, by a reintegration of each facet, now better understood, in our total vision of the reality of distinctively human formation as integrated within its formation field and its horizons as a whole.

Often people neglect to highlight the relationships of these new findings to the formation, reformation, and transformation of human life as a whole. Relative autonomy of the sciences is misunderstood by many as absolute autonomy. Preoccupied with the founding and ordering of each single discipline in its particularity, they are insufficiently concerned with the subordination of the findings of each to an integral appreciation of, in our case, the original whole of transcendent-immanent formation of character and personality in interformation with one's formation field and its inherent traditions. My appreciation of such a still-missing systematic account of transcendent empirical-experiential formation is crucial for the balanced formation of human life and world. The cooperation of both specialization and integration holds the greatest promise for the advancement of the distinctively human formation of humanity. A failure of confluence in specialization and integration of human formation may lead in the long run to the self-destruction of humanity and the earth itself.

Signs of a New Spring of the Spirit

At present there are many signs of a new springtime for humanity, of a renewed awakening to the necessity of relating particular fields to the whole of human form reception and donation in this world. Examples of such signs are mounting: ecological concerns; ethical considerations in government, business, and medicine; questions of nuclear waste; outcries for responsible physics, biology, and chemistry. New voices urge scientists to take into account the whole of human life and its cosmic condition. These and similar movements seem to converge in the demand that human life and its field should be given form in accordance with an integral vision. This vision should take into account the whole of reality as formational and as disclosed by classical transcendent formation traditions in dialogue with the formationally relevant findings of sciences, arts, and disciplines. There is an outcry for such a unitary view. I believe that my vision of transcendent human life formation as a whole will provide us with wholesome directives for the implementation and wise application in the human formation field of the formationally relevant outcomes of our pluralistic, specialized avenues of knowledge.

Formation Science and Formation Anthropology

In the light of this hesitant awakening to a more holistic vision, I moved to establish the new science of formation with its underlying anthropology. As I said in the preface to this volume, my idea took its initial, explicitly systematic form during the last year of World War II when I was hiding and working with others in the countryside of the still-occupied western and northern provinces of Holland.

The upheavals I observed in the famined population and its vanishing institutions made me aware of the always-ongoing process of the falling and rising of forms in fields of human presence and action. It made me realize that people are always in a process of giving and receiving form, even in the midst of famine and persecution. In brief, people are always in formation.

Applying that insight to my own life, I realized that I myself was in continual formation and reformation. It was obvious to me in my new hidden life in the attic on top of a stable of a solitary farm, fighting famine and Nazi terror, far away from my usual life as a protected student. I did not stay the same. I became a little more different every day. I found in myself the free possibility to receive or refuse the forming influences offered to me in this wartime situation. If I decided to affirm an influence, I would appropriate its message, making it my own. I would allow it to give form to my life. Yet I experienced also that I did not lose what I basically was in spite of all the changes I underwent. There was something in me that stayed the same. I would experience that I would in some way remain "me," even if I tried at times by mistake to take in some forming influence that was at odds with who I was fundamentally called to be. Sooner or later I would feel an inner dissonance.

In this way I learned to distinguish between what I called congenial and uncongenial formation influences. I came to the conclusion that there was in me something preformed. This lasting foundational form enabled me to assimilate the new formation I received in a fashion that was consonant with who I was deep down. In a sense I became more my own deeper founding life form in the midst of all these new life formations. What happened to me made me want to befriend the mysterious "I" hidden within me. In trying to disclose and articulate this transcendent "I," I soon defined it as our unique-communal or personal-social life call. This experience taught me that I could only address this deepest "I" by becoming involved in the reality around me, by being tentatively engaged in that which is not yet or may never be part of my inmost unique-communal life call.

Giving form to my own life always happens as I give form to something that is not yet me. I can realize my transcendent potential only when I transcend or go, inspired by the will to love, beyond my selfishness, my self-enclosure. I must go out to what I am not. I must give of myself. I must become engaged with people, events, and things, with ideas, works, plans, and projects, that will evoke the best in me and others. I can only become myself when I give content to my life by my commitments to what is not yet me. Then I begin to form my life through them, in them, and out of them. They become truly part of the content of my own life. If I truly care for people, events, and things, they do not remain outside of my unfolding form of life. They expand my own interiority and my own way of presence in my surroundings.

I concluded that every act that gives form to my care for others and for things will give form to my own life. These were ideas that I inserted in my emergent formation anthropology. Another idea that took hold of me was that of formation dynamics.

Dynamic of Distinctively Human Formation

Through all that occurred, I saw a basic striving at work—a striving to give form to my life in the best way I could. In others around me, who communicated to me their problems, I observed the same, often unacknowledged striving. I named this the formation dynamic. Reflecting on its meaning while walking over the wide grasslands or *polders* around the farm where I was hiding, I began to see more clearly in myself and others the disposition to receive and give form in life in a unique-communal fashion. As we do so, our given formation potential becomes increasingly disclosed and consonantly realized in our empirical life.

Around my observation of this dynamic and its conditions, I outlined the basic concepts of my science of formation with its prescientific formation anthropology and its postscientific applications. This science and discipline aims at understanding the formation dynamic, its conditions and modes of operation. The human formation dynamic is transcendent. This means that it makes one strive for what is beyond what one already is. Therefore, I also designated it as the "transcendence dynamic." Anytime I use the term "transcendence dynamic," I want to emphasize that I do not look at transcendence primarily from a speculative philosophical viewpoint but from a dynamic formational empirical-experiential theoretical perspective. I take formationally relevant insights of philosophies into account, but I do not concentrate on their own philosophical focus as such.

Formation Freedom

Formation anthropology, as the word *anthropos* indicates, is about the human form of life or human personhood as a whole and its unfolding. This raises the question: What is the difference between our human life form and the formation of animals, plants, and things?

Let me say a few words first about the life of animals and plants. My formation anthropology assumes that each life is meant to grow over time to the fullness of its own basic form, essence, or nature. This process demands the congenial expression of what is given in this original form. It implies also a compatible adaptation to the environment.

The formation process in prehuman life differs from that of lifeless chemical-physical forms. These are marked by rigid patterns of development. Chemical patterns of unfolding are predetermined. Therefore, we can compute and predict in advance what the formational effect of their components will be. What is missing, however, even in the most complicated physical and biological processes is the factor of creative love and freedom. The risk and vulnerability factor that goes with free self-formation, reformation, and transformation is absent.

When an animal or plant form of life is unable to maintain the proper balance between its own nature and its environment, sickness and death may destroy it. The higher the species of life, the higher and more differentiated its basic life form will be. It has to maintain and express this differentiated form in congenial and compatible ways. The human species enjoys freedom of choice. This factor of freedom thus makes the human form more vulnerable than any other on earth.

Plants and Animal Forms of Life

Plant and animal forms of life develop by means of their own nontranscendent or "non-transcendence-oriented" formation potencies. Some species develop organs of primitive appraisal, of congenial selection, of self-protection, and of adaptive compatibility. They also have certain innate fixed dispositions and directives that automatically lead to effective patterns of behavior for survival. These are called instincts. They go beyond the mechanical uniformity of reactions typical of lifeless, chemical-physical forms. Instincts represent the necessity of nature. The tension of instincts enhances the vulnerability of these higher life forms.

The higher the life form, the more complicated its structures are, such as those of instinctive dispositions. Increased complexity means increased vulnerability. The higher and more complex the life form is, the less safety and certainty these higher forms enjoy. Much can go wrong in complex instinctual and other structures as well as in their conditions for optimal functioning.

Humans and Their Life

The human form of life or personhood has a qualitatively new status, granting it a unique dignity. Person formation distinguishes itself from plant and animal formation by its relative freedom in regard to dispositional development, self-direction, flexible form receptions and donations, and transcendent openness.

Formation freedom is not a problem to be solved or the product of a syllogism or a process of scientific reasoning. We experience our inner formation freedom directly as an inherent aspect of our personhood. Still we can deny or veil that part of our "consciousness-as-persons" that tells us we are free inwardly. We can try to explain our experience in a way that contradicts its evident meaning.

Another question we ought to ask is: How is my formation freedom as a human person related to the formational conditions I meet in my life and its field? How do these limit my scope of personal form reception and donation?

Freedom of personal formation means that I am the source of my formational acts. They do not simply go through me. They have their origin in me. I am their unique source. I am responsible for them. They are the manifestation of my freedom as a human person. This freedom is the ground of my unique dignity and responsibility.

We experience our formation freedom as persons in two ways. The first is the freedom for apprehension, appraisal, and affirmation. This freedom enables us to abide critically with formation opportunities available to us. In this abiding we look at them in comparative appraisal. Then we affirm one or more of them personally as the best opportunity to be chosen for a formational act. The second mode is that of the free, personal expression of our preempirical life form, our unique-communal essence or nature. This is the process by which we can consonantly express our innermost life call or founding form in the core form of our personality as character with its empirical dispositions or virtues. These, in turn, express themselves in life directives, appearances, and acts.

Transcendent and Functional Willing

My observations and reflections in Holland compelled me to develop in my formation anthropology a distinction between free transcendent and free functional willing.

Transcendent willing or the love-will (*liefde-wil*) refers to the supreme facet of our will that is operative in the transcendent dimension of our life. I borrowed the term "love-will" from the soul friend of my youth, Rinus (Marinus) Scholtes. Trusted exchanges with him before his early death during our presystematic pondering of formation questions became a basic source of my reflections in this realm of transcendent experience.

Rinus used the term love-will repeatedly in his intimate conversations with me and in his ascetical-mystical notes. During his ascent through the dark nights of sense and spirit to the heights of mystical espousal and marriage, love-will sustained him in a year of utter desolation and devastating dryness of thought, image, and feeling. Love, in a supreme transcendent sense, becomes for this mystic the simple will to love in the midst of utter detachment. This love-will or purgated willfulness or appreciative abandonment represents the basic consent of our whole person to any consonant appeal in our formation field. To determine the consonance of an appeal, we appraise it in the light of the formation mystery, its inviting unique-communal life call, and our faith and formation tradition. This innermost choice is always rooted in our basic option to trust in the love-will of the mystery for us.

By contrast, functional willing is executive willing. It is operative in the functional dimension of our personality. If our life is consonant, our functional willing is subordinated to our transcendent willing, our higher love-will. Often, however, the functional will takes over. If not enlightened by the love-will, it tends to give rise to coercive willfulness. This diminishes our freedom and clouds our perspective. People who did not advance to their transcendent dimension are usually directed by their functional decisions. These are in part free, but they are not as free as they could be. They still seem to be dominated too much by sociohistorical pulsations, vital pulsions, and willful functional ambitions. They would be more liberated if they were open to their inherent capacity to share in the transcendent love-will of the mystery of formation.

The direction we give to our formation dynamics is also dependent on our free decisions. Each dynamic forming act of ours is only formative in a deeply human sense to the degree that it is a free act. Our freedom is limited by many inner obstacles, especially our coercive patterns of life. We should widen the limits of our freedom constantly. We should transcend increasingly the many coercive dispositions that diminish it. The more the mystery of formation enables us to transcend such coercive dispositions, the more our decisions will be rooted in the transcendent freedom of the love-will, latent in the depths of human personhood. Some measure of freedom of formation is always available to us. This gives human formation its distinctively human character.

Formation freedom has its risks. In our appreciation and affirmation of what may be most congenial and compatible for us, we may lose our way. We can give the wrong direction to our formation dynamic, to be sure, but if we could not go wrong, we would not be really free. We can even be blinded to such a degree that we lose the freedom to see and acknowledge the lack of liberation that should be ours as human persons.

The experience of choosing wrong directions made me aware of a split in the human personality. Our personhood carries the blessing of a hidden nobility and the curse of a source of perversity. We are a unique-communal call of the eternal in the depth of our personhood. This splendid origination in the love-will of the formation mystery is the true foundation of human personality, of its presence and action in all situations, the source of its consonance, poise, and peace. Our hidden splendor is the gift of the openness of our whole being to the Transcendent, who mysteriously permeates our life and world. A disposition of self-centeredness pervades us as well. It veils the radiance of our original form. It gives rise to numerous coercive dispositions, directives, and dynamics. These turn us away from our inmost call to open our love-will to the transcendent mystery and its appeals to our unfolding character and personality.

Because we are beckoned to guide our life by reason and will, our vital instincts are few. These few are far less developed in us than they are in animal life. We lack the natural poise and certainty of direction we find in animals from the beginning. The automatic flow of the processes of the instinctual life is interrupted in us by our power of free appraisal and our subsequent affirmation or rejection of the direction of the vital flow in our life.

Our formation freedom should not make us destroy or deny our vital instincts and their pulsions. Enlightened freedom must give form to such pulsions in the light of the transcendent dimension of our personality and character. Yet, unless and until sufficient subordination is achieved, we may suffer much dissonance, uncertainty, ambivalence, and vacillation.

Freedom and Nature

Human life is fundamentally a call to tradition-enlightened freedom of formation. Our formation journey is not fully determined. To be sure our corporeal existence makes us share in the unfree processes of the cosmos. Therefore, we are in some measure determined by them, yet in many ways we do rise above them. We are not mere products of a blind evolution. Neither are we the fully predictable outcomes of mere psychophysical stages of development.

Lower forms of life are different. They are encapsulated in the finely woven web of nature. Lacking in formation freedom, they cannot know what they are missing or what the whole of nature is to which their programmed formation is subjected. Programmed by nature, they execute in minute detail instinctual life directives. It is precisely in the exercise of our formation freedom that we become aware of nature as a whole. Therefore, we can acknowledge nature as a reality that we basically cannot change, a reality to be reckoned with in the free formation, reformation, and transformation of our character and personality in dialogue with all spheres and dimensions of our formation field and its horizons.

We sense our immersion in a mysterious immense whole in and beyond all things. Yet, unlike lower forms of life, we, as human persons, find in ourselves the power to give names and meanings to this mystery that transcends and carries us. We can flow with it in loving, creative ways. We are able to use in relative freedom natural processes in service of our own projects. Paradoxically, when we acknowledge our limits, we transcend them. Something within us endows us with the power to ascribe a formational meaning to these limits and to the reality they signify. We have the ability to accept reality freely: what is, *is*. We can revere it in free appreciation. We can make it a realistic point of departure in what we sense, imagine, think, feel, and do. In many ways, reality limits and resists our free powers of personal formation. It is in the experience of this resistance that we begin to sense what our freedom as persons really means.

Human freedom is a limited freedom, a freedom circumscribed but not destroyed by everyday reality, a freedom called to flow compatibly yet uniquely with reality.

This disclosure of the true nature of human formation freedom may tempt us to doubt that we are really free. We may feel inclined to believe that like all other forms of life we, too, are totally encapsulated by nature. We may fear that we are merely the prisoner of a few known but mostly unknown determinations imposed on us by fate and nature. We may speculate that we are not really free, that ours is only an illusion of freedom. Based on this belief, we may build for ourselves a whole philosophy of fate and determination, as others have done before us. This deterministic view of life and world may influence the way in which we formulate the outcome of our scientific or scholarly research on the formation of character and personality.

Mystery of the Human Spirit

If we can overcome this temptation, we may ask a few new questions: Granted that I as a human person can freely give meaning to all that is and therewith already transcend it in my mind, what is it in me that makes this possible? What in me as a human form of life or person is different from impersonal forms of life? How do I rise above matter and nature?

Evidently, nature and matter itself as they operate around us in the material universe cannot be the source of our potency to transcend them so dramatically as human persons. What is that mysterious power in our personhood that enables each of us to relate formationally to all that is and to the mystery that underlies and transcends nature everywhere? What name do we give to it? During the formation history of the human race, the source of this possibility has been called by many cultures and many faith and formation traditions the human spirit.

That such a power even exists is shocking from the viewpoint of materialism. Do we not observe the opposite in our laboratories and everywhere in the universe? All material formation is determined by predictable cosmic laws of a chemical-physical nature, isn't it? From a naturalistic perspective the idea of freedom of choice, of free personal self-formation, is an anomaly in this universe of matter and process, an oddity, an unheard-of aberration.

This in-breaking of freedom into a deterministic universe presupposes necessarily a source of power that is different from sheer material cosmic power. It must be an enigmatic potency that lifts human persons above an exclusive determination by cosmic matter alone. This is not to deny that our human form of life or personhood is also corporeal and cosmic. As such it is subject to the forming influences of matter and its chemical-physical processes. But that is not the whole story. Such processes cannot be the only, or exclusive, formators of our character and personality. These processes, insofar as they operate in us, must be complemented and elevated by free transcendent directives that emerge from another source in us.

Such transmaterial directives originate in our human spirit. They give shape first of all to what I have designated as the transcendent dimension of our personality. This dimension interforms constantly with our socio-vital-functional dimensions of life as well as with their interactions with the powers and processes of the material universe-in-formation. In this way the transcendent directives take into account lower directives, also the material ones. These, too, are an inescapable facet of *what is*. As such, they deserve our respectful attention and appraisal. Matter truly matters. Material forms and processes belong to the undeniable points of departure for our free process of personal appraisal. Such an appraisal should guide our effective life in the world. A reverential appraisal enables us to do justice to our form donation and reception in relation to events and things that emerge as significant in our field of presence and action.

Our spirit sets us free from the tyranny of mere matter. It grants us a measure of independence from nature's formators. This independence enables each human person to become a unique, free and loving formative appearance in the universe of matter. Our spirit is a source of its own formation directives for better or worse. These spiritual character and personality directives are essentially different from the mechanical form directives of matter. Yet they can complement the directives of matter, for matter can be made to serve our spiritual inspirations and aspirations. It is our spirit alone, however, that makes us distinctively human persons. Our spirit empowers us to transform nature and matter. In this work of transformation of the cosmos, our spirit moves us to respect the ecological directives we can disclose in each form of interformational matter we encounter in the world.

Our human spirit is not called to be destructive of nature. Ours ought to be a spirit of loving facilitation of nature's consonant unfolding. Nature is a sacred treasure entrusted to the loving care of the human spirit. The free spirit of the human person is meant to be a spirit of transforming love and care for people and nature everywhere. The human formation dynamic is a dynamic of loving and appreciative transformation, a transcendence dynamic. It originates in our transcendent spirit with its love-will and is directed by it. Ours is a spirit of transcendent-immanent love.

Burden of Formation Freedom

The life of the formative human spirit has its own risks, its own peaks and valleys. We may have moments of piercing awareness of the burden of responsibility. We are not allowed to sink blissfully away in the all-nurturing womb of nature. Sometimes we would like to be relieved from the pain of doubt and ambiguity that the freedom to receive and to give form entails. Suddenly we may feel lonely and unnatural in the midst of an overwhelming universe, dense with countless forms and processes of matter. As spirit, we are not any of these familiar everyday material appearances. As spirit, we are a continuous denial of the ultimacy of any of the things and processes that surround and affect us. We may feel like lonely exiles of the cosmos. We experience painfully the nothing-ness of the spirit, our own "nothingness." Initially it hurts. We feel a wrenching estrangement from the things with which we are interwoven so commonly and pleasantly, at times painfully, in our everyday endeavors. We were at home with them from the beginning of our life. As we grow up, however, they are disclosed to us as passing and relative. The ultimacy we have ascribed to them appears to be an illusion.

It is hard to detach ourselves from them because we have made our home in this world. Our familiarity with its daily gifts and assurances gave rise to some of our illusions. It hurts to leave the idealization of one's illusions behind, to leave the light of the day for the darkness of the night of the spirit. We may envy the effortless movements of animals in the wild, the blossoming-without-why of flowers in the meadows. How blissfully ignorant they are of problems and responsibilities, of free appraisals and risky options. How blindly and safely they are embedded in the great maternal web of sheer natural and vital processes.

After such a night of cosmic loneliness, we may come home again to the wonders of nature. We may return in a new way. All nature shines forth with a new radiance for our spirit-enlightened mind. We experience nature as epiphanic. It reveals to us as spirit the presence of the mystery that makes us and all of nature *be* and that calls each of us by name.

Spirit and Personhood

The word *person* comes from the Latin *personare,* which means "to sound through." The Latin term *persona* was used for the mask through which the actors in antiquity spoke their lines. In formation science, I speak analogously about the apparent life form. The mask represented the character in the drama acted out by the actor. The voice, sounding through the mask, made the person represented by the mask come to life.

This origin of the word *person* can guide our reflection on the relationship between spirit and personhood. In the measure that we allow our spirit to sound through our life, we are spirit-filled persons. Our mask of vital matter comes alive as a channel of our spirit. We are persons to the degree that our human life is transformed by our spirit. Our spirit transforms us through the transcendent dimension of our existence. It is our spirit that forms and articulates the transcendent dimension of our fleeting life.

Through our spirit we come in our transcendent dimension to candid self-transparency or self-presence. Our spirit awakens us in our transcendent dimension to hear in candor our call to free formation—a distinctively personal formation free from enslavement to matter and its processes; a formation free from coercive dispositions, from dissonant social pulsations, vitalistic impulses or compulsions; a formation rich in consonant transcendent ambitions but free from the pressures of mere functionalistic ambitions.

Our spirit makes our transcendent dimension also grow in awareness of the uniqueness of our incomparable transcendent-immanent life call as human persons. All of this makes the transcendent dimension the home of the spirit, the origin, the birthplace, the womb of personhood. We become really persons insofar as we first of all allow our unique personhood to be formed by the spirit in our transcendent dimension. Second, we become persons insofar as this unique personhood penetrates and transforms all of our life through our core form. This makes us really "per-sonal"; it enables us to "sound-through" our mask or through our apparent forms of personality. We become epiphanic personalities. Through our apparent forms, the mystery of our unique-communal transformation of character and personality begins to shine through epiphanically.

Uniqueness and Individuality

The uniqueness of our transcendent destiny ought not to be confused with our individuality. Individuality can be found in all living things. Each particular animal has its individual blueprint. My individuality goes beyond my fingerprint or voiceprint or the individuality of my DNA. Individuality extends itself on the vital-functional level to our humanly developed talents, aptitudes, inclinations, interests, and preferences. Yet I assume in my formation anthropology that uniqueness goes beyond all of that. Reflection on my experience and that of the people with whom I was hiding during the Hunger Winter compelled me to formulate a distinction between uniqueness and individuality.

Uniqueness, in my thinking, belongs to the transcendent dimension of personality. It discloses itself over a lifetime as our unique-communal life call. This uniqueness may or may not include the development of certain individual preferences and potencies. The life call will not destroy or deny our individual characteristics. What it might demand is the sacrifice of the development of certain individual abilities. For example, in a war situation in which one has to serve the survival of starving or hunted people, the pursuits of certain individual talents may not fit what one is meant to be here and now as this person in this providential life situation.

Therefore, the ultimate aim or norm of holistic formation guided by the spirit can never be mere individuation. Of course, consonant life formation has to take into account what is individually given. It is a realistic point of departure for the appraisal of all factors in our formation field. When the development of some of our individual talents happens to be in consonance with our unique life call and its demands, we ought to follow them. No matter what we do, however, with our individual gifts and idiosyncrasies, we should not succumb to individualism.

CHAPTER 3

Anthropology of
the Founding Form of Life

Our aspiration for transformation is first of all apparent in what I introduced in my formation anthropology as our *integrating forms* of life. These enable us to integrate—to bring together—what otherwise would remain a jumble of dispersed thoughts, feelings, actions, and particular research and partial theories. My proposed integrating forms are, respectively, the founding, core, current, apparent, and actual forms of our life. Each of these forms is a way of holding together what we love, want, feel, fear, hope, plan, think, say, do, research, and write about.

Our *founding form* or life call as disclosed in dialogue with the spheres and dimensions of our formation field in the light of transcendent formation traditions is the ultimate and deepest way and norm of our empirical-experiential integration. All other lower integrational forms should become more and more compatible with each other in the light of this fountain of the full meaning of our personal-communal existence.

First among these four main subordinated integrational forms is the *core form,* operating as, respectively, the centering core, heart, and matching character; it holds together the basic dispositions and affections of our personality.

The second subordinated integrational form is the *current form* of our life. It tries to harmonize our current ways of doing things. Our current form as integrative aims also at consonance with our unique-communal life call as disclosed so far. As long as these forms remain current, they are not yet enduring character dispositions or lasting virtues.

The third subordinated integrational form is our *apparent form.* It aims at the integration of the many ways in which we appear in daily life to ourselves inwardly and to others outwardly. These ways include the roles we have to take up if our life is to be compatible with the consonant demands of the society in which we are called to be effective. It is our *apparent form* that makes us socially effective. We must *appear* in adaptive ways but always in congeniality with who we are called to be. Our social appearance should not be a betrayal of who we most deeply are. What I define in my formation anthropology as the dispositions of call-appreciation and of firm and gentle call-assertion or affirmation is as critical in our appearances as in every other form of our life.

Our *actual form* of life is the fourth subordinated integrational form of our life. It guides the way in which each of us in an actual situation brings together what in our foundational, core, current, and apparent forms is relevant to our coping with the actuality of our lives here and now. Each integrational form has to participate in the transcendent transformation of life as a whole. All are, therefore, subordinated forms.

In this and the following chapter, I will consider the formational anthropology of the founding life form. In subsequent chapters of part one on transcendent formation anthropology, I shall reflect on the other subordinated integrational life forms in relation to our transcendent formation. Some of these forms, like the core and the apparent, require more extensive treatment. Hence, I devote special chapters to them. The other two forms (current and actual) can only be understood in relation to the founding, core, and apparent life forms. Therefore, I will deal with them in connection with the latter.

Our Founding Life Form

The founding form of our life is the mysterious ground of our unique-communal existence. It is the basic orientation, the providential direction, of our very being. Therefore, I call it at times our providential form. This most elementary orientation can be expressed in the countless empirical forms of life we freely and creatively initiate and foster during our formation journey. Love, peace, wholeness, and happiness elude us to the degree that these empirical forms, no matter how splendid they may be, are at odds with our deepest orientation, our love-will, and with the consonant transcendent traditions to which we have committed ourselves.

The providential depth direction of our life is not directly open to our experience. It discloses itself only gradually in the light of everyday living. Consonant faith and formation traditions illumine these experiences. They help us to envision them as transformational. Because this founding form is not directly available to our observations, we cannot elucidate its dynamics by mere empirical study. We surely cannot empirically unravel its mystery of loving transformation. However, insofar as these basic dynamics somehow become expressed in our empirical form of life, we can examine them in an empirical way.

For example, we cannot *empirically* elucidate the rootedness of our founding form in both a cosmic and radical mystery. We can, however, elucidate experientially the aspiration of the love-will of humans for the "more than." Having done this, we can then trace this yearning anthropologically to an underlying founding form of life and even point to its transforming power.

Universality of Founding Forms

One of the basic assumptions of my formation anthropology is that all beings in the world have some kind of dynamic ground form, nature, or essence that directs their ongoing formation.[1] But only humans have a unique-communal personal ground that itself is transcendent.

For example, the grounding form or essence of an oak tree gives direction to the growth of the tree. It assures that the growth of the tree in all its subforms of leaves and branches is a consonant expression of the "oak-ness" of the tree. Therefore, no matter how many individual variations of its subforms may appear, the oak never becomes an evergreen or a eucalyptus tree. Of course, the founding forms of such subhuman creations as trees are not open to conscious transformation-in-depth as human forms are.

In subhuman forms like animals, trees, flowers, rocks, and chemicals, we observe expressions of their ground form in their subforms. These expressions are necessarily congenial with their founding form. A dog that is not congenitally deformed or maimed in an accident will develop four legs and a canine tail. The same does not apply to the transcendent human life form. Because our life form is relatively free and unique, it can refuse its founding form full expression in its empirical forms of life. We can choose to be uncongenial instead of congenial with our unique-communal life call. As distinctively human beings, for instance, we are called to grow in mutual care and respect. We may refuse to express this directive in our life and instead become oppressors of underprivileged people. This will make our transcendent dimension less receptive to the transforming power of the mystery.

Origin of Founding Forms

Anthropologically, we can ask ourselves from whence do these founding forms and their dynamics emerge? Expressing themselves in our empirical forms, are they themselves the expression of something else? Different ideological and religious faith traditions posit different answers to these questions. The humanistic faith traditions that underlie, for instance, the Freudian, Jungian, or behavioristic answers to these questions are different from those of the Jewish, Christian, Buddhist, Hindu, or Islamic faith traditions. The subsequent formation traditions rooted in these various faith traditions will also be different. I want to keep the anthropological assumptions of formation science—before its articulation in various faith and form traditions—as basic as possible. I say simply that the source of all forms and formations is a mystery that we call the mystery of formation and transformation. The expressive

[1] I use the term *formation* for nonhumans when I look at them from the viewpoint of their relatedness to the formation mystery. They themselves cannot be aware of their place in the all-transcendent and all-embracing formation design, but we can. This formational view is an option. Others may opt for a merely evolutional-developmental view.

dynamics of this love-will of the formation mystery could also be called epiphanic. (The word "epiphanic" means the appearance of a higher light, power, or mystery.)

All founding forms are epiphanic expressions of this love-will of the mystery, each in its own way. We assume that each form, also each subhuman form, is empowered by the mystery to express some trace of itself. The founding human form of life, however, is not only a trace but a form of likeness to or image of this mystery. This founding likeness to a higher power implies a demand by the mystery that we follow a path of consonant unfolding in the light of our call to deepening alikeness with its forming aim for our life. This will create room for transcendent transformation. My anthropology of distinctively human formation starts out from this providential human form of life. I cannot experimentally verify this anthropological assumption or quantify it mathematically. I can only point to the empirical-experiential manifestations of transformation as witnessed to unanimously by numerous masters of formation over all centuries within a tremendous variety of cultures and traditions.

The dynamics of each unique-communal form of human life are not like those of subhuman founding forms, such as those of plants or chemicals. Foundational human forms endow each human life with the freedom to create in some measure its own empirical dynamics, directives, and dispositions. In some way, therefore, the dynamics of our empirical life will be original, new, and unpredictable. To the degree, however, that our ongoing formation becomes more and more consonant, they will be congenial with the basic overall directives of the unique founding form of our life and of the transcendent traditions that guide the disclosure of its calling. They will then serve the advent of the gift of transformation.

Transcendent Aspiration for Consonance

Human nature aspires after peace and joy. Without taking away suffering and pain, the joy of the love-will can remain in the core of our being. For this to happen, it is necessary that we attain consonance within and without. This is only possible if we grow in harmony with the love-will of the mystery. In response to this aspiration, we are initially inclined to seek substitutes for the mystery. We are unable to go beyond these "lesser beyonds" by our own powers. We must flow with the transforming gifts of the mystery. The experience of our insufficiency makes us reach out to its saving power. The human form of life, therefore, transcends itself the more it becomes consonant with the mystery. The more consonant we become, the more we will be detached from our dissonant coercions. We become a participation in the love-will of the mystery itself. It alone is the transcendent source of the fullness of peace and joy. To be present in love to the mystery is to be on the way of transformation.

To be distinctively human is to transcend oneself without extinguishing oneself; it is to be abandoned to the dynamics of the mystery and yet to be bound to the finiteness of a unique-communal human journey. To the degree that the dynamics of consonance gain in power, the dissonant dynamics of the autarkic pride form lose their hold on our existence; the way to abandonment to the love-will of the mystery is no longer blocked by the obstacles of our willfulness.

Metalinguistic Considerations

I often use in my formation anthropology the terms "epiphanous" and "epiphanic." What do they mean? From whence do they come?

The term "epiphanous" points to the potency of all appearing forms to manifest to us something of their mysterious source and its attributes.

The term "epiphanic" refers in my formation anthropology to the dynamic workings of the forming mystery, its energizing of the field, its empowering of our life by its love-will, enabling our human existence to coform itself and its world in candor, congeniality, compatibility, compassion, competence, courage, justice, peace, and mercy. The forming mystery is epiphanic insofar as it appeals to our potencies for form donation, conservation, and erasion. These latter terms, too, should be examined for the meaning they have acquired in the context of my formation anthropology.

My terms "form conservation" and "erasion" are used here for the first time. Hence, they need some interpretation. The dynamic operation of both the formation mystery and our particular formation cannot be restricted to form donation. Once a form is given, formation energy and direction must *conserve* it for as long as it is consonant with our founding form, with the love-will at its base, with our transcendent traditions, and our field of presence and action. Hence, the term "form conservation" and the phrase "form-conservation dynamics" are both related to the verb *conserve,* which comes to us from the Latin *con,* meaning "with," and *servare,* meaning "to keep" or "to save." "Conservation" and its Latin roots are closely related to the verbs "to save" and "to serve." The forming mystery saves, serves, and sustains all forms in the universe in their actual or potential consonance. We ourselves are called to save, serve, and sustain such forms in and with (*con*) the saving mystery and with the classical transcendent traditions in which the mystery instilled at least a significant part of its transformative love-will and wisdom.

The same formational intent implies that all forms of thought, word, and deed that are no longer consonant should be eliminated, usually in a gradual fashion, through a gentle but firm erasion in service of consonant reformation and transformation.

I derived my terms "erasion" and "erasion dynamics" from the Latin *radere,* meaning "to scrape." *Radere* gave to the English language also the words "abrasive," "raze," "razor," and "eraser." Scraping provides us with a striking image of the slow and repetitious dynamics of eradication by the power of the love-will. For instance, it takes a long period of time to erase the power of dispositions that are deformative. Such would apply, for instance, to racist dispositions. This particular erasion would be a necessary preparation for the gift of transformation into a transracist respectful generosity for all human beings.

Anthropology of the Dynamics of the Formation Mystery

The formation mystery comprises the comprehensive dynamism of a formation process going on always and everywhere. It operates in everything. Therefore, we cannot disconnect this all-pervasive dynamism from anything we know. Otherwise, it would no longer represent the whole of all actual and possible formation dynamics; some form or formation would remain outside of it. We cannot withhold anything—our own form and formation dynamics included—from the all-encompassing mystery of formation. We should not see ourselves as if we were standing outside the universal formation dynamism of cosmos, humanity, history, and traditions.

We cannot look upon the universal dynamism of formation as outsiders observing some alien object. Instead we should celebrate our participation in the all-forming mystery. Permeated by its power, no thoughts or deeds are excluded from its presence. Any formation dynamic in us or in our field is in some way involved in the cosmic and transcosmic dance of form reception, donation, conservation, erasion, reformation, and transformation. A merely abstract viewpoint will never bring us near to the mystery of formation and to the sense of awe-filled love in which we may experience in faith its self-disclosure within ourselves and all things.

The comprehensive universality of the dynamism of the formation mystery would also make it impossible to apprehend and appraise it from the perspective of positive science alone. Neither can we fully understand it from our involvement with the particular formation dynamics we experience in our own limited field of presence and action. We need the widest possible anthropological understanding.

All this does not mean that there is no way to be present to this mystery or that its dynamics would be irrelevant to our concrete formation and its understanding. On the contrary, its dynamics are essential to human formation. Over the millennia, the transcendent faith and formation traditions of humanity have generated directives that can facilitate our abiding with and within this mystery.

My pretheological formation science as a human science cannot elucidate the intrinsic dynamism of the radical mystery itself or how it creates, maintains, and permeates the cosmic and historical epiphanies of this mystery. What my science can elucidate are the dynamics of our experiential participation in this mystery. It can also clarify the empirical ways in which we welcome its dynamic radiation in our daily formation of life and world. It can point to our hunger for transformation by this mystery. Such an anthropology can address the radical source of these dynamics without disclosing its deeper secrets.

The atrophy of the sense of awe, human greediness, the need for power, the idolizing of technocracy, of mere utility or vital pleasure, the resentment toward anything that cannot be controlled or quantified—all these factors have paralyzed in many people the spiritual potency to abide within the mystery in humble, loving receptivity. An anxious bureaucratic and statistical contraction of life can make us myopic. An insular stand may lead to an arid existence untouched by the full power of the human spirit and the love-will hidden at its very roots.

To relieve this aridity is not a question of reason alone. Rather, it is a basic option of the will to abandon oneself in trust and awe to the mystery. We cannot escape its might. We can only refuse to flow with it, to acknowledge it in awe. Subsequent to this refusal, we can abuse the formation energy flowing into us from the mystery. We may use it only for our own pretranscendent purposes and projects.

Insulation of Empirical Formation Dynamics

The autarkic pride form veils our unique-communal call. It gives rise to contradynamics that try to absorb and use the energy flowing from our founding life form. The pride form directs this alienated energy toward its own self-centered projects. It insulates them from our foundational dynamism, exalts them in their own right, and finally totalizes them as if they were the basic foundational dynamic of human life itself. Therefore, in my anthropology I designated this autarkic form as the quasi-foundational pride form of life.

Such erratic contraction or imprisonment of the energy of our love-will in insulated pride dynamics vitiates the receptivity, flow, and flexibility of our distinctively human dynamism; it generates dissonance and deformation.

Anthropology of Expression Levels

Each dimension and sphere of our life participates in its own way in the expression of the image of the mystery in our life. I distinguish six expression levels in my formation anthropology. They are:

1. The transcendent-functional and the transcendent expression.
2. The functional-transcendent expression.
3. The functional expression.
4. The vital expression.
5. The sociohistorical expression.
6. The field expression.

Anthropology of Transcendent Expression

Our providential life form is unique, preformative, filled with the love-will, and initially preempirical. To give form to human existence, this grounding form needs first of all the mediation of our human spirit. The human spirit—transcendent mind and will as illumined by the mystery—must give form to its own transcendent dynamics in congeniality with our providential life form. These dynamics imply the embodiment or implementation of our transcendent directives in all dimensions of our life. All of them are subordinated to our transcendent dimension. Foremost among them is the functional dimension, for it directs and organizes our pretranscendent life as a whole.

In the beginning we may be closed to our transcendent possibilities. We may seek for a merely functional-vital self-actualization. Later we may discover the beauty and power of the gifts of our transcendent love-will. We may then be tempted to use them for purposes of functional individuation only. We become stuck in the functional-transcendent dimension instead of rising to the transcendent-functional dimension. This is a major obstacle to loving transformation.

I fostered the formation of this transcendent expression and implementation in my courses of spiritual formation in the Dutch Life (formation) Schools for Young Adults shortly after the war. I offered them a kind of catechetical version of my formation theology.

Anthropology of Functional Expression

The functional expression or implementation of the inspirations of our grounding form demands our competent functioning in encounters with persons, events, and things in our field of presence and action. For example, we may be inspired to promote social justice. The inspiration can become effective, functionally speaking, if I, for instance, as a lawyer, develop competence in court battles in defense of oppressed people.

Our functional expressions should become more and more congenial with our unique, distinctively human form, willed and carried by the love of the mystery, and its expressions in our spirit. We should live our transcendent traditions with transcendent love. Then our functional dynamics and directives will become increasingly transformed by the formation mystery. Our functional ambitions begin to serve transcendent aspirations and inspirations. The latter gradually transform these ambitions without destroying their relative autonomy. For example, the profane ambition of Thomas Merton to become a famous author was gradually transformed into the ambition, inspired by the transcendent love-will, to serve the mystery and its dynamics in self and others. He did so by competent publications about inchoate presystematic concepts of what I call transcendent formation.

In my formation theory about the program of the Dutch Life Schools I referred to the transcendent-immanent courses of cooking, sewing, home repairs, practical child care, responsible attractive makeup as functional expressions of the spiritual life inspired by our unique-communal call.

Anthropology of Vital Expression

The graced expression of our providential form on the transcendent and functional levels of our life affects our vital inner and outer bodily dynamics. It fosters a more relaxed flow of the organismic dynamics I call "pulsions" in my anthropology. It also manifests itself in the formative movements and expressions of our observable bodies. The resulting gentle yet firm lifestyle will make our bodily dynamism more gracious. It will be less subject to symptoms of premature aging, distress, and overexertion. This presupposes, of course, that there are no other genetic or somatic sources of such symptoms. This vital expression gives form also to our vital neuroforms, as I shall show in other chapters.

In other words, within the genetic and environmental limits of our individual vital form potencies, we will become the best expression of the mystery we can be vitally. For example, many paraplegics have become radiant examples of courage, joy, and self-forgetfulness. Within their physical limits they did better than those who gave in to discouragement. Obviously, this expression prepares the way for a transformation of our body that, in the conception of many historical formation traditions, will reach its fullness only in the life hereafter.

In my formation theory used at the Dutch Life Schools, I referred to the courses in sexuality, medical care, food selection, preparation, and diet, cooking, exercise, and makeup—all rooted in the formative spirituality of the schools—as graced vital expressions of the spirit with its love-will serving ultimately the transformation of the body.

Anthropology of Sociohistorical Expression

I call sociohistorical dynamics "pulsations." For such dynamics pulsate continuously in our society and history. They are kept alive by narration, myth, symbol, education, and the media.

Pulsations give form to many facets of the inter and outer spheres of our formation field. They affect us also personally insofar as we make them our own. Such appropriation of pulsations is preceded by our appreciative apprehension and appraisal of them. Both apprehension and appraisal can be illumined by the expression dynamics of our founding form as guided by our transcendent traditions. The same transcendent dynamics have already expressed themselves appropriately in our spiritual, functional, and vital dimensions. Through the latter they may express themselves in our sociohistorical appreciative apprehension. This enables us to select wisely, and to appropriate diligently, consonant sociohistorical pulsations. By the same token, dissonant pulsations will be depreciated in the light of our distinctively human life call as disclosed in the light of our transcendent traditions.

The result of such expression dynamics will be a participation in history and society that is enlightened by transcendent wisdom. It will be consonant with our unique-communal call by the formation mystery. For example, the socio-historical pulsation for women's rights may have generated in us a disposition either to use diplomacy or to do battle in this area, depending on our basic makeup, life call, transcendent tradition, and subsequent lifestyle. The disposition of sociohistorical consonance readies not only us but also human history and society for the wonder of transcendent transformation.

In my theory of formation and interformation, offered at the Dutch Life Schools, I referred to the expression of this sociohistorical dimension of my basic interformation program. I pointed to the courses in family-related law, in interformation with town and country, and in historical formation traditions as fostering the sociohistorical dimension of a holistic spiritual life.

Anthropology of Field Expression

The dynamics of our providential form express themselves not only in the aforementioned dimensions but also in the basic comprehensive spheres of our formation field. Evidently, they affect our intrasphere, the domain of receiving and giving form inwardly to our sensing, intuiting, thinking, remembering, imagining, and willing. They affect also our interformation with others. The more our field dynamics are competently congenial and compatible with our basic dimensional expression dynamics, the more our interactions with others will become gracious, peaceful, and joyous. The inspirations of the spirit will engender a childlike openness, a relaxed attentiveness, a loving presence to where we are here and now. Within the limits of our form potencies, the dynamics of facial expression, language and gesture, movement and bearing will become serene yet animated manifestations of the formation mystery we are called to express uniquely in all realms of life.

The dynamics of our providential form express themselves also in the life situation or the local outer sphere of our field. Our surroundings will express who we are uniquely called to be. The way in which we arrange our home, workplace, and recreational environment will manifest our interiority as influenced by our fundamental providential dynamics and traditions. Our life situation, if consonant, will increasingly carry the signature of our preformed nobility.

When we express the dynamics of our basic human dignity in our successive life situations, we participate in the dynamics of consonant world formation. We share the dynamism of distinctively human dignity with countless others. All of them are called to give form to this earth over the millennia. Each one of them is destined to do so within one's own formation field in cooperation with the formation mystery.

Consonant world formation implies courageous care for the economic, political, and cultural conditions of peace, justice, and mercy that facilitate the receptivity of the world population for transcendent transformation. In my transcendent-immanent formation theory of full field spirituality, offered at the Dutch Life Schools, I pointed to the courses in aesthetic home arrangement in dialogue with the culture. I mentioned also the critical courses in appreciation of our own and others' fields of formation as linking us with the wider world. These courses fostered the expression and implementation of the basic spheres of my interformation paradigm for the expression and implementation of a holistic full field spirituality for young women and men in the world.

CHAPTER 4

The Founding Form
and Transcendent Formation

My formation anthropology further assumes that every person is endowed with a unique-communal life call, founding form or image of the mystery of formation, sharing in its very ground the love-will of the mystery. Deep down human life wants to transcend the tyranny of our attachments to security, pleasure, satisfaction, and power. Only a mysterious power of love, greater than we are, can achieve such liberation by true transformation.

This higher power, this supreme love-will, transforms our life as a whole without destroying anything that is good in it. We talk, walk, work, share the lives of others, eat, drink, have fun, and suffer. We drive, take the bus, travel, and plan our days. Much seems the same, yet everything is different. A new meaning discloses itself. It transforms what we are thinking, feeling, doing. Everyday events begin to light up for us as allowed by a mystery that embraces us lovingly. We live everything in a new way.

Transcendent-immanent formation is a transformation not only of one or the other isolated facet of our life. It is a change of our life as a whole. Transformation is an answer to our aspiration for wholeness, for having it all together, for consonance with all that is.

According to my 1944 formation paradigm, this original form of human personhood finds itself from the beginning embedded in a complex web of given sociohistorical, vital, and functional conditions that serve to embody our unique image of the mystery in our embodied character and personality. The unique image of the mystery that we are is individually embodied in us at conception and birth. Sociohistorically, every emergent human life finds itself always, already from the first moment, influenced by a given *formation field* of family, neighborhood, culture, ideology, or religion. Vitally, each new life is preformed by genetic inheritance. Functionally, it is preformed by innate aptitudes, related potential strivings and ambitions, and given environmental opportunities for skillful functioning or the lack thereof. All of these together coform, in the light of our overarching transcendent unique-communal life call, our founding form of life.

In some way this ground form or basic life design—with its concomitant original incarnational dimensions—will direct our formation throughout our life from birth to death. What is given initially will somehow influence our further unfolding. Neither this foundation nor the reality of our field of life can be denied. Both have to be taken into account. How we deal with this reality during our formation journey depends on our freedom. But this freedom of formation is not absolute. It is always situated. This means that it has to dialogue wisely not only with the present but also with the early influences on our life. Therefore, I refer at times to our formation freedom as a finite dialogical freedom. Human persons ought to exercise their formation freedom always in dialogue with their present and their original founding situation. This dialogue is usually implicit or prefocal. It should be focal when a new situation demands an explicit appraisal in depth.

Transcendent Dimension of Founding Life Form

What concerns me in this volume is the transcendent dimension of life, the dimension of the unique image or call deep within us with its personal sharing of the love-will of the formation mystery. I shall consider formation anthropology insofar as it touches on our *transcendent* dimension of personality and on its relationship to the transformation of our *pretranscendent* personality. Our pretranscendent personality is our personhood insofar as it is not yet transformed by our transcendent-immanent personality dimension. This transcendent dimension is more fully open to our founding form or unique-communal calling.

Our founding life form as transcendent is rooted in and suffused by the mystery of formation. This mystery of transforming love dwells in each of us formatively, no matter where we are on our journey or what we have done. Usually we are ignorant of this source of loving transformation at the ground of our personality. The mystery of life itself may awaken us to this deepest reality of our fleeting existence on planet Earth. We become aware of this awakening by abiding in attentiveness to its epiphanies in our field of forming influences. The more we awaken, the more we abandon ourselves in love to what announces itself in this awakening. Thus are we empowered to live in consonance with the unique love-will of the forming mystery for our transcendent character and personality unfolding. All people want to be liberated in some way from their socio-vital-functional coercive dispositions, directives, and patterns of action and to rise to the joy and freedom of the transcendent life.

A number of classical traditions seem to have in common a certain pointing to the basic presence of a mystery of formation appealing to our transcendent founding form of personality, willed in love by this mystery. They seem to point in different symbols and images to the concept I have initiated in formation anthropology as that of our transcendence dynamic. In all of us slumbers a hidden aspiration, a longing to go beyond the limitations of a mere socio-vital-functional personality. The best in us aches to be liberated from coercions that deflect and deform our longing for lasting love. Our transcendence dynamic is a reaching out for beatitude, bliss, or happiness that may fill us with a peace that goes beyond our encapsulation in the life of our senses and functional analytical reason alone.

Transcendent and Pretranscendent

My formation anthropology does not look at the transcendent founding form as if it were something separated from my everyday personal presence in this world. It is not an impersonal thing that I "have." Rather, we should experience it as what I "am," as our dynamic deepest "I." For it is "me," not something else. This transcendent "I" is different from the socio-vital-functional "I" of our pretranscendent personality by which we manage our life in an everyday field of leisure and labor, work and play, effective presence and action. This deepest "I" is not an alien thing. It is the dynamic source of what I am ultimately called to be as a unique-communal person. This does not mean that our transcendent-immanent "I" will eclipse the managing "me," the lower "I" or executive agent of my daily functioning. The organizing "me" will not disappear. On the contrary, it is the socio-vital-functional "I" that should execute faithfully, yet in adaptive flexibility and creativity, the inspirations of the deeper "I" as rooted in the mystery. My heart is invited to awaken in faith to the deeper "I" of my unique-communal calling as a person. The mystery of formation, by its epiphanic appeals to my deeper "I," wants to transform my socio-vital-functional life. My core form as centering core, heart, and character, and my pretranscendent "I," which may have initially dominated the formation of my character dispositions, are invited by the mystery to open up to this transcendent dimension of my personality. The mystery of transformation alone can empower me to liberate fully my pretranscendent "I" from its manifold coercions, which are rooted in my autarkic pride form. I must be transformed into consonance with my deeper calling. The mystery dwells there as a source of transformation. The mystery can work wonders in history through those persons who are aware of their unique-communal rootedness in it.

Two Dynamics of Human Life in Transformation

I see the transformation of character and personality as carried by two dynamics that are in mutual dialogue all the time. The transformed person is a creative confluence of a unique-communal calling and of a pretranscendent individuality. Our individuality must give flesh in our everyday world to our personal call as inspired by the mystery. Accordingly, transformed persons grow in the awareness that their acts and patterns of action should be coformed by the directives of the mystery. In them the individual socio-vital-functional "I" becomes the manifestation of the founding "I" as sourced and resourced continuously in the transforming love of the mystery. To the degree that our nontranscendent "I" is filled with coercive dispositions, directives, and routinized patterns of action, it is not yet in consonance with our deeper epiphanic "I," the "I" in which the mystery appears.

In the measure of our transformation, we find ourselves not merely in a profane formation field but also in a field of transcendent-immanent transformation. All events in that field become filled for us with epiphanic invitations. We see them as messengers and carriers of a transforming higher power.

The mystery as uniquely epiphanic in us is our beyond "I." It keeps transforming our deepest transcendent "I" in the unspeakable intimacy of its love-will, as it were, from the inside out. At the same time, we meet the formation mystery as epiphanically manifesting itself in our field of daily form reception and donation. There, too, the all-pervasive mystery shows itself for all who have been granted ears to hear and eyes to see. It manifests itself communally, yet also personally and uniquely, in tune with each one's unique mission of life.

Between the enlightened founding "I" in me and my pretranscendent "I," there is both consonance and dissonance. We are not necessarily consonant all of the time. Often we do not do the good we want to do. We can refuse to be in harmony with our deeper calling. In other words, we are responsible for our options, dispositions, directives, and patterns of action. Our managing "I," in cooperation with the mystery, must freely opt for consonance with our deepest "I."

Sad as it is to say, most persons have not yet awakened to their inmost reality. They have neither heard nor responded to the invitation, appeal, and empowerment of and by the mystery. Contemporary pulsations may have closed their hearts to this enlightenment.

Contemporary Pulsations

In the past, people could trust a general pervasive wisdom about the transcendent-immanent unfolding of human life. This is not to say that everyone profited from this wisdom, but it was still available as an honored path, even if it was not followed by all. Our present civilization ignores this treasure of insight into the ways of transcendence. We are prone to functionalize life, to measure its worthwhileness by security, popularity, status, power, and possession. Such anxious proclivities deaden our sensitivity for the true dignity of the human person. Spiritual wisdom and the transcendence dynamic it serves become paralyzed. The transcendent core of true education-in-depth is forgotten.

Profane theories and practices of human development replace those of transcendent-immanent transformation. They foster an existentialistic (instead of a balanced existential) tendency to autarkic self-actualization, self-development, and mere humanistic self-esteem. The popular pulsations of developmental humanism and existentialistic therapism pervade the media and invade the community. The courses, techniques, and terminologies of even pastoral counseling are not immune to this influence. Pastoral training may blindly borrow constructs from the secular sciences about the profane, merely pretranscendent, life. There may not be enough room left for the wisdom of traditional spiritual direction, for formative instead of developmental counseling, and for the inspiration of classical traditions.

Contemporary Pulsations and Religion

There is in the West a scarcity of transformative wisdom. This is true even in some pastoral counselors, teachers, and preachers. They seem unable to awaken people to the deeper mystery in their lives. Many people in crisis may seek instead the assistance of social workers, psychiatrists, and developmental counselors. These experts can help to clarify and relieve the socio-vital-functional facets of their counselees' suffering. But today an increasing number of people bypass both spiritual directors and formation counselors, even as they search for answers to their transpsychological and transdevelopmental struggles.

Even the cloistered life as lived in various degrees and styles in different faith groupings does not always foster as a primordial concern the transpsychological and transdevelopmental wisdom of formation and transformation by the love-will of the mystery, a wisdom of love treasured by the spiritual masters of their traditions. This neglect diminishes the role of religious communities in the culture as centers of awakening to the transcendent love dimension of human existence. Often, unwise cults and social projects, cut off from classical transcendent wisdom about the path, take over. Frequently the lack of true wisdom born from awakening diminishes the understanding of the transformative meaning of higher symbols and disciplines. Such ignorance may sometimes tempt people to reject even such basic disciplines as those of meditation and formative reading. They may consider practices of this kind no longer relevant compared to the popularity of pretranscendent developmental theories.

The absence of spiritual awakening to one's love-will can give rise to a mainly functional ethicism not grounded also in spiritual experience. Meditation on classical texts written by the masters of awakening may be reduced to an intellectualistic text analysis. Much professional and social work may no longer be inspired by the deeper transcendent "I" rooted in the mystery.

It seems as if the average contemporary human person lives often in an implicit denial of a transcendent-immanent mystery. Yet this mystery makes itself constantly available to coform one's life graciously. This denial can also be found in people who belong to an ideological or religious faith grouping. They may color their socio-vital-functional strivings with ideological or religious symbols. Some may use holy texts and phrases without really grasping and living their deeper power of awakening and transformation. When a person awakened, empowered, and transformed by the love-will of the mystery says, "I did this or that task," he or she means to say, "The epiphanic and transforming love power has done or performed this service in and through me.

A truly epiphanic painting, sculpture, movie, poem, or musical composition transcends the conditioned creative power of the socio-vital-functional "I" of the artist. We may be empowered to enjoy and to be nourished by this expression of the epiphanic "I" of the artist in her work, an expression that remains hidden for many. But that can happen only if we ourselves are awakened and consonant with the epiphanic form of the mystery in ourselves. This presence is what enables us to share spontaneously in the epiphanic depth of the vision of the artist. Iconography by gifted craftsmen and women is a sublime expression of epiphanic art. The transcendent founding form can thus manifest itself through aesthetic form and what it brings to life in its field of presence and action.

Our transcendent founding form cannot produce coercive dispositions. As our deepest "I" is disclosed to our core form, it transforms it into consonance with itself. This leads to a lessening of coercive dispositions. These might include time urgency, task avoidance, indifference to people toward whom we have no affinity or to whom we feel hostile, and animosity toward those whom we cannot control and manipulate in service of our pretranscendent projects.

Paradoxical Presence of the Radical Mystery as Formational

In my formation anthropology the radical mystery *as formational* has a paradoxical identity. This mystery transcends infinitely the human life form and its field. Yet at the same time this transcendent mystery is in some way immanent, or within us. For it inspires, speaks, and acts epiphanically and transformatively in and through the deepest "I" of our personhood. It transcends also infinitely each human field of life and action. Yet at the same time it manifests itself epiphanically and transformatively in that field. Hence this gracing mystery appeals to the human person both from the inside and the outside.

Every human life unfolds within a field filled with cosmic energies and profane challenges. But the same field is also bursting with the power or transforming energy of the love-will of the mystery; it is blossoming with epiphanic invitations. Every nonhuman being in our field, too, is endowed with a basic form potency that is a trace of the love-will, an epiphanous sign of the truth, goodness, and beauty of the all-forming mystery. We humans carry far more than a trace. Hidden in the depth of our being is an image of the mystery itself. We are generally not aware of this awesome presence at the root of our fleeting life.

Because we are not aware of it, this founding image is not reflected in the core form of our life as, respectively, core, heart, and matching character. Therefore, we do not know the presence intimately. We do not recognize it as the epiphanic and transforming power of the love-will shining forth in our deepest "I."

I believe that all people share the basic call to consonance with the transcendent-immanent image within them. Without some basic consonance with the sustaining power of the calling, loving mystery, they would fall out of existence. When I developed my concept of consonance, I made a distinction between basic consonance and transforming consonance. Basic consonance of sustenance by the mystery is not yet a consonance of transformation. Our unique call to consonance of our life with its founding image is not automatically transforming our socio-vital-functional life. Our transcendence dynamic or our longing and search for peace and happiness does not find immediate fulfillment. The transcendence dynamic is easily deflected by our autarkic pride form from which all excessive attachments stem. It inclines us to fall back on ourselves alone, away from our will to love. We turn into insulated prisoners of our coercions. They seduce us by their promise of autonomous fulfillment of our search for happiness. Our attempts at self-development halt the flow of transcendent-immanent transformation of our character and personality by the love-will. We remain in the shadows of self-centeredness, missing wider horizons of meaning. Passing social convivialities and popularities, vital pleasures, and functional successes or satisfactions are turned by us into quasi epiphanies to which we become addicted. We endow these naively with a transcendent dimension that cannot be theirs. We expect from them a peace and love they cannot give.

Such one-sided attachments change miraculously when we allow our transcendent call to announce itself in our core form of life and through it in our pretranscendent personality. Gradually, our epiphanic founding image, carried and inspired by the love-will at its base, begins to act through, in, and with our empirical actual form of life.

The hidden call to transforming consonance with our transcendent-immanent divine image resonates in the depths of our being. This resonance is mirrored in a growing consonance of transformation of our empirical life with this image. This transforming consonance is a continuation of what is already in us in principle and a priori. The numerous informational-speculative theologies and philosophies of the various transcendent religions and ideologies—in faithfulness to their basic tradition—will offer their own more informational-speculative explanations of this process and its principles.

As adherents of such a tradition, we should be faithful to its sacred vision. In our personal life we should implement from formation science and its formation anthropology only what is compatible with the basic principles that underlie our own faith and formation tradition. On the one hand, we should live not by the science and its anthropology alone but by our own tradition as perhaps partly enlightened by this science. On the other hand, we surely remain in the shadows of formation ignorance as long as we live only on the level of pretranscendent dispositions, directives, dynamics, and coercions.

CHAPTER 5

Anthropology of the Core Form of the Human Person

Does our personality have a center of its personal experience? It surely does. I call that center the core form of human life. Three words express for me best the three main functions of this core form: core, character, heart. The "core" of our core form stands for its function of centering our experiences. The word "character" points to the core form's function to anchor some of these centered experiences in lasting character dispositions. If they are consonant, I call them virtues. The word "heart" refers to the affective sensitive and sensible qualities with which our core form endows these experiences and dispositions. These three functions of our core form work together. They enrich each other constantly. For example, a woman who loves her son centers and cherishes in the core of her personality many experiences of him as a baby, a child, an adolescent, a grown-up man. These experiences are converted by her in character dispositions of enduring love, care, concern for him. They are at the same time dispositions of the heart insofar as her core form continues to endow them with corresponding affects and feelings.

The same applies to our relationship with the mystery of formation. Our core form as core centers and cherishes all experiences of the love of the mystery. As character, our core form converts these experiences in transcendent character dispositions such as those of awe, gratefulness, faith, hope, love, commitment, and fidelity. As heart, our core form continuously deepens the affects that go with these transcendent dispositions toward the mystery.

Dissonances of the Core Form

Our core form should be consonant or in tune with our founding life form. What our founding life form stands for can be misunderstood at any given moment of life. There are many sources of misunderstanding. Among them, I would name our autarkic pride form, dissonant sociohistorical pulsations, and various coercive vital-functional dispositions rooted in the neuroform of our life. At times these will seduce us to refuse, misunderstand, or distort the message of our spirit. Our heart is not necessarily consonant. Language conveys

this possibility of dissonance by speaking of the bad, the envious, the tyrannical, the cruel heart, and so on. In my formation anthropology every human life
has a core form, but not every core form is consonant, and no human core form
is fully consonant all the time, be it as centering core or as character or as heart.

Expression of Our Core Form in Our Formation Field

We can ask ourselves, How do, for example, labor leaders who are well disposed in their heart and character effectively express their core form in the
daily promotion of social justice? It depends on the formation dynamics of
their current, apparent, and actual forms of life. The current life form may lead
one in the direction of servant leadership. Such a well-disposed servant leader
will keep in close touch with what is going on in the labor situation. The current form suggests how one should respond competently to the state of affairs
that management and labor need to address.

Servant leaders, then, allow the care disposition of their core form to express
itself in any numer of appropriate, currently required responses. Their apparent
life form is directed by their core form to show a wise and effective appearance
on the labor scene. Their appearance is permeated by the transcendent servant
sensitivity and sensibility of their heart. Finally, the actual form of their presence and action as a whole is the embodiment of all of these transcendent servant dispositions, sensitivities, and sensibilities in the actual situation a
transcendent servant labor leader faces here and now.

My formation anthropology holds, thus, that the dynamics themselves of the
core form strive to express concretely the formation field. Messages that come
from that field through the integrational current, apparent, and actual forms of
life coform such expressions of our core form.

Four Dynamic Directions of the Core Form

The dynamics of our core form are marked by one or more of four possible
directions. I refer to these as dynamic movements "toward," or "away from,"
"against," or "with."

Our acts may be directed by such "moving-toward" dynamics as hope, longing, desire, appreciation, anticipation, and aspiration. We may be moved also
by such "moving-away-from" dynamics as depreciation, rejection, condemnation, resistance, and repudiation. In other situations, such "moving-against"
dynamics may guide us as fortitude, affirmation, courage, opposition, anger,
hate, envy, jealousy, and malediction. Possible also are such "moving-with"
dynamics as those of love, openness, admiration, awe, reverence, respect, resonance, compassion, compatibility, acceptance, confirmation, cooperation,
solidarity, union, and benediction.

Some lives may be dominated mainly by one or two of these orientations.
Others may release any one of these dynamics in consonance with the

demands of each specific situation. In both cases, the affective and effective quality of our life as a whole may be distinguished by the prevalence of one or the other of these orientations. For example, people who are predominantly directed by the "moving-with" dynamics of their core form may show this in the way they meet a suffering child in need of a warm word, a loving embrace, and a helping hand. Such dynamics affect also the way we appear among people who are shy and fearful. Our actual behavior will radiate the love disposition of our core form as character. It inclines us to express this love in a responsible fashion.

Form Traditions and the Dynamics of Our Core Form

My formation anthropology holds that the dispositions of the core form are not all at once there. They are formed in dialogue with both our founding form and our formation field—above all, with the transcendent form traditions of this field. Because of the influence of our experiences in that field, we could say that our dispositions are coformed also by the people, events, and things with which we interact or interform. The way in which these facets of our field appear to us is not of our own making only. From birth on, we assimilate with a minimum of effort the way in which others around us receive and give form to the surroundings we share with them. Neither were these others alone in creating their traditions. They were not insulated from those who went before them. We all share in traditions of formation we inherited from our predecessors. For example, the dynamics of life formation favored by American Indians are different from those of Alaskan Eskimos, Kenyan Masai, French Catholics, or Spanish conquistadors. The ways handed over from generation to generation in the traditions we share will influence the ways in which we give form to our personal life, at least initially.

How do the dynamics handed over by our traditions affect our own core-form dynamics? Our core form—like every other empirical form of our life—has six dimensions. These are the sociohistorical, vital, functional, functional-transcendent, transcendent, and transcendent-functional. Each of these dimensions of the core form can be affected in their dynamics by our form traditions.

Sociohistorical Dynamics of Our Core Form
and Formation Traditions

The sociohistorical facet of our core form is rooted in those pulsations in our field that result from prevalent form traditions. For example, Muslims adhering to certain (by no means all) Islamic formation traditions may in times of holy war be moved by dynamics of self-forgetful heroism and self-immolation. This makes them less fearful in battle. Since childhood, they assimilated the dynamism of their religious faith tradition as mixed with a particular formation tradition. They have been assured that to fall as a martyr in holy war is to gain access to paradise. This dynamism has been handed over from generation to generation. Through interformation it has been imprinted in the core form of their life. It is a latent readiness for heroism the moment a holy war engages their energies.

Vital Dynamics of Our Core Form and Formation Traditions

The vital facet of our core form is rooted in temperament. For example, we may be lastingly disposed in our core form to dynamics of fast movement or to what I call in my anthropology temperamental dynamics of our "temper form." These are "givens" in our vital-genetic preformation. Parents see such predispositions for certain dynamics already in their infants. They are from the beginning fast or slow, irascible or peaceful, active or passive. These early dynamics are the temperamental seedbed of the emotional intensity and basic temperamental orientation of the dynamics of the child's core form. Often people who knew adults as little children will say, "I am not surprised that they are so anxious, fast, slow, intense, quiet, or outgoing. They were already inclined that way as children."

Basic Vital Dynamics, Expression Dynamics

In my formation anthropology I began to delineate a distinction between basic vital dynamics of the core form as heart and as character and the way in which one expresses these dynamics. Especially in the expressiveness of vital dynamics, I observed differences due to formation traditions. The expression dynamics of the core form are affected by interformation between children and the people surrounding them. Since birth, we are taught to take part in approved ways of self-expression, cherished by our family and the other people around us. These dynamics of acceptable self-expression are the result of traditions people abide by in the common or segmental field of life they share.

I observed a difference between the same basic dynamic tendencies in people and their variety of expressions. For example, a number of Moscovite Marxists, South African or Scotch Calvinists, and Italian Catholics may share by genetic preformation a similar vivacious dynamism. Yet the core-form dynamics of expression in which each of these groups allows this vivaciousness to show itself will be different.

The same is true for the average individual person in each group. One's personal core-form disposition of expression is somewhat unique, yet it depends also on the form-traditional dynamics of expression confirmed in one's formation field. For example, if a Southern Italian man expresses his heartfelt sympathy for any other man by a warm embrace and a kiss, this dynamic expression is confirmed by other people in his village. The same would not be confirmed by average Scottish people in Aberdeen or average Irish Americans in Boston.

Functional Dynamics of Our Core Form
and Formation Traditions

I saw something quite interesting at this point. Unlike our preformed vital dynamism or temper form, our functional dynamism is mainly acquired. This observation led me to three different kinds of acquired functional core-form dynamics. They are as follows:

1. *Specific segmental functional core-form dynamics.* I observed how we acquire the latter through sharing in the functional dynamics specific to the formation segments to which we belong. For example, the style of functioning of descendants of the upper classes in the city is different from that of those born and raised in rural poverty.

2. *Typical form traditional, functional core-form dynamics.* I noticed by careful observation how we take these dynamics in when sharing in the functionality typical of the form traditions to which we adhere. For example, a person born and raised in a Puritan or in a Jansenist formation tradition has a different style of functioning than a person raised in an Indian ashram or in a Pentecostal tradition.

3. *Characteristic functional core-form dynamics.* I noticed how we, personally, develop these characteristics through our own unique-communal dialogue with our formation field and tradition. By reflecting on their origin, it seemed to me that they are first of all rooted in the unique-communal dynamics of our founding form. But I have found that they are based also on our core form's characteristic dynamics, which we have already acquired during our personal formation history. For example, within each of the groups to which we belong we can still detect personal differences in the specific and typical style of dynamic functioning. I observed how people may reform in a similar way the dynamics they share with others. They make them into a distinctive part of their own personal-communal character while still maintaining their group's characteristics. The latter represent the communal facet of their personal-communal core form as character.

Specific Functional Core-Form Segmental Dynamics

The idea of functional segmental dynamics of the human core form took hold of me when I began to trace their emergence. They emerge from our participation in the formation dynamics of the *specific* segments of the population to which we belong. We are born or inserted in such segments during our formation history. For example, factory workers, ballerinas, bartenders, farmers, college professors, and artists share different specific formation dispositions and dynamics. This similarity of dynamics must be rooted in their sharing in the dispositions of their segments of the population. It appeared to me that the people who coform these segments face similar challenges, interests, responsibilities, demands, and expectations in their given or chosen formation field. I realized upon further analysis that such segmental core-form dispositions include also—with some modifications—some of the common dispositions of a wider population of which the segment is a part. Traveling through Japan, I noticed, for example, that specific business segments of the American population share certain general ways of life that make them different from the same business segment in the Japanese population.

Typical Functional Form-Traditional Dynamics of the Core Form

The *specific* core dynamics, which I conceived in my empirical formation anthropology, can be modified by *typical* form-traditional dynamics prevalent in various formation segments. For example, engineers, entrepreneurs, farmhands, military personnel, nurses, actors, and oil drillers, who are committed to Protestant, Catholic, Eastern Orthodox, Islamic, Buddhist, Marxist, or humanist form-traditional dynamics are, in my observation and study, different in some way. On the one hand, they share the specific form-segmental dynamics they have in common with people belonging to the same functional formation segments. On the other hand, I felt compelled to state that some of these form-segmental, *specific* functional dynamics will be somewhat modulated by the dynamics *typical* of their different ideological or religious form traditions in their functional expressions.

Functional Characteristic Dynamics of the Core Form

Focusing my attention on *characteristic* dynamics of the core form, I became aware that these kinds of core-form dynamics go beyond what I have called specific or typical functional dynamics. Characteristic dynamics are mainly the effect of the personal formation of our core form as character. I began to see them as a more direct expression of the stable style of functioning we have made our own in the course of time. I saw, however, also that the formation of our character is coformed by our interformation with a particular population. For example, as I observed the British in London, it was evident to me that personal character dynamics of the average Englishman or woman are more like the characteristic dynamics of the English than like those of the naturalized Pakistanis I met in the same city. I concluded that our core form as character is coformed by the pervasive formative influence of the population into which we are born and with whom we interact during a significant period of our life.

I discovered another unique aspect of personal dynamics within such common character dynamics of the core form. This uniqueness is due to some subtle and continuous selection and modulation process in regard to the way of life we share with others. This process of selection and modulation is based on an implicit awareness of the founding life call, which plays such a basic role in my formation anthropology. Our unique-communal founding form tends to express itself— dynamically as our life call—in our empirical life form. Later on, our already formed character dynamics play a significant role in the further selective adoption and modulation of traits we share with other people. Such sharing does not exclude new disclosures of the uniqueness of our life call. For example, when I studied from the viewpoint of my formation anthropology Gandhi's call to give form to a unique style of nonviolence, I noticed that this aspect of his life call was disclosed to him later in life. It inspired his own adaptation of his core form to already existing Indian traditions of nonviolence.

When I speak in my formation anthropology of the interformative influence of traditions on personal character formation, I do not first have in mind faith traditions. Far more influential, in my observation, are the formation traditions of that segment of the population in which we happen to be inserted. I see a great difference between one's shared faith tradition and the pluralistic, concrete form traditions in which this faith may be lived by various groups of faithful in the same culture.

For example, I began to distinguish in some Catholic South American populations three different formation traditions, embodied in three different core forms. Yet I saw how all three claimed the same public adherence to the Catholic faith tradition. I saw a difference between South American Catholic landowners, their not yet socially awakened Catholic campesinos, and those Catholic campesinos who have become aware of the necessity of a battle for human rights. I became aware how all three groups may consider themselves adherents of the Catholic faith tradition. Yet I observed how each group lives by a different kind of form tradition. Within each of these groups again, I saw how each individual may live the specific and typical dynamics of the group in his or her own core form's characteristic way.

I gained gradually the insight that either specific or typical dynamics become only *characteristic* dynamics in the core form of life of people to the degree that they are assimilated and coformed personally. According to my formation anthropology, this personalizing coformation would be rooted in the dynamics of our founding form, vital-temperamental dynamics, our character dynamics, and our formation traditions. Thinking all of this through, I came to the conclusion that functional character forms represent the functional consistency of our core form of life in its uniqueness. For example, a secretary knows that her boss, because of his character disposition, will respond in a certain way to what she proposes. His consistency of functional dynamics makes him predictable to a significant degree.

Studying a historical picture exhibition in the museum of Santa Barbara, I noticed that often the difference between *characteristic* and *specific* or *typical* dynamics of people are noticeable in pictures taken of them. What kind of dynamic disposition they show is often dependent on either the spontaneous or the focal-functional way they are exposed to or pose for the camera. When people are photographed unwittingly or playfully, they often show in their spontaneous posture, action, or expression more of their personal dynamic characteristics of their core form as character. When they are asked to pose as representatives of their specific formation segments, such as an administrative hierarchy or members of a social club, or as representatives of their typical form tradition, such as a religious society, the photographic expression is different. Often their form-segmental specificity and/or form-traditional type of core form dominate their official serious, pleasing, sociable, charitable, or pious expression in such pictures. My finding was confirmed for me many times over when I repeated the same research in other picture and painting exhibitions.

Transcendent Core-Form Dynamics

I experienced in myself and many others that the transcendent facet of our core form is formed by those core-form dynamics that are spiritually inspired and directed. For example, certain melodies of the music of Mozart seem inspired by a dynamic of spiritual beauty. They surpass any merely functional or vital esthetics. They also transcend any popular pulsations that pervaded his environment.

We all have spiritual inspirations to pursue goodness, truth, and beauty in our life, no matter how modest these dynamics may be and how little we may be able to express them in works of art or wisdom. In a consonantly unfolding human life, these transcendent dynamics attune and harmonize all other dynamics. The form traditions to which we adhere can have a profound inspirational impact on the formation of such transcendent core dynamics.

Transcendent-Functional Core-Form Dynamics

The transcendent-functional facet of our core form is formed by the core-form dynamics that dispose us to express our transcendent awe, love, and care for the all-forming formation mystery by loving competent care for its manifold epiphanies. For example, certain forms of transcendently inspired care for famined populations in developing countries can be expressions of transcendent-functional love and concern for these epiphanies of the suffering mystery. This seems especially true when such care is accompanied by a genuine awe for the mysterious majesty of suffering in these afflicted people. The loving care that people such as Mother Teresa of Calcutta and Martin Luther King showed to the oppressed and the poor pointed to the transcendent-functional core form of their lives.

Dissonant Dynamics of the Core Form

My formation anthropology suggests that one of the main problems with which formation researchers and practitioners should deal is conflicts between the dynamics of the core form. We may experience a dissonance between the vital-temperamental and the functional and/or the transcendent dynamics of our core form which I have been describing in the previous pages. Contests may emerge between the specific, typical, and characteristic functional dynamics of the core form which I have explained and exemplified. Such tensions between dynamics should be appreciated as a call to a search for the inner consonance of our core form. Appreciative opportunity thinking appraises this experience of core-form conflict as an occasion for its reformation and transformation. It inspires us to strive gently and firmly for transcendent integration of the core form's centering core, character, heart. A certain tension between dynamics of our core form is healthy and helpful as long as it does not become deformational hypertension.

Deformational hypertension between dynamics of our core form can lead to lasting core-form dissonance. In my experience with many people, one source of such chronic distress and tension within the very core, heart, and corresponding character of their personhood may be the impact of deformative or deformatively appraised form traditions. Traditions, even initially consonant ones, may have become deformative for our core form because of incidental accretions that have become dissonant. They cling like barnacles to the form traditions that prevail in the common or segmental ranges of our formation field. Dissonant accretions may breed a *typical* core form that is unjustly oppressive of the earlier described vital-temperamental, acquired characteristic, or transcendent core dynamics of one's core form.

Certain vital dynamics of one's core form may be instantly and automatically repudiated under the influence of such accretions. Similarly, consonant transcendent dynamics of one's core form may be refused when we appraise them prefocally as useless or harmful. Subsequently, the prefocal region of our consciousness may lose its flexibility, creativity, and spontaneity. Formation direction, counseling, or transtherapy in private or common may facilitate a relaxed access to such repudiated or refused dynamics of one's core form. It does so through a wise appraisal of prevalent form traditions. Do they show consonant or dissonant accretions that may influence our core form, heart, and matching character beneficially or badly? Did some of these harden into coercive dispositions of our core form as character?

Consonant Sexuality

Let me give an example of repudiation and refusal of consonant dynamics of our core form, heart, and matching character due to dissonant accretions. Playful and creative expressions of sexuality in marriage may be distorted by dissonant core formation. These accretions of a form tradition may have deformed one's formation conscience. Conscience falsified by one's dissonant core-form formation may release a dynamic of intrapunitive lashing out at the playful partners, a punishment ordered by the deformed sexual character disposition. Everything playful in the marriage encounter, even if it is consonant with one's faith tradition, is then falsely appraised as closed off from the human spirit by its very deviation from one's deformed core dispositions. The rejecting and punishing dynamics of a conscience distorted by the deformed core form of the person lead to an automatic repudiation of consonant spontaneous vital dynamics. These vital dynamics are also represented in the core form as dispositions but subordinated now to intrapunitive dispositions that serve the falsified sexual dispositions of the core form. These dissonant dispositions move the partners also prefocally to refuse the corresponding transcendence dynamics.

Gratefully received, the transcendent sexual dynamics of the core form would enrich and deepen the character and temper disposition of spontaneous playfulness. The character disposition of sensitive and sensible playfulness forms a substantial aspect of marital spirituality. The right *ultimate* directives of various faith traditions and of their informational theologies may be most helpful for a correction *in principle* of such dissonant accretions of the core form of life. By themselves alone, however, they are not sufficient to reform and transform in all practical and experiential details the dissonant accretions of the *proximately* lived form tradition.

My formation anthropology stimulates the science and praxis of *proximate* formation of the core form. As such, it can complement the *ultimate* formation directives of religious and ideological faith traditions and their various consonant informational theologies and philosophies.

CHAPTER 6

Anthropology of
the Apparent Life Form

I define the apparent form as the integrational structure of the various ways in which we are disposed to appear to ourselves and to others.

My war experience and the dangers threatening the Dutch people whom I helped to hide made me painfully observant of what I called the attractive apparent form of some Dutch collaborators with the Nazis or of other self-centered yet charming men and women who could infiltrate our ranks and endanger our survival. In that climate, I began to think about a theory of the apparent forms of life, which I would integrate with the principles of systematic formation science, whose seeds I developed during that fateful year.

In volume one of this series I referred to the dynamics of the apparent form mainly as operative in the *inter* and *outer* facets of the way we appear in our field of life. How do I want to appear in my interformation with my family? How in the outer situation of my public life? Basic to formation are also the dynamics of the *intra* facet of our apparent life form: our self-images, the ways in which we are disposed to appear to ourselves. This facet of our apparent form plays a decisive role in our transcendent formation as well as in our striving for intimacy with others.

Only human life carries self-images. We may fabricate pleasing images to cover up for ourselves less flattering facets of our personality. This distorts the candid way in which we should appear to ourselves. We should take into account our acknowledged as well as our refused intra-appearances. Only then can we clarify their impact on our way to transcendence.

Our self-images are thus a part of our intraformation. They deeply influence our life. Self-images that do not take into account candidly our weak, evil, or coercive leanings block our way to self-understanding. Such refusal delays the unfolding of our transcendent life. This explains why all classical masters of transcendent formation stress humility as a basic condition of true ascendance.

We must purge our store of self-images or inner self-appearances by the candid disclosure of what we have refused to acknowledge so far. I call this in my anthropology "the restoration of the refused." Unfortunately, not only restoration but also return of the refused is always possible. We can never do away with our pride form. It is the source of such refusal. Autarkic pride tempts us to exalt unrealistically the ways in which we appear to ourselves and others.

Description of the Apparent Life Form

Our apparent form is one of the five integrational forms of life I have discussed thus far; to rename them, they are the foundational, core, current, apparent, and actual forms. I reflected on these in volume one of this series. Each form integrates in its own way the structures, dynamics, and directives of our field of life. These integrational forms are distinct yet interwoven with one another. All of them come together in our actual form of life or that which attunes us to our field here and now.

Our apparent form refers to how we appear or strive to appear to ourselves and others. It differs from our foundational form. The latter points to our unique emergence out of the mystery of formation. At no moment of our life can we fully comprehend this emergence. Only part of it appears in our awareness at any one time. Our self-images give us only glimpses of who we most deeply are. Our inmost nobility is a gift and an invitation. It is a veiled epiphany of our preformation by the unspeakable mystery. Our life is directed by this epiphany insofar as it appears to us inwardly. Our right self-images or intra-apparent forms are the dim lights by which we set our course in our search for consonance with our personal-communal destiny.

Our need to respond to the challenges of our field of life compels us to define what we can and should do or not do. These definitions affect our apparent form. Such definitions tell us how we rightly or wrongly *want* to appear to ourselves and others. They do not necessarily express how we *should* appear to ourselves and others in light of our unique founding life form. The mystery can change our self-images radically. The condition of such change is that we are open to the self-elucidation of the mystery in our life. This elucidation happens through its inspiration, its intimation of our life call in our field of life, and its speaking in transcendent traditions.

Our apparent form can be erroneous in many ways. We may appear to ourselves as better than we are. This affects the way in which we function in our field. Imagine, for instance, that I have to function as a contractor. My exalted intra-apparent form—the way I appear inwardly to myself—may generate in me dynamics and directives of overestimation of my capacities. As a result, my mind becomes insulated from inputs by others that could correct this exaltation. I may be inclined to involve myself in enterprises too risky in view of my limitations, which I refuse to acknowledge. I may stubbornly stick to my own counsel, neglecting to consult knowledgeable people. I may underestimate the cleverness of competitors. A subtle arrogance, nourished by pride, may spoil my dealings with clients and subcontractors.

The more I exalt an inflated way of appearing to myself as the "real me," the deeper the attachment to my fictitious self-image may become. To the degree that I identify blindly with arrogant self-images, I will become less able to grow in the transcendent truth of my life. An exalted intra-appearance blocks the path to one's transcendent call. I need the inner freedom to distance myself from what should only be passing self-images. Otherwise, the adventure of my life will be hemmed in by attachments to what I fancy myself to be. I should grow in awareness of my fantastic phantom "I" rooted in my autarkic pride form. This "I" is a source of many delusional "I" forms.

Intra-Apparent Forms

àIn my anthropology I introduced the term intra-apparent forms for our self-images. I realized that our apparent form as a whole has various facets. Among them I began to distinguish the intra-, inter-, and outer-apparent form. I saw, however, as fundamental to all of them, our intra-apparent forms or self-images. Intra appearances are the ways in which we appear to ourselves. They play a crucial part in our formation. They are among the main coformants of our life. How we appear to ourselves influences the way we appear to others. We let shine through or we disguise for others selected aspects of our self-images.

Our personal appraisal of who we are should be based ideally on an accurate apprehension of the presently available signs of both our uniqueness and our individuality. Uniqueness is a quality of our transcendent dimension of life. Individuality is typical only of our pretranscendent dimensions of life.

In regard to our uniqueness, our appearance should be consonant with who we are called to be by our transcendent source as disclosing itself in our founding form of life. This means that our intra-apparent form should be in tune with the most probable present disclosures of our emergent life call. The disclosures of our call should be the compass of the form we give to our successive self-images.

In regard to our individuality, our intra-appearance should be coformed by the individuality, the assets, and the limits of our pretranscendent functional, vital, and sociohistorical dimensions. We should take into account the signs of this individuality.

For example, the experience of unjust oppression may be for me a disclosure of a personal calling to sacrificial courage in service of the oppressed. When this disclosure is affirmed in much reflection and confirmed by wise companions who know me intimately, it may change my intra-appearance. I look different to myself. This changed self-image as protoform will generate new acts, dispositions, and attitudes toward the underprivileged. I begin to realize the levels and limits of my individual vital energies and of my individual functional capacities. I learn how to organize my assets and limits effectively in the struggle for justice. Such insights, too, will change the way in which I appear to myself, leading in turn to change in the way in which I give form to my life and world and, in accordance with that change, to my core, current, and actual forms of my character and personality.

Consonance Dynamics of Intra-Appearance

Many dynamics play a role in the way in which we appear to ourselves. Prominent among them are the dynamics of candor, congeniality, compatibility, compassion, competence, conviction, commitment, and courage. These are operative as well in the shaping of our intra-apparent forms. They will give form also to aspects of our other formational structures. Earlier I referred to these as the dynamics of consonance. These dynamics facilitate our approach to a more consonant apparent form of life. We must allow them to improve the way in which we appear to ourselves. We may approximate, but we will never attain, perfect consonance. Our self-image is a confluence of consonant and dissonant character coformants or dispositions. Both should be acknowledged candidly as showing themselves in our life.

A first facet of consonance is congeniality. In regard to our self-image, we should strive for *congeniality* in two ways. First of all, the way in which we appear to ourselves gains in congeniality to the degree that it is attuned to our personal-communal life call insofar as it discloses itself to us at this moment of our formation history. Second, self-perception becomes congenial to the degree that it is also congruent and congenital: congruent with our functional, congenital with our vital individuality.

Consonance dynamics imply that these individual tendencies are appraised and affirmed or nonaffirmed in the light of our call. The striving for consonance implies that we candidly admit that tendencies which we cannot affirm as consonant are nonetheless still in us. We acknowledge them as challenges we should cope with candidly, courageously, gently, and firmly. I call this, in my formational anthropology, *intentional consonance*. Although we shall never come to full consonance in this life, we can always walk in the way of intentional or genuinely willed consonance.

Our intra-appearance is *compatible* if the mode in which we appear to ourselves takes into account the realities of our field. Can we let them affect our individuality without compromising our life call? Do we let them diminish or deepen our commitment to our faith and formation tradition?

Another subordinate facet of consonance is *compassion*. Is our intra-appearance compassionate? Did we choose to appear to ourselves as people of gentle respect for our own vulnerability and that of others? Is ours a participation in the universal compassion of the formation mystery? Such a compassionate self-image will gradually become part of who we truly are.

The consonance component of *competence* inspires the formation of an intra-apparent form that appreciates rightly and promotes firmly our individual form potencies as gifts of the mystery. Our transcendent-immanent life needs pretranscendent competencies to express itself in the world and to grow in balance and wisdom by such expression. We should not deny such potencies in false humility. Neither should we transpose such denied potencies and dispositions to others. The latter aberration of the intra-apparent form can lead to exaggerated clinging to people in which we magnify and admire our own unacknowledged consonant potencies and dispositions.

Exaltation of Our Apparent Life Form

In my formation anthropology, I conceive our autarkic pride form as a source of exaltation, closure, and insulation. Exaltation distorts the right appreciation of our field of life and of our presence in it. It interferes with the dynamics of consonance, namely, those of candor, congeniality, compatibility, compassion, competence, conviction, commitment, and courage. To understand the dynamics of exaltation, closure, and insulation, we must realize the dynamic powers of our inner-apparent form or self-image.

Our intra-appearance is not merely a mirror that passively represents who we really are. It functions also as a power of formation that helps us to generate in relative freedom a dynamic, intricately structured apparent form of life. Therefore, we speak not only of appearances of who we are but also of an apparent *form* of life. Like all other life forms it is dynamic in its taking on new form facets. Our intra-apparent form codirects the way in which we receive form in and give form to our character and personality. Through them, it influences the form we give to our surroundings.

Insulation of Our Apparent Life Form

Our intra-appearance tends to close itself in upon itself under the pressure of our pride form. Once it insulates itself that way, it easily hardens. Our heart will shrink. In some cases only formation counseling, guidance, direction-in-depth, or the transtherapy that I am developing may be able to break through the shell of a shrunken heart that is the victim of a hardened intra-form of self-appearance and appraisal.

For example, a fellow may have developed an exalted self-image of tough masculinity. This may be the result of antifeminine pulsations that were popular in the special segment of the field of life in which he grew up. Times, however, have changed. He may have entered a new segment of the population less frantic about male superiority. The new times and the new segment offer him numerous opportunities to become aware of his own refused, more gentle qualities. He may be too proud to admit his blindness. He refuses to listen to the new sociohistorical messages of the inter and outer spheres of his always unfolding field of life. His stubborn insulation in macho superiority and insensitivity may threaten his marriage. To avoid separation, he chooses with his spouse to enter into marriage counseling. There they experience, after many sessions, that the shell he has built around his intra-appearance may only be mellowed by in-depth therapy. The subsequently reformed intra-appearance may change his marriage and grant it new chances for survival.

Dissonance and Consonance of the Apparent Life Form

I often observed in group sessions how the consonance of human formation is imperiled if people mistake their apparent form for their foundational form of life and identify themselves with it totally and unconditionally. In that case, one disregards, first of all, the fact that we humans suffer from the dynamics of refusal that split our apparent form into realistic and unrealistic self-images. Second, we overlook the fact that even if our apparent form would be wholly consonant it would only be a limited manifestation of the life call we most deeply are. We may become attached to this intra-appearance as if it represented our total form of life. As a result of this faulty conviction, we may insulate this self-image more and more rigidly from other aspects of our formation story.

Instead, we should delineate our self-image wisely, provisionally, and progressively. We should keep this delineation in consonance with successive disclosures of our uniqueness and individuality. Otherwise, we lose our sensitivity for the ongoing call of the transcendent. We walk in the illusion that we have caught this call already in its fullness in the limited apparent forms of our life at this passing moment of our personal formation history.

I have carefully chosen the terms "appearance" and "apparent" precisely to point to the fact that our self-apprehension and appraisal can extend itself only to what at a given moment in this history "appears" to us as who we may be called to be. This limited, momentary self-understanding can never fully comprehend our ever-unfolding and surprising story of life.

Integrative Dynamics of Apparent Life Formation

The apparent form is one of the five integrational forms which I disclosed in my structuring of the human personality-as-transcending. It tends to bring together the intra, inter, and outer aspects of our appearance. The way we appear is thus not limited to our intra-appearance. We appear also to others. Usually they see us differently than we see ourselves. Because we care about both our inter and outer appearances, many dynamics and directives of our life reflect this concern. Most of our actions—for example, dressing, grooming, moving, posturing, and speaking—are at least in part influenced by these dynamics. If we are overdependent on outer appearances because of lack of inner self-affirmation, we may be exploited. Politicians, public-relations experts, salespersons, and commercials play on our need to appear impressive and attractive. If we depend excessively on them, our way to transcendence will be blocked.

The interaction of the dynamics of the intra, inter, and outer facets of the apparent form of life may be more or less consonant or integrative. An example of lack of integration would be that of a young woman who appears accurately to herself as a better student than her male classmates. This is an aspect of her intra-appearance. Yet she may try to appear to them as less of a brain. She may cultivate a less-intellectual appearance to enhance her chances for the dates she also desires. She does not want to threaten a perhaps vulnerable, masculine self-appearance. When attracted to a companion socially or romantically, she does not want to appear to him as intellectually superior.

An undertaker on the job, no matter how jolly he may feel inwardly, must appear solemn and slightly sad when dealing with the bereaved. A bartender, on the contrary, must appear jolly on the outside even when he is somewhat cantankerous on the inside. One is reminded here of the image of the hilarious clown who cries inwardly. In many instances, such divergences may be necessary for effective functioning in the community. They are the expected and needed social symbols. Therefore, they are not necessarily deceptive or inwardly disintegrating as intentionally deceptive appearances would be. However, if we falsely interiorize them as if they represent all that we are personally and lastingly, they will cut into our flight of transcendence. This insight was confirmed for me in the many transtherapeutic group sessions I was privileged to facilitate.

Affirmation, Confirmation, and the Apparent Form

Affirmation comes from the inside, confirmation from the outside. Affirmation means to assert inwardly that we are worthwhile as a unique gift of the mystery. Confirmation is the expression by others of our worthwhileness. Others show us their approval. Often we try to gain their confirmation by the way we appear to them. The more hesitant our own affirmation of a true self-image is, the more we feel the need for confirmation by others.

Such confirmation cannot substitute for our own inner affirmation. Their confirmation can complement and strengthen our self-affirmation of the way we appear to ourselves, but it cannot replace it. We can always affirm our consonant appearance in the trust that the mystery within us always affirms us; it wants us to share in this affirmation. This can make up for the lack of confirmation we receive from others.

This deepest affirmation is based on our faith and hope that this mystery affirms us lovingly in our self-appreciative intra-appearance. The mystery appreciates our striving for consonance as well as our repentance about dissonance. Such faith and hope make us grow in appreciative abandonment to the mystery. We hear much today about finding, asserting, and expressing our real self. These words often refer exclusively to our apparent form as falsely mistaken for the mystery of our true self. But this deepest self can never be seen and appraised in its fullness this side of the grave.

Anthropology of Exaltation Dynamics
and Form Appearance

Our apparent form may be insulated from our transcendent-immanent dimension of life. Such insulation is a result of the pride form. It makes us increasingly vulnerable to the pushes and pulls of exaltation. The exalted and exalting pride form may lead to excessive attachment to the inclination to identify ourselves with what we exalt. In that case anything that threatens our exalted intra-apparent form is appraised as a threat to all that we are or can be. This leads to the development of anxious security dynamics and directives, formed in such a way that they can safeguard the illusion of our exalted apparent form. Our growth in transcendent presence meets a formidable barrier in such protectionistic directives. Only an alternative growth in detachment and humility may help us to break through this barricade.

The exalted apparent form is exceedingly vulnerable because it is based on fantasy, not reality. This gives rise to the excessive need for self-affirmation and for confirmation by others. It results in a proliferation of safety dynamics. They maintain and enhance the shaky affirmations and confirmations by which we live. Other guardian dynamics are developed to explain away the threatening message of the absence of hoped for inner affirmations or outer confirmations. The dynamics of vigilance against any threat to our exalted form appearance may become excessive. As I observed in my transtherapeutic group sessions, this can cast us into the dark valley of paranoid deformation, a formidable barrier on the way to joyous transcendence.

Provisional Character of Our Self-Images

Such problematic dynamics are often compounded by the fact that we may live in forgetfulness of the reality that our apparent form, even at its best, is only provisional. It can only represent a tentative time-and-space-bound delineation of the unique form of our always-ongoing and changing formation and its participative union with the mystery. The apparent form can manifest only those dynamics and directives of the founding life form that are available to us at any given moment or period of our formation history. Forgetfulness of this fact tempts us to make our self-images absolute. We do not go beyond such images to faith in our participative union with the mystery as at least an *intimacy of sustenance.*

This union holds within it our deepest transcendent identity. An excessive attachment to one or the other absolutized appearance would make us anxious, suspicious, closed, and defensive. It keeps us basically insecure and inwardly overaffirmative. Outwardly it makes us oversensitive to any sign of withholding confirmation. The logic of such defensive dynamics may gradually generate a lasting climate of insecurity. The experience of failure or rejection can then become devastating.

Confirmation and affirmation are dialectical. One affects the other. Too much confirmation may intensify our excessive and exclusive attachment to external apparent forms that attract casual confirmations. We substitute this apparent form for our true transcendent identity. It may imprison us increasingly in the deceptive climate of exalted self-appearances. We become overdependent on popular pulsations and cheap confirmations. This dependency may be used against us by people who want to manipulate our need for confirmation in service of their own projects.

The dynamics just described apply not only to the apparent forms of individuals but also to those of formation segments as a whole. For example, a formation segment made up of religious enthusiasts may absolutize its apparent moments of shared elation. They may idolize their segment as exalted above people who do not share such transports of spirit. A shared apparent form of the elect may be rigorously insulated from the not-elected, who do not resonate with our self-enhancing excitement. The consequences of such insulation, built on a deceptive self-image, are devastating. They can become painfully obvious in certain cultic enclaves.

Current Form and Apparent Form Dynamics

Scholars, students, and practitioners drawing upon my formation anthropology may ask themselves, What is the difference between my concept of the current form and the apparent form and their respective dynamics? At first glance they may seem to be the same.

However, my concept of the current form is more comprehensive than my concept of the apparent form. Not all dynamics that give form currently to our life become part of the way we appear or strive to appear to ourselves and others.

For example, truck drivers are dynamically influenced in the way they give form to their occupational life by the current state of their physical health, by the condition of the roads they have to use, by current speed limits, the situation of their companies, their family concerns, and so on. All of these affect the manner in which truckers give form to their job. Their current way of driving is influenced by such factors whether or not these factors are assimilated into the basic ways in which they appear or want to appear to themselves and others.

Apparent Form and the Dynamics
of Refusal and Repudiation

People become excessively attached to the appearances or self-images they have absolutized. Such attachments are dissonant if they are at odds with one's unique-communal transcendent life call or with one's individuality as manifested in the lower dimensions of life. People may mistake their apparent form for "the real me." Accordingly, their clinging to it is intensified. Any threat to it generates tension, crisis, and frustration. What they prefocally fear most is the unmasking of the deceptive facets of their apparent form. Such disclosure would make it impossible for them to maintain this form in its solidified state.

The dynamics of refusal and repudiation enable us to escape such painful self-disclosures. These dynamics are concerned with the denial of any inspiration or aspiration of the transcendent life dimension that would cast doubt on one's intra-appearance. Repudiation is the denial of any individual vital, functional, or sociohistorical reality that threatens the illusionary facets of one's apparent form.

Refused and Affirmed Apparent Form

I began to observe and understand that the result of the dynamics of refusal and repudiation was a split in the apparent form of those who came to my transtherapeutic formation sessions. I saw in them two apparent forms: a refused and an affirmed one, each with its own dynamics. Available to focal consciousness is the affirmed self-image with its exalted facets. Infrafocal are the refused or repudiated features of our life that threaten this exalted intra-appearance. They coform an infrafocal, unacknowledged apparent form. The exalted intra-appearance looms larger and larger in one's focal and prefocal consciousness than one's real life form does. It excludes all denied features of a person's life. They have been exiled into the arena of refused and repudiated self-images.

I speak often about the *refused* apparent form, intending it to cover both the refused and the repudiated aspects of our apparent form. This use can be justified by the fact that all repudiation implies some refusal, but not all refusal implies repudiation. For example, I may refuse the inspiration to spend more moments with a sick member of my family. But I may not necessarily repudiate my guilty awareness of the fact that I would have the time and the means to be with her. On the other hand, a repudiation of my guilty awareness would imply some deeper refusal. I refuse any aspiration or inspiration that could possibly move me to direct my mind and heart to be more generous. True transcendence begins with a process of candid appraisal of our refusals, with a dying to our exalted self-images.

Transposition of the Refused Apparent Form

What I do not allow to appear to me as a part of my true call of life is not absent from me. It does not vanish in thin air. One hidden dynamic of coping with denied facets is to transpose them from me to something outside of me. The dynamics of deformative transposition may dominate at this phase of the process of refusal. They move me to give form to a particular transposition of a facet of my life that threatens my exalted self-image. For example, I may have a tendency to manipulate people in subtle ways. I cannot admit this inclination to myself. This facet is at odds with the exalted image I have formed of myself over the years. One way of dealing with this refused feature is to transpose it to others. Unwittingly, I become sensitive to any deed or expression of others that could be seen as manipulative. This enables me to condemn, hate, and reject in other people what I cannot accept as a negative facet and challenge in my own life.

What can I do to overcome this division in myself? I must reappropriate the transposed dynamic. By making it my own again I can reintegrate it into my acknowledged apparent form as one of its depreciable but real facets. I can affirm the refused dynamic not as a consonant but as a still-dissonant feature of my life, a challenge to be taken into account gently and firmly in the further direction of my life. I call this kind of affirmation the *affirmation of intentional consonance*. I distinguish it from what I call the *affirmation of attained consonance*. Intentional consonance, unlike refused consonance, does not interfere with the road to transcendence.

Dynamics of Rage and Despair

A threat against our exalted self-image may persist and grow stronger. When such perseverance begins to overwhelm our barricades of safety directives, we may be moved to irrational rage. Pent-up rage may be released toward any person, event, or thing that happens to be near. Persistent rage tends to deplete the formation energy available to us. Depletion leads to fatigue and despondency. If rage cannot be released effectively it may turn inward. It overpowers the dynamics of our intrasphere. They turn against the intra-apparent form itself, which we cherished for so long in such an exalted and exclusive fashion.

The appreciation of the apparent form turns into depreciation and doubt. Because this inner apparent form or self-image has been mistaken for our basic identity, our whole self-appreciation is threatened by our depreciation of our apparent form. We may sink into depression or erupt in destructive actions, even suicidal attempts. We lose our sense of form potency. Yet we cannot live effectively and healthily with a constant mood of form impotence.

The dynamics of rage and despair heighten the dynamics of irrational fear. The fear is due to the impression that one's personal life—falsely identified with one's apparent form—is beyond control. The fear becomes formation anxiety when it extends itself to the very mystery of our life and its basic meaningfulness. Formation anxiety has no well-delineated object because the mystery and its call cannot be reified or made into a thing-like object. One has a vague, all-pervading, usually implicit feeling of abandonment *by* the mystery.

My formation anthropology distinguishes this depreciative sense of abandonment *by* the mystery from appreciative abandonment *to* the mystery.

Distortions Due to Field Deformation

When the inwardly apparent life form of people which they have absolutized is severely threatened, their whole world seems to go to pieces. I have tried to show in my anthropology that my 1944 paradigm of the formation field in its sphere of interformation has a universal, common, segmental, and personal range. The field as a whole, even in its nonpersonal ranges, is initially apprehended and appraised from the viewpoint of one's personal range. This is often a source of subjective distortions.

Growth in maturity and objectivity diminishes gradually our personal distortions of these nonpersonal ranges. This dynamic of purification of distortions is diminished when the apparent form of life is absolutized. The field as a whole is then fashioned in terms of our absolutized apparent form. This form makes us strive after a field that confirms it and that fosters its corresponding unfolding. Any threat in the field to the absolutized apparent form implies a threat to the field that we are. For this field is partly shaped by the perspective of our intra-apparent self-image. If one's deceptive apparent form is dissolved by such threats, one's whole field seems to dissolve. Recall such popular expressions of this experience as "My world is falling apart," or "It seems as if my whole world is going to pieces."

Formative Solution of the Crisis
of Field Deformation

The excessive attachment that brought on the crisis of field deformation should be reduced to normal attachment. It is normal that we be reasonably attached to each successive apparent life form. After all, we have directed our formation energy along the lines of that apparent form during a significant period of time. The apparent form, moreover, is the only light we can live by as long as our foundational life form does not manifest new pathways of formation and therewith new self-images. Fidelity to our apparent direction implies necessarily some attachment. We attach our formation energy to what here and now appears to us as fostering our consonant formation of life. Suddenly or slowly, it may be disclosed to us that the mystery, which ought to be the sole focus of our absolute attachment, demands a change in certain facets of this apparent form and in our conditional, relative attachment to it. This means that we have to detach formation energy from some of its facets and redirect it to a new attachment.

Such detachment is painful. It gives rise to suffering that is unavoidable. This normal suffering should not be confused with the unnecessary suffering of excessive, stubborn, blind attachment to an absolutized apparent form or one of its facets. Normal suffering can be transformative. It can lead us to deeper abandonment to the mystery. In this suffering, we may be gifted with a new appreciation of our founding form as emerging uniquely from the formation mystery. In appreciative abandonment we may experience at moments that we are loved into uniqueness. A great feeling of relief and freedom may flood our heart when it no longer has to mourn an apparent life form from which it was painfully detached by the transcendence dynamic. Crisis is at the same time danger and opportunity. Detachment presents us with an opportunity for homecoming in the radical mystery that underlies its epiphanic manifestation in our unfolding life.

Anthropology of Extreme Dissonance

Our lack of abandonment to the mystery in the midst of detachment may lead to desperate attempts to maintain our apparent self-image in all its facets as ultimate. In terms of my formation anthropology, the willingness of abandonment gives way to the willfulness of management of life as we want it, no matter what. Our refusal to flow with our changing life story becomes adamant. This leads to the dynamics of extreme dissonance. Rather than giving up control in trusting abandonment, we may be plagued by suicidal inclinations. In such cases, suicide may be the ultimate act of defiance, a last spasm of final control. The gift of life can be defied in direct or more often in indirect ways, such as neglect of our health, constant overwork, hypertension, overeating, drug abuse, neglect of sufficient exercise, recreation, friendship, and aesthetic enjoyment.

Another form of extreme dissonance is the flight into total withdrawal, a kind of paralysis of life. The symptoms may be so striking that they seem like those of catatonic patients. In my science of formation, I make a distinction between excessive withdrawal due to a process of deformation and the withdrawal due to psychosis. If and insofar as the latter is the result of biochemical causes, it falls outside the competence of my transcendent experiential anthropology and my transtherapy. Its solution belongs to such fields as medicine, neurology, psychiatry, and clinical psychology. They did most of their research in the pretranscendent realm of our life, including its biochemical factors.

The same applies to a third possibility. I call it the flight from the reality coformant of the formation field into the dissonance of delusion. In this case, people fashion by means of fantasy a new apparent form or they change fancifully some aspects of their already-existing apparent form. This self-deceptive form or form aspect is totally out of touch with the reality aspects of the inter and outer spheres and with the real universal, common, and segmental ranges of one's field. This delusional form gives some deceptive sense of effective control of one's life.

Anthropological Coformants
of the Intensity of Attachment

Attachment implies adherence to the direction our formation energy assumes in our life. Attachment to our apparent form or to its aspects implies our clinging to the formation energy we have directed toward this form.

According to my formation anthropology, the degree of intensity of attachment depends on various factors. One of them is the formation energy available to people. Another is the amount of energy they are willing to direct to the critical appraisal of their apparent form and its dynamics. How much energy do we invest in the appraisal of this form in comparison with our appraisal of other forms and dynamics? To what degree is our intensity wisely tempered by abandonment to the mystery? This intensity is also dependent on our preformation. Preformed characteristics may incline certain people to be more attached and determined in their attachment.

Some persons, for instance, developed a character disposition of tenacity. This inclination can be an effective aid in the functional control of the manageable matters of one's field of life. It becomes destructive when it is used also to force what cannot be managed in a functional sense. In that case, one may experience many frustrations of one's preferred apparent form. This is often accompanied by an erosion of security feelings and of one's sense of control. It may lead tenacious persons to desperate, willful attempts to preserve their dissonant self-image.

Willfulness compels us to cling stubbornly to an apparent form or form facet of life that no longer makes sense. Such tenacity can ruin our life or at least its effectiveness. If the stubborn will does not mellow in time, spiritual life in gentle abandonment becomes impossible. We should realize that the mystery's gift of gentleness enables us, at least in the long run, to soften this willfulness. Then we may reach some measure of abandonment, even if we are inclined by temper or character to tenacity.

Often we are trapped in the mixed dynamics of both a refused and an affirmed apparent form. The pride-empowered striving to appear to ourselves and others in a favorable light makes us selective in what we acknowledge as part of our real form of life. Our pride form tempts us not to admit to dispositions that are at odds with the exalted appearance to which we give form in our imagination. This tension nourishes conflicts between our affirmed and refused apparent form. As I showed earlier, the solution to this conflict is often mistakenly and unwittingly sought for in a dynamic of transposition to others of what we refuse to see in ourselves.

Example of Dynamics of Transposition

The dynamics of transposition can be illustrated by an example. John wants to force a career for himself as a famed scholar. He is overambitious because he is unrealistic about his limited abilities and his lack of affinity to a life of scholarly solitude and discipline. All of these insights are relegated to his *refused intra-appearance*. He declines to admit these ways of appearing to himself. He also refuses to acknowledge a hidden embarrassment about his own excessive and unrealistic ambition, the more so since he has not succeeded so far. He does not acknowledge the overambitiousness of his personality. He is coerced to deny the rootedness of this excessive ambition in a deep sense of insecurity, in self-doubt and feelings of inferiority. He transposes to others his own inordinate striving and the shame it generates. In accordance with his acknowledged self-image, he sees himself as a modest, unassuming person not interested in a conspicuous career but only in serving others by developing his talents in this chosen field. Because of his religious upbringing, he is able to beautify this pleasing intra-appearance with self-congratulatory images of the virtues of humility, serviceability, and self-forgetfulness. They substitute for his sense of insecurity, self-doubt, and inferiority. Abuse of virtue and its true meaning throws the religious person off the path to true transcendence.

What gives his refused intra-appearance away is his resentment, bitterness, and gossipy behavior when colleagues are successful in their chosen field. He is prone to accuse them of careerism, pride, and self-centeredness. Such persistent resentment is hidden in spiteful remarks. He pretends to himself that he is objective. Nevertheless, some aspects, as, for instance, the tone of voice, disclose his unacknowledged and refused apparent form and its transposition to others. In short, John transposes his own overambitiousness and its inferior motivations to others. He apprehends and appraises it as existing in them, not in himself.

Self-Depreciation and Self-Exaltation

The refusal to acknowledge certain formation dynamics in our life has thus led to a split in our intra-apparent life form. Facets that are at odds with our exalted positive or negative self-image are split off from our acknowledged intra-appearance. They may now be transposed to others as if they were not really operative in us but in them. We disown them in our apprehension and appraisal. Such unacknowledged dynamics form together an infrafocal constellation, which I called earlier our *refused intra-appearance*.

This refused intra-appearance contains the appreciation or depreciation dynamics with which we are no longer in touch, those we have forgotten. We have exiled them from our focal and prefocal awareness. The refused intra-appearance may thus encompass not only dissonant facets but also consonant ones, such as noble inspirations, aspirations, and desirable dispositions. We refuse to acknowledge and affirm them as invitations of the epiphanous mystery to become our own unique, limited life form, no matter how modest and simple. How is this depreciation of our own limited qualities related to the dynamics of exaltation?

Depreciations can be the negative expressions of exaltations. The exalting pride form may have led to the formation of an unattainable image of perfection. We may tire from our own perfectionism; we despair of ever scaling such impossible heights. Yet we do not want to give up this idealized intra-appearance. Proudly we refuse to be satisfied with our own real qualities that cannot match the idealized image conjured up by the perfectionistic pride form. Rather, we deny these limited qualities and transpose them in an idealized form to others. In them we celebrate our idealized self-image by boundless exaltation of our own transposed qualities. The logic of the dynamics of transposed exaltation leads usually to an excessive clinging to the exalted persons.

Anthropology of Interformation
and the Dynamics of Transposition

Although we may deny all deformational facets of our intra-appearance, they nevertheless remain a part of our nonfocal consciousness. Any attempt to disown them will remain futile. Because these facets remain secretly with us, they continue to give form indirectly to our life. We cannot escape apprehending them in some nonfocal fashion. Since we refuse to acknowledge them as belonging to us, we may deal with them as dynamics that are operative in other people. In this way our refused self-image plays a significant role in our *inter*-appearance and subsequently in the story of the dynamics of our interformation with others.

Effective interformation will be served by awareness of the dynamics of the refusal and of the transposition of self-apprehension that play in the interforming action and reaction between ourselves and others. An effective approach to the disclosure of such dynamics is to be attentive to what we condemn or exalt in others, especially when such condemnation or exaltation has emotional overtones. Of course, this does not mean that such condemnation or exaltation of others is necessarily always a disclosure of our own refused dispositions. It means only that there is a real *possibility* of such a transposition. If signs that point in the same direction begin to accumulate, this possibility of transposition may turn into a *probability*. We are cautioned that people who interform with us also may transpose their own refused dynamics to us. This tendency in ourselves or others contaminates the interforming relationship.

The transpositions may be so complete that people have become utterly unaware of them. They no longer realize that what they condemn in others may be their own afflictions. Each of us may become the unsuspected focus of such transpositions. We may find ourselves treated as either the despised embodiment of some people's own refused defects or as the adored embodiment of their denied qualities.

Human Freedom and Refusal Dynamics

Our acknowledged intra-appearance is one of the bases of our acts, disposi-tions, and attitudes. The dynamics of refusal and transposition reduce our for-mation freedom. An accurate knowledge of the dynamics that are active within us enlarges our range of free decisions in regard to these dynamics. Lack of their acknowledgment reduces our freedom of effective form reception and donation in daily life.

These unacknowledged dynamics now operate beyond the range of our free decisions. A significant part of our formation energy has been externalized. We now feel threatened or overly fascinated by these transposed dynamics of ours. They now appear to us as energized in others. In reality, it is our own dynamic formation potency and energy that gives form to these imagined external threats or fascinations. What we refused to acknowledge and to deal with in our own intra-formation now turns against us from the outside through our experiences of inter and outer formation. We can no longer see that we our-selves are the source of these imaginary threats or fascinations by others.

As we conclude this chapter on the formation anthropology of our apparent life form, we should remember that this form—like all other integrational forms—differentiates itself not only in terms of the pre, intra, inter, and outer spheres of our formation field but also in accordance with the dimensions of the human personality and their articulations. The same applies to our intra-appearance. Our apparent form manifests itself basically in the intrasphere of our formation field. It shows up in the transcendent, functional, vital, and sociohistorical dimensions of our intra-appearance. Each of these dimensions modulates the appearance of our apparent form in tune with its own dimen-sional directions. Each of them has its own modes of refusal and of concomi-tant exaltation, insulation, totalization, and identification in relation to the unacknowledged dimensional facet of the intra-apparent form.

In the course of these considerations of my anthropology of the intra-appar-ent form in this chapter, I highlighted the foundations of the dynamic for-mation process as a whole. This process is related to our foundational life form in its emergence from an *intimacy of sustenance* with the formation mystery and in its striving to *intimacy of consonance* with this mystery. The process is related also to our all-pervading quasi-foundational pride form and its dynamics.

The insights thus gained will facilitate a critical appraisal of the different approaches to reformation and transformation of the intra-apparent life form developed or to be developed by my formation science and formation theology in dialogue with the findings initiated by auxiliary sources. Above all, it can help us to facilitate our transcendent journey.

In this chapter I did not deal with the secret guardian that guides and super-vises our apparent form of life, our conscience. No formation anthropology can be trustworthy and complete without dealing in detail with this complex, powerful structure of human consciousness and the fascinating story of its formation and deformation. Therefore, I will develop in the following chapters my empirical-experiential formation anthropology of conscience and its vicissitudes.

CHAPTER 7

Anthropology of Formation Conscience

Formation conscience represents a particular set of ought dispositions. They show us how to give direction to the giving and receiving of form in our life. This conscience tells us what to do and what to avoid concretely, how to carry out in daily life the principles of our faith. It makes us feel guilty when we turn away from it; it works as a compass on our walk toward the land of consonance.

Formation conscience implements our moral conscience in our proximate as well as in our immediate formation field. Moral conscience draws directly on natural law and our faith traditions. Moral theologies and ethical philosophies shed light on this foundational aspect of conscience. We do not give form to this basic moral conscience by ourselves alone; we draw always on moral or ethical traditions of humanity, often unwittingly.

Formation conscience formatively implements the principles of basic moral conscience in the empirical-experiential coformants of our particular field of presence and action; it turns our attention to concrete ways of giving form to the basic moral directives in our life here and now. Formation conscience thus takes into account moral directives; it tells us how to adapt, refine, detail, and amplify these in such a way that they give form most effectively and soundly to our personal and shared lives in a wide variety of particular situations.

Our form directives are not developed in a vacuum. Knowingly or unknowingly, we always fall back on formation traditions that have touched us during our lifetime.

Pretranscendent and Transcendent Formation Conscience

I make a distinction between two general levels of formation conscience: the pretranscendent functional formation conscience and the transcendent formation conscience.

The pretranscendent functional formation conscience shows us how to give form to our lower powers of development. It enables us to handle practical situations effectively.

Transcendent formation conscience guides our lower functional formation conscience. It does so by means of higher dispositions. Examples of such transcendent dispositions are intuition, contemplation, wisdom, love, peace, endurance, and enjoyment. This formation conscience carries also the transcendent dispositions that we took over from our traditions. Transcendent formation conscience gives a decisive direction to functional formation conscience. Our transcendent conscience helps us to keep our functional life in line with our higher aspirations and inspirations.

These two kinds of formation conscience tie in with our formation traditions as distinguished, though not separated, from our faith traditions.

Anthropology of Socialized We-Conscience

Our pretranscendent formation conscience does not put itself at once under the direction of our transcendent formation conscience. In many formation traditions—as lived by divergent groups of people—our formation conscience goes through a phase of what I call the "we-conscience." This is still a pretranscendent phase. The "we" I speak of here does not stand for the transcendent "we" of the mystery all of us are called to share explicitly. Neither does our "social we" necessarily tie in with the "we" of the pervasive flow of the mystery in which all of us participate. It can remain merely a "socialized we."

Social we-traditions may mark the formational life of a community as a whole. They may typify, for example, an Islamic community, an ancient Spartan bent, or certain cults arising in the course of the formation history of Christianity.

In some communities, the social we-tradition touches people early in life. Children are caught up in it from the beginning. Many stay in it for a lifetime, never enjoying to the full their own transcendent form potencies. They do not come to the awareness of their unique-communal life call as flowing in and with the utmost and widest "we" of the mystery. To the degree that their call remains hidden, it cannot lift them beyond their merely socialized life. Unaware of their unique destiny and personal responsibility, instead of moving upwards, they may fall from an initially flexible social formation conscience into a fixated, merely collective, formation conscience. They become easy preys for demagogues, rabble rousers, undemocratic leaders, or fanatic religious and ideological gurus.

Anthropology of Collectivistic "We" Traditions

In collectivistic formation traditions, our formation conscience does not inspire us to develop truly social or individual potencies. Instead, it only lets the "we" of a collectivity run our life. The self-esteem of the merely socialized person does not draw upon the deeper resources of self-appreciation in the light of one's personal-communal call by the mystery. There is little or no personal self-appreciation. One's individual sense of worthwhileness is tied up with the appreciation, the honor, the achievements, the true or imagined glorious history, origin, or project of the group to which one belongs. Neither does the merely collective "we" break through to the deeper and wider "we" of our unique-communal life call. Without this transcendent we-appreciation people fall easily into a shared rejection of those who do not link up with the formation tradition of their group or who seem to threaten it. They cannot bear with any show of doubt by outsiders about the glory of the in-group. It strikes them as a threat to their collectivistic self-esteem. This hostility draws its energy from our innate need for appreciation. Everyone looks naturally for appreciation, though not necessarily in this collectivistic style.

In collectivistic we-traditions of formation, every reproof of the group is felt as a reproof of one's own life. For one's personality is excessively merged and identified with the formation directives of the group. There is also a fear of how outsiders would view the apparent form of the group adherents. Will the bad appearance of one of us shake the repute of the group as a whole? It is an unwritten rule that every member of the group should follow the public path in such a way that they uphold the honor of the collectivity. Self-esteem in followers of we-traditions draws heavily on the standing of the group as a whole. A public scandal of one, especially a ranking figure, will deeply shake many. Sometimes it makes them deny the wrongdoing as, for example, some people even now deny that the Holocaust ever happened.

Anthropology of Transcendent Formation Conscience

Our transcendent formation conscience sends out directives that guide our everyday formation conscience. Some are ought-not-to directives; others are ought-to directives.

Our life call as formational is coformed in its everyday implementation by communal and personal directives. The general features of our basic moral conscience are implicit in our formation conscience. They are communicated to us in the symbols, doctrines, and rites of our faith traditions. The particular features of our formation conscience, however, depend on the unique-communal aspect of our call as situated in time and space. As such, it cannot be fully covered in all details by the general ethical precepts of our shared faith and formation traditions.

Our formation conscience directs us to give form to our unique-communal formation call in tangible ways. Our actual life situations signal to us suggestions of how to give palpable form to our call. This form should be compatible with the truth of ethics as well as with those consonant demands of the situation that are in principle, but not in each and every possible detail, covered by our ethical precepts. To the degree that we cast our life in the light of our call, we can cut down on the number of "ought-not-to" directives." Recall the renowned words of Augustine: *Ama et fac quod vis,* "Love and do what you will." Meant here is our love-will as already transformed by the call of the mystery.

At the peak of transformation, our pretranscendent functional formation conscience and our transcendent formation conscience are at one. The transforming mystery reigns supreme. This mystery shows our core form as heart its unique destiny and shapes it in such a way that it can only will this inspiration. The functional conscience can only guide the execution of this inspiration faithfully and effectively.

Few people come in their lifetime to this peak of transforming consonance. The further down they slip from this height, the more they fall back on their practical everyday conscience alone. Their transcendent formation conscience takes on some of the features of a merely pretranscendent self-actualizing conscience. They fall back, under the pressure of popular traditions, on the directive of a pragmatic individualistic conscience. The directives of their transcendent tradition no longer radiate their inspiring power into their formation conscience.

In some cases practical conscience casts higher directives wrongly in the form of perfectionistic self-actualizations. One pushes oneself to instant ethical perfection by sheer individualistic willpower. One turns the deeper meanings of a transcendent form tradition into mere functionalistic meanings with subsequent willful control and containment of any spontaneity of life.

Coercive control carries with it the danger of crippling deformation. The merely functional formation conscience strikes back in fright when threatening insights, feelings, and strivings break through its control. Often people fall into a pattern of anxiety that keeps deforming their life in a hidden way. Their functional conscience pushes them to multiply safety directives. These keep them going in the midst of anxiety, holding their fears down so that they do not get the best of them.

Problem of Safety Directives

If we run our life by safety directives, a wide array of symptoms can wear us down. These symptoms run the gamut from hysterical-impulsive to coercive-compulsive features; from cognitive to somatic glandular, neuromuscular, organic, and bodily behavioral problems.

Needed is a candid appraisal of the functional formation conscience of self or others: Is it driven by a fretful concern for mainly the functional facets of transcendent form traditions? We drive ourselves to carry out functional projects that are not appraised and approved by our higher wisdom. We fall down from reasonable functioning that is necessary into crass functionalism that is self-defeating. We push away any reproof by our transcendent formation conscience that threatens to slip into our functional formation conscience. We set up all kinds of safety directives. To push away a guilty awareness of, for instance, hostility, anxiety, greed, and envy, we work out a great variety of protections. We develop patterns of blocking our awareness of such dissonant strivings, desires, and emotions. For they do not fit our exalted self-image. Such blocking does not remove these bothersome emotions. It is in our mind alone, not in our life, that we break the link with their original source.

Transposition of Guilt to Others

Sudden feelings of hidden rage about always having to function well may shake the onesidedly functional person. Feeling guilty about feeling guilty, he or she blames other people, events, or situations, thus removing the guilt from its original intraspheric source. This gives form to a disposition to look toward people and situations as the cause of our failure to carry out perfectly the functional form directives of a tradition. Yet the guilt feeling stays with us. Even if we let go of our awareness of the real source of the guilt, it keeps returning. To suppress its accusation of us, we keep alive the disposition of accusing others. This outburst may relieve, but it will not extinguish, this disturbing emotion in our own life.

Such false free-floating deformative guilt drives some to find relief in symbolic obsessive cleaning dispositions, such as repetitive compulsive handwashing. In others it gives rise to a self-punishing irrational kind of asceticism or mortification. In some cases I have found that my transtherapy or formation counseling—over and above the effective use of other necessary therapies—proved helpful. This kind of therapy made it possible for some people to disclose the deepest source of their disturbing feelings. It helped them to heal the rift between their transcendent call conscience and their functional conscience.

Dynamics of Form-Traditional Rage

We can push our harsh conscience demands for perfect formational self-actualization so much that our life becomes emotionally unbearable. Frustrated people may get into a rage at their form tradition itself instead of at the deformation of that tradition in their rigid formation conscience. Unaware of the real inner source of their frustration, they direct their anger only to insiders or outsiders of their own form-traditional communities. They cannot bring themselves to talk about their outrage. For this would be incompatible with their self-image of perfection. The checks of their functional form conscience are too strong for that. The hidden rage pushes some of them into mob explosions of fury and violence against the "infidels" or the "revisionists" or those to be cleansed ethnically. They dress their discrimination in the splendid vestments of spiritual absolutes, which they identify with their relative particular form directives. The sharing of the enraged "we-ness" feelings of a ranting crowd shakes them loose from their curbs of conscience, allowing them momentary relief. Such outbursts of shared frenzy tell the story of lynchings, pogroms, and persecutions. The fury of the crowd may choose to vent itself on minorities such as Jews, Gypsies, blacks, or immigrants.

Often people lay their guilt, anxiety, anger, and hostility on others within their own community. The stories of the devils of Loudon or of witchcraft trials, such as that of the witches of Salem, show us examples of such shifts of guilt to others. I worked these thoughts through in my theory of the differences among community, crowd, and collectivity. These views came to me during the horrors of the Dutch Hunger Winter when many of my compatriots were imprisoned or tortured to death.

Any community can be caught in collectivism. Stuck on the level of only functional conscience, the collectivity turns its bad feelings toward one or more persons within the group. They are cast in the role of the "black sheep" of a community or family. Many times the victims themselves come to believe the role in which they are caught. In the darkest moments of its history, a collectivity turns into a murderous *crowd*. Religious or ideological wars and pogroms can be the horrifying outcome of this breakdown of true transcendence of the dissonant forms of communities and collectivities.

The vicissitudes of our formation conscience, considered in this chapter, made me aware early in life that I should probe its phases of empirical unfolding. I expanded my empirical-experiential anthropology of conscience formation to, respectively, its parental, collective, and individual phases.

In the next chapter I shall present the anthropology of these phases in the overall formation of conscience.

CHAPTER 8

Anthropology of Parental, Collective, and Individual Formation Conscience

Parental Conscience

In early infancy, a primitive vital empathy prevails. It is based on a felt inter-wovenness with one's surroundings. This seed of vital formation conscience is soon overlaid by messages of the traditions to which the child is exposed.

By the time of birth, the infant is inserted in a specific group of people, for example, African Americans or Irish Americans. This fact was the source of my introduction in my formation field paradigm of the concept of the segmental ranges of interformation. Within a segmental group the child will be exposed to the particular *pulsations* alive among its members. Initially, such segmental pulsations are communicated mainly by parents. Young children identify with their parents. Hence, they go through a phase in which their emergent formation conscience is formed prevalently by the conscience dispositions of their parents or parental substitutes. I call this in my formation anthropology the phase of *parental formation conscience.*

Because the conscience of young children is not yet sufficiently illumined by their own founding dynamism, they have to fall back on the teachings, warnings, and sanctions of their parents. In this phase their formation conscience depends mainly on their parents' prohibitions, wishes, and ideals.

People who are still mainly directed by parental formation conscience show none or only a few dynamics of their own functional, collective, individual, or transcendent conscience. They have assimilated the formation directives of parental conscience without personal appraisal. Later in life, appraisal of adopted directives is part of the process of maturation of one's formation conscience. It enables this conscience to be formed by either free ratification or reformation of parental directives. For example, the everyday conscience formation of one's white American parents may have been deformed by prejudices against foreigners with strange customs and accents. Instead of blindly continuing such dispositions of parental form conscience, we need to reform them by exposing ourselves to the transcendent demands of social justice, peace, and mercy. This is part of our transcendent formation.

Parents themselves may be victimized by an unappraised parental formation conscience, which was taken over in turn from their parents. A prejudice against foreigners, for instance, may be linked to conscience dynamics handed over from generation to generation. They instilled generalizing images of untrustworthy, unpatriotic, lazy outsiders, or of threatening ambitious immigrants from overseas. These dispositions dictate that anybody of "good" conscience should watch foreigners carefully and keep them in their place. Such parents communicate by appearance, word, and deed that the formation conscience of children should be in rigid conformity with the formation conscience of their prejudiced ancestors. People may be permanently crippled by a mere parental conscience that rules their life direction, even if their parents are deceased or absent. Their life-style becomes rigid and unbending, a sterile repetition of the dispositions of the formation conscience of those who lived before them. Therefore, in some forms of tribal life, we can observe an adherence to the conscience directives of ancestors that blocks the creative unfolding of new dispositions of conscience.

The child's inner formation of a parental conscience is a necessary step on her or his way to a fully integrated formation conscience. It is the main means of assimilation of the consonant dispositions of the formation conscience disclosed by former generations. Nothing can replace it. Our transcendent conscience does not bypass wise and balanced directives of our interiorized parental formation conscience. It integrates them, permeating them with the light of the spirit. Transcendent people implement these consonant directives in daily life. While trying them out, they reform them in congenial, compatible, compassionate, and competent ways. No healthy formation conscience exists without the facet of one's sufficiently appraised parental conscience as made consonant with one's basic moral conscience, life call, purged tradition pyramid, and unfolding formation field.

Functional-Collective Formation Conscience

In the next phase of my theory of conscience formation, the dynamics of parental conscience will be complemented by those of ever widening groups of people. Interformation with these groups gives rise to what I conceived as a functional-collective formation conscience. Not the dynamics of a parental conscience alone, but those of others, such as playmates, friends, neighbors, and teachers, begin to coform our formation conscience.

A formation conscience that is onesidedly collectivity oriented fosters only form directives that are in rigid conformity with those of the group with which people identify. The reward of such conscience is confirmation by the gang or collectivity, often mistakenly called community. Their directives become the unquestioned norms of one's formation conscience. A collective conscience grants insecure people a sense of belonging. The group becomes the source of their formation conscience. Changes that take place in the conscience dynamics of the group are automatically absorbed into one's own merely collectivized functional conscience. There is little or no personal appraisal.

Loss of group affiliation can bring a person who is overly dependent on the collectivized conscience of the group to the point of panic. Exposed to another group, one does not find the reward of confirmation for directives of conscience taken over from the previous group. As a result, some may have no choice but to advance to functional individual conscience; others fall back to a mere parental conscience; still others may establish an identification with the formation conscience of the new group, allowing them to mold the formational dispositions of their own conscience accordingly. A striking example can be found in the case of some hostages, who, after a time, identified with the formational conscience dispositions of their captors.

It has been my observation that people with a merely functional collective conscience tend to cling to the group where collectivistic directives of life are rigorously determined and confirmed. They may be able to bend somewhat with changes in other facets of their own life, but they are always afraid of reaching the point beyond which to bend is to displease the group and diminish one's confirmation by them.

Irresponsible surrender of one's formation conscience to preferred collective directives replaces personal guilt with the guilt of a merely collectivized conscience. As long as one feels that the code of a gang, club, segment, country, or collective institution is fulfilled to the letter, no personal guilt or shame is felt for transgressions against one's basic moral conscience.

One of the basic presuppositions of my formation anthropology is that in every human person, a transcendent conscience is present in seed, as it were, transfocally. Hence, some vague, alien guilt feelings—transcendent in origin—may in a disguised fashion affect the dynamics of a collectivized conscience. However, these guilt dynamics cannot be identified by this conscience as such. I found in my transtherapeutic group sessions that they are often transmuted into diffuse anxiety dynamics. At certain moments of life, they may torment the heart of collectivized people, setting them up inwardly against themselves.

At any time, the call of one's unique founding dynamism may try to awaken the deepest responsibility of the heart. For some, life may become a tension between the dynamics of an insulated, merely collective conscience and the soft yet persistent voice of underdeveloped transcendent dynamics of an unacknowledged consonant formation conscience. I saw this happening in some of the distraught people I helped to escape from the threat to their freedom. Coming from an urban social upper class environment, they had to hide in the attics of simple rural farm laborers to avoid deportation to labor or concentration camps. Some of them began for the first time to question various directives of their former collective functional class conscience.

The dynamics of a collectivized formation conscience are powerful enough to block awareness of possible directives that are not exemplified in the segment of a society with which one has identified one's formation conscience unconditionally. An example may be found in groups of well-to-do families who are guided by the social-economic dynamics of their group conscience to invest money profitably in totalitarian countries that suppress Jewish, black, foreign, Muslim, Hindu, or Christian minorities. Some of their sons or daughters may dream of ways to alleviate the suffering of such minorities discriminated against under totalitarian systems. They may think about changing the investments of their parents. But for many, the dream soon fades. Before long, most fall back on the myopic dynamics of the collective economic conscience of their class-conscious families, where how much a person is worth in terms of status and possessions really matters. The price one must pay for fairness seems too high: loss of confirmation of form potency, less security, rejection by one's own kind, and diminishment of economic gain and standing. Soon the guilt of not living up to the conscience dispositions of their parents' formation segment suppresses a newly awakening guilt disposition in the upcoming generation. They silence the muted whisper of their underdeveloped transcendent formation conscience.

A striking portrayal of this predicament is given by the wife, daughter, and colleagues of Ben du Toit in the movie *A Dry White Season*. When Ben transcends the collective formation conscience of white supremacists in South Africa, they betray him. In the end his own wife and daughter share in this betrayal because they experience it as being a betrayal of their collective segmental conscience.

Functional-Individual Formation Conscience

The transition from the dispositions of a functional collective to those of a functional-individual conscience may be gradual. I observed in the Dutch Life Schools for Young Adults how I could make them aware of their individual interests, inclinations, tastes, and aptitudes. On the basis of this awareness, they began to realize that certain directives of formation conscience, exemplified in their field of life, are more in tune with their individual preferences than others. They began to feel responsible for their emergent individuality. As a result, they developed a more individualized functional formation conscience.

Both a parental and a collectivized conscience may have led to an identification with the conscience dispositions of others. Now the formation conscience becomes more selective; it is no longer a mere replication of the conscience dispositions of parents or peers. The formation of this more individual type of conscience can be facilitated by the expanding awareness of one's basic moral conscience and of the formation consciences of other people of various social backgrounds, cultures, and sociohistorical periods. It can also be stimulated by an awareness that is evoked by imaginary situations and characters in novels, plays, movies, and the media. One begins to appraise critically, at least implicitly, one's own merely parental and collectivized form conscience. As a first step, persons begin to ratify certain form directives of this newly emerging personal facet of their formation conscience. They start to appraise if these directives are consonant with their individuality. At the same time, they reject other directives as uncongenial. What is still missing in them is an openness to the unique-communal dynamics of transcendent formation conscience. This facet of conscience responds to the founding dynamism of our life call as illumined by our basic moral conscience and by the wisdom of consonant faith and formation traditions.

The new functional-individual facet of our formation conscience strives to absolutize itself at the expense, not only of the collectivized or parental formation conscience, but also of the higher transcendent facet of our own conscience. The dynamics of conscience are then merely selected on the basis of individual preferences. They may be mistakenly considered to represent one's transcendent formation direction itself that is in consonance both with one's life call and one's basic moral conscience. In fact, these people may not yet be aware that the dynamics of their true transcendent form conscience should overrule those of their individual preferences.

The domination of conscience by the absolutized dynamics of individuality makes for a strong type of personality—one committed to individual directives and, when necessary, in opposition to parents or society. Guilt is experienced when a person wavers from his or her chosen path. Because individualized functional conscience is not illumined by the dynamics of transcendent conscience, it may generate rigidity, drivenness, righteousness, or even fanaticism.

The hold of individualistic conscience dispositions may be so overpowering that this type of formation conscience is able to blot out awareness of other functional, vital, and transcendent needs in self and others. The pride form may exalt individualistic conscience dynamics out of proportion with reality. False guilt is experienced at the slightest deviation from the individualistic conscience principles and goals one has set for oneself. This type of formation conscience may make people overaggressive in their drive for ruthless self-actualization and their attempts to coercive control of others and their surroundings. Adolph Hitler has become an extreme example of a person fanatically driven by an overindividualized vitalistic-functionalistic conscience.

Exalted Individual-Functional
Formation-Conscience Dynamics

My personality theory stresses that the autarkic exalting pride form may affect one's individual functional conscience; it may breed an exalted functional self-image, which may generate in turn waves of false guilt when one fails to live up to this inflation.

I saw in extreme cases how dynamics of anxiety and despair led to a mental and emotional breakdown. I also observed how the false guilt dynamics of an exalted image of functional self-perfection led sometimes to a pietistic or ethical narcissism. It clarified for me why such individuals tried to give form conscientiously to the dynamics of perfectionism. Their conscience became stern and righteous, hurting themselves and others in its insulation from the mellowing transcendent spirit and from their basic moral conscience.

This radicalism generates in some a dynamic of almost constant scrutiny of their daily performance. In extreme cases, the victims of an individualistic conscience examine themselves over and over again. They measure themselves against their absolutized pretranscendent self-directives. Their individualistic conscience becomes tyrannical. Any failure may lead to harsh self-reproach and in the long run to an emotional collapse. It may breed dynamics of deformative scrupulosity as distinguished from clinical obsessive-compulsive disturbances, which may sometimes be mixed with it.

In the end, the deepest motivations for the maintenance of one's dynamics of conscience may change. The motivation may no longer be that these dynamics are thought to be connected with authentic life directives. I discovered that the new motivation of fidelity to these dynamics became in many the need to escape the torture of false feelings of guilt, especially when this deceptive guilt experience had led to the deformative dynamics of obsessive scrupulosity.

There is a notable difference between the guilt feelings evoked by either parental or collective conscience and those evoked by a merely individualized conscience. People who have absorbed parental or collective formation-conscience directives without sufficient appraisal may feel excessively guilty when they are not faithful to these directives borrowed from others.

People who are embedded in mere individualized conscience may, however, be burdened by guilt feelings because of unfaithfulness to their now self-imposed directives. The guilt can be overwhelming if one has exalted these dynamics deceptively to the status of the transcendent or of the basic moral conscience. In both cases, the dynamics generated by an incomplete conscience lead to deformation.

Dynamics of Formation of Transcendent Conscience

The dynamics of transcendent formation conscience awaken people to the unique gift of the mystery they are. Transcendent form potencies are latent in their founding form. Disclosures of this founding form evoke the experience of responsibility, of "oughtness," in regard to the deepest longings of our distinctive humanness. This responsibility of the heart is translated into the transcendent facet of formation conscience.

Dynamics of transcendence lift us out of the insulation of a formation directed merely by the vital, parental, functional-collective, and functional-individual facets of formation conscience. Unlike the directives of the other facets, these transcendent form directives emerge primarily in our intrasphere. Unlike basic moral faith directives, formation directives are not at once compelled or planned. Their source is the disclosure of our founding form or unique-communal life call rooted in the mystery and its epiphanic disclosures in the consonant faith tradition we have embraced. This life call reveals itself also in the messages of the mystery that come to us through all the spheres, dimensions, ranges, and regions of our field of presence and action. They may be experienced as coming from "beyond" because they flow from our formation conscience-as-openness-to the indwelling mystery. They form us by modes of subtle appeal, not by modes of coercion or seduction used at times by those who want merely to collectivize our formation conscience or strive to remake it in their own image.

Transcendent form directives are disclosed in a climate of silence. Stillness clears the way for listening to a deeper responsibility. Its message enables us to experience transcendent guilt. The heart becomes aware of a unique responsibility for one's life as a whole. Suddenly, we are faced with the probable disclosures of our personal-communal life call, which no one can take from us or live for us. In this depth of our distinctively human formation conscience, we experience the radical aloneness of the responsible heart before the mystery. Our heart's deepest responsibility transcends that of the collective facet of formation conscience. Similarly, the heart begins to respond to more than mere individual marks of a vital-functional life. The historical, vital, and functional facets of conscience lose their exclusive autonomy; they become subordinated to transcendent dynamics in openness to our founding dynamism. Their exclusive autonomy becomes, therefore, a relative autonomy.

The transcendent formation conscience is not without collective, vital, and parental facets. It takes into account the consonant dynamics of these dimensions. However, they are no longer the exclusive or only sources of conscience. Collective and parental dynamics are appraised in the light of our transcendent conscience. Neither are individual-functional dynamics of conscience eliminated indiscriminately. They are dropped, modulated, or complemented in accordance with our unique-communal dynamics of transcendence. These dynamics, while always in accordance with our faith-traditional basic conscience, *transcend* both conformity and nonconformity on the mere formational level of life. Fidelity to the unique dynamism of the mystery in one's life may prove compatible with wise conformity to certain consonant facts of various formation traditions. True compatibility will be affirmed by transcendent conscience. If not compatible, the transcendent dynamics of conscience move us to accept serenely the sometimes unpleasant consequences of our refusal to be diverted by some collectivity from our heart's primary responsibility.

Among the first signs that the dynamics of transcendent formation conscience begin to assert themselves is a diminishment of vulnerability to the opinions of crowd and collectivity, to the praise and blame of people around us. When our responsibility is rooted first of all in our transcendent formation conscience, as attuned to our basic faith-traditional moral conscience, we become less easily wounded by criticism, less self-conscious, no longer excessively concerned with the praise or reproof of others. We find that we become less intensely self-observant, less victimized by an individualistic functional conscience inclining us to incessant self-probing. Similarly, the dynamics of the vital sympathetic conscience are no longer overwhelming. We feel less driven to be excessively pleasing to others, to be overly sensitive to their feelings, to hunger inordinately for human love and liking. In regard to the collective facet of our conscience, we are no longer weather vanes moving anxiously or eagerly with every pulsation.

Generally, the more the dynamics of transcendent conscience predominate, the less driven we are by rigidity, anxiety, impulses, and compulsions. Formation guilt becomes less paralyzing, more enlightening. Past failures do not remain dead history; rather, they serve to disclose what our dynamic direction should not be. These dynamics do not turn us toward the past in futile ruminations but rather toward the present and the future. They foster what I call corrective-opportunity thinking.

Dynamics of Transcendent Formation Guilt

The dynamics of formation guilt gain a whole new quality in the light of the transcendent dimension. Dominated by functional formation conscience, our guilt may have been shallow. We may have felt guilty mainly about mistakes in the functional execution of our collective and technical-ethical obligations. While this was important, it told us little about our failures to be faithful to life as a whole, to respond to the disclosure of our distinctive destiny by the forming mystery. We may have lacked a sense of guilt when failing to live up to our unique, inmost formation responsibility.

We are now ready to open ourselves to the gift of the dynamics of transcendent conscience and the corresponding richness of the dynamics of higher formation guilt. A first preparation is to distance ourselves periodically from our immediate inclinations. We must step back from the stereotypes that populate our collective conscience and from the dictates issued by our individualistic functional conscience. In wise and relaxed appraisal, we should weigh each of these lower conscience directives until we see what should be our direction in the light of transcendent conscience as enlightened by our consonant faith and formation traditions. Retreating somewhat from the social whirl, creating moments of silence, we may be gifted with the illuminating experience of personal-communal formation guilt. This guilt is like a beacon of light on our journey into the darkness of an unknown destiny. Subduing the noise of exclusive, individualistic functional dynamics of conscience, we may grow in transcendent self-presence. We may be able to distinguish between mere functional guilt experiences and the recognition of having failed the dynamic directives of our transcendent formation conscience. Functional guilt is merely issue-oriented; transcendent guilt is not only issue-oriented but open also toward life in its mysterious unfolding wholeness and in its rootedness in the sacred.

Gradually we gain a deeper insight into the dynamics of transcendent guilt. We come to know that we are guilty not merely because we have done something of which parents, the collectivity, or our own functional conscience would not approve. We are guilty in the distinctively human sense of failing our transforming life call. The dynamics of transcendence make us sense that we have violated the call we most deeply are, that we have betrayed the source of our true nobility. We have halted the formation history of universe and humanity by refusing to interform with it in our unique-communal way as meant by the mystery. This depth of formation guilt is transcendent. It is rich in formative dynamics, holding us in awe and humility, moving us toward reformation and transformation. This latent deepest guilt, this sacred indebtedness, is always with us, albeit transfocally. It implies an elevation and intensification of what can be found in every guilt dynamic that in some measure goes beyond the dynamics of mere functional, vital, or collective guiltiness.

Transcendent Facet and Other Facets of Formation Guilt

Often I have witnessed how the dynamics of transcendent formation guilt may be numbed by teachers and counselors in misled and misleading compassion. Not only are guilt dynamics themselves dulled in this way; also dulled is one's receptivity for the expression dynamics of one's founding life form. The dynamics of transcendent guilt underlie every person's true experience of formation guilt, tangled though it may be with distorting dynamics of mere individualistic, collective-functional, or vital guilt. To deny the depth of transcendent formation guilt is to deny the founding dynamics of one's life form and of its responsible core form as character. Such dismissal of the dynamics of transcendent formation conscience makes it difficult for us to tune in to the classic transcendent traditions of humanity, as expressed, for example, in the Hebrew psalms or in the doctrines and rituals of Christian churches. We condemn ourselves to giving form to our life under the cover of only our collective or individual conscience dynamics. We do not rise into the light of our spirit as the mirror of our foundational dynamism. We can evade the light of transcendent formation guilt, but only at the risk of not approaching the unique-communal form or expression of the forming mystery we are called to be in empirical human history.

The dynamics of exclusively functional formation guilt can be insulating; they fill our lives with anxiety and frustration. Transcendent guilt dynamics, on the contrary, are never insulating. They open us to the compassionate outflow of the mystery in our field of life. They enlighten us about our potency for improvement, always present in our unique founding call of life and its latent form potencies.

Transcendent formation conscience inspires us to escape the prison of functionalistic guiltiness, to become who and what we most deeply are. We disclose the directives of our transcendent conscience in the very admission that we have violated them. We begin to sense the relation of the dynamics of our transcendent conscience to the life around us as well as to all that is. The realization dawns that through our refusal to follow the lead of these directives, we diminish the consonance of the universal formation dynamics of humanity, history, and world. To regain consonance with our own transcendent conscience direction is thus to regain consonance with the overall formation dynamics of cosmos, humanity, history, and its classic transcendent formation traditions.

Transcendent guilt becomes the core of a new, dynamic life direction. It is a forming light disclosing to us dynamically what we have to be and what obstacles should be watched in fidelity to this light. Gentle abiding in transcendent guilt grants life depth and meaning. It is a dynamic factor in the ongoing history of our formation.

Functional formation guilt is not abolished but transformed by transcendent guilt. We begin to live more in the awareness of our present possibilities and opportunities. We are less often trapped in impotent regret over the neglect of opportunities that are no longer there. Formation guilt ceases to be mere self-condemnation originating in our functional conscience alone. It is a loving appeal from the mystery at the root of our existence.

Those who live in fidelity to these higher dynamics begin to appraise candidly what is congenial with their unique-communal life call yet compatible, compassionate, and competent. They radiate transcendent social presence, practice, and prudence. The vital, parental, collective, and individual-functional facets of their formation conscience become the servants of their transcendent conscience. These partial dynamics enable persons to be effectively and competently present in their formation field in tune with their individual vital sensitivity and functional dexterity. The final decision in regard to this effective individual presence is made in dialogue with one's unique life call as radiated through the spirit into one's transcendent conscience.

Anthropology of Faith-Traditional Conscience

The vast majority of people adhere to one or the other ideological or religious faith tradition. Inherent in each faith tradition are specific conscience directives. These differ from one another to the degree that the underlying faith traditions differ. For example, there is a considerable difference between the conscience dynamics fostered by Marxian, humanistic, Freudian, Jungian, Adlerian, Maslowian, Rogerian, and managerial-ideological faith traditions. The same can be said of religious faith traditions. We cannot claim that all the implied conscience directives of, for instance, Hinduism, Buddhism, Confucianism, Judaism, Islam, Catholicism, and various denominations of Protestantism are absolutely identical in all their facets. In certain regards, the difference between conscience directives of both the ideological and the religious faith traditions are more considerable than those between certain aspects of the religious faith traditions themselves such as a shared faith in an all-embracing transcendent mystery. Still, it would be confusing to use terms of the metalanguages of any of these traditions without careful appraisal both from the general scientific viewpoint of formation science and from the formation theology of one's own faith tradition. Otherwise, one may communicate unwittingly as identical the different connotations similar terms have acquired by their specific use in the tradition concerned. A Buddhist, for example, will not feel at ease in borrowing from the metalanguage of Maslow the term self-actualization. Its Maslowian connotations do not cover what the Buddhist feels in conscience to be the deepest dynamic of human existence.

Anthropology of Form-Traditional Conscience

Generally, when we move from a faith to a formation tradition we find more points of agreement. The reason is that the practical application of the principles of any faith tradition is coformed by the demands of an empirical formation field. This field is shared by the adherents of various traditions and in part open to empirical examination. Hence, we can often find a common ground in proximate practical concerns. This makes a limited common science of proximate human formation possible. We can find some consensus on certain preferred, proximate formation directives. A statistically significant number of adherents of different faith traditions may agree on them. Over and above this consensus many differences remain in formation traditions. Those that do remain are rooted in certain unique aspects of each faith tradition. This is especially noticeable in religious faith traditions that adhere to a belief in divine revelation. Consequently, adherents should form their conscience dynamics in the light of that specific revelation and its interpretation by the legitimate authorities of the tradition concerned. The moral theologies of these traditions explain what conformity to the basic tenets of a religion entails. There are as many different specific moral theologies as there are different religious faith traditions. It would be impossible for a general science of proximate human formation to evaluate at once all of these divergent moral theologies. Even if it were possible for them, such a task would fall outside their field of competence.

Adherents of each tradition should consult the generally agreed-upon communications of the authorities of their own church and the acknowledged theologians or the ethical thinkers of their own ideological community. They should examine the formation of the faith-traditional facet of their conscience in the light of the ultimate directives of the belief system to which they adhere. What followers of my formation science would agree upon is the necessity for fidelity to the faith tradition to which one is freely committed. This commitment implies fidelity to the basic and necessary implications of these "oughts" in our corresponding form traditions. For it is through such form traditions that we can implement our faith into our empirical-experiential fields of life. Deliberate, constant infidelity to our own free and convinced faith commitment not only evokes inner dissonance; it is ultimately self-defeating.

The empirical-experiential considerations of my formation science and its formation anthropology should remain sufficiently general. Only then can they be acceptable to a significant majority of well-educated adherents of various basic consonant faith and form traditions. Some formation scientists may be interested in exploring a special area of interest over and beyond their general knowledge of formation science. For example, they may explore the possible articulation of its empirical findings in terms of a more-specialized attention to a particular tradition. They may consider the formation tradition of the particular ideological or religious faith to which they themselves belong or in which they are formationally interested. Others may want to read the eighth volume of this series. It will feature an introduction to the Christian formation theology I initiated in 1944 and then complemented with a formation science conducive to and compatible with it. I developed the science for those spiritually minded people hiding with me, who could not share my Christian formation theology.

Articulators of a specific formation tradition should not contest the informational moral theology or ethical philosophy of the tradition they are studying. They may only point out the practical effectiveness of conscience formation within the concrete formation field of the adherents of that tradition. For example, a scientific-empirical interest in the concrete-proximate formation of conscience and its consequences, as practiced by Islamic people in a specific Muslim culture, will not extend itself to a critique of the doctrine or theology of Islam as such. This would be a task for informational theologians. It is definitely not the focus of empirical-proximate formation science.

My Christian formation theology can critique the implicit and explicit formation theologies of the form traditions of other religions and ideologies as long as it does not claim professional expertise in their informational speculative theologies. Similarly, informational speculative theologians ought not to pretend that they are experts in the empirical-experiential formation theology of transcendent character and personality formation.

Recapitulation

My formation anthropology sees the core form as respectively centering core, heart, and character of the human person coformed by two dynamics: those of responsibility and sensitivity. Subsequently, in dealing with the dynamics of formation responsibility, I was led to consider the dynamics of human formation conscience. Both character formation and conscience formation belong to the core form of human life. The dynamics of conscience could only be understood in the light of the various phases of conscience formation considered from the viewpoint not only of typical but primarily of distinctively human formation. I tried to show that the dynamics of formation conscience imply dynamics of formation guilt. I asserted that formation conscience is usually formed in the light of the dynamics of faith-traditional conscience. The majority of people freely adhere to an ideological or religious faith tradition and derive from it the basic structure of their moral conscience over and beyond the natural laws of basic moral conscience that is already in principle innate in them.

I would like to repeat again that the ultimate justification of particular faith directives and the particular moral applications of such ultimates belong to the legitimate authorities of one's tradition in dialogue with its informational and formation theologies or ideological philosophies. My formation science as a pretheological-empirical discipline can only examine the general formation dynamics, conditions, and consequences of various ways of empirical-experiential implementation of such particular moral ultimates. It researches how this implementation affects people's formation conscience. It studies especially the related empirical-experiential formation of their transcendent character and personality.

The two coformants of the heart are interdependent. Responsibility and its subsequent formation of conscience influence our sensitivity. Sensibility is the affective responsibility of the core form as sensitive heart. Our sensibility affects in turn our responsibility and conscience. This is strikingly exemplified in the fact that most people speaking about their conscience seem really to be speaking about their *feelings* of conscience. They usually tell of their responsibility insofar as it is expressed in or affected by the sensibility or affective responsibility of their heart. For the sake of clarity, I have to discuss my anthropological view of these two interacting coformants separately. Therefore, the next chapter will deal with my anthropology of the dynamics of responsibility and sensibility in relation to conscience formation.

CHAPTER 9

Characteristics of Formation Conscience

My previous chapters on formation conscience make it easier for me to introduce some of the most desirable characteristics of this kind of conscience. As I have tried to make clear, formation conscience is an integral part of my anthropology of transcendent character and personality formation. Let me, therefore, review briefly some of my basic concepts of person and personality. This may clarify the place and the specific characteristics of formation conscience in my anthropology.

Transcendent Person and Personality
from a Formation Perspective

My formation science and its anthropology are formational, foundational, empirical,,experiential as well as descriptive. Therefore, my formation science lends itself to the formulation of a unified formation theory of person and personality and of the role of a qualified formation conscience within this formation.

I applied my formation theory of the person first to the life schools in Holland. In the United States, I used it as the basis of three of my earlier books on formation theology, *Religion and Personality, The Transcendent Self,* and *The Vowed Life.*

The basic idea in my later American publications on my Dutch pretheological formation science is that personhood and its unfolding can only be understood in its continual interformation with all spheres and dimensions of my 1944 formation paradigm, by now well known to the students of these volumes. The fundamental concept of this paradigm is the formation mystery at its center. I see this formation mystery as beneficial, as the Good, as Love and Loving. The secondary fundamental concept, the first one to the right of the formation mystery in my paradigm, is the human person or the human life form in its deepest inwardness and solitariness before the mystery that loved the human person into being.

What do I conceive as the ground of this personhood? In my anthropology I call this inmost ground of the person the founding life form. Dynamically speaking, I call it our continually forming life call. It guides us in our unfolding of the true unique-communal image of the formation mystery. It grants us the dignity and nobility of being irreplaceable persons called forth uniquely. As such, each one of us is an end and not a means. Therefore, people are never allowed to use any human person as merely a means for something else.

Basic Quality of Human Personhood
and Formation Conscience

What, then, should be the basic quality of human personhood and therewith of its formation conscience? This deepest quality is the disposition that I call the love-will. I borrowed this expression from the unusually graced soul friend of my youth, Rinus Scholtes, whose influence on my thought and my life still lingers. In intimate conversations and in his notebooks it became clear to me that it was his mission to purge the concept of the essence of love from any identification with mere feeling, imagination, thought. These may be included and should be gratefully accepted when granted, but they are not the bare essence of love. The love-will inspires in the depth of one's soul, at the very root of one's founding life form, an unconditional willing of love. Rinus paid his dues for this insight during a full year of a dark desert night of sense and spirit in which he was granted the understanding and acceptance of his love-will (*liefde-wil*) at the peak of his purged personhood. It happened to him during the period of transforming union only two years before his edifying death.

How do we let this love-will receive form and give form to our personality and its relatively lasting character at its core? Our love-will should strive to give form to all our character dispositions and to all our current responses to our formation field. How do we know what the forming mystery of love wants us to do, to give, to receive in our personality and through it in the inter and outer spheres of the fields of life it readied for us? We know it basically from the classical transcendent formation traditions of humanity. But the everyday formation of each unique-communal person goes beyond this general wisdom. The mystery of formation wants to enlighten each person about the unique-communal way in which he or she should implement the general ethical wisdom of humanity. It should be wisely implemented in one's own particular formation field without compromising, however, the basic ethical truths disclosed by humanity over the centuries in the light of the formation mystery.

Formation Conscience as Implementation Conscience

And it is here that my concept of formation conscience comes in. This implementation conscience should use the formationally relevant knowledge of informational disciplines such as informational theologies, philosophies, physical, social, medical-clinical, educational, and lingual disciplines. They can help the person-in-formation to disclose the particular features of his or her personality in its effective interformation with the particular inter and outer conditions of providential formation fields. That is the reason why my formation science and formation theology consult so often arts and sciences. Our formation conscience, enlightened by such disclosures, is indispensable as a power of direction for the human person who should always be in ongoing formation. It tells the person the particular formative directions his or her love-will can ethically choose from when implementing concretely the basic moral wisdom of the classical transcendent formation traditions.

My theory shows how formation conscience itself is derived from the person's primordial love-will, which in Rinus's experience and understanding includes and goes beyond concepts, images, feelings, moods, and consolations.

As I have shown in these chapters on formation conscience, I observed in the phasic formation of children's conscience a phase of proto-formation conscience. Later in life such basic proto-formation directives gain explicit power and meaning through formational reflection.

Hallmarks of Formation Conscience

In the light of this brief consideration of the basis of my formation anthropology of the person I shall now consider some of the desirable characteristics of our formation conscience.

I have argued that the love-will of the formation mystery is the ground of our personhood. Not only that, the inmost depth of our personhood is endowed with a share in the love-will of the mystery. Our love-will strives to love all that is in ourselves, in others, in the world. Therefore, the love-will strives to find the most effective way to give form to our formation field in love. Formation conscience is coformed by a love-will that wants to remind us of the right way of effective personal implementations of love. Thus, the first quality of formation conscience is that it is guided by the love-will. All other qualities are forms of this primordial will to love. This love should guide us via our formation conscience when it generates ought-directives for our everyday formation. It should enlighten us through our formation conscience when we appraise our acts, dispositions, and attitudes. Such appraisals, inspired by the love-will, are at the root of responsible formation directives in our formation conscience.

This love implies a loving openness to the universal formation directives that come to us from our classical transcendent formation traditions as well as a receptivity for the particular implementation insights we gain from other sources of information.

Out of the same love-will grow other characteristics of formation conscience, such as compatibility, compassion, competence, and firmness. I shall briefly comment on these few. After that I will add some reflections on alienation of formation conscience, its phasic unfolding, types of formation conscience, and current dynamics of conscience.

Compatibility of Formation Conscience

Our formation conscience is compatible insofar as it is in tune with our life situation as illumined by our inmost call, including our unique love-will. For example, Thomas Merton's formation conscience had to be compatible with the situation of Cistercian life to which he had committed himself. His autobiography and journals provide a striking illustration of Merton's struggles, successes, and failures to establish compatibility between his unique call and his situation in a community less intellectually and artistically inclined than he himself was.

Compassionate Formation Conscience

Compassion is a coformant of our unique transcendent love-will. It should express itself in our conscience. Therefore, a mature formation conscience is compassionate. Its directives become gentle and flexible if we begin to temper ardent, impatient, rigid, and ruthless strivings. Pitiless rigidity has to be mellowed by compassion for our own and others' limitations. The dynamics of compassion rescue our responsibility from willfulness, harshness, and fanaticism. The responsive sensibility of our core form as sensitive heart tempers the potential rigidity of our formation conscience.

In Thomas Merton's story, we see a gradual gentling of his appraisal of both his own striving for perfection and the limitations of his community and its administrators. He grew also to a more benevolent appraisal of the sins of his past, youthful university years.

Competent Formation Conscience

The dispositions of a responsible conscience are competent insofar as they are enlightened by continual transcendent reflection, experience, application, and study, especially in times of transition in formation traditions. One is responsible for the expansion of the competence of one's conscience, not only for one's own sake but for the sake of others. Merton's dynamics of formation conscience changed for the better by transcendent reflection on his own experience and on the new insights offered by the changes in his monastic formation tradition as a result of Vatican Council II. It is clear from his writings that he grew in transcendent life formation.

Firmness of Formation Conscience

A firm formation conscience is based on a disposition of free and flexible appraisal and ratification of consonant directives, while rejecting dissonant ones. For example, Golda Meir's formation conscience became firm when she was able to appraise transcendently her bent toward a life of service to Israel. This decision implied in turn a depreciation in her own life of the attractive possibility to establish a well-to-do life in America, a disposition promoted by the form tradition of her family in Milwaukee. Other family dispositions, however, could be ratified by her as fitting her life call. For instance, the sobriety of the life-style in her parental home became a lasting conscience directive, even when she, as prime minister of Israel, strove to be a servant leader. The dynamics of formation conscience in her case were firm enough to be maintained steadfastly in the midst of resistance, fallibility, vulnerability, and limitation.

Firmness grants responsibility its sober steadfastness. People like Golda Meir, Gandhi, and Martin Luther King are outstanding examples of a firm formation conscience in regard to their transcendent life call.

Alienation of Formation Conscience

There is always the danger that our formation conscience may become alienated. This peril deepens to the degree that we do not establish a disposition of candid appraisal of our conscience directives, at least implicitly. For example, people on the road to success, wealth, and power may succumb to popular pulsations that are dissonant with their transcendent call including its deeper, unique love-will. They assimilate such alien pulsations in their formation conscience. During this process they are afflicted by dissonances and tensions. The source of such tensions remains hidden from them as long as they do not focally appraise what is happening.

What are the possible sources of such alienating dynamics of formation conscience? To name a few, they are the impact of dissonant formation models; popular or academic subjectivistic codes and philosophies; sociohistorical pulsations; formational literature; the media and propaganda; pressure groups in the common and segmental ranges of our field—aberrations of the perceived directives of one's love-will.

Some blindly borrowed directives may later prove to be consonant. They may foster the formation of genuine personal and social presence. In that case, they are worth personal ratification with or without correction. Thomas Merton ratified in this way most of the dynamics of life in his community while maintaining a sense of the need for contemplation in a world of action.

We may borrow blindly from impressive others directives they are called to realize in their life. On closer inspection they may prove to be alien to our own unique preformation; they are not merely possible complementary counterforms but harmful contraforms to the personal-communal form of life to which we are called. Merton could not ratify in personal conscience as ideal for his own life the anti-intellectualism he found among some of his fellow monks. Nor could he confirm the initial depreciation some felt for his aspiration to live a more solitary existence. Neither could Golda Meir ratify as a leading dynamic for her life certain bourgeois directives that initially guided her parents' aspirations for her future.

Phasic Aspect of Formation Conscience

Our formation conscience unfolds over time through a succession of different phases. For this reason I had to introduce the concept of phasic formation conscience. I have already distinguished in my empirical anthropology of formation the following phases: vital-parental; functional-collective and individual; functional-transcendent; transcendent unique-communal; and transcendent-functional. In each one of these phases, the developing corresponding aspect of formation conscience temporarily predominates. It is possible, however, that we become fixated on a facet of conscience that would then mark our life more than any other facet.

The struggle between unfolding modes of conscience within us can intensify at critical junctures of our journey. Golda Meir, in her autobiography, describes the struggle she had to go through as a young girl between her own interiorized parental conscience telling her to stay with her family and the individual coformant of her formation conscience telling her to run away from home to another city in order to be able to get the high school education her parents did not deem necessary.

Types of Formation Conscience

In my formation anthropology I relate the phases of conscience formation to different facets of the structure of conscience, one or the other of which may prevail at any given time.

The types of formation conscience I identified offer tentative descriptions of what people would be like if they were ruled exclusively by one or the other facet of their conscience. Descriptions of types shed light on our understanding of how conscience comes to be both formed and informed. These enable us to highlight the tendencies human conscience may assume in different persons lastingly or during certain phases of their life. Usually, formation conscience is not dominated exclusively by one of these types. The prevalence of any one type of conscience does not necessarily exclude some secondary influences by other types.

Succession of Current Dynamics
of Formation Conscience

Something similar can be said of the succession of one current dynamic of formation conscience by another. This sequence is not the same in each person. There may be a phase in which one type of conscience prevails for the time being, only to become latent again during another phase in which other dynamics take the lead.

For example, the dispositions of a primitive vital formation conscience emerge in the early phases of childhood. After that, children enter a phase of conformation with parental conscience. If the parental conscience repudiates expressions of vital warmth and sympathy, the earlier vital dispositions become submerged. When they become older, children may rediscover their repudiated vital dynamism. A facet of formation conscience that once dominated their early childhood may be reawakened later in life when they mellow with age. When purified from childishness it can become a significant coformant of one's second transcendent childhood. This transcendent childhood formation conscience is guided by the love-will which transcends yet takes into account the vital facet of formation conscience.

Vital Conscience Formation

The vital facet of formation conscience is basic for our growth in spontaneous cordial empathy for people and things. Early in life we are not yet able to form either a well-organized functional or a transcendent conscience. We have not yet at our disposal the necessary neurons, concepts, and skills. What emerges, however, is a prefocal sense of the vital-sensitive interwovenness of our life with all other forms surrounding it. If the conditions in the child's field are favorable, a flood of sensitive and imagistic sympathy and empathy with the things one encounters may pervade prefocal consciousness. This lays the foundation later for a genuine interest in and a vital compassion for people, animals, nature, and things.

Vital formation conscience is not yet guided by powers of apprehension, appraisal, and affirmation as illumined by our spirit and by our basic human and faith-traditional moral conscience. It marks, however, an important beginning in the shaping of a sensitive and sensibly responsible formation conscience. This original seed will enable the human life form later to experience guilt when it violates the directives of vital sympathy. The vital facet of conscience as sensibly sensitive fosters a feeling of responsibility for the expression of kindness to people. The vital coformant of our formation conscience fosters cordial receptivity in response to others' showings of warmth and sympathy or of their experiences of pain or pleasure. Vital sympathy moves us beyond mere tolerance; it generates an outgoing feeling of vibrant consonance, of concerned and sensitive presence and its effective expression.

This first phase of vital conscience formation has to be complemented and corrected by the functional and transcendent facets of conscience. Otherwise, vital dynamics may blind us to everything else because of the overwhelming sympathy we may feel for family members and friends, children and victims of crimes and accidents. The dynamics of higher functional or of transcendent conscience may demand that we limit or modulate wisely the expression of vital dynamics. In emergencies, for instance, such as a fire or shooting, we have to control our vital feelings of compassion and their warm expression in order to function effectively in our rescue efforts or in damage control. Physicians, police officers, and fire fighters are professional examples of such modulation of their expression of vital feelings.

To give another example, a beloved friend or family member who is an alcoholic may move us vitally to protect her or him at all costs from failure or discovery. Yet our empirical formation conscience may tell us that it will take nothing less than "tough love" to make them face their addiction and its embarrassing consequences and to seek a path to healing.

A charming person exuding warmth and friendliness toward us may incline us vitally to give her a position others are better able to handle. In this case, the higher dynamics of our formation conscience should direct us not to betray social justice because of vital dynamics of warm, personal involvement. Great harm can be done to cultural, social, judiciary, and religious institutions and to human rights because of socially unjust court and jury decisions or appointments of charming, flattering persons or sport, movie, and TV heroes who prefocally played on the vital facets of the immature formation conscience of superiors, supervisors, judges, jurors, or adulating fans.

The vital facet of our conscience as sensible can become overpowering when we refuse to listen to our founding form with its basic love-will as illuminating our core form as core, heart, and character by means of our spirit with its wisdom, wit, and memory.

We can deny our transcendence dynamic with its yearning love for the infinite. Its denied love energy can then attach itself to our vital-sympathetic formation conscience. This results in an absolutizing of this lower facet of conscience. It becomes quasi-transcendent. When vital sympathy rules over us uncontrolled, everything is allowed that gratifies its insatiable hunger. This problem highlights again the importance of the love-will. As "will" it is not seduced by vital sympathy feelings.

Vitalistic Formation Conscience

A vital formation conscience can thus become vitalistic and self-destructive. This shift is linked with our vital care dynamics. Some vitalistic people feel overcome by deformational guilt feelings when they do not exhaust themselves unwisely in excessive affective care for others. Or we may feel resentful if others say or do anything that might diminish the endless vitalistic care and sympathy we ourselves expect from them irrationally. We anticipate such vital outpourings because we ascribe to others a vital formation conscience similar to the one we ourselves overcultivated in our own life.

Briefly, a onesided supremacy of a vital conscience will generate an oversensitivity for our own and other's emotional needs. At first sight, vitalistic people may charm us because they seem so attractive, charming, dynamic, open, flattering, and outgoing. Their vital enthusiasm is contagious. Gradually, we may discover that their excitement, their expressions of warmth, their countless spontaneous offers of assistance are not necessarily complemented by the dynamics of discipline, firmness, effectiveness, wisdom, stability, perseverance, solidity, sobriety, reliability, task commitment, and controlled concentration—dynamics characteristic of other facets of a stable formation conscience with its related character dispositions.

The dynamics of a vital formation conscience are an asset, provided they are consonant with the sociohistorical, functional, and transcendent phases of conscience, which respond in turn to the demands of the founding life form and of the love-will at its root. The loving responsibility of our heart—as illumined by the spirit and its expression in consonant faith and formation traditions—finds in the vital facet of conscience a proper guide by which to express warm, attractive feelings in daily interformation with others in our shared field of presence and action.

When vital conscience becomes vitalistic, it is a hindrance to the unfolding of transcendent conscience. Its emotional dynamics leave little room for the silence, stillness, recollection, and solitude we need if we are to keep in touch with our founding dynamism or founding life form. The vital directives of formation conscience should not prevent us from retreating periodically from the demands of sympathetic social togetherness. Neither should they seduce us to idolize our sympathetic social compatibility with others as above anything else. We should not pretend to have feelings that are not really in tune with our own founding ground or with our true, best will for the others even if we cannot always feel it vitally.

The vital facet of conscience may prompt us to overidentify with others by sharing in their enthusiasms. Michael Mott, in his biographical work *The Seven Mountains of Thomas Merton,* gives striking examples of Merton's own struggle with the dynamics of overidentification as a result of occasional dominance by dynamics of vital sympathy. The price we pay for exciting togetherness with those to whom we have little basic affinity is often the betrayal of our transcendent self. We may be unmindful of our life call as resonating in our responsible and sensible formation conscience.

A responsible-sensible sensitive formation conscience not only gives form to our everyday formation acts but more importantly to our enduring character convictions and dispositions. Such dispositions guarantee the continual ease of our corresponding acts. This brings us to the problem of character formation in the light of our transcendent responsible-sensible conscience. An anthropology of character formation can deepen our insight into these problems. Therefore, in the following chapter, I will consider my anthropology of transcendent personality and character formation in the light of what I have said about formation conscience in this and the preceding chapters.

CHAPTER 10

Anthropology of Transcendent Conscience and Character Formation

A consonant transcendent formation conscience is the source and guardian of the consonant transcendent formation of character.

Earlier I distinguished a transcendent from a pretranscendent conscience. I mentioned also their interformation. How do we prepare children for their growth in both pretranscendent and transcendent conscience? In many traditions children up to the age of six or seven are regarded as not yet fully responsible for their actions. We realize that neither their pretranscendent nor their transcendent conscience is sufficiently developed. Therefore, parents have to direct their children in the light of their own adult conscience. Mothers may try to prevent undesirable comportment by distracting young children from mischief. They gratify them in some other way. By such diversions they aim to draw attention away from the harmful action in which children may want to indulge.

Preventive Formation

It is one of the principles of my formation anthropology that constant prevention of unwanted behavior can lay the groundwork for future character formation. It may dig the furrows of routines in the germinal character of children. Later in life they may appropriate personally such channels of prepersonal customs by filling them with the personal affirmation of a corresponding character disposition or virtue. A wise mother spontaneously tries to prevent actions that would be in conflict with her own pretranscendent and transcendent conscience as formed in her by her own tradition. Such preventive formation cannot yet form a true tradition-based transcendent conscience in children. What it can do, however, is to affect their neuroformation in ways that can later facilitate the carrying out of directives of their own awakening pretranscendent and transcendent conscience.

Another facet of preventive formation is the development of a greater sensitivity in children. They become more sensitive to any sign of displeasure they may evoke in the people who try gently to prevent them from harmful acting out. The methods preventive formators try to use are kind, loving, and even-mooded. Children begin to sense if and when they have hurt their guardians. They feel it even when hardly discernible signs of disappointment and disapproval shine through.

This growing sensitivity to the moods and feelings of parents and guardians derives from the loving mode of preventive formation. Such perceptivity prepares children for the development of dispositions of sensitivity to nonverbal or symbolic communications later in life. This same sensitivity enables them to be touched by the ethical symbols of their formation tradition and, in later life, to be receptive to traditional transcendent directives of appreciation and depreciation. Such wise preparation is crucial in the formation of a tradition-based transcendent conscience. In the meantime, the development of a pretranscendent conscience is not neglected. However, development of the latter is not made ultimate in transcendent traditions as it could be in merely self-actualizing or so-called nondirective ones.

The seeds of transcendent conscience are sown in interaction with a family that images for the children a transcendent tradition. By contrast, families that live by mainly self-actualizing traditions tend to foster in children dispositions for autarkic decisions without wise dependency on classical traditions meditatively absorbed through inspiring stories and examples.

Tradition-rooted parenting creates a loving, form-traditional climate. Such an ambience can diminish the magnitude of the split infants normally make between good and bad maternal forms of their mother image. This split has been described in all its intensity by psychoanalytic theorists. They base their theories necessarily on observations of the pretranscendent self-actualizing form traditions prevalent in Western societies.

Transition from Preventive to Demanding Formation

The age when children become capable of taking responsibility heralds a new unfolding of their formation conscience. The style of formation becomes less preventive and more demanding. In some cases, demands can engender conflicts. Children may experience a clash between the lost paradise of early childhood gratification and the demands now put upon them. They want to please their parents, and yet they do not feel sure about their own ability to comply effectively with every parental demand. In this new phase they experience the withholding of some earlier gratifications. They also miss now the customary adult excuses for unwanted childish behavior before they had entered the age of responsibility. Such changes can be experienced as rejection or as punishment.

This process is compounded by the emergence of strivings for more independence. A new school environment, for example, may lead to comparisons with the freedom allowed to certain classmates by their more lenient families.

Considerable anxiety may be generated because of all these experiences. This can lead to a suppression of the emerging lower "I" conscience. In extreme cases the formation anxiety may be channeled into various rituals. One may unwittingly indulge in frequent handwashing to maintain purity, a ritual that can become compulsive. In that case, it may be rooted in a coercive core disposition of dysfunctional coping with formation anxiety. Such a core disposition may become increasingly obsessive. Coercive neuroform facets parallel such obsessive character dispositions.

Parents may use shaming, scolding, and physical punishment to force prematurely the formation of conscience. They can use these means to compel blind submission to their authority. They will not countenance any expression of anger toward them. Children learn to become extremely guarded around such parents. Away from them they can be quite expressive of their pre- or infrafocal angry feelings. They may transpose them to others who cannot or will not punish them, particularly when they feel assured that their parents will not learn about their out-of-sight outbursts. Such behavior may foster the deformation of what I designate as apparent form conscience.

Apparent Form Conscience

This kind of conscience represents a onesided concern for looking good in the eyes of others. It can be consonant or dissonant. If consonant, it provides wise directives of compassion and reasonable compatibility with others because its directives flow from a deeper, more inward level of conscience whose directives are in tune with one's faith and formation tradition.

A dissonant apparent form conscience, on the contrary, can be split off from one's higher conscience. It may tend to be in constant flux, anxiously intent on pleasing others, no matter what directives come from one's own tradition-inspired conscience and from the reasonable limits of compatibility and compassion.

To prevent the formation of an exclusively apparent and, therefore, deformative conscience, parents should be circumspect in the communication of praise or blame. Excessive praise or blame can build a dependency that deflects children from disclosing, albeit in an imperfect, childlike fashion, slight intimations of elementary facets of their unique call. This overdependency may carry over in their core or character dispositions toward significant others later in life.

Tradition-Based Transconscience

An initial, vague, tradition-based transconscience reflects the unique founding life form or life call of children. Crucial in its primal formation is the revelational or intuitive orientation of the faith and form tradition of the family. This orientation is symbolized in the holy writings, parables, symbols, rituals, and prayer formulas of their tradition. Frequent recital of stories in which this orientation is illustrated is crucial for the formation in children of transconscience ideals that are tradition compatible. For Christians, the stories in the Bible contain an exemplary number of such ideals. Adapted to the children's mind and imagination, they can serve as models for identifying their as yet indistinct, incipient transcendent conscience. Other religions have their own storehouse of adaptable exemplary narratives. It facilitates the later replacement of pretranscendent self-esteem by transcendent call appreciation. This humble esteem of the undeserved nobility of our unique life call fills us with joyful gratitude and boundless call appreciation. It overcomes the anxiety engendered by our vulnerable pretranscendent self-esteem.

Transcendent Formation Conscience and Intraformational Internalization

Our formation conscience is identifiable by internalized dispositions, attitudes, ideals, and directives. People who are directed by Western pretranscendent form traditions have been the topic of study by the psychologies, psychiatries, and sociologies of the pretranscendent life. They have tried with some success to identify the dispositions generally internalized by these particular populations. Some tend to make this particular internalization the universal norm of any internalization in formation conscience by any population influenced by any culture or tradition.

Some may deny that people with a transcendent conscience develop also personally independent dispositions. Others seem to insinuate that the formation conscience of adherents of transcendent traditions suppresses their uniqueness and inventiveness. They may imagine that such people depend only on external controls and guides provided by representatives of their traditions. They may not realize that any kind of consonant or dissonant formation conscience, also of self-actualizing secularistic persons, is ultimately rooted in often unacknowledged form traditions or fragments thereunto. (I developed this research in great detail in my fifth volume, *Traditional Formation*.)

Unique Personalization of Transcendent Conscience

A consonant, tradition-illumined, transcendent conscience is profoundly internalized. It becomes personalized in accordance with one's unique-communal life call as appraised in the light of one's tradition pyramid. To be sure, the intraformational dispositions, ideals, prohibitions, and directives of transcendent conscience are formed in a different way than are those of a merely pretranscendent conscience. They function differently than do the life directives of adherents of mainly pretranscendent traditions. The ultimate orientation of a tradition-inspired transconscience is also different. The stories, symbols, and rituals of a transcendent form tradition are deeply internalized in one's formation conscience. They give rise to an inner unique-communal field of tradition that carries representations supporting one's unique formation conscience.

The transcendent conscience, like the pretranscendent, grows by an intraformational process of unique-communal assimilation. This process results in an intraformational field of images or forms. They are unique, and yet, insofar as they are communal, they manifest some implicit affinity to one's form tradition. For example, many unique artworks of Africans, Eskimos, Scots, Russians, and Arabs may show certain affinities with the images or forms of their traditions. I call images that affect our formation conscience formational representations. They exercise a form-directive impact on our empirical life form in all its dimensions. They affect the form we give to our thoughts, memories, anticipations, feelings, perceptions, and actions.

I call the totality of our field of formational representations a "field of intraforms." This field comprises both our uniquely personal and our personalized traditional representations. For example, a mother may carry within her certain uniquely personal representations of her private experiences as a mother. She may also cherish traditional representations of motherhood as, for instance, found in a devotional book. If her conscience is transcendent, she will relate all such representations spontaneously to the transcendent mystery as celebrated in her own faith and form traditions. Such lived transcendent traditions generate in her a certain mood. I call this a transcendent mood or affect. This mood touches and transforms the experiences of all representations in her field of intraforms. All things represented in that field may appear to her as interforming in the light of the mystery as communicated by the symbols of her own adhered-to faith and formation traditions.

Loving interformation rather than abstract universalization is central to transcendent attention, awareness, and appreciation as contrasted to pretranscendent conscience. Everything in one's formation field is believed to be basically epiphanous of the forming will of the omnipresent mystery. The outer boundaries of one's lower "I" become more and more permeable. One lovingly interforms with all that is. Epiphanic awareness and appraisal of one's formation field does not imply a passive attitude. It demands a disposition to work with any and all disclosures of the mystery and of one's life call as rooted in it.

Traditional Transcendent-Functional Character Formation

So far I have dealt mainly with the formation of conscience. I am now ready to consider the formation of character in the light of our formation conscience and our formation traditions.

By now it ought to be clear that my anthropology of formation is as different as night and day from so-called transpersonal anthropologies, psychologies, or therapies. They tend to be in an explicit or implicit way cosmic-pantheistic, functional-transcendent instead of transcendent-functional, subtle ego- or self-centered approaches. They are not rooted in the mutually complementary history of classical formation traditions as a whole.

My contrasting anthropology was developed years ago in Europe—long before I knew anything about the transpersonalistic trends so prevalent in America and elsewhere today. My work in all respects is radically different from their approach. It is rooted in and oriented to the transcosmic and trans-Self rooted not in an impersonal cosmos, but in the radical mystery itself. The cosmic epiphany is in my thinking only a secondary expression of the radical mystery. It is subordinated, in other words, to the radical, transcosmic formation mystery.

My theory of personality rejects the transpersonalist assumptions that we are centered in a so-called higher Self. In my opinion, their concept of our higher Self is no more than the expression of a sublimated subtle ego, cosmically expanded and blown up in its pantheistic importance. It is to my feeling the most poisoned spiritual fruit of the autarkic pride form of life. Many seek its release with the best of intentions, but such a self is bound to disappoint.

My formation anthropology, unlike transpersonal anthropologies and New-Age spiritualities, is nourished primarily by the classical transcosmic formation traditions in which our higher Self is never perceived or imagined as ultimate.

I came to America with my formation anthropology intact. I had the good fortune, in the meantime, to become friends and debate partners with the then newly emerging transpersonal psychologists, such men as Carl Rogers, Abraham Maslow, and Sidney Jourard. I argued, in some cases for years, about the differences between my own and their anthropologies. I respectfully yet wholeheartedly rejected their basic faith and subsequent formation assumptions. In spite of our differences, Maslow invited me to take over his courses at Brandeis University for a year. I was free to teach them in my own way. Shortly thereafter, he entrusted me with his personal journals for safekeeping until he found it less controversial to publish them. The day a trusted student of his arrived at my campus residence with a bag full of Maslow's final journals was for me a clear indication of the trust that existed between two original anthropological theorists, who could remain friends while being far apart in regard to some significant assumptions underlying their theories.

The same essential differences show up also in my anthropology of character formation. This part of my thinking was sparked during the Hunger Winter in Holland when I was living with people whom I helped to hide from deportation. We discussed the characters of those who collaborated with the enemy, of profit-mongers, and of the uncommitted who did not share our care for the underprivileged. We reflected passionately on the impact of their traditions, for better or worse, on their character formation. Our conclusion was that after the war a concerted effort of representatives of many traditions should foster my form-traditional transcendent character formation (*karakter vorming*) guided by a well-formed moral conscience (*moreel geweten*).

I felt that people's basic moral conscience should be complemented by a corresponding formation conscience. Such an expanded ethical conscience ought to guide them in their minute-to-minute, empirical-experiential implementation of the directives of moral conscience. This practical application should take into account their own particular, ever-changing formation fields. This formational expansion of moral conscience should include facets of character formation that may not have been formulated as such specifically and categorically in the basic moral codes of one's faith and subsequent formation traditions.

Formation Conscience
and Traditional Character Formation

This insight led to my conception of a formation conscience (*vormings geweten*) intimately interwoven with our rightly guided or misguided ethical conscience. An example of misguided formation conscience was exemplified for us by some church-going Christians who at the same time functioned in administrative positions in the Nazi party or as SS soldiers, camp doctors, prison guards, and executioners. In spite of their claiming a faith conscience, they were victims of a misdirected formation conscience. Their repeated inner and outer acts of oppression in the name of that conscience resulted in dispositions that deformed them. It nurtured in them a fascist formation conscience and subsequently a fascist character form. This experience inspired me to develop my theory of a tradition-based formation conscience. Its focus was not on one's higher Self nor on a higher or cosmic union. It was on the trans-cosmic, radical mystery of formation as operative in all people of good will, even if not acknowledged as such.

At the center of my formational anthropological theory of personality, I put what I conceived as the core form of the human personality. I saw it as co-constituted by its coformants of, respectively, the core, heart, and matching character of one's personality. I emphasized that the consonant core form as character was, according to my findings, a hierarchical set of consonant dispositions or virtues. These virtues should be marked by inherent references to one's formation conscience as rooted in unconditional faithfulness to the radical mystery of formation. I insisted on the distinction between virtues and values as understood by certain contemporary trends in, for example, psychology and education. Values in the latter way of thinking are what people personally and arbitrarily value without reference to classical wisdom traditions.

Initially, there was little interest in this unfamiliar approach. Later, long after the war, as the crime rate rose in many countries, the character deformation of gang members with criminal leanings or dispositions through misleading conscience formation became obvious. A number of administrators, politicians, psychiatrists, sociologists, psychologists, educators, clergy persons, social workers, writers, and journalists began to develop misgivings like mine in the last phase of the war. I no longer felt alone in my concern for tradition-inspired, transcendent-functional character and conscience formation. Some began to opt with me for character virtues instead of character values in the sense of individualistically chosen norms of living.

My 1944 Paradigm and Character Formation

My formation science and anthropology, as well as their theory of character and conscience, were based on my original 1944 paradigm. This paradigm began to make sense even to students and other audiences who had not gone through the war experience. It can be added to the paradigms already existing in the social, clinical, and educational disciplines, complementing and correcting them as necessary.

One of the main models of the scientific mind, the one most familiar to us, is the informational paradigm. Guided by mostly quantifying methods of research, it informs us as to the measurable aspects of human life and its development.

My anthropology of character and conscience formation is based on my paradigm of transcendent human formation as critically compatible with, though not identical to, consonant classical human formation wisdom. I distinguish, but I do not separate, such formation wisdom from other sources of information. My paradigm complements the indispensable contributions that have been made and that are in the process of being made on the basis of the time-honored models of quantifiable information and philosophical speculation.

Any paradigm in the social, clinical, and educational disciplines challenges us to approach the object of our study from a specific angle of cognitive and experiential interest. It determines the way in which we focus our powers of attention, observation, and disciplined reflection on selected phenomena.

My paradigm of full-field interformation influenced my observing, thinking, and theorizing about human character and conscience. It affected the choice and development of my research methods. It also directed my critical attention to the prescientific assumptions one has to assume in any characterology.

To my knowledge, no other modern empirical personality theorist starts from the assumptions I have made. One of my main presuppositions is that the basic, ultimate dimension of character should be the transcendent-functional dimension as nourished implicitly or explicitly by classical formation traditions and that it should be rooted in and oriented toward the radical transcosmic formation mystery.

In my thought, this founding dimension is a unique-communal expression of the transcosmic mystery. It inspires and guides through its transcendence dynamic the lifelong process of character formation. Over the millennia it illumines also the slow and uneven development of human wisdom about transcendent character and personality formation. The fruits of this wisdom are sedimented in classical, potentially classical, and classical-compatible formation traditions.

Formation Anthropology of Paradigmatic Shifts

Paradigmatic shifts or the emergence of new paradigms in the history of character formation, as long as they are consonant, can complement one another. Historical changes in paradigms can be traced to experiences, needs, demands, dynamics, and insights that emerge in and through the ongoing formation history of humanity. A paradigm shift in our conception of character and personality formation is usually linked with a change in the overall perception of a significant number of people in a society, a change in their worldview or mindset. Therefore, I attempt to explain from the viewpoint of cultural change the emergence of any new approach to character and conscience.

Presently, in the case of the West, culture is either functionally or functionally-transcendently oriented, predominantly informational, and neglectful of classical transcendent traditions. It tends to underestimate the essential role of such traditions. Without them, in my view, character formation cannot be understood and appraised objectively and realistically within a sociohistorical context.

To subordinate again the functional, pretranscendent dimension of character to its traditional, transcendent dimension—without debilitating the former in its own unique function—is the main challenge of tradition-compatible transcendent character formation. Hence, I initiated the concept of a transcendent-functional dimension of character with its corresponding dispositions as distinguished from mere functional or functional-transcendent dispositions.

Basic Concepts of the Anthropology
of Traditional Transcendent-Functional
Character Formation Rooted in the Transcosmic Mystery

In my formation anthropology, I make a distinction between character form, proform, temperform, and neuroform. Of these four forms, character form and proform are more directly available to our focal consciousness, temperform and neuroform less so.

Our character form consists of a more or less integrated set of dispositions that define our enduring basic stands in our formation field, whether they are consonant or dissonant.

The proform (or protoform) contains our hopes, aspirations, dreams, and plans for the future. They guide our short- and long-range projects. They may partly represent some of our already-existing character dispositions, but they are not identical with them. In the process of their realization, these proformational tendencies may generate additional character dispositions and reform or transform existing ones.

Our temper form or temperament is part of our vital dimension. It represents innate properties of our genetic neuro-muscular-hormonal system, such as the inherited range of our minimal and maximum rate of speed of mental and physical movement. Another example of one of the properties of our temperform is the particular range and intensity of our vital emotion and passion. We can exercise some limited control over the conditions and expressions of our temperform. At present we cannot alter it basically and enduringly. We cannot change our temperament lastingly above or below its innate ranges of experience and expression.

I felt the need to initiate my new concept of a tightly structured neuroform. I conceived it as interwoven with, but different from, our autonomous nervous system as such. As I argued earlier in my presentations of formation anthropology, the neuroform as I conceive it functions among other things as the vital neurological referent of our character dispositions. It functions as the infrafocal informer, selector, guardian, and executive neural-hormonal agent of our character dispositions. In and through our conscience and character, we have conditioned our neuroform. It is not the chance outcome of our autonomous nervous system only. We have preset its automatic preappraisal process. This preappraisal extends itself to the millions of stimuli or wave forms that impinge every second on our inner and outer senses. We oriented and empowered our neuroform to present for focal conscious appraisal among other things those inputs we deemed relevant to both our conscience and character dispositions.

Our neuroformational dispositions can be either relatively available to our formation conscience and freedom or they may be coercive. If coercive, they give form to a character and conscience that are at least in part rigid and less flexible.

Neurodispositions that are not coercive are relatively available to our focal conscience and free will. I say relatively available, for they cannot always be recognized immediately and directly changed. Often, a process of disclosure has to be initiated through carefully nurtured attention to our experiences of repeated events of formation ineffectiveness. We have to trace our failures patiently until we can identify possible factors left out by our preappraising neuroform. This effort may enable us to detect how we should update its conditioning. The transformation of our neuroform should be in tune with our growing insight into the ineffectiveness of certain facets of how we are present in our formation field. Such updating usually implies corresponding changes in our conscience and character dispositions.

Tradition-Compatible, Transcendent-Functional Character
Having distinguished character form from proform, temper form, and neuroform, I move to the next question: What is a tradition-compatible, transcendent-functional character? Character is transcendent-functional insofar as a basic shift has occurred. The result of this shift is that its socio-vital-functional,

and functional-transcendent dispositions are now ultimately oriented toward the transcosmic mystery of formation.

Our character is partly given and partly acquired. The basic disposition of a consonant or virtuous character is one that inclines us to disclose and implement our founding life form or, dynamically speaking, our unique-communal life call. This sustaining ground is symbolized for us by our faith and formation traditions. The founding life form is our unique-communal expression, image, or mirror of the transcosmic formation mystery. Most deeply we *are* that unique image. The center of our tradition-compatible, transcendent-functional character is formed by the disposition to implement our founding life form in dispositions and attitudes that elevate and integrate our pretranscendent character dispositions.

At no moment is our founding life form fully transparent to us. It takes a lifetime to disclose a significant part of our life call. It is hidden in the unfolding formation history of our existence. Our basic tradition-compatible, transcendent-functional character contains the secret of our unique-communal life call. But this secret is only known to us insofar as it is disclosed to us and implemented by us in our character and personality at this moment in time. This implementation is guided by a continual implicit or at times explicit dialogue with our internalized and consonantly harmonized pyramid of formation traditions.

This tradition-inspired, transcendent-functional character or core form is like a continual refrain. It invites us to return to it regularly in contemplative equanimity. Such regular returns to the true center of our character formation in the "more than" restore and reenergize our core form. The unique-communal orientation of our core form extends itself to all the character dispositions that guide and energize the realization of our form-receptive and form-giving potencies.

Neuroform and Character Formation

Character dispositions may put a strain on our neuroformational system. We have to express and execute consonant or virtuous character dispositions in an often resistant and asocial world. To do so effectively, we need the informational, selective service of our neuroform. More often than we would wish, we find ourselves overextended, stressed out, driven by a neuroform that has become overactive and agitated. We no longer feel in tune with our basic character orientation. Dissonant, deformative character dispositions take over. We begin to sense that it is high time to return to our home base. The necessity of moments of character recollection dawns upon us.

Detached Recollection

Character recollection means that for a time span of say between fifteen and thirty minutes we detach ourselves as completely as possible from any exercise and execution of our pre- and post-transcendent character dispositions. For these moments we do not want to be carried by the stream of excitations that come to us from our formation field. At the same time, we try to silence as much as possible all incoming and upcoming neuroformational excitations with their corresponding inner and outer sense impressions and thought processes. Momentarily, we replace both introspection and reflection with a silent presence to our unique life call by the transcosmic formation mystery that is always "more than" we are. Character recollection means for me a literal re-collecting of the transcendent energy dispersed in our dispositional exercises, expressions, and executions. In equanimity we re-source ourselves in the basic character disposition, our love-will, which reflects our response to the call-that-we-are and to its permeation by the transcosmic mystery of formation, whose love wills us and calls us continuously.

Principles of Tradition-Inspired, Transcendent-Functional Character Formation

The formation of a consonant character depends on the following principles:

1. Such a character is formed through transcendent formation symbols, alive in classical, potentially classical, or classics compatible wisdom traditions. They invite transcendent acts. These acts may lead to a tentative, initial formation of corresponding character dispositions, attitudes, and directives.

2. Such a character is formed in interformation with the transcosmic formation mystery as epiphanically calling in one's unique-communal life form, in one's field of life and its formation events, and especially in the consonant elements and symbols of its formation traditions.

3. This character integrates through its basic transcendent dispositions all other consonant or virtuous dispositional character responses. The dispositional responses to be integrated transcendently are directed to the pre, intra, inter, and outer spheres of our field as well as to the sociohistorical, vital, functional, and functional-transcendent dimensions of our character formation.

4. Such a character form integrates, in the light of the appraisal of one's life call, the various formation traditions that affect the unfolding of its dispositions. My formation anthropology refers to the consonant outcome of this character integration as the increasingly harmonized, hierarchical pyramid of one's traditional character dispositions.

CHAPTER 11

Implementation of Character Formation

My formation science is designed from the start not only to be pretheological but also to be eminently practical. Therefore, I would like to show in this chapter how the principles of character formation can be implemented in formation programs. The following ways and means are relevant to my concerns:

1. The principles of character formation should be communicated not only intellectually but also symbolically. The personal example itself of effective and affective teachers of character formation, inspired by classical formation wisdom, should be a touching symbol of what they try to communicate. Their heartfelt words, tone of voice, gestures, and facial expressions should express their lived experience. Other symbols can be found in plays, poems, music, art reproductions, and aesthetic surroundings.

2. The principles of character formation should come alive in well-guided interformation groups. The participants should charitably and wisely interform by reflecting together on the tradition-inspired character dispositions they may have in common. They should facilitate for one another the disclosure and appraisal of insufficiently appraised pyramids of character dispositions. To guard against subjectivism, they should be guided in this interformation exercise by objectively classical, potentially classical, or classics-compatible popular texts relevant to my holistic view of transcendent-immanent character formation.

3. The principles underlying this character formation can be clarified in interformational discussion groups. Participants reflect together on formation anthropology and its related principles and explanations in formation science as made simple, attractive, concrete, and popular. If the participants happen to adhere to the same belief system, this discussion can be extended to corresponding texts in the specific form-traditional

articulation and the formation theology or ideological philosophy of the system concerned.

4. The principles of character formation in regard to social character disposi-. tions can be highlighted in social projects to be performed by interforming teams. Before, during, and after each shared project performance, the team members should appraise, in the light of formation anthropology, the absence and/or presence of transcendent-immanent, social character-forming dispositions, attitudes, acts, and their effectiveness. If the team members happen to adhere to the same belief system, the social character appraisal should be enlightened by the form-traditional articulation of that system and by its formation theology or, in case of a humanly transcendent belief system, by its formation ideology.

5. Implementation of my original principles of transcendent-immanent character formation in a program can be assured by appropriate courses. The Gemert division of the Dutch Life Schools for formation (*levensvorming*) operated as an institute of tradition-inspired, transcendent-functional character formation. One of its two core course cycles was a simplified version of the main principles and applications of the anthropology of this type of character formation. The other core course cycle was of a catechetical nature. Courses were taught on transcendent character formation in the light of my general Christian articulation of formation science. These were integrated as well with a specific empirical-experiential formational theology. It was shown to be related to, yet different from, informational speculative theology.

    Should participants adhere to another religious or ideological belief system, it was the responsibility of the teacher adhering to that system to articulate formation science and its anthropology in the light of their basic tradition, its formation theology or ideological philosophy.

6. Transcendent-immanent character formation demands, above all, the implementation of the principle of integration, which binds life together in the peaceful inner and outer consonance of universal interformation.

Implementation of Character Dispositions in Everyday Life

The sociohistorical, vital, functional, functional-transcendent, and transcendent-functional dispositions of life, as discussed in the two core cycles, need to be related to one's preparation for everyday life. This means that the character principles communicated in the core course cycles have to be complemented by practical, character-related life courses. They must teach the possibilities and ideals of post-transcendent integration of character dispositions and their implementation in everyday life. In these courses, experts train young people in the everyday skills and aptitudes necessary for an effective life in the different spheres and dimensions of contemporary society. These experts have been exposed beyond their professional expertise to the anthropology and the corresponding theology or ideology of character formation. They enable the students to appreciate transcendently their practical everyday chores and cares in family and society. They help them to appreciate these as opportunities for character and personality formation and for loving service of others. They facilitate for them the realization that a transcendent-functional character increases their practical effectiveness in daily tasks. They learn to unfold their life call joyfully through commitment to service and to loving interformation.

These courses also sensitize them to consonant dispositions for health care insofar as they enhance their physical, mental, and emotional life. All courses taught in the Life Schools represented the sociohistorical, vital, functional, transcendent, and transcendent-functional dimensions of my paradigm. For example, in the Gemert division of these schools, experts in facets of sociohistorical character formation gave courses on different facets of this dimension of life. They explained how people could profit from the history of their culture and of their families when it came to creating attractive homes and pleasant surroundings within the limits of their finances and form traditions. Experts in the legal aspects of sociohistorical development, notably lawyers, would focus on the facet of legalities that might affect the protection of one's family life and of one's position in the workplace. In accordance with the two core course cycles on simplified formation theory and on catechetical formation theology, experts would stress the importance of developing in one's character a transcendently motivated disposition of seeking and implementing legal care. The instructors discussed with those taking their courses how they could do the same for themselves, for the people entrusted to them, and for the underprivileged who might need their concern and advice.

In regard to vital character dispositions, medical doctors and other health experts taught young workers how they could implement the principles of character formation in dispositions for health care, right diet, exercise, and the sound, wise, and respectful celebration of their human sexual gifts in conformity with the guidelines of their own faith and formation traditions.

Shown and exemplified over and over again was the intimate interformation of these practical dispositions with the traditional transcendent dispositions or virtues expressed in a person's faith and formation tradition as taught in the core courses of catechetical formational theology and ideology.

Functional character formation was served by a variety of courses in everyday, practical, functional endeavors that were seen as expressions of one's transcendent love and care disposition. Of great concern was how to prepare healthy, nourishing, tasteful meals; how to function as effective house managers and economists; how to sew; how to make home repairs; how to beautify one's garden and care for a shared environment; how to dress well and to decorate homes and workplaces in the light of the transcendent dispositions discussed in the two core course cycles. Well-trained experts in these fields had to acquaint themselves with the anthropology of tradition-inspired, transcendent-functional character formation.

All of the courses were designed as avenues to the integration of transcendent and pretranscendent character dispositions. Transcendent, tradition-compatible character integration was the thread that bound together a wide variety of interests and responsibilities.

Growth in tradition-rooted transcendent dispositions enabled the participants to go beyond self-preoccupation. They learned to live with genuine care and concern for others, especially their future husbands, wives, and children.

The girls, for example, would take the course in the development of a spiritually motivated disposition for appropriate and attractive makeup. They should not use cosmetics as only a source of excessive self-interest. Makeup should be applied first of all as an expression of how their caring love for others disposed them to appear in a gracious and pleasing manner so as to enhance their everyday, formative interaction with husband, children, visiting relatives, friends, and acquaintances. Especially in the later years of a pressured married and/or career life, it was suggested to the girls that they grow in the disposition or asceticism of appropriate makeup seen as a task of love to highlight the special beauty of advancing age.

Implementation of Phasic Character Formation

In accordance with my unifying interformation paradigm, I will distinguish in part two of this book six formation phases, ranging from the first primal type of sociohistorical and vital formation in the neonate to the final post-transcendent or (to say the same) transcendent-functional phase of character and personality formation. Often this final formation phase may be only fully approached in the last quarter of one's lifetime. To be sure, partial attainments may be realized at any moment in our faith and formation journey.

Each character phase, when it is appraised in the light of our transcendence dynamic, is marked by a crossover crisis. The transcendence dynamic generates a crisis of transition, a passage from a lower character disposition to a higher one. Each consonant character disposition or virtue represents a new formation potency of one's core form as character.

From the viewpoint of my paradigm, the phases of character formation match my sociohistorical, vital, functional, functional-transcendent, transcendent, and transcendent-functional phases of personality unfolding.

Each of these phases contributes its own consonant character disposition. Of course, consonance presupposes that each crossover crisis be resolved in a way that is compatible with the classical, transcendent wisdom of character formation. This way should get its bearing from the transcosmic mystery of formation.

Each phase is marked by a shift. The passing supremacy of a character disposition in the former phase gives way to the passing supremacy of another character disposition unfolding in the next phase.

I introduced the concept of passing supremacy to point out that what is left behind in the crossover is not the character disposition as such. What is given up is only its brief supremacy in the story of our character formation. Once the transcendence journey comes to its transcendent-functional end only the transcendent character dispositions will be supreme. All lower dispositions will share in the transcendent bearings of one's character. No lower disposition, however, would lose its potency for its own contribution to our character as a whole.

To understand this fine point of my personality theory, it is necessary to see that each character has its own hierarchical structure. The subordination between character dispositions within each character depends on one's call of life. In the end, only transcendent dispositions are supreme; under them, lower dispositions may exercise a relative or subordinated supremacy. For example, transcendent athletes, poets, business managers, and doctors may favor, under their ultimately supreme transcendent dispositions, relatively supreme dispositions. Usually these are related to the vocational and professional aspects of their life call. They may have to subordinate some of their other lower dispositions in service of other relatively dominant character dispositions. For example, an athlete may have to subordinate various, otherwise legitimate, vital dispositions for drinking, the enjoyment of rich deserts, and late-night parties to his vital-functional character dispositions for outstanding sports performances the day after.

To be sure, one should never subordinate transcendent dispositions to pre-transcendent ones. Transcendent dispositions could never be subservient to relatively dominant, lower dispositions in one's character hierarchy. This would represent a backsliding from one's supreme transcendent character form to the earlier phase of passing supremacy of merely functional-transcendent character dispositions.

Formation Anthropology of the Six Character Phases

I would like to comment briefly on the six character phases. I shall delineate them in relation to the courses I taught on transcendent character formation (*karakter vorming*) in the Gemert division of the Dutch Life Schools for life formation (*levens vorming*).

The preparatory formation of sociohistorical or form-traditional character dispositions starts already in the neonate and even in some measure in the fetal situation within the womb of an always already sociohistorically conditioned mother. The human being is essentially a sociohistorical or traditional form of life. As I argued at length in my fifth volume on traditional formation, to be human is to be traditional. Earlier in my European formation anthropology, I added that a human character, no matter how transcendent, is always a traditional character.

In any phase of character formation, the striving for tradition-compatible, sociohistorical character dispositions is always at work. For the neonate, the crisis of this first crossover is one of passing from the ambience of fetal life in the womb to a life of constant interference by one's family and its traditions. This first exposure to tradition lays the infrafocal groundwork for the later development of form-traditional character dispositions.

Then the vital phase of character formation takes over and becomes temporarily dominant. This phase plays on the slumbering character potency for intimacy dispositions. Children grow in some kind of spontaneous intimacy with people, animals, events, and things that appear in their environment. This implies some crisis of transition. They are compelled to move in some measure from their disposition of passive receptivity to a more intimately responsive, form-receiving and form-giving way of life. They have to go a little beyond unquestioned acceptance of the appraisals in their field. These are implicitly given to them by the sociohistorical patterns of family life. Spontaneous intimacy awakens certain latent form potencies. Among them are the potencies for dispositions of intimate form receptivity and of some beginning intimate form donation within the limits of the sociohistorical field of family life. Such rudimentary awakenings are a necessary condition for later growth in character dispositions for transcendent presence to the epiphanies of the mystery in the everyday events of one's formation field.

The next functional phase of character formation activates the slumbering character potency for dispositions to appreciate and to develop functional ambitions of mastery and form effectiveness. These imply a first awakening to the skills and dexterity that can serve expression and execution of incipient, childlike ambitions. The crisis of transition entails a passage from the delightful, passing supremacy of vital intimacy to that of functional control, discipline, order, and restraint.

In the course of time, one may enter the functional-transcendent phase of character formation. This phase activates character potencies for functional-transcendent dispositions. They move the character form beyond full dominance by mainly functional dispositions of religiosity and morality. They dispose us to explore some of the consoling or exciting side benefits of the beginnings of a life of fuller transcendence. The crisis of transition entails moving away from mere functional discipline and mastery and venturing into the beginnings of fuller transcendent character dispositions without yet giving up the prevalence of the functional.

One may then be lifted by the mystery of transformation into the temporarily dominant, purely transcendent phase of character formation. This phase activates the character potency for the development of the disposition of full transcendent presence. In this phase the crisis of supremacy is rooted in the invitation by the mystery to relinquish any ultimate functional control over transcendent experience, to abandon oneself in love and appreciation to guidance by the mystery.

Finally, one may reach more fully and lastingly the transcendent-functional formation phase. This phase activates the character potencies for transcendent implementation and integration dispositions. They foster the ongoing integration of one's subordinated sociohistorical, vital, functional, and functional-transcendent character dispositions. This shift sets up its own crisis. For it entails a crossover from the bliss of pure transcendent presence to the never-ending and often failing task of integrating old and new subordinated character dispositions with transcendent ones.

New Paradigm of Formation Anthropology and Transcendent Character Formation

The graph on the following page represents the adaptation of my 1944 interformation paradigm to transcendent character formation.

Transcendent character formation is rooted in this paradigm. So is the anthropology of its implementation in schools and programs of transcendent character formation. I developed this approach when I was freed from other duties to apply my empirical experiential anthropology to the Dutch Life Schools on a full-time basis. I already explained how I used the dimensions of the intrasphere of my paradigm for the aim of these schools, exemplifying it in the Gemert division. I still have to clarify how other coformants of this paradigm, such as its spheres, consciousness regions, and ranks of human interformation, are related to character formation.

The expression "interformation paradigm" indicates that character formation, as all formation, is conceived by me as interformation. Our character comes into being by interforming with the five spheres of our formation field.

First in importance of my paradigmatic spheres is the central sphere of our preformation by the mystery of formation. Our founding life form is rooted in this preforming sphere. This founding preformation is the hidden ground in the secret depths of our soul. Our core form as character form should basically be an expression of our unique-communal form of life. This life call is enshrouded in the impenetrable depths of our soul and in the mystery of formation from whom this founding formation flows constantly. This most sacred ground of our being summons us by inimitable wake-up calls.

Our intrasphere comprehends, among other things, our core form as character with all its dispositions, be they virtues or vices. This intraspheric character

GENERAL INTERFORMATIONAL
CHARACTER FORMATION

Cosmic and World Sphere:

Apprehension and appraisal
of events and dynamics as affecting
and affected by character dispositions

Intraformation ←←	Mystery of Preformation →→	*Human Interformation*
Sphere →→	of unique-communal ←←	*Sphere*
	character call as guiding	
Unfolding character	consonant character	People and commu-
with all its	formation	nities insofar as they
consonant and	↑ ↓	affect formation of
dissonant dispositions.	↑ ↓	character dispositions
Its impact on our	↑ ↓	and are affected by
perception of		them. Their impact on
and receptivity to		our perception of and
the mystery		receptivity to the
		mystery

Situational Formation Sphere:

Life situations insofar as they
symbolize formation traditions
that affect our character
formation via our form-
traditional pyramid.
The feedback of this
character formation
on our here and
now situations.

form is in constant interformation with our founding central sphere and the other spheres depicted in my formation paradigm.

The interpersonal or communal interformation sphere represents people who symbolically or directly, and especially form-traditionally, affect our character formation via our interformation with them.

The situational sphere of character formation represents the formation directives embedded in the challenging appearances and events that coform our life situations. Influential among these are symbolically situated formation traditions. Their situational symbols are carried by events and acts, by the media, the arts, demonstrations, movies, plays, books, heroic and criminal events, news, gossip that colors and permeates our everyday environment.

These situationally expressed traditions become internalized in our character through what I introduced in my formation anthropology as the concept of a form-tradition pyramid. This pyramid contributes mightily to our consonant or dissonant character formation. It is especially influential when it joins forces with the interformational communication of similar form-traditional character dispositions. One developing disposition is that of ecological and aesthetic concern for the immediate environment. It affects directly our daily situation, which is, of course, dependent on our care as its stewards.

At the apex of my formation paradigm stands the wider cosmic and cultural world. This world is communicated to us through science, education, literature, the media, and other channels. The media in particular make the mediated world a continuous part of our formation field without necessarily making it an integral aspect of our everyday life situation. It is a remote but real part of the field to which we give form and by which we are formed constantly.

This world sphere contributes to our character dispositions. For example, media news of people who suffer calamities in faraway places can dispose our character to planetary concern for victims who do not share our own immediate life situation. Similarly, news about threats to the wider cosmic world can dispose our character to care for environments that are not part of our own immediate situational surroundings. We may become involved in saving whales, preventing the destruction of rain forests, or protecting the ozone layer. Such acts, when they are sufficiently repeated, may result in lasting character dispositions insofar as they are compatible with our personal-communal life call.

Thus far I have outlined the main principles of my anthropology of transcendent character formation. Implementing this anthropology in the Gemert division of the Dutch Life Schools enabled me to develop a formation anthropology of transcendent character formation insofar as we can share it. This sharing can be served by the arrangement of interformation seminars and lectures. What ought to be their focus?

1. They should facilitate for participants the awareness and appraisal of their own consonant and dissonant character dispositions as well as of the relationships of these dispositions to their internalized form-tradition pyramid and to their personality as a whole.

2. They should enable them to understand and appreciate ideal transcendent dispositions—dispositions that are consonant with one's own basic faith and formation traditions.

3. They should point to the final aim of one's advance on the way to full transcendent consonance of character and personality. In properly focused

interformation sessions, participants aid each other in disclosing and striving after ideals of traditional transcendent character formation.

4. They should highlight three kinds of ideals: first to be pursued is the overall ideal of character consonance; second, in service of this overall consonance, they should disclose and strive after such subordinated or "subideals" of consonant character formation as candor, congeniality, compatibility, compassion, courage, commitment, joy, and appreciation; third, they should strive after ideal dispositions of competent and effective implementation of both their transcendent and their subordinated ideals.

5. They should foster intermediate ideals that help people to be realistic in their attempts to facilitate character formation. Intermediate character ideals for effective implementation should be sufficiently modest and workable. They should be realizable in due time within the limits of one's present strength or weakness of character. They should be adapted to one's formation phase, time availability, energy, and environmental conditions.

Subideals of Character Formation

In my formation anthropology, I speak of J.N.I.s or Just Noticeable Improvements. Such simple, realizable subideals prevent discouragement and disappointment. Certain subideals of character formation should be built into a formation program as a whole. Others should be the result of interformational discussion between the participants. These programs should foster ways of formation that give them insights into the phases of character formation, its crises of transition and how to deal with them.

1. They should enable people to attune their character dispositions to the consonant needs and demands of the spheres, dimensions, and consciousness regions of their field of life and of each one's personal-communal life call within that field.

2. They should give them sufficient insight into the main principles, conditions, and dynamics of transcendent character formation as rooted in formation science and formation anthropology.

Subideals are imaginative, workable expressions of transcendent ideals of character formation. Participants may aspire after these ideals, but only a few of them may ever fully be realized. This does not mean that one's character is not transcendent and consonant at all until one has realized one or many transcendent ideals. To the degree that one genuinely strives to grow in tradition-compatible, transcendent dispositions through gradual realizations of workable subideals, one's character formation is *intentionally* consonant; it embodies one's genuine love-will.

Transcendent character formation has one overall ideal, several subideals, and numerous implementation ideals. The overall ideal is to grow—through consonant interformation with all the spheres and dimensions of one's formation field—in character dispositions that foster and protect one's advance in transcendent love-will and wisdom. Formation anthropology expresses this overall formation ideal in the word "consonance." Consonance or the quality of sounding together (*con-sonare*) points to the constantly growing harmony in wisdom and love between one's transcending character and the formation mystery as epiphanically calling in the spheres, dimensions, and consciousness regions of one's field of presence and action.

The subideals of this overall ideal of consonance are the character dispositions of transcendent candor, courage, congeniality, competence, commitment, compatibility, compassion, joy, and appreciation. In the following section, I shall discuss another kind of ideal related to implementation.

Servant Implementation Ideals

A basic assumption of my formation anthropology has been that the human person is innately endowed with the capacity to receive and give form, transcendently and pretranscendently. To be human is to receive and give form constantly, to be always in formation. This unifying principle of my anthropology, formation science, and formation theology applies also to character formation.

First of all, we are able to receive form; we are form receptive. Our transcendent mind is endowed by the mystery with the gift of receiving insight and wisdom; our transcendent will has been granted the power to receive gifts of love-will and appreciation; our transcendent character has been enabled to receive gifts of consonant dispositions.

We have also been provided with the remarkable power of giving form. Our powers of receiving and giving form work together. Often they interact. Many of the forms we receive come from the people, events, and things we meet in daily life. They emit to our senses, so to speak, physical wave forms. Our neuroform decodes them in such a manner that our mind can register them as the events that send out the waves that have touched our senses. Our mind is not only able to receive such forms; it also gives form to them. It can even reform and transform them. In relation to transcendent character formation, such transformation of received forms is guided by many horizons. To name the more important ones: the horizon of our ideal and subideal character dispositions; of our faith and formation traditions; of our unique-communal life call; of our powers of imagination, memory, and anticipation. All of these assist us in transforming received forms transcendently, consonantly, imaginatively, and inventively.

We are called to give form inwardly and outwardly—inwardly in our minds and hearts; outwardly in the inter and outer spheres of our formation field. One facet of our donation of forms is their effective empirical-experiential implementation in our life and world. By disciplined reflection on our own empirical experiences as well as on those of others and on their reflections, we disclose effective ways of implementation.

How can we concretely express here and now some facets of our transcendent ideal and its subideals as guiding us through our character dispositions? Seeking for new ways to express such ideals disposes our character to generate what I call "implementation dispositions." To distinguish them from subideals I call them "servant" ideals.

Our subideals themselves are consonant, partial expressions of our main ideals. By contrast, our servant implementation ideals represent ideal ways of serving the implementation of ideals and subideals in everyday empirical-experiential life. Usually the disclosure of implementation ideals will be accompanied by an enrichment of formation conscience. We realize that a certain way of implementing our transcendent ideal and its subideals *ought* to serve the disclosure of facets of our personal-communal life call. This insight turns spontaneously into an "ought to" or "conscience experience" of an impelling implementation ideal of conscience.

Formation conscience has two sides: an ideal one and a guilty one. The guilty side may be activated when we fail to heed the ideal. Any new implementation ideal enriches the ideal side of our formation conscience. In turn, this now enriched conscience will keep coforming the corresponding character dispositions that incline us to this particular, effective way of empirical-experiential implementation.

Dimensional Striving and Character Formation

From my original conception of phasic character formation, it may be obvious that our character is formed in its dispositions by our dimensional strivings. Each of the sociohistorical, vital, functional, functional-transcendent, transcendent, and transcendent-functional coformants of our character form can be frustrated in its phasic striving for fulfillment. Such frustration engenders conflicts. We try to deal with these by repeated acts of solving something or coping with something. Such solutions become sedimented in our character as more or less enduring dispositions or virtues.

In others words, these patterns of coping can result in the particular structuring of our character form of life. As we have seen, all character dispositions may be influential in the formation phases of our life. In certain phases, one or the other of them is more dominant than in others. Any phase can leave a lasting imprint on a character's prevalent dispositions. Accordingly, I speak of a sociohistorical, vital, functional, functional-transcendent, transcendent, or transcendent-functional character form. All of these character structures can be either receptive or executive; they may manifest a balance of receptivity and execution.

In accordance with my principle of the possibility of a relative dominance of one character set of dispositions over others—of course, under the ultimate supremacy of the transcendent life call—I conceived the following character typology.

Sociohistorical Character

The sociohistorical-receptive character is marked by absolutely or relatively dominant dispositions of taking on attitudes, directives, and symbols that can be found in the form traditions of one's society.

The sociohistorical-executive character tends to be active in its participation in sociohistorical issues and events.

Vital Character

The vital-receptive character is marked by a dominant disposition for vital-emotional gratification and consolation. This can be so strong that one's adherence to a transcendent tradition later turns mainly into strivings for consolation and warm feelings.

The vital-executive character is disposed to overwhelm the inter and outer spheres of our formation field by boundless or explosive expressions of vital emotions, such as loving, romantic, charming, aggressive, enthusiastic, angry, and resentful feelings. If this disposition prevails, functional reason may lose its independence. It can become the slave of the vital-executive character trait.

Functional Character

The functional-receptive character directs functional reason and powers of observation to gather and order information. This character form as receptive limits its dispositions of functional observing and reasoning to intraformational operations. Without coming to functional execution, it may communicate to others on a sheer logical or informational level some of its functional thought processes in conversation, teaching, or publication.

The functional-executive character is disposed to collect information eagerly and to devise cogent reasons. It uses them to strategize in order to change its formation field in practical ways. In transcendent traditions, its adherents can be resourceful in terms of administration, organization, accounting, and the development of projects of social justice, provided they can subordinate this character trait to transcendent dispositions.

Functional-Transcendent Character

The functional-transcendent character is inclined to subordinate the side benefits of the initiating stages of the transcendent life to enhanced functioning, both receptively and executively. An example can be found in the promise of certain spiritualities that transcendent living will foster physical health, increase one's property, and make one more attractive to others. Some of these side benefits may come true in favorable situations. For the functional-transcendent character, however, these side benefits are not merely "at the side"; they become one of the main motivations for one's spiritual concern.

Transcendent Character

The receptive-transcendent character is marked by a contemplative openness to gifts and manifestations of the transcendent mystery. The executive-transcendent character is distinguished by its focus on anything that can directly advance the conditions for such receptive openness.

Transcendent-Functional Character

The transcendent-functional character is disposed to strive for the harmonious subordination of all character dispositions to transcendent dispositions. This is not to deny that one or the other of the aforementioned character dispositions may still exert more influence than some others. The difference is that these dispositions are no longer absolutely dominant. They are only relatively dominant insofar as they are subordinated and permeated by transcendent dispositions. For example, a vital core form does not lose its vitality when it is pervaded by ultimate transcendent dispositions. This vitality is only purged, enhanced, and completed by a transcendent orientation. The same can be said of a functional character.

Without such subordination, character dispositions may give rise to deformations. For example, a onesided excessive reliance on a vital-receptive character structure may lead to weakness in performance, to overdependency on attractive and gratifying people and movements, to excessive emotional generosity, and to extravagant socializing that may harm one's concentration on the tasks at hand. The need for vital gratification may make a person overly demanding, placating, and compliant. One may feel averse from the directives of functional rationality.

Interformation and Character Formation

All character formation is for a great part rooted in the initial interformation patterns between parent and child. These patterns are internalized in the child's pretranscendent conscience of how things should be done to live a propitious life. Such child-parent patterns are in turn dependent in some measure on the form-traditional pyramid of one's parents.

My formation anthropology is critical of deterministic drive theories. They tend to overvalue the power of drives because of false presuppositions that do not leave sufficient room for the powers of human spirit and tradition. My formation theory and anthropology have been tested effectively by less driven members of non-Western societies. The results convinced me that many Western drive theories need serious amending. The early shaping of the pretranscendent and tradition-compatible transcendent formation conscience depends profoundly on the interformation patterns that evolve between parents and children. Formation traditions play a central role in this story of initial interformation. Therefore, I do not believe that core form or character formation can be reduced to vital biological drives alone.

Character Reformation

How can we disclose to ourselves our core form in the light of the anthropology of character? The first fruit of my anthropology should be the awakening and deepening of our character awareness. We begin by being attentive to regularly recurring tendencies to act or omit to act in certain predictable ways. We must ask ourselves if the consistency of this tendency points perhaps to an enduring disposition in our core form of life? The next thing we should be attentive to is the emotional reaction that usually accompanies these acts. Do we feel good or uneasy about them? Do they foster our overall feeling of consonance or dissonance? Recurrent experiences of displeasure, such as feelings of disease, dissonance, guilt, or reluctance, tell us that we ought to look into the character disposition at the root of these acts. Should it be reformed or transformed? Are we perhaps the victim of a deformed conscience that makes us mistakenly feel guilty about a character disposition that is actually or potentially consonant?

The next step to be taken is to calm down, to rise above the disturbing emotions. We must inwardly distance ourselves from them. Only when we are sufficiently detached are we able to explore directly and objectively the underlying disposition and its correlate in our formation conscience.

Our exploration may lead us to the insight that our character and/or our corresponding formation conscience needs to be transformed in some respect. At such a moment, we should enter into transcendent self-presence. This goes far beyond the introspection in which we may have been involved when we were first shocked into the awareness that a transformation of our character might be required. In transcendent self-presence we connect with our unique-communal life call. We look at its root in the formation mystery that resides within us. There is an intimate connection between that ever-calling mystery and the consonant dispositions that should mark our unique-communal core of life. Dwelling on our call we become gradually bathed in the wisdom and understanding that are gifts of the mystery. In due time they grant us insight in what should be changed. Now comes the hard time.

To implement our concrete call to transformation, we must die to cherished or even coercive dispositions with which we were at home for a long time. We are invited by the calling mystery to let go, to set free and relinquish anything in our character that has been born out of bad will or formation ignorance in our life so far. This period of purgation represents a trying episode of radical surgery involving our whole life of memory, imagination, and anticipation. It is like subjecting oneself to root canal treatment without a sedative.

Until such episodes are worked through radically, no matter the pain this may cause us, our dissonant dispositions will not be uprooted totally. Slowly these roots will grow again. They will reproduce in our character the old dispositions that were merely truncated. They will bring back as well their related memories, imaginations, and anticipations; we will be aware of their subtle spread in our neuroform. Sooner or later they may drive us back into past patterns of deformative action.

At the end of the dark tunnel of character purgation or radical reformation, we may be blessed with the grace of formation freedom, of growth in wholeness and consonance.

Part Two

PHASIC PRETRANSCENDENT, TRANSCENDENT, AND POST-TRANSCENDENT FORMATION

CHAPTER 12

Phasic Process
as Transdevelopmental

I invented the term phasic formation to point to successive phases of life insofar as they are related to our transcendent journey. Phasic formation gradually sets us free from ignorance of our true transcendent nature. During times of crisis, our transcendence dynamic may awaken us to a gnawing dissatisfaction with the way we have received and given form to our life so far. We may be successful or unsuccessful, popular or misunderstood, wealthy or poor, gifted or average; but somehow we are not at peace. An anxious foreboding of dissonance breaks into our awareness. The true meaning of life begins to stir in us. In the midst of this distress, functionally speaking, a longing for transcendence tugs at us gently yet firmly. We feel a nostalgia arising in us to be faithful to our founding life form or call, whatever this is and wherever it leads us.

Our deeper formation began when this longing announced itself in times of transition and crisis. The dissatisfaction we felt about being fixated on one or the other phasic form of life or being caught in a lower form dimension could no longer be denied. This awakening from formation ignorance made us aware of deformations, dissonances, and deceptive complacencies.

This experience alters our view of life. It enables us to ponder anew the transcendent direction of our formation phases. We come to see more of the inner call that prods us toward deeper consonance.

In the past few millennia of Western civilization and certainly since the Enlightenment and the Industrial Revolution, people became more encapsulated than in previous eras in the functional dimension of life. Anxious attachment to possessions, their appropriation, management, and enjoyment, overshadowed the transcendent direction of their existence. This made it impossible for people to appreciate the transcendent meaning revealed in every phase of life's formation. Through phasic transitions the formation mystery makes us gradually ready for its entrance into our life. The mystery hides in what I have defined as our transfocal consciousness until its transforming power touches on what I called, by contrast, our prefocal and focal consciousness. Each phase of transition can be seen as an inlet into the welcoming sea of the transforming mystery. How this eternal sea hungers to turn each of us into a unique epiphanic outlet of its love, peace, and joy!

Shared Blindness to the Mystery

Part of the problem is that we are conscious not only in a personal way; we also have to take into account the consciousness we share with one another. We are bound together in a special way by what I introduced in my science as our interconsciousness.

My concept of interconsciousness implies that we share not only common insights but also a common blindness. Our shared blindness to the directives of the transcendence dynamic has drawn our civilization into a shared crisis of formation. Two millennia of development of Greco-Roman functional rationality has enriched immensely our functional formation power. It is proper to cherish this enhanced power and its amazing fruits in positive science, technology, informational theology, and philosophy. What must now be overcome is a onesided functional formation and our irrational, exclusive attachment to conceptual-analytical and technical performance only. Our extension of the analytical and technical approach to any realm of life, even art, literature, religion, and the life of the spirit, blinds us to their higher transtechnical message.

Such onesidedness makes us overlook the vital and transcendent directives that ought also to guide our life. This neglect makes us unhappy and unhealthy, at odds with the mysterious unfolding of cosmos and humanity, and, in the long run, ineffective. Functionalism does not allow us to appreciate phasic crises also in the light of our more basic transcendence dynamics and transcendent traditions.

Today, the number of people being drawn beyond the barrier of formation ignorance is on the rise. Such writers and thinkers may be in the forefront of the millennia to come. I believe a period may be in the making in which the search for the transcendent will be the new frontier for many. Certainly this search has been my life's work. This openness to the "more than" will complete and bring to fruition our remarkable assimilation of the gift of functional rationality during the last two millennia. When we make it serve humanity's transcendence dynamic, functional rationality will have found its proper place in the ascent of our race.

Transcending Mechanistic Models
of Human Development

We should not restrict ourselves to mechanistic models of human development. In the light of transcendent traditions, we can begin to sense, from the inside out, as it were, the deeper meaning of crises in our life. Mechanistic models that would see humans merely as biopsychological machines to be tested, analyzed, and cleverly repaired are no longer convincing. My science calls for the appreciation of human life as also a unique-communal mystery of dynamic phasic formations. All of these imply that we are in a flow of interaction with the formation mystery at work within and without our unfolding fields of life.

This view calls for the paradigm shift I have been calling for in my science since the 1940s. I am struck by the fact that the major crises of our civilization go unresolved most of the time because of our shared formation ignorance. The once helpful but now insufficient Cartesian-Newtonian worldview kept the blinders over our eyes. Its assumptions made us appraise reality as a mechanistic collection of solid particles. The new physics tells a different story. All forms we observe are fluctuating, dynamic, ongoing formations. Sometimes they are continuous with one another. At other times they are discontinuous in a creative way. They give rise to moments or periods of crisis. At no time are the forms that appear in our universe solidly enclosed particles without any relationship to one another.

Human forms of life are not just biopsychologically functioning machines. They, too, are called to be transcendentally unfolding forms of life within everchanging fields. Human life is empowered and illumined by the mystery, and by the transcendent traditions this mystery grants all the time to struggling humanity. The dynamics of formation under consideration in these chapters show us that we are free, conscious forms of life passing through formation processes from birth to death.

At the appropriate times, new formation phases break into the continuous flow of our ongoing formation, creating discontinuous dynamics that interrupt it. Such dynamics of disruption press us to look at the process of formation. In contrast, a life of easy, continuous flow may not compel such reflection.

The numerous minor changes that take place between the upheavals of new formation phases are also important. Still, they never struck me as being as crucial as the breakthroughs we experience at the onset of a new formation phase.

The mystery helps us to deal consonantly with new dynamic directives, no matter the staying power of past formations. We should not be enslaved to blockages that are only passing accretions of past formation phases. We can be formatively present to the past, to the here and now, and to the anticipated future all at once. We can strive for a transtemporal vision. What makes this vision possible is transcendent presence to our unifying life direction. Formation traditions help us to clarify this vision. The seeds of a wider vision lie buried in our unfolding life call and the mystery that shines forth within it.

Dissonant Dynamics of Exclusive Attachments

My formation science emphasizes that a new message accompanies each phase of our life's journey. It suggests that the moving force that stimulates us to go beyond our phasic formation crises does not come only from without. It comes first of all from dynamics deep within our transcendent founding form of life. These dynamics gradually push themselves upward. They point to our founding life call, which carries within itself the promise of the hidden treasures that are our formation potencies. They are unique gifts of the mystery. Different potencies show themselves more strikingly at different formation phases. We go through a succession of such phases. The higher the phase, the nearer we get to our distinctively human forms of life.

Refusal to cherish and use these potencies and energies makes us feel guilty, frightened, and ill at ease. We try to escape in attachments that turn us away from the invitation to ascend. This evasion gives itself away in our refusal to think much about ultimate questions pertaining to the purpose and meaning of life. Such questions are evoked, at least in a roundabout way, by formation crises. What happens goes something like this:

1. We get caught in a tighter and tighter net of distracting or blinding attachments.
2. These desensitize us, at least at the start, to the painful feelings of willful dissonance in relation to the disclosures of our own deepest life call.
3. Before long, we feel shaken and shamed by formation guilt.
4. This makes us lose ourselves in frantic pursuits of pleasure and possession to dull the inner torment, even if it does not take it away. Maybe we cling to a leader, a lover, a movement, a friend, to an ideology, science, art, hobby, career, cause, project, thing, or intoxicating substance, as if it were ultimate. We turn one or the other person, thing, or event into the exclusive directive force in our life.
5. Such willfulness, rooted in the pride form, blocks our awareness of the transcendence crisis originating from deep within ourselves.
6. Exclusive attachment to anything less than the transcendent deforms our life. It recreates us, so to say, in the image of that to which we attach ourselves as ultimate rather than transforms us into the form and likeness of who we are called to become.

Escape in inordinate attachments turns out to be the wrong solution to a phasic crisis of transition. It sets us on a detour from our ascent; it makes us avoid a phase of transformation to which our inner dynamics invite us. The tension between transcendence dynamics and attachment dynamics to our past is something we all have to face when a crisis of transcendence strikes. We must learn to draw formative directives and energies from our founding form and the mystery that is its ground and center. These will help us to let go of the dynamics of mechanical attachments that encapsulate us.

The dynamics of transcendence invite us, step by step, to be faithful to the disclosures of our life call. We no longer mistake any fragmented developmental stage for the meaning of our life as a whole. We do not attempt to cling to any phase as such. It becomes for us a passing station along the way, a pointer to a higher consonance. Gradually the unifying directives of our founding form come to the fore. They make us feel more consonant with the mystery in the midst of the necessary dissonance of any transient phase.

Pretranscendent Sciences and Disciplines

Often the sciences and disciplines of the pretranscendent life explain our higher experiences only from below, for example, as sublimations of the libido. My own science assumes that the ultimate source of all transcendent changes of life is from above, not from below. "Above" does not mean, in my science, a Platonic universe replete with archetypes. The source above is each human life form's unique dynamics of transcendence. I look at these dynamics as embodied in the socio-bio-vital-functional whole of our life, but beyond all of them as rooted in the unique epiphany or appearance of the mystery in a unique life call that each of us is asked to disclose and implement.

In contrast to my science, the theories of positivistic psychologists as well as those of some ancient and contemporary platonists or gnostics have woven beautiful tapestries of partial truths into whole theories of life. They advance our journey to a degree, yet often at the price of dimming the deeper, unifying direction underlying all transcendence crises. They may actually stand in the way of a direction to which our consonant traditions are pointing us.

Our recovery from exclusive attachments may enable the spontaneous coming to the fore of successive disclosures of the basic call of our life. These disclosures point to a transcendent form of life. The latter always benefits from pretranscendent insights but not from attachments that are exclusively pretranscendent.

I have sought for years a deeper understanding of phasic formation than is presently available in the developmental theories of social, clinical, and educational disciplines. A more profound insight has made me aware that sheer functional control of the symptoms of attachment and its immediate causes, while helpful, is only an intermediate means to some clarity, not an entrance to the fullness of light. By itself alone, such symptom control can serve to foster pretranscendent consistency, but it cannot expose us to the high lights of transcendent ascent and its fruits of increasing consonance and harmony.

Once we, in coformation with the mystery, allow our founding call to come to the fore, the dynamics of attachment can be transformed into transcendence dynamics. I look at attachment dynamics as an abuse of the deepest dynamics that inspire us to attach our lives to the transcendent mystery itself. Each of us is called to give form to life and its field in consonance with a unique-communal life direction. Every crisis in our life, even its faulty solutions and attachments, comes to us as an opportunity for transcendence. Everything can be used for our consonant life direction by the healing, merciful mystery. Its transforming power waits respectfully upon our free consent and willing coformation.

Return to Our Intrasphere

Often we falsely imagine that the inter and outer spheres of our formation field impose a crisis on us. We like to believe that they drive us into the popular attachments that pulsate through our culture. We are always tempted to blame others for our deficiencies. The truth is that our own free, intraforming sphere coforms our field as a whole in a unique fashion, not the other way around. Widening our focus from only the inter and outer spheres of our field to also and primarily our own intrasphere is the beginning of the process of transformation. Our option for this inner expansion sets us in principle free from the bondage of exclusive attachments.

Crises may appear to be caused merely by inter and outer events in our field. Of course, they should be taken into account, for they may indeed be the occasion, if not the ultimate cause, of our crisis. They also provide an opportunity for our becoming aware that our founding form or life call, through our spirit, nudges us further on our ascent to full transformation.

Detachment Dynamics

To the degree that we are enslaved to our lower attachment dynamics, we may be afraid to venture into an unfamiliar phase of life. Dictatorial or seductive people around us, bent on molding us mechanistically, not on setting us free for the mystery, may enflame our fears. They seem to prefer that we suppress the dynamics of higher directives, that we prevent them from coming to the fore in accordance with the unique pace and peace of our personality, character, and temperament. They do not endorse in us the creative emergence of our unique-communal call of life.

Parents blinded to the transcendence dynamic in their own life may, for example, thicken in their children the suffocating powers of depreciation. They do not help them to appreciate each possible disclosure of their own ideal form of life and its congenial pace of unfolding. Such depreciation tempts children to inflate a false apparent form, instead of their consonant public appearance, so as to please their parents. They cover up their true form of life. Thanks to transition crises later in life, such inflation of mainly one's deceptive apparent form may be transcended and one's true upward ascent can continue.

We should help one another to open up to the ongoing, probable disclosures of our life call, to appraise them critically, to try them out in everyday practice. We can only do so when the crisis of phasic formation makes us ready for this work. Formation wisdom rooted in openness to one's life call can be taught in some measure, but beyond that it must also be caught. It is only caught when the moment of personal insight has come. We must cultivate a refined radar, a special sensitivity, for this moment of readiness in ourselves and others. We should cultivate a disposition of patient attentiveness to the signs of unfolding of life by means of new formation phases.

All of this confirms the conviction at the core of my science that we should not base our life merely on the theories and methods of clinical, social, and educational disciplines. While truly appreciating their insights, we must look at them from the perspective of a deeper kind of understanding. We may then begin to see that such insights are meant to serve the transcendent purpose of our overall life direction. How does this direction show itself in the formative meaning of a crisis with its invitation to courageous detachment?

It does so by drawing on the wisdom and practices of classical traditions and on their experience of the ascent to freedom. When it is desirable, we may also consult compatible clinical, social, scientific, and educational insights that bear on our journey, its dynamics, obstacles, and conditions. This research in the literature of pretranscendence makes us more sensitive to the moment of receptivity for a different decisive phase of transcendence when it emerges. Receptivity means that our heart is ready to take in something of the inner life direction that is pushing upward into our focal consciousness at this juncture of our journey.

In a civilization that turns onesidedly to mechanistic mastery and management of the inter and outer spheres of our fields of life, this readiness to respond to the mystery may be hard to come by. Mechanistic mastery depends on constantly fueling the functional powers of our life and the practical know-how of our functional individuality. Often we mistake this important lower aspect of our personality for the whole transcending person in his or her unique rootedness in the mystery.

Phasic Formation and the Dimensions
of Our Life Formation

My formation science, I repeat, looks at all dimensions of our life's formation. It pays special attention to phasic formation dynamics because these carry life from one dimension to another. Phasic bridges are indispensable on the journey to full transcendence. On the one hand, attachment to our lower dimensions without attention to their hidden transcendent orientation would stall our flight. It would bind our life to a mundane whirl of everyday pulsations, pulsions, and ambitions. On the other hand, higher transcendence dynamics, without their embodiment in the lower ones, would be just as ineffective. They would be like inflated balloons drifting in an endless sky with nowhere to descend. Without embodiment in these lower dynamics, the higher ones may remain formless and out of touch with everyday life. Pretranscendent sciences and disciplines may enlighten us greatly about the lower developmental ranges of formation, but they can never fully satisfy our quest for the "more than."

The mystery enables us through a succession of formation crises to put the dynamics of formation and reformation of our lower dimensions at the service of the transcendence dynamic. Every time the mystery effects this integration-through-detachment within us, we enjoy some transformation of life. Gradually, we are ushered into the transforming phases of our journey.

Pretranscendent Disciplines

The dynamics of formation should be pervaded by those of transformation. This happens when we draw upon the universal energy flowing from the formation mystery. We can do so explicitly, but usually we rely implicitly on this energy. The forming energy of the mystery is always ready to stream through people inwardly. It also permeates the inter and outer spheres of their formation field and its horizons. It wants to heal, transform, inspire, uplift, and console. Each formation phase is a potential opening to this loving dynamic of transformation. Each phase affects and is affected by one's field of presence and action.

We should respect, but not overemphasize, our pretranscendent personality. We should not ascribe to it the exclusive and final meaning sometimes ascribed to this lower servant structure by pretranscendent disciplines. The latter, to use the example of a Jungian approach, may adorn itself with some transcendent concerns. Such insights into human development, no matter how sublime or edifying they may be, are placed inevitably at the service of our functional-transcendent, gnostic personality instead of disclosing to us our true transcendent and transcendent-functional identity.

In my formation science, the lower personality is profoundly meaningful as the flexible servant of the higher "I." What we are meant to be is hidden as a seed in our life call. This call is the transcendent source of our unique-communal life formation. To disclose our destiny step by step and to express it consonantly in empirical life is the function of each and every formation phase.

The dynamics at work in these phases, more often than not, lead to faulty solutions of current crises, "solutions" that prove to be counterproductive in the long run. Formation energies become constricted in dispositions of exclusive attachment dynamics. They lose their receptivity for permeation by the dynamics of transformation. Our ascent is bogged down in the mire of exclusive attachments. Before we know it, our transformation is delayed.

We must do what we can to release blocked dynamics. Once freed, we can regain our receptivity to the permeation of the lower "I" by transcendence dynamics rising from the fountain of life deep within us.

Those who base their counseling and teaching exclusively on the theories offered by pretranscendent disciplines restrict themselves to the extensive development of their socio-functional-vital and functional-transcendent personality. They may show little or no appreciation for the transcendent person and his or her transformative relation to the lower personality. A behaviorally trained therapist, for example, may deny the existence of this deeper, less definable founding form or call. Tests and experiments do not detect or measure it. Hence one may conclude it does not exist. Subsequently one may mistake the fragmented socio-functional-vital and functional-transcendent personality for the human personality as a whole.

CHAPTER 13

Formational Process
as Dynamic and Phasic

Our core form, heart, and its matching character are meant to mirror our basic or founding form of life as a gift of the mystery. Initially, this founding form is still preempirical and transconscious. A succession of what I call "current formations of life" makes it possible for us to discover over a lifetime what we are called to be. I distinguish two kinds of these formations: the situational and the phasic.

Situational Current Formation

A new situation may push us into a giving and receiving of forms that bring us more in tune with the changing conditions of our life. Situational current formation refers, for example, to an illness, new employment or unemployment, failure or success, a conversion, migration, change of school, loss of a beloved one, ecclesiastical, political, or economic upheaval.

Such situations affect and change our formation field. They push us beyond our familiar ways. For a time they take up much of our formation energy. Other concerns stay in the background. Change brings to focal consciousness aspects of our call of which we were thus far not clearly aware. Take, for example, people who are put unexpectedly into a position of leadership. They go through a period of assessing their new responsibilities. At first, they have to go along with the people under and above them, but soon there may awaken in them dormant predispositions for taking charge. The current situation has set in motion unsuspected leadership possibilities they have yet to explore.

Phasic Current Formation

The other kind of current formation is phasic. Its dynamics set the stage for advancement to the next phase of transition in our life's unfolding, namely, from a lower form of presence and action to a higher one.

Phasic formation dynamics script or program the successive phases we have to pass through on our journey. They bring us nearer to the unique-communal call that is ours in this life. As I mentioned earlier, this dynamic progress is, in principle, common to all people within certain age ranges. Its timely working out, however, differs in people because everyone's field of life, traditions, and history hide unique challenges.

Phasic current formations, unlike situational formation changes, are linked to vital-genetic predispositions in our makeup. As a result, they are somewhat predictable and common in most people in the same age range who share the same cultural situation. By contrast, we cannot foretell situational life formations. Their number and variety are inexhaustible. For that reason I will confine my considerations to the dynamics of the *phasic* currents we have in common with one another. These phasic dynamics can be seen as lower and higher stepping stones on the ascent of human life as a whole. In this chapter, I will thus reflect in a general way on the basic dynamics of formation that mark human unfolding phasically. I shall go into them in more detail in the following chapters.

Neuroformation and Phasic Formation

Phasic reformation, unlike situational reformation, is linked with changes in our vital neuroform. My concept of the neuroform refers to our infrafocal, biophysical form of life; it is partly acquired, such as in the development of neuroformational dispositions, and partly congenital due either to general human factors or to family inheritance.

The age-bound awakening of potencies for each specific phase of human life follows neuroformational pathways. These have been evolved in humanity by the cosmic formation mystery over billions of years. Age-bound phasic formation is thus very much a function of neuroformation. There is a direct correlation between the emergent functions of specific neural structures in our neuroform and the formation phases I am describing in this volume, but this is not the whole story.

Each emergent phase is coformed in its concrete appearance by all the spheres, dimensions, ranges, ranks, and regions of our actual field of life. We should take them into account. First of all, we must reverence the preforming mystery at the center of our field in which is grounded our unique-communal founding life form, life call, and life project. The intrasphere of our field contains the way in which we inwardly respond to phasic awakening. The interformational sphere is the way in which others model for us formation traditions. These traditions can guide us in our unfolding of a new phase of life. Also, the situational and wider world spheres of our field affect our apprehension and appraisal of new phasic challenges.

At predetermined times in our life, phases programmed by the cosmic formation mystery over eons of time are triggered by neural structures that emerge in our neuroform. These enable us to experience new form potencies that make it possible to receive and unfold a new form of life that is different from former ones. As we will see in the following chapters, the vital-emotional child may suddenly phase out and become a child ruled by the first stirrings of functional reason. The neuroform triggers this change in the child. At each pre-programmed age range, it initiates the neurological possibility for the appropriate new phase of formation.

The same can be said of the formation of the lower "I." Its emergence at the appropriate phase is a function of neuroformational changes. It starts when the formation field of the child stabilizes itself. This can happen between seven and eighteen months of age. Then, seemingly out of the blue, the willful "I" emerges as a first manifestation of this new lower "I." The adult logic that will later be typical of the same functional "I" is not yet available to the infant at this age, known as "the terrible twos." A tremendous sense of the power of the pretranscendent will of the lower "I" is suddenly breaking into the relatively quiet unfolding of the child. I explain that breakthrough by the neuroformational shift that automatically expresses the agenda of the cosmic mystery of formation.

Once this age phase emerges, its shape is modulated implicitly by other interforming dimensions. For example, the slumbering transcendent dimension of the child is implicitly touched by the transcendent dimension of the motherly presence.

This breaking through of the lower individual "I" is a great gift of the cosmic formation mystery. It may be bothersome to the parents, but it is necessary. The structure of the lower "I" is guided in the neuroform by the limbic structure of the brain. This structure of our neuroform contains the emotional potencies of the human form of life. This explains why the two-year-old, devoid still of the logical power of reason, may whimsically manifest boundless excitement, rage, love, hate, and other emotions in an unpredictably willful fashion. It is the way in which the cosmic mystery through the neuroform stirs the infant for the first time beyond its vital beginnings. It is the first announcement of a pretranscendent "I" that will enable human life later to control its vital dynamics and to respond to them with lower functional reason in the light of and in the service of the higher transcendent-immanent "I."

The almost exclusive dominance of this willful phase is as passing as all other formation phases; it, too, prepares the way for the next phase. Each new phase dominates formation almost exclusively only for a certain period of time. When it has accomplished its forming task, the cosmic mystery of formation shifts us to a new, temporarily dominant phase of formation.

I prefer to use the word "formation" instead of "development" because in formation science I relate all development to transcendent-immanent formation by the mystery. The moment we do so, the vitalistic or functionalistic meaning of human development basically changes, at least for us transcendent observers, even if the person concerned is not aware of this change. The transcendent dimension of life slumbers already in children. They can be touched implicitly and indirectly in the nonfocal region of their consciousness by the transcendent-immanent faith, hope, and love of their parents or parental substitutes.

Our lower "I" is thus formed in its various structures under the influence of our neuroform at specific periods of our life. During these periods each new structure rules supreme. Each new phase complements and moderates the former one. The whole history of phasic unfolding is marked by the emergence of new enriching phases and ultimately by our higher or transcendent "I." The *dominance* of the lower "I" is not transformed but made obsolete; it is transcended by the newly emerging dominance of the higher "I." The lower "I" itself is not destroyed or passed over. On the contrary, it becomes the indispensable executive servant of the higher transcendent-immanent "I."

The cosmic formation mystery, which, in my science, is the gift to humanity of the radical mystery, uses the neuroform to awaken in us the formation potency that more fully enables us to strive personally for transcendence. This potency for personalized transcendence does not unfold automatically. As a general rule, no potency disclosed by the neuroform will give consonant form to our life unless it is guided by the formation wisdom of humanity as expressed in formation traditions attractively and convincingly modeled in our field of life.

For example, at a certain moment of our history the neuroform awakens in us the potency for language formation. But we cannot give form to a language until we have the benefit of a lingual tradition modeled for us in our field by parents or their substitutes.

The same holds for all other phases of formation. Appropriate formation traditions must be modeled appealingly if the crucial neuroformational functions are to unfold. The cosmic formation mystery has endowed us in utero and at birth with the whole system of neuroformational predispositions necessary to awaken us over a lifetime to the successive phases of our journey. It will not do us any good if these potencies are not stimulated by the form traditions, models, and symbols that can activate them.

To activate these predispositions, we need persons around us who in some measure in their own life have given form to these potencies—people who have done so in the light of humanity's wisdom as condensed in consonant traditions. Their example inspires us to learn from life what the triggers are that activate these predispositions of our neuroform. Initially, we have to imitate their approach until the use of such stimulation and inspiration becomes spontaneous in us. Then we can dispense with the model and give personal form to the phase concerned in the light of our own unique-communal life call and project. This call is slowly disclosed by us in dialogue with the consonant formation traditions to which we are personally committed.

In early childhood, the parents model the traditional wisdom of living. Later, the neuroform disposes the child to expect a change in direction from familial to social models. During the midteens, the lower "I" becomes established more firmly. This makes the growing child ready for a new phase of life. Beginning at twelve, thirteen, or fourteen, and reaching its zenith around fifteen, an adolescent experiences that the cosmic mystery of formation (as kept operative by the radical transcendent mystery) evokes through the neuroform a longing for the "more than." This vague desire is a first disclosure of the transcendent dimension and the transfocal region of consciousness. The transcendent beckons; the life of the spirit opens up; a higher "I" begins to emerge; the deeper meaning of a unique-communal life call and project may reveal itself.

Adolescents try to make sense of this experience in terms of their current form traditions shared with their peers, no matter how shallow these companions may be. They may feel this awakening as a kind of churning, vehement idealism, but they do not realize to what this experience is really pointing. They feel that nobody understands them. They do not understand themselves either.

Western functionalistic tradition does not recognize what is stirred up in its late adolescents via their neuroform. Unlike original African and Asian traditions, many present-day Western traditions do not offer generally accepted symbols, institutions, form traditions, and models that can inspire the formation of the higher "I." Western young people, confronted with the birth pangs of their spiritual life dimension, wait unwittingly for persons to model appealingly the wisdom of spiritual traditions. Most of them look in vain. Such models are rarely to be found in functionalistic societies.

The tragedy of Western civilization at this point resides in the priming of young persons by the neuroform for higher formation and an absence of the models for whom they are looking prefocally. The longings of the awakened heart are misunderstood and abused for the support of unworthy causes. The consumer society tells them that all longings can be fulfilled by acquiring and consuming more and more material goods, by pursuing promising careers, and by sharing in popular hedonism.

Formation Dimensions and Current Formation Phases

What is the difference between form dimensions and formation phases? The former stay intact whereas the latter are passing. Phases of formation change from one phase to the other by driving powers or dynamics. Let me explain this process step by step:

1. The transcendence dynamic sparks our awareness of a higher dimension of life. Each disclosure of such a dimension brings us nearer to the transcendent founding form of our life or life call.
2. Phasic dynamics make us somewhat familiar with the transcendent

dimension of life, at least implicitly and indirectly, by preparing us for it. They stimulate us to try out newly unveiled potencies. They foster our tentative use of probable aspects of a new life dimension in terms of where we are in our formation field and its traditions. They urge us to disclose the rightful place of this newly emerging dimension in the overall order of the dimensions and dynamics of our life. Thus, "phasic" is another word for "dynamics-of-transition." They give form to a passing transitional trying out of probable facets of the emergent dimension before the new dimension itself is fully active.

3. The dynamics of any passing transition phase call into question the ruling power of the dynamics of the foregoing dimension. This preceding dimension both directed and absorbed much of our formation energy. Now the upcoming dimension demands our attention. For the time being, its emergent dynamics center our life as a whole and help us to begin to focus on the new, higher dimension.

4. Dynamics of purification, illumination, field articulation, and consonance-dissonance polarization also come into play. Take, for example, the beginning of the new dimension of the functional-rational. It can only break through the shell of the foregoing functional-vital dimension if we purify ourselves from its control of our life.

5. Purification dynamics lead to illumination. In this example, they bring to focal awareness the light of reason illuminating rational functioning. These lights are hidden from the beginning in our founding form of life, but now they can become a source of corresponding lasting dispositions of character and personality. Under the illumination of our awakening reason, our powers of reasonable functioning take into account the particular features of our formation field and its consonant traditions that require us to function rationally.

The dynamics of consonance are always at work in such phasic transitions. They press toward harmony between our new dimension, first in its current and tentative, then in its lasting form, on the one hand, and our other dimensions as well as our traditions, on the other.

Some dissonance in this process is to be expected. It, too, plays a role within the various phasic dynamics. We have to accept the challenge of dissonances we cannot yet go beyond. In this way dissonance can serve deeper consonance. Acceptance of the challenge of discord in our life keeps us on the path of sound, humble, and realistic formation.

End of a Current Formation Phase

Dynamics of initiation into a new dimension of life involve a great deal of trial and error before they turn into a lasting new dimension of life. As this dimension gains in stability, it becomes linked more and more with the core form, especially as not only core and heart but also as the corresponding character of our life. The new dimension adds its own lasting dispositions and directives to our character. Yet this new dimension remains sufficiently independent to allow for new articulations in our ever-changing formation field. For example, to function reasonably in the new situation of caring for a husband suffering from coronary disease, a wife must take into account the practical demands brought about by this change and adapt her characteristic way of functioning in the family accordingly. She must express her character disposition of care in a new, specifically goal-oriented care attitude.

We should let go of our tentative, transitional formation phase as soon as a higher phasic form has been established. The preceding transitional phase should no longer be the main ruler of our outlook on life. It is a new form that now takes up our formation dynamics. The previous phasic form remains with us as a familiar, highly appreciated, but no longer supreme formation dimension. While being basically stable, the new dimension is peripherally adaptive to changes in the field.

For example, an adaptive change in the dimension of rational functioning happens when a teenager turns from school work during the day to working in a fast-food restaurant at night. Her general disposition of rational functioning expresses itself in a different rational-functional attitude toward school assignments and a different one for serving effectively restaurant customers.

The basic direction of our current dynamics is the same as for that of all formation dynamics. Their final aim is to prepare us for transformation to the fullest degree of consonance possible for us. Usually, we have to bear with some dissonance. We cannot resolve each dissonance totally. Yet, in spite of that, consonance may pervade our life more and more as we attune it to the transcendent. Above all, we must remain present to the formation mystery in itself, in its epiphanies in our field, and in our consonant formation traditions.

The final phase of formation will bring us closer to the limited consonance possible for us in this life. It does so in principle, for we may not arrive there due to such unfavorable circumstances as childhood deprivation, severe general deformation, or excessive forms of social injustice. While this consonance is always limited, it is in some measure granted to people who keep trying to be faithful to their call insofar as it is disclosed to them.

Core Dynamics and Phasic Dynamics

The phasic movement of current dynamics differs essentially from that of core or character dynamics. The movement of character dynamics is basically one of preservation. Character dynamics preserve, deepen, and amplify certain dynamic directives that are basic to our particular way of life or, in other words, that have become characteristic of it. Many of these directives of our heart with its corresponding character emerge during the unfolding history of current formations. Over time, we turn them into character dispositions, each with its own proliferation of attitudes. We should only do so if they prove to be lastingly congenial with our founding form of life and the consonant traditions to which we are freely committed. We look at them as gifts of the mystery in which our unique-communal formation as a whole is rooted.

Cosmic and Human Formation Fields

The cosmic epiphany gives rise to a cosmic formation field stretching over unimaginable eons of time. Humanity gains knowledge of this field and its dynamics only gradually. Insofar as cosmic formation enters our immediate field of presence and action, it becomes known to us. It shows itself as a coformation of subfields and forms in constant formative evolution. It involves a continual rising and falling of forms, each of which is a segment of a larger story. Each field interlaces the other, and every formation event intersects in some way with other events. Cosmic formation is dynamic, creative, and epiphanic. Its dynamics of formation give rise to ever higher forms of consonance, simultaneously more inclusive and more finely differentiated. This overall cosmic process unfolds in space and time through countless formational dynamics empowered and directed by the cosmic mystery. In my science, I define the dynamic of cosmic consonance as the ongoing movement toward the formation of ever-higher fields and forms of consonance along a gradient of currently forming and reforming dynamics.

Human life is the highest epiphany of the mystery we know. It, too, like everything else in the universe, is driven by dynamic movements of formation, reformation, and transformation. The difference is that our distinctively human formation does not depend on biophysical powers alone. It is lifted beyond other instinctual life forms by the power of the human spirit as gifted uniquely by the mystery.

CHAPTER 14

Phasic Formation as Dimensional and Spiral

Each new phase of formation is marked by its own directives and dynamics. Those of a higher phase do not emerge in isolation from those of a lower. For example, the dynamics of practical functioning in the functional phase of child formation take into account the directives of vital formation the child acquired in the earlier vital phase. Therefore, a vitally temperamental child will be more vivid and headstrong in its style of functioning than a child with a gentle vital temperament. Interformation occurs between the dynamic directives of all dimensions. This is especially true in relation to the directives of the transcendent dimension. In my science all previous phases of formation are animated and marked by the transcendence dynamic. It guides our formation as a whole through each pretranscendent and transcendent phase of life. It plays its indispensable role in the gradual ascent of our transcendent character and personality from its founding source. The transcendence dynamic is, therefore, the only adequate means for the full integration of our personality.

Each phase of formation is integral to the spiral of ascent. The ongoing impetus of ascent moves each lower dimension to go beyond itself and its own basic orientation. Each prepares in its own way for the advent of the higher dimensions called forth by the transcendent. For example, vital animation formed initially in one's vital phase of formation and appropriate use of functional reason acquired in the functional phase prepared one for a well-balanced transcendent life that is alive, animated, reasonable, and truly incarnational.

Transcendent Affirmation of Lower Dimensions

We must not view each newly emerging higher direction of life as merely a negation of the directions that preceded it. Consonant higher dimensional dynamics reform or transform consonant lower formation potencies and energies. Far from destroying or paralyzing them, they lift them up while leaving intact their unique contribution to the balanced formation of human life as a whole. Each higher formation thus implies some reformation or transformation of what went before it. The ultimate orientation of this step-by-step ascent is the fulfillment of the inmost longing of human life. Our life aspires after ultimate peace and joy in supreme consonance with the mystery that gives form lovingly to our unfolding existence.

Dissonant Compromises

Our ascent is by no means an uninterrupted growth in consonance. As we have seen, our travel upward is often derailed by dissonances rooted in our self-idolizing pride form. Pride exalts our autarkic attempts to gain the fullness of joy and peace by some limited increase in power, pleasure, and possession that deceives us into thinking we can do it alone. Caught between the pull of transcendent consonance and the push of dissonant pride, we tend to substitute, already in childhood and adolescence, false forms of fulfillment or, in other words, forms of pseudoconsonance. These represent at best a compromise between our hunger for consonance with the mystery that transcends us and our temptation to autarkic insulation and anxious enhancement of only our pre-transcendent self. All such efforts at compromise inevitably create dissonance in our life.

Each successive formation phase may develop its own particular type of dissonant compromise. The loving and liberating power of the mystery invites us to use these detours to bring us closer to true consonance. It lets us experience formation crises that alert us to the dissonant path we have chosen. Crises like these are usually linked with a significant event of loss, failure, humiliation, pain, or disappointment. They open the way to either reformation or transformation of our compromised character dispositions.

Each authentic reforming process in which we freely engage can be seen as a consonant expression of our formation energy. This healing energy is always available to us. It flows abundantly from the transcendent compassionate mystery in which our life is sourced.

Dimensions and Their Articulations

Each dimension enables us to be present in a specific way to our formation field as a whole. For example, the vital dimension is a specific mode of presence rooted in the biophysical substructure of our life. It makes us present, for instance, to our biophysical need for food; it alerts us to what kind of food can still our hunger.

In each dimension we can further distinguish a central direction and a more peripheral articulation. Consider, for example, the functional. Basically, this dimension actualizes our potency to manage and organize everyday details. By itself alone, our functional dimension cannot do anything that is not more or less concerned with managing life in some way. This specific potency can give rise to many articulations of its forming power, all of which are particular expressions of this basic dimension. For instance, we may articulate our potency for functional management of our life in regular physical exercises that protect our cardiovascular health in dialogue with the messages of our vital dimension. This is one kind of articulation of our overall functional potency to manage our life and its conditions in ways that foster our general wellness.

In fact, I posit as a general hypothetical law of my formation science that *articulations of our life dimensions are restricted in their forming power by the limits of the potencies of the dimension they articulate.* Within the limits of this restriction, each articulation gives form to a variety of corresponding acts, dispositions, and attitudes. In my example, the articulation of exercise is restricted in its power by the individual limits of our potencies of dexterity and aptitude preformed in our functional dimension since conception.

Through the functional dimension, we shape and form our acts, dispositions, and attitudes of logical reasoning, mathematical computation, technical sophistication, manual skills, philosophical systematization, and so on. What all of these articulations have in common is that they are particular actualizations of the basic functional form potency of human life. In relation to its articulations, therefore, a form dimension is like a basic design or prototype. It carries within itself, like a code, all the limited possibilities of the articulations to which it can give form. At the same time, it is one of the basic integrational form potencies of our life. As such, the functional dimension enables us to integrate all functional aspects of our existence. Therefore, I distinguished in the new theory of personality integration, which I initiated in the Netherlands, between dimensional and overall transcendent integration of the personality. I highlighted their integrating interformation.

Distinctions between Personality Dimensions and Their Articulations

Form dimensions are distinguishable from their articulations. Unlike the latter, these dimensions are not learned as such. They are inherent in our human life form as essential modes of human presence. Being latent in us as basic potencies, they are disclosed to us in the course of our formation journey. However, their manifold possible expressions in concrete articulations can be learned. I do not acquire by a learning process, in the strict sense of this term, sociohistorical, vital, functional, and transcendent dimensions. As such, these dimensions are not the result of a learning process without which they would not be there at all. In principle, I am all of these already potentially. They reside in my founding form of life as plants reside in their seeds. During the history of my ascent, they are disclosed to me by their emergence in my empirical form of life.

The same is not true of the numerous particular articulations or concrete diversifications of the potencies inherent in these dimensions. These are acquired by processes of learning within one's concrete formation field. In the vital dimension, for instance, I can learn to like certain kinds of food more than others, to play, walk, or run in a unique way that is still compatible with the form traditions that exert their influence in my field of life. Similarly, my functional-dimensional presence can be articulated in various concrete ways, such as cleaning, organizing, building, typing, reading, or using a computer. I learn these skills also in interaction with traditions of practical form donation or how to give or evoke form appropriately in my field.

This distinction helps us to understand all the basic dimensions of life. No higher one can be seen as merely the sublimation of a lower one, for all dimensions flow from and return to the transcendent founding form in service of which each exerts its own particular mission. Therefore, my formation science is very cautious with the various ways in which clinical, social, and educational disciplines use the term sublimation.

Reformation and Transformation of the Vitalistic Life

I can illustrate what I have said thus far by referring to the formation of images in the vital dimension of our life. This formation is ruled at first by bodily pulsions that are relatively undifferentiated. In later formation phases, the images formed in infancy in relation to bodily experiences do not disappear. Our fantasy life may be amplified in countless ways in reaction to later events and experiences. In some measure infantile images may keep operating as a hidden factor in adult ventures and relations.

The vitalistic life of the infant's formation phase must be reformed and transformed in subsequent formation phases. In this process the intrasphere or inner sphere of our life has to differentiate itself from the other spheres of our formation field. It must open up to sociohistorical, functional, and transcendent dynamics in response to the intraspheric call to reformation or transformation. If we refuse to respond to this call, we may be in danger of becoming encapsulated in fantasies and their impulsive or compulsive satisfactions via particular, symbolically amplified, oral, anal, or phallic orientations of an initially bodily organismic nature.

Such infraconscious orientations are subject to the dynamics of symbolic amplification. For example, an intrasphere still dominated by the infantile oral image of satisfying its form reception needs by feeding may amplify out of proportion its maternal object pole. The vitalistic "I" then tends to include symbolically in the maternal image all kinds of sources of nourishment as a means of satisfying certain emotional needs. This infraconscious pulsion may then give rise to an obsessive-compulsive need for eating indiscriminately whenever one is under emotional stress.

Originality of Dimensional Formative Symbols

Certain forms of psychologism are inclined to constrict formative symbolic amplifications to infraconscious or infrafocal dynamics alone. They may apply this reductionistic principle even to functional-transcendent symbolism.

It is true that our infrafocal region of consciousness and its dynamics is in great measure linked to the survival region of infantile consciousness. Throughout our formation history, our infraconsciousness remains the region of an inmost link between our initial vitalistic absorption in our field as mainly a bodily presence and the symbolic meanings of that field. Such meanings are in the beginning confusing. They are bridges between organismic experiences of infants and vital symbols of other human realities experienced in the widening field of the life of children.

My science emphasizes that the vital dimension is not the only possible source of symbols. Other dimensions of our life form are original sources of symbols, too. They complement and supplant for a great part merely vitalistic imagery. Another hypothetical assumption of my science is its denial that what emerges first in empirical formation represents what is ontologically first, what is most basic or distinctive in the preempirical founding form of life. As I have said, our intrasphere can become encapsulated in initial vital dynamics. In that case we tend to give form exclusively to symbols that are amplified representations of vital pulsions. I do not deny that all of us can be influenced in some measure by this aspect of our infrafocal formative consciousness. This may happen especially during formation crises. What I oppose is the exclusive reduction of all symbolism to vitalistic symbolism.

My science assumes that the highest, most distinctively human forms of life are always already present in seed in our first original or foundational life form. Timewise, however, they come to the fore last in the sequence of our empirical-experiential formation phases. These highest forms usually emerge only after the lower forms of human life have prepared us for them. Our transcendence dynamic prepares these lower forms as future channels for concrete implementation of higher inspirations and aspirations in our formation fields. Our transcendence dynamic thus uses the lower dimensions of life to prepare us for the higher ones.

Having clarified in these chapters the principles of my phasic formation theory, I shall use the following chapters to comment in detail on each specific formation phase. For only after we have become somewhat familiar with these phases in a more general way can we go into the complexities of each distinctive phase.

The successive phases of life formation that I will present in the upcoming chapters follow generally the sociohistorical, vital, functional, functional-transcendent, transcendent, and transcendent-functional dimensions of my 1944 interformation paradigm. These dimensions are inherent, essential human formation potencies. If our formation story unfolds unhampered, these potencies will be actualized. They become, then, more than potential dimensions; they give rise to actual formation phases that in turn actualize our potential dimensions.

Our first dimension is the sociohistorical. Why is it first? Because we all are conceived and born at some definite point in time and space. This point in time embodies us instantly in a web of sociohistorical traditions. From the viewpoint of transcendent formation, the transcendent traditions among sociohistorical traditions are the most important. They influence to the very end the way in which we will experience, appraise, and live each subsequent formation phase in the light of our transcendent call. In that sense the sociohistorical traditional phase is all-embracing. Therefore, I shall discuss the implications of the exceptional position of sociohistorical traditions in their initial phase as well as when this phase is transcended yet continued as an inescapable constant companion of every following or simultaneous phase.

CHAPTER 15

Sociohistorical Dimension

I feel ambiguous about writing of my concept of a sociohistorical formation *phase*. The reason is that it is far less of a well-delineated, dominant phase than other phases such as the vital and functional. Social historicity is from the beginning to the end of human life a condition of all human formation. All other phases presuppose this condition and are penetrated by it. Therefore, in some way, it is not a clearly describable phase of formation dominance but a presupposition of all phases. I would call it a dominant condition, that is, inevitably operative as a guiding coformant in every phase. I say this because all phases of human life as human are unavoidably colored by the sociohistorical condition within which they appear and are processed.

Another problem I encounter here is that of providing descriptions about what happens in this phase. One can do so at length for the other phases, but not so here. The reason is that infants are passively exposed to sociohistorical conditions. They cannot yet respond to them personally. That leaves one with little to say about the formational viewpoint of the infant.

Therefore, in this chapter, I plan to speak about the sociohistorical dimension as an overall condition. I shall only linger briefly on its early phasic dominance at conception and birth.

Our Sociohistorical Form of Life
Never in my life could I be called a fully isolated individual. I was, am, and will always be a person who is sociohistorical through and through. From conception on, I was situated somewhere in time and space, inserted inescapably in a sociohistorical context. The family into which I was born could have been black or white, rich or poor, farmers or city folks, Arabs or Israelis, Christians or pagans. Such sociohistorical backgrounds affect the way in which they experience their life. They affect also the way in which parents give form to their infants and children. Our life is not a blank, empty page on which people can write anything they want. Parents, too, are influenced in their child formation by the laws of social historicity.

From the start, social historicity permeates the life of infants by a process likened to osmosis. This sociohistorical dimension infiltrates all their spontaneous reactions. Often, I call these early sociohistorical life directives "key directives." They offer us a key to the understanding, correction, or further unfolding of the social and historical factors that began to coform in infancy the character and personality of any person we meet.

Social historicity touches infants deeply. They are, as it were, dipped in it until it has saturated their little incipient personality. For example, some children may have been conceived, born, and raised in a Christian family in the dynamic American context of democracy and free enterprise. Their country, church, school, neighborhood, and, above all, their family spun an atmosphere around them filled with human and Christian faith, hope, and love. These social, historical surroundings—suffused with the presence of the formation mystery—coformed their childhood. Infants are helpless. Without skill or experience, they are dependent on grown-ups for everything. They cannot yet take a stand in life. It is not the infants themselves but their social historicity, as represented by their families, that make up their mind for them. Their parental sociohistorical situations orient their life without their knowing what is happening to them. The beginnings of their character and personality formation is thus coformed by the social history in which they are inserted.

Changes of the Germinal Sociohistorical Character Form

The dominance of this early sociohistorical dimensional phase will disappear to make room for other dominant phases. It is important to realize that the formation of one's life is by no means fixated once and for all in this first sociohistorical germinal period of life. On the contrary, many later sociohistorical influences can alter significantly what infants adopted by osmosis. Therefore, to prevent an overestimation of the power of this early phase of formation, I want to call attention to a variety of later sociohistorical dynamics that lead to change in this earliest structure of character predispositions.

Sociohistorical Formation Phase, Its Lifelong Variations

To repeat, the first phase of typically human formation of all children is the sociohistorical one. All children are born somewhere among people in a definite segment of time and space. They have to come to terms with the sociohistorical dimension of human existence lived by the people around them. It constitutes the first phasic challenge to the form children give to their life. This challenge dominates the earliest beginning of their formation journey. This first dominance will give way to the dominance of other successive phasic dominances. Still, a strong influence of the early sociohistorical influences on their life will always be with them. It will accompany all their future formation phases. Their original sociohistorical conditioning will always be in implicit dialogue with the ever-changing sociohistorical context of their life. This dialogue will modulate their responses to each new formation phase. For example, even their final phase of supreme transcendent formation will be colored in its experience and expression by specific transcendent structures of the formation traditions to which they have been exposed in infancy or later in life.

As children, we absorbed spontaneously the formational meanings our families imposed on us, on themselves, and on the people, events, and things around us. Such meanings were mediated by the sociohistorical form-tradition pyramid of our parents, which may have been more or less transcendent.[1] Their pyramid was a mixture of their own sociohistorical traditions and their personal adaptation of them. Their own outlook on life, their temperament, character, and personal history, as well as the history of their families and surroundings, affected this adaptation.

It stands to reason that people formed in different sociohistorical traditions will also differ in character and personality. Such variety is indeed the "spice of life." It can be a source of cross-sociohistorical fertilization. For example, the Christian, Moorish, and Jewish sociohistorical life dimensions in medieval Spain gave rise to a fertile ground of new thought, literature, art, and architecture.

Most people turn first to the sociohistorical tradition they learned as children. It may remain the decisive tradition by which they basically want to life for a lifetime. As I have shown, they will later draw on elements of other traditions, especially when these are compatible with their original sociohistorical conditioning. We live, as it were, by a whole set of offerings from different sociohistorical trends. These will be arranged, as I indicated in volume five, in a kind of pyramid of traditions.

By comparing the bases of different sociohistorical dimensions, we lay the groundwork for crossdimensional enrichment. Ecumenical dialogue among various Christian churches is an example of such mutual enhancement. Adherents to the various communities try to find aspects of their Christian sociohistorical dimensions that are compatible. They seek ways to adapt these to their own tradition without compromising the basic doctrines at its core. Similar dialogues can take place between adherents of other religions or ideologies, who differ in their sociohistorical embodiments of their own shared faith tradition.

People, even if committed to the same faith and basic formation tradition, may show considerable variations in the way in which they give form to it sociohistorically in their everyday life. What causes this difference are elements of other traditions that people superimpose on their own basic sociohistorical dimension. For example, a Presbyterian artist may add to her Pres-

---

[1] To understand my construct of the pyramid of traditions, consult volume five of this series, *Traditional Formation*.

byterian form of life elements belonging to a sociohistorical artistic form tradition.

One person who lives by an American-Islamic form tradition may become a scientist, another a laborer or a farmer. All these take on different sociohistorical professional traditions. This decision affects the way in which they give form to the same basic faith and formation tradition. Each of them puts a personal stamp also on the social traditions they share with others. Of course, our sociohistorical personality, character, temperament, and unique life call play a role, too, in the way we live out the traditions we share.

Publicly Apparent Sociohistorical Dimension

The symbolic point at the top of my pyramid of sociohistorical or formational traditions stands for the way in which we let our traditions appear in society. I have identified this as the publicly apparent sociohistorical dimension of our life. Many facets of the formation traditions in my concept of the pyramid touch on our public appearance. We all adopt certain sociohistorical public forms of life. This makes a difference in the way we appear in public. What again should come into play in this selective adaptation are our own transcendent life call, our unique-communal life situation, and our guiding traditions.

Usually, people take on different *apparent* sociohistorical forms in different situations. Hindu businesspersons in the West show another face when they worship in a Hindu temple than when they go to their office, store, or factory. In the work situation, it is their sociohistorical professional tradition that comes to the fore. In this public sphere they function as well-adapted employers or employees. For example, a university professor who adheres to the Hindu form tradition will also take on a sociohistorical academic form tradition when he or she functions as an academician in a Western university. This all goes to show how our first sociohistorical formation phase does not take away our flexible receptivity for other traditions later in life.

The pressures and enticements of sociohistorical pretranscendent traditions in our society can be overwhelmingly onesided. Even staunch adherents to transcendent traditions may succumb to them. Even in their transcendent sociohistorical traditions their main interest may be in the functional and pleasurable facets of these traditions. This happens especially in Western societies where many people function almost exclusively on the lower pretranscendent level of their life. Their functional managing "I" may take charge for the most part.

Most social, clinical, and educational disciplines have evolved through observation of populations that live on the basis of these sociohistorical pretranscendent structures. As a result, their researchers and practitioners know well how most people sociohistorically live, imagine, think, and feel today.

This kind of insight helps social workers, counselors, and therapists to look for solutions to some of the problems typical of pretranscendent Western existence. Such answers appear to be sufficient until the moment that excessive suffering touches one's life. Loss and profound disappointment force us to face our hidden, deeper longings. We come to sense something of our own transcendence dynamic when a loved one dies, when we are struck by a terminal disease, or when we have to let go of our belongings after a hurricane or earthquake. Suffering can break through the illusion of self-sufficiency. Such suffering can bring us back, at least momentarily, to the deeper meanings of our sociohistorical traditions and their symbols.

Intraformation by Life Call
and the Sociohistorical Dimensions

In my science, I have put forward the idea that an inner, founding life form is secretly calling us from the beginning to the end of life. This call contains directives that affect first of all the appraisal of our vital life. We begin to detect and accept its limits and possibilities. In life-and-death emergencies, our call shows itself precisely as a call to *life,* to stay alive, to keep as healthy as we can in our vital-bodily sphere. Beyond and in some way before and after this, the call inspires us to look for the unique direction of our existence. The mystery of formation gives us this deepest direction, though seldom directly! It is usually a transcendent sociohistorical tradition that lights up our call. Enlightened by traditional wisdom, we hear the whisper of our calling the moment we rise above the chatter of pretranscendent desires and beyond the babel of subsequent pretranscendent sociohistorical traditions.

Views of life derive from various sociohistorical sources. These give form to structures of the sociohistorical dimension of people's lives. To comprehend this seemingly unmanageable variety of sociohistorical dimensions more fully, formation science consults with other arts, sciences, and form traditions. It draws together some of their relevant insights and findings and works them over thoroughly in the light of its own transcendent vision of the sociohistorical dimension. One could compare this approach with an intricate dance. Its steps change with each new information and insight. The dance of life's ongoing pretranscendent development has even more twists.

One error of personality theories may be what I call sociohistoricism. In that case, the sociohistorical dimension becomes the exclusive explanation and determinant of all formation. To counter this tendency I introduced the idea of the founding life form or life call as one of the organizing principles of transcendent character and personality. A consonant sociohistorical dimension is guided by this call. I prefer the notion of a unique-communal founding form or call to the concept of "self-identity." The latter is used as the theoretical base of some pretranscendent social, clinical, and educational disciplines. An example is found in the work of Erik Erikson. His concept of identity, while helpful in many ways, cannot provide a full picture of our transcendent life call as served by our sociohistorical dimension. It leaves out the deepest dimension, that of our founding form of life, which comes to light in transcendent traditions. The latter are, of course, necessarily colored by the sociohistorical content in which they emerge.

I do not deny that pretranscendent concepts like those of Erikson can yield important insights. They make us familiar with the struggles, conflicts, and solutions of many people who live mainly by sociohistorical pretranscendent traditions. The same applies to those who live their transcendent traditions sociohistorically in mainly a pretranscendent way. This may be the case in the lives of a great number of present day North Americans and Western Europeans and of those in other countries touched by the social history of the West.

Interformation with
the Sociohistorical Dimensions of Others

Daily, we come across people who either hold to our own sociohistorical dimensions or who turn away from them. Their stance touches our own sociohistorical life. So do their social symbols. Usually, we filter such symbols through the symbols of our own social dimension. For example, during World War II people who lived by the symbols of a tribal social history in New Guinea saw for the first time American planes. Some dropped food and other gifts. The tribal men and women filtered the symbols of generous American cargo planes through their own sociohistorical symbolic forms. They stood in awe of them as exotic, majestic birds bringing gifts. They organized religious ceremonies to draw their attention. The new symbols set in motion a process of reformation. Each reformation of this sort—as in the case of the New Guinea tribes—puts into our sociohistorical dimension affect-laden forms or images. These give rise to new appraisals, dispositions, attitudes, and directives. They bear on our relationships, rituals, and symbols. In the case I have cited, what happened led to the so-called cargo cult. Its rituals were carried out to keep the "exotic birds" coming because they brought heavenly gifts of food and tools.

Not only tribal but also personal assimilation of social symbols can take place in our life. Two principles can help us protect the consonance of our changing sociohistorical dimension. The first is the ongoing appraisal of this dimension in the light of our life call and traditions. The other related principle is how we put new social symbols into practice in a way that is compatible with our life call and consonant traditions.

For example, some people may feel called through sociohistorical movements to live and work as social reformers. When they read such basic books as the Upanishads, the Qur'an, or the Bible, they find there also some meanings relevant to their own calling to social action. They choose and read these texts in the light of what they believe their call to be at this moment of their life. They ask themselves how they can bear fruit here and now in their field of presence and action in a way that is enlightened by their own sociohistorical traditions. New social symbols and relationships can thus be filtered into our given sociohistorical dimension in a way that is compatible with our life call and tradition.

Sociohistorical Interformation

Let us look again at the sociohistorical interformation that goes on between us all the time. What can we say about the ways in which we carry ourselves in time and space? How do the ways in which others appear strike us? Do we take certain patterns over from one another? Is there some mutual give-and-take between the social appearances of people of different sociohistorical backgrounds? Do Indian doctors living in London, for example, take over something of the British style of medical appearances? Take, as another example, the different public ways in which undertakers and bartenders are sociohistorically expected to appear when doing their jobs. This does not rule out that such social forms may also mirror their personal life. The undertaker and the bartender may feel inwardly what they portray outwardly. Our sociohistorical dimension thus directs us to appear in different ways at different social occasions, for example, at a picnic, a funeral, a board meeting, a church service.

The more whole our life becomes, the more our social appearances will emerge out of a transformed heart. For example, spiritually mature devotees of the Quaker tradition live not only in public conformity to the pledge of non-violent behavior they learned from the sociohistorical dimension of their religion; they also strive to become nonviolent, loving, and peaceful in their heart.

How does the way in which people take in sociohistorical traditions turn their thoughts and character dispositions around? How does a "tradition-as-assimilated" change one's sociohistorical dimension? To answer these questions, let me bring to the fore three important aspects of the dimension of life in question:

1. The *inter*formational aspect refers to the sociohistorical dimension as carried on within families and other groups of people. They keep forming each other in and through this dimension. What does the common sociohistorical dimension of another society do to people as they move into it? Take, for example, a young person formed in the Amish sociohistorical ambience. Circumstances that require him to live and work in New York are bound to make a difference!

2. The *outer*formational aspect refers to the sociohistorical dimension as it is brought out or "felt to be brought out" in languages, myths, rites, practices, and customs, in world and cosmic appearances, stories, and symbols. What shared meaning do these outer expressions carry for the

followers of a shared sociohistorical dimension? For example, what was the meaning of the buffalo for warriors brought up in the American Indian faith and form tradition?

3. The *intra*formational aspect refers to that part of a sociohistorical dimension that is taken in by us personally. What personal meaning does a shared sociohistorical dimension carry for me or any other person? How do I or anyone else personally feel about it? For example, what does the common social custom of the veiling of women in certain Arab countries mean to an individual Islamic believer in an Arab country?

Pretranscendent and Transcendent Implications

Each of these three aspects of a sociohistorical life dimension can be more or less pretranscendent or transcendent. For example, many nonpracticing Jews, Muslims, Buddhists, or Christians may still live by the pretranscendent inter, outer, and inner sociohistorical dimension of their religious community. At the same time, they have split these routines off from the deeper transcendent meaning of these expressions as carried in their religions. I recall a Jewish acquaintance who became not only a Christian but a priest, yet who could never bring himself to eat pork. His sociohistorical conditioning kept his eating patterns in check even after he had given up his commitment to a Judaic formation tradition.

Others fall into the opposite extreme. They live only by the transcendent sense of their sociohistorical dimension. They do not bring that deeper sense down into their pretranscendent life. They do not let it transform their life as a whole. In Western traditions, on the contrary, forgetfulness of the transcendent root of their sociohistorical dimension of life seems to be the main problem for many believers.

Arts and sciences in the West often show a diminishment of awareness of the transcendent depth of their sociohistorical dimension of life. Clinical, social, and educational disciplines tend to ignore, underestimate, or treat reductively the original ground of a transcendent sociohistorical dimension.

Those who share the same dimension may bring to the fore at different times and places its inner, outer, or intra forms. A contemplative Hindu in the Himalayas emphasizes the interior forms of the sociohistorical dimension; a Hindu businessperson in London chooses to stress its outer and inter facets. Any onesided emphasis, if carried too far, may miss one or both of the other aspects of the same social dimension. Our life form as a whole would then fall into disharmony. It would differ considerably from that of people who take into account all three aspects of their sociohistorical dimension in a balanced way. They, too, may draw on one aspect more than the other two because a person's life call may imply this preference. This does not matter as long as they do not deny in principle the other facets of their social dimension. To illustrate such an absolutized denial of other facets, imagine a contemplative hermit who would mistakenly look at daily labor in the world or on marriage or social action as necessarily unspiritual, even for those called to these ways of life.

The way of transcendence transforms the pretranscendent life, including its sociohistorical dimension. All that we are and do is increasingly touched by our deepest call. Strivings for pretranscendent individuality should draw more and more on the inspired aspirations of our deepest dimension. Our transcendent traditions set the pattern for this transformation of our sociohistorical dimension. For example, Islamic rulers, in touch with their call, look at the sociohistorical scope of their tradition as setting the tone for their leadership. They put their power under the wing of Islam as shining forth in the Qur'an and its masters as well as in the social history of Islamic traditions. In that light they take stock of their own personal tastes, gifts, and limits as well as their realistic struggles and labors in a particular setting.

The Islamic Moors, for instance, conquered southern Spain. There they built their own palaces, mosques, and gardens. In their architecture they attuned the sociohistorical range of their tradition to their own taste and environment while still upholding its basic tenets.

Appraisal of the Sociohistorical Dimension, Conflict, and Crisis

Conflicts arise alongside of new appraisals of one's personal or shared sociohistorical dimension. The more complex and diverse our sociohistorical background is, the higher the probability of crisis. An adolescent in Los Angeles will bear with much more conflict than a pygmy growing up in the forests of his ancestors. Conflicts between the sociohistorical dimensions of people are more likely to occur in a metropolis like Los Angeles, New York, London, or Paris. The rate of transcendent reformation of the initial sociohistorical formation phase in young adults slows down in such urban environments. A large city gives one more chances for the enrichment and differentiation or for the deformation of this dimension. We must find a way of blending wisely a wide variety of urban experiences. I say a "way" because transformation of life, in checking its sociohistorical dimension by the wise blending of traditions, is a never-ending story. We never arrive at the fullness of a unified life; we are always arriving.

At present, we live in an age of turbulent expansion and feverish mingling of sociohistorical dimensions. Asians and Africans drop the customs of their familial and social traditions to update their life. They take over from Western sociohistorical dimensions all kinds of elements that break into their own formation space. On the other side of the coin, some Europeans and Americans open up once again to lost aspirations. They look at the failure of many of their sociohistorical ideologies and projects. Some turn to the transcendent aspects of the African and Asian sociohistorical dimensions. In the process they become aware of the deeper sense of transcendently illumined sociohistorical dimensions in their own denied or forgotten past.

From this struggle between the social life dimensions of individuals and populations, a new spirit makes itself known. A new vision lights up the social history of individuals and groups. From them it trickles down to wider populations. Many Americans, Africans, Asians, and Eastern Europeans, as well as people from the republics of the former Soviet Union, push for change in the sociohistorical structure of their character and personality. They look at new ideas, styles, and customs that may partly expand, partly change their historical view. This development is in great measure the outcome of a worldwide meeting of various sociohistorical traditions of humanity.

Changes in our everyday field of life also widen our social vision. For example, women's striving for equality alters the onesidedness of some sociohistorical dimensions of womanhood. Changes in society help also to spark women's social drive for fair play. These changes give women access to education in fields formerly closed to them. Women begin now to play leading roles in professions that used to be open only to men. They share in the work force at large. Machismo in public life has been exposed as a cause of social injustice. All of these changes make for a new female style in a changing sociohistorical scene.

Crosstraditional Research
in Sociohistorical Dimensions

Keep in mind the distinction I established already in Holland between inter-, outer-, and intraformation. I applied this first of all to personal life, but I also used my newly found distinction to draw out the inter, outer, and intra spheres of social dimensions. If we look at any one of these spheres, we may catch a glimpse of what the other two aspects of the same sociohistorical dimension may reveal. Let us say I grasp some inner sociohistorical aspect of the adherents of the Amish tradition, for instance, their disposition to look at the attractions of the modern world as potentially fatal temptations. My new insight brings me to a better understanding of some outer aspects of their social dimension, too, such as no cars, no makeup, no luxury, no power tools, no clutter in their homes. The interformational aspect of the strict education of their children outside the public school system becomes clearer to me as well.

This threefold approach makes it easier for us to understand the differences between various formational social dimensions within the same faith tradition. For instance, how do the Shiite and the Suni sociohistorical dimensions of life in their inner, outer, and social life-styles compare with one another within the same basic Islamic belief system they share? Finally, this triad of appraisal gives us a practical way of looking at changes in people who took over elements of other sociohistorical form dimensions. Take, for instance, the differences between people of the same Islamic sociohistorical dimension. They lived for generations in lands like Ethiopia, the Soviet Union, or North America. It is no wonder that they differ in the social form dimension of their life.

This tripartite approach works also for persons who come to properly trained experts for formation counseling or therapy. One may ask: are they coming from a social form dimension where one or the other of these inner, inter, and outer spheres stood out more than another?

Many sociohistorical dimensions of different human life forms show strong vital-affective bonds. For example, the sociohistorical dimension of human life in India promotes mutual dependency within families. So do Mediterranean sociohistorical form dimensions in Europe. The Japanese sociohistorical dimensions of the human personality compel lasting affective bonds, even with a person's employer or company. I call such sociohistorical types of the human personality a fusional social dimension. The fusion shows itself first on the pretranscendent level. Such traditions carry weight in great parts of the world. Therefore, I want to look at them more closely.

Fusional Pretranscendent Sociohistorical Dimensions

Fusional sociohistorical dimensions give form to relationships of intimacy. People stay connected affectively with one another. A fusional social dimension can turn up in groups of people who adhere to the same faith tradition. By the same token, some people, sharing the same faith, may not fuse spontaneously because of the different, less fusional, social dimension of their life.

One example of a fusional social form dimension is the charismatic. Charismatics do not feel as strong a separation between one another as do people who live by other Northern European or American social dimensions of their life form. Their heart drives them to vital affectiveness.

The affective need of fusional social people often meshes with their sensitive-vital temperament. A vital-emotional sub-"I" rules their heart. It brings out dispositions of empathy, exuberance, and warm self-expression. They may show a higher degree of suggestibility, dependency, and codependency. Some bond together so intimately that they feel themselves to be almost totally a "we-form" rather than an "I-form."

Generally, fusion makes for we-form attachments, appraisals, dispositions, directives, and fascinations. Great concern with the qualities, reputation, and honor of one's family and community can mark any shared we-form. We find this to be the case in many families of Mediterranean descent. This perception of such qualities of one's family and community may be real or imaginary. Usually, this view of family life is a mixture of realistic apprehension and affective imagination.

Another mark of social fusion can be an adulation for the hierarchy of authorities within the group. Unscrupulous leaders of fusional social groups and communities can awaken and abuse such affective attachments. This happened, for example, in Mafia families, in communities in the excessive militaristic period of Japanese fusional form traditions, and in the taking of poison by all members of the cult in Jonestown.

Other examples that come to mind are similar obsessive attachments of many people in the Soviet Union to Josef Stalin, of many Germans to Adolf Hitler, of Iranians to Khomeini, and of Iraqis to Saddam Hussein. Propaganda pushed followers into excessive social fusional relationships with their leaders and their illusions of grandeur.

Excessive Fusion of the Sociohistorical Dimension

These examples show that social fusion can become onesided and excessive. It may cast aside outsiders. An excessive appreciation of the idealized ingroup and its leaders takes over, destroying one's appreciation for one's own and other's unique calling. The life call does not strike one as in some way unique or personal. The social fusional form dimension of one's group turns out to be the only true context by which one can live. One cuts the fullness of a life call down to merely a social-contextual or sociohistorical fact. The group and its leaders lay out for all people concerned what this alleged group-defined call should foster or not.

The fusional social dimension defines one's public apparent form as well. In excessive fusion, one's apparent form may be totally determined by the public, fusional show of adulation of one's group and its leadership. In some situations this tendency can be fatal. This is evident from the reports of many Soviet and German people during the totalitarian phase of their history. Even people who knew better, who had moments of doubt about the regime or who were imprisoned by it, could succumb to public, fusional symbols and appearances. A large number of Soviet citizens, even many in the concentration camps of the Gulag Archipelagos, confessed later to crying about the loss of a great beloved leader when Stalin, the murderer of millions and their own cruel jailer, died.

The apparent fusional life form shows up also in the public ceremonial conventions that celebrate an adulated hierarchy. An example would be the past ceremonial veneration of the emperor of Japan.

Fusional dispositions, through our sociohistorical dimension, touch on our vital-functional life. They define and direct vitalistic anger, enthusiasm, indignation, aggression, and defensiveness as well as affective and sexual expression. They keep such expressions in tune with the demands of the extended family, group, or regional relationship. For example, marriages may be arranged by families, by covenant groups, or by the party. Modes of communication in such traditions can develop on two or more levels. One type of public communication is directed by the shared climate of a fusional, highly suggestive affectivity; the other type of expression is inspired by latent remnants of doubt inwardly.

I recall interviewing fugitives from the Nazi regime who fled to Holland before it was occupied by Germany. Some of them would talk in roundabout ways. In accordance with the German patriotic, sociohistorical dimension, they would still show admiration for Hitler and his hierarchy of ministers, who made the fatherland so ordered, so powerful. As our conversations became more intimate, latent doubts would come to the fore, bringing about some concerns about the regime. These secondary concerns pointed to the possibility of some reform of their sociohistorical dimension.

The particularity of each tradition explains the great variety of fusional sociohistorical dimensions. For example, there are notable differences between such dimensions if they are Chinese, Japanese, or Indian; Southern Italian or American Indian; African or Mexican.

The opposite of a fusional sociohistorical dimension is an individualistic one. In the following section, I shall look at the individualistic sociohistorical dimensions insofar as they appear on the pretranscendent level. Later in life, the excesses of an individualistic structure of their sociohistorical dimension may be emended and even transformed by the transcendent dimension of their life.

Pretranscendent Individualistic Shape
of the Sociohistorical Dimension

Individualistic sociohistorical structures are neither transcendent nor ruled by the fusional interformation I just described. Self-protection holds sway in such structures of human life. It makes people inordinately attentive to what they can get from any group they belong to. They may value even spiritual exercises only in terms of their own self-actualization. Sheer individualism governs the formation of their character as well as of their corresponding conscience. It rules their socio-vital-functional as well as their functional-transcendent dimensions of life. As an example of the perversion of their transcendent intentions, they may practice meditation merely to become more relaxed, to enhance their health and conserve their energy. They meditate only to improve their calm effectiveness in business or heighten their winning charism in social and political life.

Such individualistic dispositions and directives begin to mark their character more or less continuously. They set boundaries between people. These boundaries are defined bureaucratically or pragmatically. The individualistic character differentiates sharply between appraisal of oneself and appraisal of others. It experiences little of a transcendent at-homeness with others. The individualistic tradition directs people toward the formation of a "managing me" that is almost exclusively self-directive. It breeds separation; it inflates ambitions for self-enhancement in a functionalistic fashion.

The individualistic structure of one's sociohistorical dimension does not give form to an affective appreciation of one's life as part of a group with which one wholeheartedly interforms, of course, always within the limits of one's unique-communal life call. Neither does it evoke the joyous praise and appreciation of each one's call and vocation, as transcendently illumined social structures tend to do. Instead, it instills in its followers a kind of lower self-esteem based on insulated self-actualization. It breeds arrogance. On the other hand, it makes the individualistic person less dependent on the need to mirror and idealize the group and its leaders. This latter tendency would be more typical of the fusional social dimension.

The sociohistorical dimension of the transcendent life strikes a healing balance between these two extremes. We should be aware that all sociohistorical dimensions of parents affect the conditioning of the sociohistorical dimension of the germinal character of their infants and children.

CHAPTER 16

Vital Dimension Phases

The vital aspect of life rules the early unfolding of fetus and infant alike. I distinguish different phases of the formation of the vital dimension of human life. Some overlapping of these phases can be expected. It happens usually between one phase and the one that comes after it. Such an in-between or crossover stage can be very ambiguous.

The Phase before the Differentiation of the Infant

Our life, as I envision it formationally, is an ever-differentiating and integrating field of personal-communal unfolding. This field is composed of what I call "spheres of formation." In my 1944 interformation paradigm, I distinguish a sphere of pre- or preparatory formation, one of intra or inner personal formation, another sphere of interformation with persons and communities, and finally a sphere of outer situational formation signifying the integration of our unfolding life with what happens in our life situations. I distinguish also an outer mondial and cosmic formation sphere of interaction with our wider world and with the cosmos we share with all unfolding forms in the universe. A fetus or an infant at birth is, of course, unaware of such distinctions. Totally embedded in its vital phase of life, it does not know of its own inner life as distinct from its life with others and with the environment. To put it briefly, an infant dwells in its field of life in an undifferentiated way.

In this beginning phase the different spheres of life of just born children are indistinguishable for them. Once the inner or intrasphere of the child is opened up, it will become the personality dimension in which one begins slowly to discover one's unique life call. But this happens only fully later in life when a transcendent, so to speak, second childhood begins to dawn. In this early stage, infants are not aware of their individual or personal distinctiveness. This is the primitive slumbering phase of human life. Only slowly do infants learn to adapt their life to the differentiations of the field in and with which they are born. This gradual adaptation is the condition for personal formation.

I also want to point out here why just born infants cannot yet share an adult's experience of space. One can only experience spatial forms when one can make distinctions, appraise distances, and observe separations in oneself and one's environment. Without such experiences of spatial forms it is also impossible for newborns to share an adult's experience of time. We, on the contrary, observe a temporal succession of forms within our ever-changing life. Such observed changes make it possible for us to measure time by linking such changes in ourselves and our surroundings with such spatial changes as, for example, the spatial changes of sun, moon, stars, and planet Earth. It is thus the absence of awareness of forms as spatially distinct that makes it impossible for the newborns to experience separate moments of time as we adults do.

Because newly born infants have no sense of space and time as such, nor of their separations, they are also unaware of their own limitations in space and time. This ignorance of limits makes for a vague, implicit sense of magic and omnipotence.

This phase is short in duration, but, like all phases, it will never be wholly forgotten. At crisis moments later in life, desires for this lost paradise may come to the fore and influence the direction of one's desire, imagination, attention, observations, and appraisal. Such a regression may even reduce one's spiritual life to an illusory exercise in self-gratifying fantasies of a religious nature.

The Beginning of a Phase of First Distinctions

The first dynamics that direct neonates beyond the phase of vitalism are those of incipient differentiation, leading to the emergence of a beginning intrasphere. This rudimentary intrasphere is almost exclusively identified with bodily experiences. The body of the infant no longer seems to be wholly fused with the body of its mother. This does not mean that either the functional or the vital dimensions are now sufficiently differentiated. A preponderance of vital, prepersonal dynamics still dominates in this bodily intrasphere. Only in the course of successive phases will the functional and the transcendent realms of life come into view. Gradually, they will gain in independence from the substructure of vital dynamics. The phase I am speaking about now contains merely some seeds of individuality and personality. One's field is, however, no longer totally undifferentiated. Infants begin to sense some vague possibility of differentiation, but nothing more.

Global Spheres

Dynamics of detachment are not yet strong enough to enable the infant to separate the inner sphere of life definitively from the field of life as a whole. It experiences only an elemental disclosure of some global intra, inter, and outer spheres. The infant is aware of these in a vital prepersonal fashion. The previous phase of vitality was marked by total undifferentiation of the field; the current formation of starting field differentiation marks the beginning of the breakup of this original homogeneity into vague, global intra, inter, and outer spheres, which are only vitally apprehended and appraised.

As I suggested already, the differentiation dynamics of this phase foster some vital apprehension of a separate bodily intrasphere. There are some moments of dim awareness of their own separate, corporeal being. This awareness awakens a corresponding, if fleeting, awareness of some sphere of interaction between this body self and that of others. In that in-between experience, others appear bodily as somehow different from the infant's own bodily being.

Similar moments of fleeting awareness start to give form to a weakly differentiated outer sphere of things and events. They seem no longer the same as the vital bodily life of the infant itself. This pristine, hesitant awareness of differentiation is not strong enough to lift the infant's consciousness beyond passing, momentary impressions of a dawning awareness of some overall differentiation of its life and its environment. The dynamics of vital fusion, prevalent in the previous phase, while beginning to lose slightly their hold on the infant's consciousness, are still dominant.

Vital-Oral Form Reception and Donation

In this phase, the main vital means of form reception and donation is oral. Therefore, another good name for the incipient bodily intrasphere would be the oral sphere. The functional dimension of this sphere is not yet formed. Hence, what prevails in this phase are the dynamics of the vital dimension with its preformed instincts and primitive emotional effusions. Nothing is as yet experienced inwardly in any individual or personal way. There is not yet an enduring awareness of an inner or intraspheric dimension of life.

The field of life as a whole shelters, nourishes, and carries infants in this phase. They can scarcely be said to attend, apprehend, appraise, affirm, or act. Consciousness is almost wholly nonfocal, which means there is no personal sensitive attention, apprehension, or appraisal. All of these can be sources of human suffering. Therefore, ideally, if a child is not living in an abusive setting, this is at least in part a blissful phase. Formation responsibility and therewith guilt are still unknown; sensibility of the heart does not disturb the sweet slumber of prepersonal existence. Most of the time, well-cared-for infants live in vital embeddedness. Theirs is in part a blissful life of full vital consonance or harmony with their surroundings. This vitalistic consonance is different from the consonance granted to people who live predominantly in the transcendent phase of their life.

Emergence of Anxiety

Despite many moments of vital euphoria, already the roots of anxiety begin to show themselves. Anxiety is awakened by the first awareness of the threat of differentiation or breakup of the paradise of unquestioned embeddedness in vital life. There really seems to be an "otherness" which limits the magical feeling of omnipotent form potency. The limiting other may be experienced as threatening, demanding, overwhelming, or, in the worst case, as abusive. The main vital means of form reception and donation at this stage is, as we have said, vital-oral. Therefore, anxiety may be expressed in symbolic fears of being eaten up, swallowed, and destroyed by vaguely apprehended others, no matter who they are. In response to these fears, indications or pulsions emerge that are linked with the fantasies of consuming or destroying the other. The latter reaction is a defense against the fear of deformation or annihilation by the other.

At this stage, the infant's potency for well-focused attention, apprehension, and appraisal is still decidedly limited. Its vital life is only in the earliest stages of sensory motor development. It is dominated by physical reflexes and their primitive elaboration. None of these physical reflexes is as yet precisely oriented in time and space.

Gradually, the innate human dynamics of transcendence will push the infant beyond this primitive form of life. They will lift the infant into the new current form of a more functional and individual intrasphere.

Meaning of the Intrasphere at this Stage

The beginning intrasphere exemplifies in what sense I use this term in my formation science. It does not refer to a spiritual life that would be exclusively interior. A sphere suggests something wider than a closed-off interiority. It refers to what is more directly or intimately related to one's own emergence in one's own field of life. Only after that does the infant experience within this field the emergence of others with whom it will share its life. Later in life the intrasphere can contain a highly transformed, spiritual sensitivity, for example, to a deeply assimilated, and hence interiorized, form tradition. In this just-starting differential phase, however, the primitive experience of otherness can be restricted to the awareness that the food in my mouth is in some way more connected with my body than is the food in the mouths of my parents. Infants may begin to experience that the breasts of the mother or the bottles nourishing them do not belong to them as does the thumb they suck. They become dimly aware that the thumb seems somehow to occupy another sphere of their field than the mother's body does; it feels more intimately connected with their own body than does their mother's breast.

This beginning experience of certain things falling within one's own vital bodily sphere gives rise to the initial formation of a faintly separate intrasphere. Often the popular phrase "the interior life" is restricted in its connotations to an exclusively spiritualistic, separated inwardness, untouched by the other spheres of one's field of life. Hence, I found it necessary for my formation science to prevent a dualistic Platonic or Cartesian misunderstanding. For this reason, I use the term "intrasphere" purposefully in the metalanguage of my formation science to avoid a deformative spirituality in which "the interior life" is split off from its intimacy with the vital-functional inner, inter, and outer spheres of one's life as a whole.

Basic Differential Phase

The dynamics of formation begin to shift the rudimentary differential openness of infants away from the merely vital to the vital-functional phase. The first emergence of what I call a prefunctional phase occurs. It awakens the potency of infants to become aware of the prefunctional autonomy of other people in the interforming sphere of their field. The infant gradually gains some awareness of the prefunctional role of events and things, of family members, strangers, and friends, in the outer spheres of his or her life. Vital emotionality is still a strong force in this just-emerging functionality. Yet the bodily intrasphere is now amplified sufficiently to allow for the emergent awareness of a bodily-functional or vital-functional intrasphere. This marks the beginning of typically human formation, although this stage is still in great measure vital, that is to say, it is only partially functional.

Momentarily Anchored Object Poles

In the previous formation phase, there were moments in which an intrasphere connected with the body was differentiated, albeit in a hesitant, passing fashion, from other spheres in the same field. The latter were experienced as perhaps not related so intimately to the felt body of the infant. Around the age of four to six months, this bodily sphere is fleetingly formed by the infant. A definite demarcation of one's own body and of what falls within (intra) its own sphere does not take place until around the age of fifteen to eighteen months.

Formative Imagination

I cannot overemphasize the importance of formative imagination as an auxiliary formation source in this regard. All formation processes imply the formation of correspondingly formative or deformative images. In this phase, the emergent intrasphere is somehow imagined in the form of central or pivotal images. These enable infants to experience their perceiving and sensing body as anchored within their own sphere. Correspondingly, they see objects out there as anchored in spheres interconnected with, but somehow different from, their own intrasphere.

In the vital-functional phase these differently anchored object poles are only experienced as such when they are present. I call them "anchored" object poles because infants experience them as anchored only in their not-lasting or passing appearances to them. This anchorage in their actually perceived presence makes it difficult for infants to embody them enduringly in their cognitive region of recall. When these different objects disappear or are lost from sight, their form image is lost too. For example, when the mother leaves the infant, her form image tends to disappear too.

New current formation dynamics, however, will push the infant beyond this stage of forgetting. They will give rise to images rooted in their field of life as a whole in all its spheres. These enable infants to give some stable or enduring form to the spheres of their field. As a result, a vital bodily sense of one's own intrasphere with some functional form-receptive and form-productive potencies now becomes a more definite and stable experience.

Emergence of Basic Emotions

Likewise, the basic emotions of this vital-individual intrasphere begin to unfold. They complement and partly replace the cruder formative reflexes and instincts of the previous formation phase. Feelings are still rudimentary. Cognitive sensory-motor forms are still elementary. They cannot yet give rise to any of the higher, more complex affects characteristic of either typical or distinctively human formation. These kinds of feelings and cognitions belong to a preaffective, emotional realm. The infant experiences and expresses emotion-laden forms, such as explosive anxiety, fear, pleasure, displeasure, satisfaction, dissatisfaction, rage, tension, appetite, vital comfort or discomfort. At this stage, the infant is guided by the limbic brain structure of its neuroform that triggers primitive emotional reactions.

Formation of Time Experience

The formation of time experience at this stage is related mainly to the present appearance of objects in the field as perceived. Emotions related to short, temporary appearances are quick and short-circuited. They often give rise to unrestrained, effusive expressions. The infant has as-yet-not-available concepts, constructs, continual images, memories, and anticipations that can give a rich and a stable form to these eruptive time-bound emotions. Only later will their intraform be deepened and enriched by more fully and focal ideas, images, memories, and anticipations. This will make the formation of temporarily more enduring affects possible. Until such further formation has taken place, there is nothing in the infant's time experience to prevent the unmitigated discharge of primitive emotionality.

Two Prevailing Formation Dynamics

Both the bodily character of the intrasphere and the impermanence of the temporal mode of this phase are related to two prevalent dynamics, namely, those of instantaneous survival and of the pleasure-displeasure cycle.

Instantaneous survival dynamics make infants vitally receptive to any vague threat to their individual bodily intrasphere, which has become the focus of their attention. The same dynamic gives form to any reaction or primitive response that is meant to protect one against such threats. In accordance with the limited time sense of infants, they cannot develop long range, protective directives. Living from moment to moment, their vitalistic form reception and donation in relation to threats is instantaneous and passing.

Intimately related to the vitalistic bodily experience is the dynamic of plea-sure-displeasure. This makes infants vitally receptive to anything that causes them to feel bodily gratification or deprivation. From the viewpoint of my con-cept of vitalistic form donation, this dynamic moves infants to favor any reac-tion or response that procures bodily pleasure and avoids displeasure. In the previous formation stages, this dynamic did not prevail because the bodily intrasphere was not yet differentiated from the other spheres in one's field. The new differentiation leads to new awareness of other spheres of the field and the infants' relation to them. At this stage, what most appeals to infants are the pleasureable qualities of things in their field of presence.

The apprehensive appraisal of the field tends to change with every new cur-rent phasic period. So do the images and symbols in which these changes are expressed. The latter, in turn, foster the phasic processes of human unfolding.

In this basic differential phase, detachment from the former both prediffer-ential and incipient differential fields of life means facing, no matter how vaguely, a new kind of field that holds unknown threats and possibilities, dan-gers and discomforts. The nascent bodily intrasphere becomes more keenly attuned to the experience of pleasure and pain. In the measure that the field becomes more differentiated, it also becomes more ambivalent and ambiguous in its possibilities. From this moment on, the ambiguity of human life forma-tion will not disappear; it can only deepen. Focal and prefocal awareness of this basic ambiguity can be refused or repudiated. In previous stages of phasic formation, the dynamics of perfect fusion and vital consonance prevailed. Now the dynamic of pleasure-displeasure reforms the former dynamic of fusion and becomes dominant. In my formation science, all formation dynam-ics are directed ultimately by the transfocal dynamic of transformation. Hence, in my formation system both formation and reformation patterns in this vital phase, as in all phases, are affected by the transformation dynamic. I see this dynamic as sourced in the all-pervasive formation mystery.

Primal Integration

The basic differential phase thus generates a faint sense of one's own intras-phere. This sense is still bodily, vital, and organismic. It receives and gives form in vital-emotive, sensate, and proto-affective ways. The dynamics of pre-focal and focal self-consciousness are also rudimentary. At most, they give form to a disconnected collection of biovital moods, protoaffective effusive emotions, sensate impressions, and vitalistic appraisals. Primal integration of the above elements cannot compare with the nuanced, well-integrated self-awareness typical of higher formation phases. A relative centering of these affects and moods happens at first around some part of the body that is vitally central in its relation to the field. This is most often the mouth. Gradually, this sensate, oral form reception is complemented by vital-functional form dona-tion to patterns of motor behavior that arise in relation to the forms appearing in one's field. What this leads to in turn is the formation of a primitive intras-pheric motor identity.

Imaginative Differential Phase

The emergence of an infant's imaginative form potency gives rise to a new extension of the field and the emergence of forms within it. Formative imagi-nation enables infants to extend the presence of such imaginary forms beyond a momentary perception of their objects. Such perceptions can now be held as present in imaginary forms within the intrasphere, even if the represented objects disappear from an infant's immediate field of perception.

Imaginary forms contribute to the infant's growing ability to fashion some sort of time awareness. The dynamics of extension, via the emergent imagina-tive potency, enable infants to make the original momentary, passing forms in their field more constant and enduring. By means of formative imagination, infants initiate a remarkable reformation of their field. The sensory-motor col-lection of objects, once disconnected in the vital intrasphere, becomes inte-grated within the infant's imagination. These integration dynamics are stimulated simultaneously by both consonance and transcendence dynamics. Under their impact, the intrasphere moves beyond its former encapsulation within mere sensory-motor dynamics.

Image of the Mother

The first image or form received by the infant in its unfolding intrasphere is that of the mother. This first form leaves one with a vague impression of another who is mothering. Gradually, this image is etched more sharply by the dynamics of differentiation and detachment. These enable infants to apprehend the form of the mother as no longer merely a part of their own intrasphere. This imaginative apprehension of the mother as other is followed by a primal, vital appraisal of her or her substitute as also other.

If formative mothering is experienced as generating a feeling of well being, the infant will appraise her as good. If her mothering seems to be the origin of discomfort or displeasure, her presence and action are appraised as bad. What typifies this stage is a tension between one's own unfolding intrasphere and the other spheres of one's field as momentarily dominated by the overwhelmingly formative or deformative presence of the "good" or "bad" mother.

Of special significance here is the emergence of what I have identified in my other volumes as the foundational formative triad of initial faith, hope, and consonance played out between the mother and the child. I discovered in my transtherapy sessions that these appreciative dynamics conflict with what I had defined earlier as their depreciative counterparts: the dynamics of no faith or anxious self-encapsulation, of primitive despair or hopelessness, and of disturbing dissonance. In my conception, the dynamics of transcendence, are dimly present in infants. They manifest themselves as elementary evocations of faith, hope, and love to be realized more fully later in life. They lend, as it were, a mysterious background music to the primal experiences and conflicts of infancy.

To be sure, the infant is totally unaware of this deeper directive to ascend. Later in life the conflict between these two opposite sets of the foundational triad will be influenced, but not totally determined, by the outcome of this conflict in early childhood. I shall later, in volume eight, look at the same from the viewpoint of my Christian formation anthropology and formation theology. I shall explain there that in my form-theological point of view this conflict points to a graced transhuman formation always already operative in every human form of life, at least as an anonymous appeal and an offer. In such early stages of prepersonal development, transhuman formation operates mainly as a remote, graced preparation for consonant options of human freedom, to be awakened later in life.

The foundational triad of faith, hope, and love in regard to the mystery itself—as appearing in the mother-child relationship—gives form to or reinforces the Great Mother symbolism that one can observe in many traditions.

Somatic Self-Images

The infant begins to give form to a complex of images and vital-functional impressions of the mother, as well as of other forms in its field of life. In response to these external images and impressions, infants begin to give form to somatic self-images. Such images cannot be reflexive. For the cognitive potencies of the infant have not yet developed beyond sensory-motor and imaginary knowledge. Self-awareness is still based on form images of the physical body. The form receptive potency of infants is actuated at this stage by both outer tactile and inner sensory apprehensions and appraisals. This input enables them to give form to their own body image with its unfolding intrasphere.

The body image helps the intrasphere to differentiate itself more definitely than it could in previous stages from the pre, inter, and outer spheres. The integration dynamic gathers the various representations of the bodily form or image together into the mental form of a vague, primitive vital-functional "I."

This vitalistic "I" will be a precursor of and a contributor to the later functional "I" as well as to the unique "I" of the transcendent dimension of life.

Initial somatic images usually take shape in interformation with the mother image. In accordance with a momentary positive or negative image of the mother, the latter gives rise to the images of, respectively, the appreciable, the depreciable, and the negligible "I." The *appreciable somatic "I"* is a vague, primitive bodily image of the infant as somehow acceptable and appreciated by the mother and/or significant others. This appreciation is communicated to the infant by gentle and affectionate bodily care. In contrast the *depreciable somatic "I"* is a vague, primitive bodily image of the infant as somehow not acceptable and appreciated by the mother and/or significant others. This is communicated to the infant in a lack of gentle and affectionate bodily care. The third possibility is that infants experience themselves as a *negligible somatic "I"*. They develop a vague, primitive bodily image—one of being neither appreciated nor depreciated but somehow neglected or deprived. They experience or imagine faintly that others give them a functionally correct but emotionally cool, distant, or indifferent bodily care. Alternately, each of these three somatic images may dominate consciousness. If one of them gains a lasting, prevalent influence, it will exude a corresponding controlling impact on later character and personality formation.

Form Images

The dynamics in this imaginative differential phase thus operate preferentially through images or forms that are not present to infants at all times. By means of image formation, it is possible for them to maintain these images in their own intrasphere. In the previous formation phase, the pivotal center of the field, the body, was present only to that toward which it was turned. In that period of infancy, potency for nascent formative imagination could only give shape imaginatively to forms that were actually present. The image disappeared with the disappearance of the form that was within the immediate sensory-motor reach of the infant. This preceding instantaneous, passing imaginary form reception can be viewed as a kind of preparatory exercise for the actualization of the formative imaginative potency proper to distinctively human life. In the present phase of image formation, infants are able to hold on to many forms in their field by virtue of their evolving imagination.

I hold in my formation science that our field of life in general is formative for us through the symbols and representations of it that we hold in our formative imagination. By means of them, the inter and outer spheres of the field enter into our intrasphere. They expand and deepen it and therewith enable us to be in touch with the other spheres of our field. The basis of our compatibility with the inter and outer spheres of the field can be traced to this happening. It is also the ground of our temporal and spatial experiences.

The infant is still far away from such symbolic and representative functions of formative imagination. Its just awakening dynamics allow infants only to expand their intrasphere with chance images of past events and equally chance images of what may happen or appear in the future.

How do such unconnected, or loosely connected, images actually give form to an infant's life? It does not happen in a logical fashion. Such images direct the unfolding of infants insofar as they are experienced as representative of their field of presence and action. The form-receptive potency at this stage is mainly passive; it lets life be formed by disparate vital-functional moods evoked by momentary sensory-motor apprehensions and appraisals. These are prolonged now also by a number of disjointed symbols and representations floating in the infant's nascent imagination.

Prelogical Formation
and Primal Integration Dynamics

This prelogical formation does not totally escape the integration dynamics which begin to emerge. These dynamics generate a primal attempt toward some kind of organization. Because the dynamics of integration cannot yet draw upon or use the gift of reason or logic, they are restricted to sensory-motor ways of combining forms into some kind of tenuous collection. Forms are vitally apprehended and appraised as manifesting a sameness that allows for some kind of prelogical integration. The nonfocal search for a likeness that would make possible some sort of integration scans aspects of reality that appear to one's sensory-motor experience to be somewhat similar.

This primitive integration attempt, because of its partial apprehension of forms and due to the absence of logical form donation, necessarily becomes confusing. For instance, the primary integration dynamic may base its perception of elongated, pointed, straight, potentially piercing, penetrating forms, such as pencils, cigars, knives, cotton swabs, or fingers, as belonging to the same category of things. They all have in common a certain elongated, pointed, penetrating appearance. All of them fall under the sensory-motor category of "longishness" and "piercingness." Thus, each of these forms appearing in the field may be vitally-functionally apprehended and appraised as similar to all other forms in the same category.

On this level of imaginary form reception and donation, one form can be apprehended as the same as any other in the same category. By the same token, one form can also be apprehended as being the whole of any sensory-motor category. Conversely, the prelogical category in its totality can be seen as the one form of the category as such. Form images at this stage are subject to such a primary integration process. What goes on here helps also to explain certain deformations resulting from the limits of the primal manifestation of integration dynamics.

One deformation is due to faulty transposition, that is, one form in the field or its representation in the imagination is mistaken for another because of the transposition of the qualities of the one to the other. The other deformation is the result of compression, that is, a whole category is compressed entirely within one of its forms.

During our later formation journey, we may still be influenced infrafocally by these primitive integration attempts and their lasting traces in our imagination and memory. Under pressure, we may fall back on them. In a disturbed religious person, for example, one may see such a transposition and compression of integration dynamics. It leads easily to a primal integration of delusions about the similarity of extraordinary religious experiences. Those who have worked in mental hospitals are aware of the distortions this primitive urge to integration may generate in religiously or ideologically educated persons.

The formative imagination, under pressure of the primary integration dynamics, can be a matrix of deformation. However, later in time, the same imagination, when stimulated by the dynamics of tentative integration in service of consonance and transcendence, can be a wellspring of creative unfolding of character and personality. This reasonable and intuitive integration can be greatly formed and sustained by consonant classic formation traditions and their symbols.

Insufficient Differentiation
and Imaginative Confusion

The same primary imagination of infants tends to confuse the pre, intra, inter, and outer spheres of their field of life. These are just starting to differentiate themselves more fully in this phase. The differentiation is not yet sufficiently effective to prevent cognitive confusion. All spheres, while somewhat differentiated, are still close to each other. The outer spheres of the field may be imagined as filled with a kind of consciousness of their own: the intrasphere transposes its own power of consciousness to things. The nascent intrasphere is, after all, still saturated with the thinglike facets apprehended in the outer spheres.

Each progress in the differentiation of the field leads to increasing divergence. Yet the differentiation dynamics never effect a total separation between the spheres, neither in the child nor in the adult. In every formation phase, there remains the tendency to transpose certain facets of the intrasphere to other spheres in the field.

This fundamental and inevitable confusion of spheres is one of the marks of the *preverbal differentiation dynamic*. Infants only begin to form images around the seventh month. For instance, they are able to look for a toy when it is hidden under the cover of their crib. This action implies that infants can give form to the toy in their imagination. Toward the end of the second year, their potency to form images has been so highly developed that the images children form may be given a corresponding permanence in their field of presence and action. This certainty—repeatedly confirmed by their reality testing—enables children to assess the forms in their field in a formative and reformative fashion. They begin to realize that these forms maintain their own identity in spite of any well-meant manipulation to the contrary by the children. This effectiveness comes about through the dynamics of formative imagination.

Emotional and Motivational Formation

Image formation exercises a considerable influence on the emotional and motivational dynamics of the infant's life form. Emotional reactions and responses can now be elicited not only by present forms in the field but also by their images. The latter can extend in time and intensity the emotion evoked by one or the other outer form in one's field. As a result, the infant can for the first time give form to such lasting emotions as anxiety or of feeling either at ease or disturbed, even when the persons, things, or events that evoked these emotions are no longer available to their perception. Similarly, lasting desires can be formed by imagining what is desired. This happening marks the beginning of formative anticipation. Along with formative imagination and memory, it plays an immensely important role throughout the unfolding of our personality.

The pleasure-displeasure dynamic, which had such an influence during the previous phase of formation, is now reformed into the dynamics of fulfillment of desires and diminishment of anxiety. These become formative motivations.

In my own formation science, I call the motivational dynamics of the vital dimension, in this stage, *pulsions*. The dynamics of restraint and discipline are still not strong or effective enough to prevent an explosive, instantaneous unloading of compressed formation energy in these emotions and motivations. Because of their increasing force and dominance in this period, I refer to this phase as one of *pulsion prevalence*.

Gradually, infants begin to leave behind them the homogeneous experience of their formation field. They experience a germinal sense of some difference in spheres, no matter how feeble this awareness may be in the beginning. Their sense of being the magical, omnipotent source of events and appearances starts to weaken. No longer do they feel as if they are the whole of the field in an autarkic, indiscriminate fashion. No longer do they sense without doubt that other field spheres and the forms appearing in them are identical with themselves. Neither do infants now—if they are not autistic or otherwise damaged by birth defects—fall into the opposite extreme. They do not sense themselves as fully insulated from the field, as isolated bodily intraspheres.

As is the case for all human life forms, so infants, too, experience in some way the field that they are, even if its inter and outer facets are sensed as differentiated from them. The truth is, they are their field and its horizons in a participant way. They share always already in its spheres and horizons. They are in their field as prepersonal intraspheres. They will potentially grow into a certain freedom to give and receive form within the limits that are imposed on their freedom by all the spheres and dimensions of their field of life. Their relative, just-awakening potency for freedom springs from the depths of their transcendent founding form. At this stage of their formation journey, any actualization of this potency is still tenuous, intermittent, and often erratic.

CHAPTER 17

Recapitulation of the Vital Formation Phases and Lingual Formation

Looking back at the phases of vital formation considered thus far, I see in all of them the dominance of vital pulsions. These are intertwined with biogenetic processes. The vitalistic apprehension and appraisal of infants is still mainly a matter of chance sensations and perceptions. In the realm of feelings, they are capable of only proto-affective emotions that are effusive and explosive. Infants are also unable to interform with others in a personal sense. Their life is presocial. Motivationally, they are driven by sensory-motor impressions and by dynamics that are mainly vital pulsions for comfort and survival. Their intrasphere is still first and foremost corporeal.

Infants find themselves initially also in total fusion with the inter and outer spheres of their field of life. They do not even recognize it as a field in the way older children and grown-ups do. In this phase of blissful embeddedness, there begins to emerge a vaguely differentiated field. Their own emergent intrasphere, even within these differentiations, retains an almost exclusively bodily character. It does not yet become differentiated within itself. Functional and transcendent mind and will, while potentially in place, show only minimal influence because of their lack of development.

Hence, contact of this intrasphere with the other spheres of the field is almost exclusively through bodily modes and modalities. Infants suck, spit, push, pull, hit, cry, seek bodily pleasure and comfort, undergo oral, anal, phallic, or clitoric sensations and only gradually begin to sense that, for instance, beating a toy too severely does not hurt the toy but their hand. It appears to them in due course that there is a difference between their bodily sphere and the sphere to which a toy or anything else belongs. This marks the emergence of a first intraspheric sense. As we have seen, only gradually do infants learn to distinguish this inner sphere from the other spheres of their field of life. Now these other spheres begin to feel different from their own immediate bodily sensations.

Remote Preparation for Transcendent Formation

I came in my formation science to the conclusion that every formation phase can be seen as a remote preparation for the spiritual ascendance of human life. In my view, the human transcendence dynamic is operative also in this phase. The emergence of a faintly individualized, bodily intrasphere transcends or goes beyond the phase of mere embeddedness in the field. This formation is a first step on the long road of pretranscendent preparation for fuller human transcendence. This phase is part of a succession of pretranscendent dynamics. All of them are a gift of the mystery of formation. They prepare the human life form for increasing consonance and intimacy with the mystery.

This first lower, preparatory level of transcendence enables infants also to give some form to things within their field. Around the age of two, the sensory-motor stage comes to an end. The spheres of the field are sufficiently differentiated to enable children to develop images within their intrasphere of what they see and touch. Through these images, which represent forms in their field, they begin to realize the constancy of such forms even if they cannot actually see them any longer. Awareness of their more or less steady appearance helps children to deal with them compatibly. They coordinate through neuromuscular movements the way they handle these stable appearances. This enables them to use things as dependable instruments to give some form to their life and world.

My observations so far are intended to provide a basic paradigm of effective form reception and donation. I initiated these two concepts in Holland on the basis of my observations there. I explained them briefly in the first volume of this series. A first condition for this effectiveness was, in my observation, that the intrasphere differentiates itself from the pre, inter, and outer spheres of life and from the forms appearing in and through them. Simultaneously, the intrasphere as a form receptive potency begins to become aware that both these spheres and their forms are distinct and stable, and hence manipulable. This recognition in itself is a mode of transcending, of being empowered, as a form donating potency, to deal with things formatively. My growing insight in these processes contributed greatly to the conception of my 1944 interformation paradigm.

How form is given to these appearances depends on the modalities of the concrete formation powers available to the individual at any specific stage of life. In infancy, mainly sensory-motor and vital modalities of form donation are available. Neurologically speaking, in infancy all form reception and donation is directed by the limbic system of the brain.

The overall thrust of human transcendence and its integration and consonance dynamics exert their influence here anonymously. They facilitate the emergence of a certain vital unity of bodily feeling, a kind of bodily consonance, as it were. It represents a first faint epiphany in the intrasphere of a mainly somatic individuality. Out of this shadowy ground there will emerge later an apprehension of a personal life call, which is a dynamic appeal of the indwelling mystery. This call is hidden in the founding form of life. In its push upward, it has led in this phase to the emergence of a dim, somatic individuality. What makes all of this possible is the loving operation of the mystery in the current phases of fetus, neonate, and infant unfolding. The mystery's forming power is most effective if the conditions in one's field are favorable for its implementation. The next phase—ending the centrality of vital formation—will be a transition to the functional dimension of the human life form. This transition begins with the phase of lingual, verbal, or, along with it, a far more extensive form-traditional formation.

Form-Traditional Formation

The human formation field, as I conceived it, is permeated and profoundly influenced by formation traditions. Without them, neither a typical nor a distinctive human formation is possible. These traditions are already indirectly influential in the vital phase of life. They touch the child through the style of motherly presence it receives as guided by traditional customs of infant care.

The formative power of tradition comes really into its own in a more direct way with the emergence and acquisition of language. This enables the infant to share more intimately in traditions. Language itself is an outgrowth and gift of tradition. It is a lingual treasure of form-traditional attentions, apprehensions, appraisals, affirmations, symbols, directives, and dynamics.

The unfolding of one's lingual form potency is the most decisive event of child formation from the viewpoint of the anonymous, preparatory transcendence dynamics of my formation science. Lingual formation is the condition for many other growth processes in the life of infants. Examples are new and increased modes of attention, apprehension, and appraisal; a lengthening of one's experience of time; the emergence of a more integrated and individualized intrasphere; an expansion and deepening of the emotional modality of life, preparing for the affects of intimacy; and the emergence of rudimentary forms of reflexive conscience. All are related to a first and more direct sharing in formation traditions by means of lingual interformation with the people around us.

Lingual Formation

The language spoken in the infant's environment embodies a particular tradition, a specific way of attending, apprehending, appraising, affirming or denying what appears in a field that is shared with others. Language formation reflects a tradition as nothing else can. Correspondingly, the formation of the intrasphere of infants mirrors in this stage what is assimilated through the language of the traditions alive in their surroundings. In other words, language defines both the child's field of life and the child's intraspheric formation within that field.

It is mainly through language that children become implicitly aware of themselves as participants in a community of people who share certain form traditions. The imaginative and vital-bodily modalities of apprehension and appraisal no longer dominate awareness in an exclusive fashion. Language provides the intrasphere with the means of slowly interiorizing the patterns of apprehension and subsequent functional-rational thought sedimented in the language children begin to assimilate. This stage still belongs to the vital dimension; the child's mind is not yet dominated by functional, linear thought. This is still a transitional stage insofar as only the beginnings of functional apprehension and appraisal announce themselves along with the beginnings of language assimilation.

Transitional formation phases in infancy are marked by mainly prefunctional and, hence, prelogical apprehensions. These are pervaded by magical, animistic, and imaginary apprehensions and appraisals. The formation of the infraconsciousness of the intrasphere is influenced deeply by this prefunctional language and hence can still radiate its latent power later in life.

Transitional language is utilized by our hidden integration dynamics to give children some vague consciousness of the connectedness of their experiences. We saw in the previous phase that the dynamic led to a primary integration process by means of nonlingual images. In this phase, the apprehension and appraisal process often seeks for some primitive integration. It makes infants look for external similarities that seem striking and obvious to their immature apprehension. The difference with the previous type of integration is that this primal and primitive integration becomes now for the most part lingual; it is no longer restricted to nonlingual images.

Symbols and Symbolized Forms

The potency for formation of language and other symbols has been awakened. Infants in the beginning of this phase have difficulty in differentiating symbols from the forms in their field to which these symbols refer. They may identify names or other symbols with the forms themselves to which they point. In certain instances or cultures, prolongation of this tendency later in life can lead to a deformation of the spirituality of people. The identification of symbol and symbolized form plays into the dynamics of magical thinking and acting. People can get stuck in such identifications. They may imagine that they can control the formation field, its forms, and even its transcendent horizon by a magical manipulation of names or images.

Identification through such magic plays a role in certain primitive forms of religion and in people who, under emotional stress, take refuge in this early magical formation phase. Identifications like this can lead to pathological behavior. For example, compulsive-obsessive people may try to control their fate or their adversaries by manipulation of symbols which, in their imagination, stand for that fate or for such enemies. They may invent ceremonies of their own, such as compulsive hand washing or the obsessive repetition of prayers in an incantatory fashion. They may develop elaborate rituals to avoid cracks in the pavement or abuse the customs of their religion as powers to exert control over the deity. They may craft images representing their enemies and believe that they can hurt them by stabbing them with pins.

Initial Dynamics of Abstraction

Early lingual formation depends on some rudimentary dynamics of abstraction. These enable children to take from manifold forms facets that seem similar. By means of these abstracted similarities, classes of forms can be shaped conceptually instead of mainly imaginatively, as in the previous phase. Initial abstraction dynamics are far from accurate. In this phase of prefunctional thinking, confusion between the abstracted facets and the forms as a whole from which they have been abstracted is quite common.

Gradually, this confusion will be clarified. Verbal interformation with parents and others improves the abstraction process and strengthens the lingual dynamics. In the course of this current formation, the prefunctional thought process is slowly reformed. A more rational-functional type of thought, mainly borrowed from others, begins to take its place. Prefunctional thought, because of its borrowed character, will reflect somehow disconnected fragments of the thought traditions of the child's family and field segment.

Briefly, conformation with the language of others in one's field implies conformation with their field and its traditions. A field of life is a demarcation of reality limited by our actual sociohistorical potencies of form reception and donation. The demarcation of such a field is reflected in a particular language. In my thinking, I have come to believe that our language represents the actual ranges of our field of life. Children learn to coform with others around them the language that mirrors their shared field. In so doing they assimilate the particular field range reflected in this language. It gives form to their prefocal conviction that this language represents not only a particular range of that field, that is to say, reality as formationally demarcated by this limited segment of humanity, but all of reality.

Functional attentions, apprehensions, appraisals, affirmations, and directives are repeated until children in their initial childhood phase functionally coform the field in the same way people around them do. First of all, what is formed are the segmental and common ranges of the field of first childhood in their functional dimension. These ranges will be gradually penetrated and reformed by those that are personal and universal. All of the above may be transformed later in life in the light of the horizon of the field which I have conceived as one's second or transcendent childhood.

Dynamics of Recognition and Recall

At first, children can exercise only the dynamics of recognition of forms, their names and symbols. Then dynamics of recall begin to complement those of recognition. Now the field, in its segmental or in its common range, becomes for children the uncontested reality which remains constant in their formative memory. Because of this constancy of symbolic input and its interiorization in their intrasphere, young children tend to believe that all people apprehend and appraise reality in this same way.

Through ongoing lingual formation, this objectified field becomes more and more interiorized in their intrasphere. The lingual form-traditional phase tends to render the phases I have discussed previously less accessible. The prelingual apprehensions of former stages lose much of their forming potency in comparison with the power of distinct lingual expressions. By means of language, children can become well-accepted participants in the field in which they are verbally reared. In regard to the former prelingual experiences, neither children nor adults can recall them at will, precisely because they were preverbal. Hence, schools of depth psychology devise a specific symbolic metalanguage to point to these early lingual forms and to their potential influence later in life.

The ascent of the empirical human life form happens through a hierarchical succession of current formations. This can give rise to problems and conflicts. Each phasic formation dynamic leads to a newly emergent form dimension or subdimension. The dynamics of integration and consonance compel us to integrate each new dimension or subdimension with those previously formed. New current dynamics initiating a higher dimension on the ladder of ascent tend to ignore or repudiate the dynamics of the previous ones.

This diminishment of attention to former dynamics serves one of the purposes of any current transition dynamic. It enables us to make a new, emergent dimension central for the time being to our focal attention. This effect may be temporarily useful. If this exclusive attention is unduly prolonged, it interferes with the possibility of effective integration of both present and former dynamics. For example, the emergence of lingual form-traditional dynamics can lead to an ignoring or repudiation of previous current dynamics and their recall in our memory. Prolonged ignorance or repudiation interferes with the effectiveness of our integration and consonance dynamics. Excessive, lasting fixation of attention on only current transition events can lead, in turn, to lasting dissonance and subsequent deformation. This will be especially the case if the process of right formation is not restored in due time. An opposite danger is that the dynamics of lower dimensions, which were prevalent during their current formation period, can overwhelm higher phasic dynamics. Healthy formation seeks always for the middle way between these two extremes.

Formational Memory and Anticipation

In the lingual phase now under consideration, I observe a more pronounced unfolding of formational memory and anticipation. These are two servant formation powers, which, along with that of imagination, play such a basic role in my formation science. Both powers gain now in constancy within the intrasphere of the children. They make possible a first awareness of the temporal dimension of their field. Only what unfolds in time can be remembered or anticipated.

To understand this rule of thumb, let me reflect again on my concept of the formation field. A formation field represents for me a limited expression of the formation mystery in time and space. I believe that the mystery allows such fields to emerge through historical human forms of life. They form these fields in dialogue with their own inner and outer experiences as well as with those that gave rise to the knowledge and wisdom traditions of the human race. Each particular field should be formed over time in fidelity to reality. In my thinking, such a field is not at once there in one indivisible act of instant full and perfect formation. On the contrary, I believe, on the basis of my observations, experience, and reflections, that formation fields unfold in time. My notion of ongoing human formation implies a temporal sequence of formation events and of intimations of formation traditions as well as a corresponding sequence of our responses to them.

Consequently, effective presence in our field depends, among other things, on realistic apprehension and appraisal of its temporal dimension. Such appraisal is possible only when the sequences just mentioned can be represented by us symbolically in our own intrasphere. The formation dynamics of first childhood and infancy prepare us for this ability. Through the dynamics of language formation, children are able to make sense of the functional dimension of time in their field of life.

In the previous phase, formative imagination brought together disparate moments of time. It did so by extending imaginatively within the children's intrasphere the sensate forms they had perceived selectively. Children grow beyond this limited imaginative capability. Their expanding intrasphere becomes empowered by abstract representations—lingually acquired—of formation events and one's response to them. This response generates a sense of the duration and placement of actual or potential events in time that succeed one another in a line of symbolic representations from past to future.

The dynamics of lingual representation enable children to understand for the first time the past modality of time. They tend to recall the past by means of lingual symbols insofar as it is relevant to their present formation needs. Lingual dynamics make it also possible to apprehend and utilize the future modality of the temporal dimension. This apprehension actualizes one's potency for formative anticipation and proformation, enabling one to give a more enduring direction to one's present formation efforts. Children, for example, can anticipate possible future effects of their efforts and actions. Such anticipation is due to the intraspheric manipulation of language symbols. In this instance, symbols reflect the accumulated experience of one's formation segment in regard to things to be expected as a result of certain acts or happenings.

Differentiation of the Intrasphere

In this phase of transition, lingual dynamics effect not only a sharper differentiation of the pre, inter, and outer spheres of the formation field. I noticed also a differentiation of the empirical intrasphere itself. In the previous phases, this sphere was almost exclusively bodily, sensate, and vitalistic in its relation to the pre, inter, and outer spheres of the field. The functional dimension, with its functional mindedness and its articulations, now begins to announce itself in the intrasphere. Through this announcement—mediated also by lingual dynamics—the intrasphere begins to experience some inkling of a primal freedom from total determination by intraspheric vital determinants as well as by those that are pre, inter, and outer. The interaction with these spheres becomes less automatic, less impulsive or compulsive, less bound to what happens only instantly, here and now.

Lingual dynamics expand the awakening of the intraspheric consciousness by means of the apprehension of temporal and spatial dimensions of the field. Through this extension children open up to new directives and dynamics, transcending those that are merely vitalistic. The latter were ladened with many types of pulsions and pulsations evoked by vital sensations in the here and now.

Dynamics of Formation Anxiety

Lingual dynamics foster the awareness of the temporal dimension and with it a certain hint of beginning freedom of the intrasphere from other spheres. I am convinced, after many years of observation and reflection, that any hint of formation freedom is accompanied by a heightening of formation anxiety, usually nonfocally. As a result, a first faint sense of responsibility and vulnerability begins to dawn. A kind of proto-conscience in relation to children's interaction with the now more distant spheres of their field begins to disclose itself prefocally. At such moments, children feel in some way that they can be thrown back on themselves. This gives rise to a tension and anxiety which, in this form, were unknown previously.

Awareness of time gives rise also to anxiety about what may happen in a future filled with hidden threats and promises. This marks the remote beginning of some apprehension of the possibility of disappearance—a primitive experience of mortality with the anxiety it can evoke. Formation anxiety will deepen over a lifetime, at least nonfocally. Its definite mitigation is possible only beyond the functional dimension. Mitigation may later be granted by the gift of abandonment to the mystery in the faith, hope, and consonance of what I have identified and named a second transcendent childhood. The increment of anxiety in this crossover phase explains the familiar nightmares almost all children suffer at times.

Dynamics of Control

Lingual formation makes it possible for children to have more control over their vital pulsions and to delay their response to them. The rise of such dynamics of control is again facilitated immensely by the emergence of language. Language embodies various possibilities of delayed responses. These may have become standard in the traditions of the segment of the population in which the child is born and reared.

Such dynamics are crucial in the gradual formation of a relatively free functional consciousness. This facet of consciousness now begins to awaken in the intrasphere of the child. Any moment that children do not immediately release their vital pulsions in equally vital reactions, there is room for the development of more or less realistic responses. Such responses replace blind reactions. The delay of release creates time for a functional apprehension and appraisal of the situation that evoked the vital pulsions in the first place. The accumulation of such appreciative apprehensions, during repeated moments of delay, advances the formation of functional consciousness. The exclusive domination of children by their vital dimension is thus gradually transcended.

Proto-Conscience

The dynamics of controlled delay of vital reactions foster the formation of what I introduced in my science as the proto-conscience. This conscience is formed by interiorization of the directives of the person in charge of the child's formation field and representative of its traditions. Usually, this is the mother for the young child. The phase of awakening of formative imagination disclosed the forerunner of proto-conscience. This precursor of the child's proto-conscience consists of a loose coformation of various mother images, such as those of the good and bad mother form.

The proto-conscience which emerges in this phase represents a more coherent coformation. It consists of lingual representations that complete and nuance the formerly dominant vital images. These lingual representations point to form directives of the tradition that are embodied in the language structure itself or are conveyed by means of it. I gave this facet the name of proto-conscience to distinguish it from the later developing functional and transcendent facets of conscience. The proto-conscience differs from the latter in a variety of ways. For one thing, its organization is rather defective and feeble. The proto-conscience tends to disintegrate when the person in charge of the child's formation field is absent for any significant length of time. It is also prefunctional. I see it as an intermittent crossover to the functional conscience. The latter will be more coherent and stronger. It will be enlightened by the functional facets of one's form tradition. Last, but not least, the proto-conscience differs from its forerunner, the imaginary vital facet of conscience. Unlike imaginative conscience, it carries some explicit formation directives mediated by lingual dynamics.

Dynamics of Motivation

Both lingual dynamics and the subsequent, emergent dynamics of primal abstraction expand children's potency for emotional presence in their field. The disclosure of the dimension of time through these dynamics expands the range of available feelings considerably. Time-related emotions and motivations now become a distinct possibility.

For example, children may form felt desires for this or that to happen in the future, such as receiving some reward in the evening if they behave well during the day. These dynamics may give rise in turn to worries about what they did wrong that morning for which they may be punished later when it is found out. Such emotions give rise to corresponding motivations to behave in certain ways.

Lingual dynamics also expand the realm of our functional selection of preferred events and of our responses to them. When we experience our field of life in its temporal dimension, it will offer us through our use of language various specific possibilities of past, present, and future form receptions and donations. These different opportunities are embodied in form-traditional language as assimilated by the child. Rudimentary patterns of functional selection of such possibilities are also embodied in language. These lingual directives begin to complement the more scattered impulsive wishes for things that struck the child's senses and imagination in the former vital phases. The exercise of selection prepares the child for the emergence of functional willing that makes responsible choice possible. It goes without saying that all of these formative experiences differentiate increasingly one's intrasphere.

Fourfold Struggle in Current Formation Phase

Current formation dynamics imply a fourfold struggle:

1. A struggle against dominance by the vital dynamics of the previous phases. They try to pull children back into the safety of vital embedded-

ness. They make them fear the adventure of a more independent intrasphere.

2. A struggle to follow the call to give form to some rudimentary childlike originality despite the pressure of absolute conformity carried by certain lingual communications.

3. A struggle against lack of confidence in one's own ability to be oneself, albeit in a prefocal, elementary, and childlike way.

4. A struggle to bear, without discouragement, embarrassment and debasement when bold or timid attempts to lingual and functional form donation are met with failure, ridicule, or depreciation, real or imagined.

Such struggles and disappointments, failures and setbacks, are unavoidable. They are part of everyone's formation story. This phase offers us an early introduction into the discomfort that we cannot escape during our precarious journey through life. It prepares us for the lifelong demand to turn apparent failures into formation opportunities.

At this point, the intrasphere is only beginning its process of a more refined, inner differentiation—a process that will be complicated by clashes and reconciliations, by consonances and dissonances, with other spheres. The inter and outer spheres remain always integral to any human formation field as well. The matter, the unique depth, the originality and richness of differentiation of the intrasphere cannot take away the necessity of continual interformation with these other spheres of one's field.

Ascent toward Consonance with the Mystery

As I have shown, the intrasphere begins to differentiate itself by means of lingual dynamics and dynamics of abstraction. These give rise to an unfolding of the formative attentions, apprehensions, appraisals, affirmations, and directives of the child. They are typical of the segment and of the traditions of the population into which a boy or girl is inserted by birth.

The lingual, traditional differentiation of the infant's intrasphere awakens a rudimentary functional consciousness. This consciousness is gradually formed and reformed by the increasing lingual communication of form traditions.

Through the assimilation of language, the intrasphere of the child begins to raise itself slowly beyond its mere vital dimension and its dominance by the vital imagination.

Prelingual presence is complemented by the beginning lingual mode of presence. In the future, the functional lingual mode will be complemented by the potency for translingual moments of presence. This happens when the transcendent dimension of the intrasphere is more fully awakened and starts to assert itself in a new second transcendent and transformed childhood.

Through prefunctional language, children slowly become able to distance themselves from their vital pulsions and reactions. They have some time in-between for the birth of formative responses, for recall of the past, and for anticipation of the future in service of their present form reception and dona-tion. Their life is no longer dominated by vitalistic dynamics and their explo-sive, thoughtless release.

All this means in my thinking that the formation mystery has begun to awaken the life form to its functional dimension, and therewith to a basic, new differentiation of its intrasphere. In the context of my formation science, this phase is an important step in the long ascent toward full consonance with the indwelling mystery always present as the center of one's field. Through cur-rent dynamics, the mystery begins to draw out formation potencies that were hidden from the beginning in the foundational life form. It prepares the child for later functionally effective participation in, and for donation to, human for-mation fields and their formation history.

Segmental, Common, Poetic, and Metalanguages

Children depend on the formative dynamics of a segmental language or the language spoken by the segment of the population into which they are born. All of us, of course, depend on the dynamics of the common language of the field and of its consonant traditions that constitute our birthright. I have kept stressing over the years that in my opinion this does not mean that humanity is imprisoned by existing lingual dynamics or that we cannot rise beyond their boundaries through innovative thought and creative expression. Humanity reanimates, expands, and deepens its language forms constantly. It reforms and augments its lingual treasures through poetic language and metalanguages.

For me, poetic language, in the broadest sense, refers to any creative rearrangement and placement of common words in such a fashion that they disclose a new facet or depth of human experience. This happens by means of existing lingual symbols. Every person, not only the poet by special talent and profession, but even the child, can cultivate moments of original use of com-mon parlance. Such use renders a potential meaning of a familiar symbol sur-prisingly new or translucent.

Similarly, sciences, arts, scholarly and practical disciplines can thrive only by creating metalanguages of their own. Metalanguages disclose and sustain humanity's organized attempts to discover and name new facets of reality. What a metalanguage makes us see is not yet or not accurately enough covered by the experiences and observations represented in the symbols of common language at this moment of a society's formation history.

To learn a new science, art, or technology is to learn a new language. If not, one would not be learning a new science, art or technology but only repeating what is already known in common conversation. Metalanguage transcends common parlance. Once the dynamics of metalanguages have made it possible for humanity to gain and express accurately new perspectives on life and world formation, people can enrich and renew common language by adopting and popularizing some of the relevant expressions of such metalanguages. Then they become part of the always-unfolding common language.

Such renewal of common language happens, first of all, by a new descriptive use of already-existing words to point to what has been discovered. If desirable, certain expressions of the metalanguage can be introduced in the common language. Such introduction should be accompanied by sufficient explanation. This will make the newly disclosed knowledge available to those interested in it, who, however, are still unfamiliar with its metalanguage. I have, therefore, advised that those who study my pretheological formation science or my corresponding formation theology should be bilingual. That is to say, they should be sufficiently familiar with my metalanguage and also able to translate it in common language. I myself try to do so both as a thinker and a communicator in many of my other, more popular publications.

The segmental and common lingual formation of children when they grow older should be complemented by the awakening of some rudimentary awareness of both poetic and metalanguages. They should learn to respect these languages, for their dynamics prevent the paralysis of human ingenuity by encapsulation in a common language that may have lost its power of renovation. Without constant renewal by the dynamics of poetic language and metalanguages, common parlance becomes the grave of creative human formation. Paralyzed common language vulgarizes culture and civilization. Therefore, from time immemorial parents and sages have known the importance of storytelling.

This chapter and the one preceding it dealt with the complexities of the vital formation phases from the viewpoint of formation science. When appropriate, I made references to the transcendence dynamic and to the sociohistorical role of formation tradition. Obviously, the phase of vital formation has a lasting impact on our formation story.

From the former volumes detailing my science of basic transcendent life formation, it should be clear that a significant role is played by the functional dimension, especially in its relationship to the transcendent. The next chapter, therefore, will pay special attention to the emergence and the dynamics of the functional dimension in childhood. This focus will refine our understanding of a dimension powerfully developed in Western civilization. It will clarify the position and meaning I created for this dimension in my 1944 interformation paradigm that is at the base of my formation theology and its sustaining formation science.

CHAPTER 18

Functional Dimension

In the previous two chapters, I discussed the vital-formation phases. In this chapter and the following, I shall consider the phases of functional formation.

The last chapter ended with a consideration of the final stage of the vital phase. This stage of transition guides us from the vital to the functional dimension of life. In the previous phase, children began to differentiate their intrasphere. They felt stimulated in this work of initial differentiation by their more individual sharing of traditions to which they were exposed in their surroundings. The accelerated assimilation of the language of their families facilitated sharing of this sort. At the same time, children developed a first tenuous sense of their own individual functioning in family situations. They can now listen more intently to a name of their own. Before this time, they apprehended their name only as a kind of external labeling. The new awareness of a more personal meaning of their name makes them feel less anonymous.

Dynamics of the Functional Dimension

This sense of individuality keeps unfolding and differentiating. In this stage the awareness of one's life form begins to center itself around the emergent functional dimension. Centering and integration dynamics are now shaped mainly, though not exclusively, by the functional facet of their traditions. This facet is now communicated more verbally by the parents.

The appropriation of language implies an assimilation of the traditional dispositions of attention, apprehension, appraisal, affection, affirmation, application, conformation, communication, confirmation, collaboration, and concelebration as well as of imagination, memory, and anticipation. The varied contents of all of these are interwoven with the traditions that permeate the life of children. Functional assimilation prevails at this time. It is interspersed with moments of what I call *transcendence resonance* or a resonating of faint signs of transcendent meanings hidden in traditional languages. The mystery grants all of us transcendence dynamics. They are with us from the very beginning of our life. These dynamics are the secret source of the current dynamics of any formative phase insofar as they are consonant. All consonant human formation is from the start to the end of human life directed toward transcendence, at least implicitly and silently.

Shift to Mental-Lingual Functionality

The previous phase of vital formation, toward its conclusion, is marked by crossover features. Therefore, the beginning of functional awareness is somewhat fleeting because it is still submerged in the vital but is beginning to cross over to the functional dimension. That is why I designated this previous stage as the vital-functional phase.

The now newly emerging functional phase proper shows a definite shift from vital to mental-lingual functionality. The vital-functional, sensory-imaginative dynamics of the previous phase no longer dominate one's life as a whole. Neither do they totally disappear. Gradually, these dynamics will be subordinated to those that are mental and lingual. Their former, almost exclusive influence is replaced by an influx of linear, conceptual, abstract lingual dynamics. Children no longer apprehend and appraise their own life as a more or less amorphous form. They go beyond experiencing themselves as a loose constellation of images. They no longer feel labeled by a name that has only external significance. Their own name now has a different quality for them than the names of other things already labeled in their surroundings. Now their own name points to an individually functioning "I" that is a source of their feelings, thoughts, presence, and action within their surroundings.

The emergent functional dimension gives them a sense of a life form of their own that gains increasingly in internal consonance. Initially, this newly emergent sense of form is embryonic, tenuous, and ill-defined, yet in due course it becomes more solidified. Intricate lingual-conceptual dynamics, replete with symbolic power, give direction to the child's ongoing functional unfolding. Children assimilate from the traditions in which they are submerged lingual appraisals of what makes them functionally significant in their surroundings. They begin to learn their functional role in family and neighborhood. They learn how to gain appreciation from others as effectively functioning individuals within their environment. Such appreciative apprehensions, with their concomitant affects and images, memories and anticipations, make up to a large extent a child's sense of his or her own life form and its functional significance. Children no longer see themselves only as vitalistic forms or as things labeled in a particular way. They begin to sense themselves as dynamic powerhouses of appreciative and depreciative apprehensions and subsequent directives. This lingually acquired set of apprehensions and directives demarcates their sense of being also a functional form of life.

Sense of Functional Form

To me this functional sense of form could be described as a more or less coherent cluster of appreciative and depreciative apprehensions of one's functional capacity within one's field of life. The appreciative/depreciative facet of such apprehensions both generates and is sustained by corresponding images, memories, and anticipations, by pulsations, pulsions, and ambitions. The dynamics of consonance and integration make children try, moreover, to bring together the often-dissonant strivings of their functional dimension. This leads to the tentative development of some of the functional dispositions of their character.

The functional formation sense of children differentiates itself gradually from its vital underpinnings. In some measure the vital formation sense will keep pervading one's embodied intrasphere as does the functional. However, this vital sense will no longer exclusively control one's thoughts, feelings, and actions.

In regard to intraspheric vitality, the functional formation sense relates itself specifically to the voluntary neuromuscular facet of the vital dimension. The formation of muscular dexterity in service of effective functioning is important in this phase. Serious failure of or dissonance between one's emergent functional formation sense and one's neuromuscular dexterity can affect adversely one's overall growth and self-appreciation. Sooner or later one has to learn that such failure has to be relativized. The light of the transcendent dimension and of one's transcendent faith and formation tradition is the most effective source of such relativization. Children can indirectly participate in that light through the transcendent example, word, and storytelling by loving grown-ups, first of all their parents.

The current dynamics of the functional dimension are thus guided in great measure by appreciations and depreciations that are mainly functional in nature. These are directed in turn, albeit often implicitly, by the always-present transcendence dynamic. In this phase the transcendent dimension helps to raise indirectly the intrasphere beyond its previous encapsulation in only the vital dimension. It prepares the human life form to embody later more fully and focally the inspirations and aspirations of the mystery in one's field of presence and action.

Functional Facet of Formation Conscience

Earlier in this volume, I introduced my notion that human conscience as formative has many facets—sociohistorical, vital, vital-functional, functional, functional-transcendent, transcendent, and transcendent-functional. I had much to say about this in my chapters on the anthropology of formation conscience. The functional phase of formation is conducive to the emergence of the functional facet of this conscience. It consists of a lingual-conceptual cluster of intraspheric functional directives. These functional conscience directives point out what constitutes appreciable or depreciable functioning, for example, within one's family or neighborhood. I have conceived this facet of functional conscience as representing the input of familial and segmental functional directives. At this stage, these are, in the main, directives of traditional functioning. As such they are symbolically expressed by the parents or their substitutes. Gradually, such parental directives insert themselves in the conscience of the child's intrasphere. If they are not obeyed, they evoke guilt feelings. They prepare one for the implementation, later in life, of the inspirational and aspirational directives of the mystery revealed more fully and focally through one's transcendent dimension.

Interiorized Parental Appraisal of Children

Children appraise in their own way what their parents seem to appreciate or depreciate in them. They become aware of such parental appraisal in the interformational processes that occur constantly between parents and children. The parents' appraisal is absorbed by the children in the functional-formative facet of their emergent conscience.

I have found that the processes themselves of parent-child interformation do not remain totally outside the intrasphere of the children. They become partly interiorized as inner processes within the child's own expanding and contracting intrasphere. Parent-child talk and its forming or deforming effects continue inwardly, even when one's parents are absent. Interformational dynamics thus become, in part, intraformational dynamics.

Interiorized parent-child talk continues as a forming or deforming force well into adult life. It remains as a nonfocal process deep within us. It can distort not only our relationship with others but also our relationship with the mystery. It may compel us to reduce our idea or imagery of the mystery to the inner parent. For the parent may still be talking within us, even when we pray, without our realizing that this is happening. We then take on the childish (not childlike) features that dominated our interformation and the formation of our functional conscience at an early stage in our history. By the same token, one can be tempted to reduce religion to only a religion of functioning well while neglecting its spiritual-depth aspect.

The formation counselor, director, or transtherapist should be attentive to the potential presence of directives that may have been inserted into consciousness and conscience by early dynamics of interformation. Some childish directives may have infected the religious practices of people with vestiges of anxious functionality. Others may abandon religious practices altogether. They reject them along with the rejection of other functional childhood directives. They may have repudiated the latter when they sensed their paralyzing impact later in life. They began to experience such directives as uncongenial with their life or incompatible with their unfolding field and with the new traditions entering their pyramid of formation traditions, a point I made in the preceding volume of this series, *Traditional Formation.* A person's overreaction to this negative experience may be due to the fact that one never wisely worked it through. Instead of purifying one's religious mind-set and practice or letting it be purified by the mystery of formation, one threw away vestiges of faith that seemed only to reinforce the functional directives of childhood conscience.

The inward continuity of parent-child talk can also distort our relationships with others. We have to watch the dynamic of flight into the repetition of the familiar. This often happens when we are confronted with threatening situations. For example, meeting new or important people whom we appraise as superior or inferior may cause us to regress to the interformation dynamics of childhood. These are still available to us because of their insertion in our early consciousness. Thus, we may feel inclined to slot others into the role of either the parent or the child. We cannot see them for who they really are. Neither are we able to assess realistically the actual parameters of the relationships in which we find ourselves here and now.

Current Intra- and Interformation
in the Parent-Child Relationship

In previous chapters, I tried to work out how our *intrasphere* and *intraformation* become inwardly differentiated. Now I want to stress as well that the *intersphere* and *interformation* between parents and children are differentiated too. This differentiation is due to the fact that formative interaction patterns between parents and children become more effective with the learning of language. The clearer and more precise the language of the parents is, the more able they are to nuance their formative directives clearly and distinctly. Children absorb these and insert them into their expanding intrasphere, thus fostering its further differentiation. In interformation, parents nuance verbally and symbolically the various appreciations and depreciations they express about their children and their behavior. For instance, parents may manifest anxious depreciation of a child's normal questions about sexuality. Children are prone to insert this depreciation into their own conscience. Lingual symbols enable them to take on inwardly the function of depreciation exercised by parents outwardly. In this example, children may become depreciative of themselves when sexual curiosity pricks their consciousness. The opposite is true too. If parental words or patterns of conduct express sexual addictions, they poison by interdeformation the child's conscience and character formation.

In other words, dynamics of parental appreciation and depreciation can lead to self-appreciation and depreciation in children. In the light of assimilated parental appreciations, they may adopt certain thoughts, feelings, images, and actions that rightly or wrongly feel consonant to them. Conversely, the depreciations they absorb may give rise to feelings of dissonance, guilt, or self-depreciation whenever such depreciable thoughts, feelings, urges, and images about their self-worth are awakened. This current functional dynamic in childhood readies us for the ultimate concerns of conscience. For these are related to transcendent appreciations and depreciations of the mystery as disclosing itself in transcendent faith and formation traditions. These ultimate concerns can be healthy, life giving, well balanced, and invigorating, even if one sometimes fails to live up to them. The condition is that one then feels sustained by his or her joyous faith in the forgiving, healing, and strengthening presence of the transforming mystery.

Parent-Child Differentiation
of Formation Conscience

By inserting the directives received from their parents in their own intrasphere, children differentiate increasingly the functional dimension of that sphere. There are two facets to this differentiation: one stands for the interiorized appreciative or depreciative directives that emerge in interformational interaction with one's parents. The other represents the child's appreciative or depreciative responses to the parents during this process. At certain moments these directives function as if the children were parenting the child-image in themselves. In prefocal imitation of the parental voice, these conscience directives inwardly reproach their inner child-image for not behaving in some particularly parental, approvable fashion. At other times they function as if the children were behaving in accordance with their interiorized parent-image. They praise, in prefocal parental imitation, their already-established inner child-image as making them think, feel, and behave in what they believe to be a way that is in tune with their inner parent-image. This intraspheric dialogical functioning is based on the original external interformative functioning that occurred between parents and children.

I have conceptualized this as the *paradoxical dynamic of intraspheric expansion:* on the one hand, new form directives expand one's consciousness; on the other hand, the same directives add paradoxically to the restraining dos and don'ts of the functional, legal facet of one's conscience. Directive facets of parent-child interformation that were at first only present in the intersphere are now absorbed in the intraformational, functional consciousness and conscience sphere of the child.

Interformation of Imagery

Interformation between intraspheric parental images and children's self-images is directed by a host of appreciative and depreciative dispositions. For example, one image of the interiorized parent may be that of a compassionate, caring person. Another may be that of a cold, indifferent, distant or abusive parent. Appreciative memory of the caring parent influences formation in the child's conscience of altruistic ideals. Ideals of a tough, self-centered life may be formed by a conscience that harbors the internalized image of a disciplining, intimidating, legalistic, overly restraining parent. The forbidding, inhibiting aspects of the children's internalized conscience could exclusively dominate their formation.

Something similar can be said of children's self-images. One may experience oneself as, respectively, a compatible child or a resisting child, a congenial child, or one who is competent or incompetent. These intraspheric apprehensions are also appreciative or depreciative as are the affects, images, felt memories, and anticipations that are connected with them.

Typical of this phase of formation is, thus, not a total absence of feeling and imagery but their emergence in connection with functional mental apprehensions. Imagination and feeling as such are, thus, no longer primary, more or less isolated sources of conduct as they were in the previous vital phases of formation.

This functional phase in the unfolding of human life should ideally prepare us to affirm our childhood freely in relation to the all-forming mystery and to the unique-communal life call, project, and consonant tradition it gradually discloses. The later gift of a second and fuller empirical transcendent childhood will liberate us from certain unfree features of the vital and functional phases of our first childhood. At the same time, it enhances and elevates immeasurably its prototypical features of free, loving abandonment to the presence of the mystery in one's life and world.

Intraspheric Child-Parent-Adult Dynamics

I have worked out in more detail how interformation between people can be internalized in their intrasphere. This process inserts in the inner life of the child what was and is the outer parent-child relationship. Later this parent-child interaction within will be superseded by a second transcendent parent-child awareness, which is itself a gift of the mystery. This gift ought to be foreshadowed by the earlier first parent-child relationship. Our second transcendent childhood is meant to symbolize the parenthood of the forming mystery and our trusting second childhood in relation to this loving presence.

On the path to fulfillment of our transcendence dynamic, there are many hurdles to cross if we would grow to adult maturity. This dynamic detaches people from their fascination with certain childish (not childlike) patterns of their first childhood as still operative within their intrasphere. The release of, for example, childish expressions of blind obedience does not exclude their free affirmation or refusal of certain consonant or dissonant directives and character dispositions absorbed in the family.

Growth to adult maturity is a long process, announcing itself already in one's emergent functional dimension. The inner child-parent dynamic is thus joined by the dynamic of growth toward mature adulthood. This adds, as it were, a third voice to the voices of the interior parent and child. From that moment on, functional life will be directed also by an inner dialogue between the parent-child dynamics and those of the preadult growth dynamic that resonates especially in young adult life.

For example, sexual dynamics in the marriage of a young couple may still be directed by this threefold dialogue. Early parental condemnation of any sexual curiosity may give rise to some initial withholding of full sexual expression of marital affection. This dynamic collides with that of rebellion, which may develop in the child as a reaction against the parents' excessive withholding of any information and qualified appreciation in this regard. Angry revolt breeds excessive dynamics of resistance. These goad young people to break through parental taboos in an almost violent, willful fashion. Confronting both of these opposing dynamics are the emerging adult dynamics. Their role may be to enable the couple gradually to rise above both excessive withholding and willful forcing tendencies. Maturing adult dynamics may dispose one to express warm intimacy feelings for the beloved in a marital relationship that respects the wisdom of a couple's transcendent tradition and reflects the radiance of the loving mystery in their love for one another.

Such growth in maturity and in detachment from the exclusive dominance of dynamics of one's first childhood takes time, but it is an essential part of one's preparation for transcendent adulthood.

Functional Project of Formation

It is my personal contention that the internalized parent-child-adult dialogue enables us to give form effectively to more balanced functional projects of formation. I define the latter as a purposeful appraisal of various directives in service of the functional goal one wants to achieve. For example, as they grew up, children may have been admonished by their inner parental directives to make the acquisition of money a priority in life. The voice of the interior resistant child may whisper: "I like money, but I hate to be a copy of my father, who wants me to take over his business." The beginning preadult voice may say: "If I become a professional, I can help people in a way that suits me and that is in line with my aptitudes. At the same time I will receive a sizable income, which should please my father." My independent choice thus shows my parents the autonomy that the resistant child in me wants to demonstrate somewhat defiantly.

The inner dialogue that goes on among these three dynamics remains mostly nonfocal. This example illustrates the way in which this disclosure may generate a more balanced functional result. At its center, one can often find some possibility of compromise among these three interior dynamics.

Infiltration of the Intrasphere
by Interspheric Agents of Formation

Agents of formation, other than our parents, who are active in the inter-sphere of our life can infiltrate the triple dialogue occurring there. Let me expand on this important idea. The dynamic desire to expand and enrich our *intrasphere* by disclosing and assimilating new appearances in our *intersphere* offers interformational agents their entrance point.

For example, powerful, suggestive personalities may infiltrate the conversation going on between the child's interiorized parental voice and his or her interiorized response. Such people appear to be aligned with and to amplify in the child's intrasphere this parental voice. They may cajole, command, charm, or seduce the earlier first child in us. It is still inclining us to listen with some docility to what sounds like the familiar parental voice within. Advertisers, administrators, salespersons, and even quacks may take advantage of this inclination. Politicians, cult leaders, dictators, and demagogues may sound spellbinding to their followers. It is as though they are the amplified expression of powerful inner parental figures. Other examples are spiritual directors and counselors who unwisely play the role of all knowing fathers and mothers for their spiritual children. For them they are children not in the sense of a second transcendent childhood, but in the sense of the early first childhood. Often such directors and counselors themselves did not grow beyond their first child-hood conscience. They transpose this childish childhood image to their directees or counselees.

Other leading figures, too, may infiltrate the voice of interiorized first child-hood but now as sounding over against the parent. Some of them may insert themselves in the dispositions of interior rebellious children. They may play on their dynamics of smoldering anger so as to turn them into followers of vio-lent, subversive movements.

People should be cautious when they suspect any, perhaps unintentional, play by an interformational person on their inner dynamics. They should be doubly cautious when this play sounds too patently transcendent in expression and motivation. Clever infiltrators are most effective when they give us the impression that they are aligned also with the transcendence dynamic of our second childhood. They cover their identification with the inner voices of par-ent, child, or preadult by using pseudotranscendent symbols. Examples are the ceremonial symbols of Nazism, Fascism, and Stalinist Marxism. Another instance might be the abuse of Christian symbols by certain dictators. Cult leaders often infiltrate the intrasphere of their followers by the use of general religious symbols that have a strong emotional appeal. In this way they touch the emergent dynamic of transcendence. They abuse it to dispose people to abandonment. In this case, their deceptive abandonment is not to the mystery, as in the second childhood sense, but to a leader, director, cultic master, counselor, therapist, or spellbinding teacher, as in the second childhood mode.

Such surrender tends to silence former familiar directives that have proven to be beneficial. It perverts the essence of the transcendence dynamic by turning people away from its only proper object: the mystery itself.

I must add to this that, in accordance with my fifty years of observation and reflection, our vital dynamic may emerge as a fourth participant in this intraspheric dialogue. Some infiltrators may play especially on this voice. They promise one food and fame, vital security from the cradle to the grave, full employment, if one only gives up the freedom and the wonder of a second transcendent childhood. Certain Fascist and Marxist regimes have been temporarily successful in placating large numbers of people by infiltrating the urge for vital security crying out within them. Blind conformity allows people to escape the pain of adult maturation and the burden of responsibility it entails. They also forgo the peace and joy of a second transcendent childhood, which is for me exemplified in the life of my soul friend, Rinus.

CHAPTER 19

Advanced Dynamics of the Functional Formation Phase

As I contended in the previous chapter, functional conscience continues to form and reform itself during the early stages of child formation. Within the intrasphere, the will begins to assert itself in its functional facet. I call this the *executive* or *managing will* to distinguish it from what I designated early on as the *transcendent will*.

The managing facet of the will can be touched indirectly by transcendent directives. These are implicit in the other directives we receive as children. They are spontaneously absorbed from the transcendent traditions that permeate our surroundings and are modeled by our parents. I studied carefully how such directives may be personalized later in life. The appraisal powers of our second childhood make such personalization possible. I associated this transcendent childhood with the transcendent dimension of our personality.

Functional-Transcendent Willing and Conscience Formation

The managing will begins to assert itself in the emergent conscience of the child. The child-as-willing begins to make some decisions in the light of his or her limited, pristine conscience. In other words, as they grow up, children begin to choose some of the directives that will guide their life. By the same token, they reject others and, for right or wrong reasons, relegate them to the infrafocal region of their consciousness. Later in life, their transcendent dimension awakens more fully in their second childhood. They come under its direct influence. Transcendent directives will then be proposed to them by their higher reason and intuition through their transcendent will. Their lower functional reason and its managing will are consulted by the transcendent reason and will: what are the practical consequences of the implementation of such transcendent directives in one's everyday field of life? The consulted managing mind may advise the transcendent mind and will for or against proposed ways of executing such directives. But, in the end, the person decides in and through his or her transcendent will.

Dynamics of Centering and Decentering

So far I have carefully reflected on conscience dynamics as they begin to operate in the emergent formation conscience of children. I looked at these dynamics and their directives from the viewpoint of either their affirmation or repudiation by children.

Now I want to go a step further and ask, once certain directives have been affirmed, do they all play as central a role in the emergence of our formation conscience? My answer to this question is no. Children learn to decide implicitly and mostly prefocally that some, not all, of these directives ought to play a major, if not some minor or continuous, role in their life. More or less prefocally, they assign to other directives a marginal formative power. I conceive of a hierarchy, not only among central conscience directives, but also among those that are marginal. Lowest in the hierarchy of marginal directives are directives that are only affirmed as undesirable tendencies to be reckoned with realistically. They are appraised as challenges to be overcome, as directives that will hopefully drop out of our formation conscience. For example, children may sense that they should not take the toys of others. This directive may become central. Yet a former directive like "I ought to have or I ought to take what I want to play with" may still be influential. Children have not as yet overcome totally the effects of such a former directive, but neither may they relegate it to the region of infrafocal consciousness. Such suppressed (not repressed) *prefocal* (not *infrafocal*) directives, unless they are dealt with maturely, can grow in hidden force.

Children thus allow certain "ought" directives to take a leading position in the center of their formation conscience. Such, usually prefocal, selective centering implies a decentering of other "oughts" less related to or even opposed by these central ones. The dynamics of centering and decentering of formation conscience can both be exercised in a way that is either consonant or dissonant with what a child is called to be and with the legitimate demands of the child's field of formation and its traditions. Accordingly, I distinguish a consonant centering and a dissonant decentering of formation conscience. What is the difference?

Say a child decides wittingly or unwittingly to relegate an ought dynamic to the infrafocal region of consciousness where it festers as a hidden source of dissonance. To prevent such dissonance from getting the best of one, a child has to learn from stories and examples something about the dynamics of humility and candor. Courageous candor and humility imply openness to what is true, no matter how painful it is; lying to oneself deforms conscience at its very root. Children must be taught to reorganize and reject dissonant directives without denying that they are still not able at once to overcome their power. The candor of humility should enable parents to acknowledge and accept dissonant directives not only in themselves but also in their children. Otherwise, their irritation and impatience may push children to deny their problems. As in the case of dispositions in general, so, too, dissonant ones may disappear over perhaps a long period of time if one tries to diminish their lead.

In a way, all of us are composites of consonant centering and dissonant decentering dynamics. Take, for example, a student who decides to become a fair-playing, outstanding athlete. His striving for fairness may be dictated by the internalized urgings of his parental tradition. His own intent to excel in athletics and not in academic pursuits may be in part dictated by the voice of the rebellious child in him. His father perhaps had neither the time for nor the love of sport. The decision made by him to form his functional conscience in the directives of fairness makes it possible for the son to compete for a place on the local team without cheating. However, these central directives are not necessarily the only ones guiding him. Dissonant, less central ones may be influential, too.

Another directive inclines him to try to obtain a preferred spot on the team, even at the price of lowering his grades. He may also be tempted to flatter the coach by pretending to admire his leadership. The directive of cunning flattery may remain a decentering influence at the periphery of his conscience, only intermittently activated. In that case it is not too destructive. It is also possible that awareness of this dissonant directive is relegated to the infrafocal region of the young athlete's consciousness. From there, now hidden from local checks and balances, it may begin to pervert his conscience. It may even worm its way into its central dynamics. Dishonest flattery can become one of his basic ways of functioning. No longer acknowledged as such, it generates a fraudulent apparent form that creeps up on him insidiously. Because of this sly invasion of a deceptive way of appearing to himself and others, it becomes more and more difficult for him to know who he really is.

Consonant and Dissonant Dynamics
of the Apparent Form

Formation of the functional dimension starts in childhood. It is in great measure a formation in appearances that are compatible with the expectations in one's surroundings. Each individual develops a constellation of diverse apparent forms, for example, as a student, a teacher, a spouse, a parent, an administrator, a member of the golf club, a churchgoer, an employer, an employee. Such apparent forms express compatible modes of presence in these different situations. An effective functional dimension consists to a large extent of easily available apparent forms. They facilitate our compatible functioning in the situations that make up our specific field of life. The development of each apparent form discloses to us a facet of our potential for interforming with others.

A dynamic of integration influences our formation. It moves us to harmonize our different apparent forms into an overall sense of our appearance potency. Once the transcendence dynamic awakens more fully, it will inspire us to choose effective apparent forms that are congenial with our life call and compatible with the situation in which we find ourselves.

Apparent forms are vulnerable to deformation; they can be self-destructive if they are uncongenial with who we most deeply are or incompatible with the consonant traditions to which we are freely committed or with the situation in which we must appear. For instance, we normally do not act hilariously at a funeral, dress as a bum for a solemn marriage ceremony, wear formal attire at a picnic in the wilds, and behave as a nightclub comic in the pulpit of a church.

The apparent form lacks the gentle power of compassion if it lets rudeness and indifference dominate, for instance, toward family members in genuine distress. Another example of lack of compassion in appearance is to flaunt one's wealth in the face of the less well-to-do, or to be self-righteous in front of people humiliated by an incident of moral weakness that exposes them to derision.

An apparent form may miss the competence necessary for its effectiveness if one does not develop the necessary competence that enables one to appear credibly as a doctor, teacher, or laborer one moment and as a father or mother the next.

A subtle source of deformation of the apparent form is the excessive prevalence of one specific way of appearing over any other way. This can result in a kind of professional deformation. The apparent form that has proven to be effective in one's profession is then carried over into other situations without care for situational compatibility. One appears, for instance, everywhere as the preacher, or as the undertaker, the politician, the commander, the teacher, the police officer, the salesperson, the administrator.

Dynamics of dominance of the apparent form can also be traced to the takeover by one or a few dispositions of one's intrasphere. For example, one may be tempted to let shine forth in one's appearance only the disposition of rationality. In that case, dispositions fostering warmth and tenderness, or spontaneity and enthusiasm, are not allowed to enter one's formation conscience or to direct one's everyday appearance in a variety of situations. A marriage will most likely flounder if one or the other partner refuses to let the disposition of tenderness appear in moments of intimacy. The tenderness may be there, hidden in the intrasphere as a neglected disposition, while one's opposite preferred way of appearing may have been conditioned by the macho appearance of rational functionality. Thus, any appearance of tenderness may have been suppressed, thereby paralyzing the marriage relation in one of its essentials.

Counter- and Contraconscience
and Apparent-Form Deformation

Dispositions we constantly reject become split off from our apparent life form. Gradually, they drop out of our focal and even our prefocal consciousness. These rejected form potencies and dispositions gather in the infrafocal region of the intrasphere. Studying these "rejects" more carefully, I felt obliged to introduce my distinction between counter- and contraconscience.

I define my concept of counterconscience as infrafocal conscience that holds in check refused directives that are congenial, however, with our life call. As such, they ought to be made available to our focal and prefocal regions of conscience so that they can counterbalance any onesided set of congenial dispositions we may have assumed due in this case to our apparent form of life. In contrast I call my concept of contraconscience "contra" insofar as it harbors, unlike counterconscience, dispositions that would be at odds with our unique founding life form, life call, and project.

These congenial counterforms and uncongenial contraforms should be made available to our focal powers of appraisal. We should look at them with the courage of candor. Gradually, we should try to bring the counterforms as complementary powers into the composition of a rich and diversified life of healthy conscience formation. The contraforms should be faced with equal courage and equanimity. They may keep disclosing themselves to us as sources of dissonance with what we are basically called to be. Then we must accept the challenge to bear with them as long as we cannot go beyond them. We must also accept the challenge to do all we can wisely and gently to let them drop out gradually. We should be attentive to the beginning development in our children of a similar counter- and contraconscience. When these dominate our own conscience formation they easily infect our children by contamination.

The counter- and contraforms of our infrafocal conscience have an impact on the formation conscience of parents as well as of children. They influence secretly certain aspects not only of our own but also of their apparent form. Accordingly, our apparent form is coformed by a combination of unacknowledged submerged directives and acknowledged ones. Both may be misdirected by the dynamics of the pride form and those of seductive field pulsations. The pride form wants us at any price to look exalted in the eyes of ourselves and others. Field pulsations may try to sway us in this or that insufficiently appraised popular direction.

This diversity of dynamic directives stands behind the apparent form and makes its unfolding often somewhat ambivalent. Hence, our appearance may shift, depending on which dynamic prevails in a given situation. For example, a married man may appear as macho to his comrades, as an unreasonably soft touch with his children, as helpless and frightened when disaster strikes. Neither he nor others may come to know what he is really like. Only disjointed facets of his intrasphere come to the fore in a disordered fashion. This man did not wisely shift modes of appearance in realistic and competent response to the situation. He took them on under the tyranny of a merely functional formation conscience dominated by the exalting pride form, popular pulsations, and unbalanced pretranscendent form traditions. It is difficult, if not impossible, for children in the vulnerable phase of their conscience formation not to take on the ambiguity of the conscience of their parents and of the community or collectivity their parents belong to.

Compatibility and Congeniality
in Relation to the Apparent Form

Toward the end of this stage of formation, the dynamics of consonance and transcendence begin to manifest themselves in a new way. They are specifically related to the functional facet of the apparent life form. Before this final phase of functional dominance, young adults may try to give form to appearances that seem compatible with the various situations confronting them. They may assume these forms as though they were fully congenial with who they really are.

One of the crucial tasks of the functional phase is to develop forms of effective interaction with one's field. To be optimally effective, these appearances must be compatible with the situations with which we have to cope without betraying a basic congeniality with our unique-communal life call. Otherwise, functional competence and effectiveness will be lost or diminished.

The dynamics of functional compatibility are often more operative at this stage of formation than are those of congeniality. The mastery of complex compatible forms of effective appearance absorbs most of our focal attention. The problem of this current phase is the tendency to confuse what is compatible and what is congenial. One source of this tendency is a new, stronger emergence of the congeniality dynamic. It inclines people to identify mistakenly mastery of their compatible effective appearance with who they basically are. "Because" I appear as a competent, effective businessperson, I must be congenial in my whole personality with all I am called to be.

Another cause of dissonance is the pride form. It inclines people to identify their apparent form with appearances that are applauded and rewarded. An added seed of dissonance is the pressure they feel from parents, peers, and other formation models. They may laud one or more apparent forms so highly that young people are inclined to betray what they are really called to be. They may succumb to the false assumption that one or the other appearance really represents or exhausts their congenial form potency. For example, young successful college athletes may assume that athleticism and its admired appearances fulfill everything they are and can be. As a result, they neglect sufficient formation in the arts and sciences, even if they have the form potencies to excel academically. They become only sports' enthusiasts.

The uncritical assumption that our wished for apparent forms represent what we can and are called to be may lead to a split between congenial and uncongenial apparent forms. This split may infiltrate and falsify our intraspheric life. Later, the formation mystery itself may have to purgate our secretly arrogant and pride-filled existence.

Relativizing of Functional Modes

Toward the end of the phase of exclusive dominance by the functional dimension, other dynamics such as those of transcendence, integration, consonance, and congeniality begin to reassert themselves. Gradually, they enable us to appreciate yet relativize our managing modes. We begin to appraise them as subordinated instrumental ways and means of functioning wisely. Such appraisal enables us to subject their use to our deeper foundational life form. This founding form begins to manifest itself as our transcendent life call and project. It gives rise to dynamics of relative decentering in service of higher centering. Effective compatible managing modes and their corresponding appearances lose their central, exclusive power in our formation conscience. The dynamics of decentering make room for those of integration and of consonance with the transcendent formation dynamics that now begin to assert themselves in our intrasphere.

Before this happens, our integration dynamic moves us to bring into mutual consonance all facets of our managerial modes and appearances. The intended outcome is a unified formation conscience that guides us in becoming a well-disciplined, effective person in our field of presence and action.

A functionalized civilization tempts people to be satisfied with an intrasphere that is dominated by the managerial conscience. This satisfaction may extend itself even to the moral facet of one's conscience. Membership in one or the other religious or ideological faith and form tradition may then be apprehended and appraised only in terms of mere technical compatibility with rules, regulations, and usages. The dynamics of the pride form tend to favor this spurious satisfaction with a merely functional-religious or functional-ideological conscience. It gives us an exalted sense of autarkic control of our life and its field.

The ongoing transcendent dynamics, nourished by the formation mystery, tend to push us beyond this stage, no matter how effective and well integrated it may be. Formation is called to become transformation. Effective functioning should remain a basic concern. But, instead of dominating our life as a whole, functionality should become subordinated to and transformed by the mystery of formation that begins to manifest itself more explicitly in the transcendent phase of formation.

Summary of Functional Formation Phase

The functional formation phase is marked by a process that is similar to that of the formation of the former vital stage as temporarily dominant. It is a process of first initiating and then growing beyond this relative dominance. Under the influence of the overall transcendence and pretranscendence dynamics, the intrasphere keeps differentiating itself. Initially, newly emergent functional dynamics are central, if not necessarily totally exclusive. They are gradually decentralized as we relativize more our functionality and ready ourselves for the emergence of the functional-transcendent dimension. The current dynamics of each emergent higher dimension subordinate the dynamics of the lower dimensions. This makes them more subservient to the higher without taking away their specificity. What it does remove are their centrality, their temporal dominance of much of our life.

Between the ages of four and seven, we see a rather consonant managing dimension emerging and differentiating itself from the vital dimension. This dimension enables children to exercise increasing control over the vital facets of their life. They become also able to control in some measure the corresponding biophysical facets of their field. In service of this initial control, they learn to utilize simple, practical apprehensions, appraisals, and actions. Usually around the age of seven, concrete practical thinking in appreciative apprehension enables children to manage their lives in their surroundings with an increasing degree of effectiveness. This mode of thought prevails in the middle stage of formation of the functional dimension. Because functional modes as well as apparent modes of presence and action begin to develop, I conceive of this in my science as the initial functional-apparent stage of formation.

During the next adolescent phase of formation, another change occurs. The managing "me" begins to differentiate itself within the intrasphere from functional-appreciative apprehension and cognition processes. This enables adolescents to go beyond mainly "managing me" processes and to exercise some control over them from a higher functional-transcendent center.

During the initial stages of formation, the functional process was still bound to the lingual formation traditions that dominated their field. These traditions were communicated by functional language in which the child becomes increasingly proficient. In this final stage of current formation of the functional dimension, there is a first beginning of transcendence of field traditions under their merely functional aspect. The formation dynamics initiating the next dimension of transcendence will amplify and deepen one's independence from the relative dominance of functional-lingual apprehension and appraisal and their pretranscendent form-traditional moorings.

CHAPTER 20

Functional-Transcendent Dimension

There is no abrupt passage from the dynamics of a lower dimension to those of a higher one. Our initiation into the beginnings of a more explicit transcendent dimension of life gives rise initially to a new crossover phase. This phase is still functional, yet it is more explicitly touched by a nascent awareness of the deepest potency of human life, that of full and focal transcendence. I conceived this as the functional-transcendent dimension. I saw in my observations that the first pointers to it emerge during the functional phase if the conditions of life happen to be conducive to this passage. This first phase of transition can be roughly situated between the ages of twelve and twenty-one.

During that time, at some point, the transcendence dynamics of our supreme founding form of life begin to announce and assert themselves more explicitly in their uniqueness. They enable the intrasphere to rise more explicitly beyond its apparent forms without rejecting all of them. It is more a question of relativizing their dominating role in our life. We feel invited to subordinate their functioning to our evolving deeper personality. We no longer identify our pre-transcendent apparent forms of life uncritically with our unique identity. Instead, we purify, modulate, and integrate our functional appearances in the light of a growing consciousness of our true identity, our unique, transcendent calling. These apparent forms have made it possible for us to run our field of life effectively. They will always remain necessary for such managing, no matter how much they may have to be reformed or transformed in accordance with our inchoate transcendent awareness.

Dynamics of Detachment

Prefocally we begin to experience some difference between our apparent forms and who we may be called to be uniquely. This detachment entails a process of disidentifying with our functional appearances to create room for a new functional-transcendent awareness. This means that we are no longer so much inclined to identify ourselves uncritically with the functional-apparent forms that made us effective and acceptable to ourselves and others. We feel more free to modulate, subordinate, and integrate such forms under the canopy of our emergent personal-communal life call and project.

This crossover phase, provided we do not close it off prematurely, prepares us for an even higher form of disidentifying detachment. I mean a later detachment from the functional-transcendent dimension itself insofar as we mistakenly may appraise it as the peak of distinctively human character and personality formation.

Relative Consonance
of the Functional-Transcendent Personality

During this final stage of the functional phase, we may be able to integrate into a larger whole our diverse controlling functional and vital strivings. This leads to a higher form of consonance within our intrasphere. We begin to experience that the sphere of our interiority, in its depth, seems somehow to transcend the vital-functional expressions of our life. Our intrasphere becomes relatively consonant within itself. We see and accept that the powers of our lower-level strivings are too limited to fulfill the deeper aspirations that now come to the fore.

At the same time, our transcendence dynamic, in my observation, begins to prepare us to go beyond our now more integrated pretranscendent personality. This newly awakening tendency deepens our experience of personal autonomy in relation to our emergence thus far. Our managerial-transcendent dimension makes us sense a new hidden power. We experience that we can actualize our form potency in line with a transcendent life call. This call begins to be disclosed in a veiled and piecemeal fashion. As long as we remain in this crossover phase, the consciousness of transcendent personhood will be translated mainly in terms of vital-pragmatic effectiveness.

Blockage of Further Ascent

This experience of a beginning uniqueness and deeper self-disclosure can be exhilarating. I have repeatedly noticed how such excitement can be abused by the pride form. Our pride may exalt our newly gained power of control to the point of self-sufficiency even in spiritual matters. Such exaltation will block further ascent to the highest personality dimension itself. Full transcendence will leave in its wake an exclusive dominance by the managerial-transcendent dimension. If we block this path to full transcendence we may imagine that our relatively integrated pretranscendent personality itself, with its experience of lofty individuation and beginning transcendence, is the highest phase of formation. That will tempt us to stay encapsulated in this crossover phase. Our highest life directive will be a sublime but limited self-actualization or individuation, with perhaps a transcendent-aesthetic flavor.

This is unfortunately the fate of large numbers of people who strive after spirituality in Western societies. These societies are permeated by pragmatic, materialistic, vital-aesthetic, and gnostic traditions. They excel in categorical conceptualization, technical mastery, and aestheticism. They may celebrate the existence of a transcendent power in the human person. This latter awareness is kept alive by certain religious and humanistic form traditions that may not be able to help us escape totally the prevalent managerial, popular-communicative, and vital-aesthetic orientation typical of the West.

To gain attention and approval, persons thus captured may highlight the pragmatic-conceptual and vital-aesthetic formulations of these traditions. They may stress mainly the informational-theological, philosophical-categorical, the legal-practical facets of religious or humanistic regimentation of life. Laudable and necessary as these are, the transcendent-inspirational facets represented in the same formation traditions and in formation theology may be less frequently brought to one's attention. Such bankruptcy of the spirit may spell the decline of the deepest sources of Western civilization. It may turn its citadels of learning into "bottomline-driven" bureaucratic schools. These may prepare people for high-paying jobs, technical theologies, professional cleverness, but not for the wisdom of living and for the transcendent character and personality formation that accompanies and makes possible true transformative learning.

Fixation on Self-Actualization and Individuation

It has been my observation that many educational faith and formation traditions assume that the managerial-transcendent personality in its individuation and effectiveness is the spiritual end point of personality formation. In this view, the highest life directives become sublime autarkic self-actualization and integration of vital, functional, and aesthetic potencies. The importance of will and freedom are acknowledged, but they are seen as transcendent potentials and dynamics to be put in service of one's pragmatic-vital self-actualization or individuation, instead of the other way around.

Such educational traditions may believe and claim that they are fostering the actualization or individuation of the full spiritual potential of each individual. Yet, they seem to be unaware of the distinctive character of the transcendent potential of the human person. They do not apprehend appreciatively its absolute primacy and rootedness in the energizing formation mystery and in the consonant formation traditions inspired by this mystery over the millennia. They neglect the gift of the deepest transcendence—that of childlike full abandonment to the mystery in whose light all of life unfolds constantly. Neither is sufficient attention given to the corresponding potency of grateful appreciation of the pretranscendent personality without making it dominant and ultimate. This passing personality form should be seen as an intermediate step along the way; it is called to become a highly appreciated instrumental form of our transcendent life in and with the mystery that hides our founding life form, call, and project.

Desirability and Limitation
of the Functional-Transcendent Dimension

I conceived of this intermediate station on our journey as an important bridge to full transcendence. I value within my personality theory its lasting instrumentality as long as I see it subordinated to this peak dimension of the human personality. If our intrasphere remains encapsulated in our pretranscendent personality, it cannot enjoy the widest and most radiant horizon of human life.

The kinds of willing and freedom fostered by many educational traditions, if they foster them at all, rarely include as most profound our higher will. Central in our intrasphere should be the will to abandon ourselves in abiding attentiveness to the mystery and its forming will. This mysterious will should be the primordial source of our formation. Our deepest will to sacred surrender leads to the relativizing of any only partially transcendent, spontaneous, or pragmatic willing that restricts itself merely to the individuation of a functional-transcendent intrasphere.

Limited Use of Symbolism

What I conceived as the crowning dimension of the functional level of the pretranscendent personality draws upon formative imagination in a special way. It uses it to express the limited wholeness of only functional-transcendent individuation. Dreams, images, symbols, psychological archtypes, and myths are appraised as reflections of the lower, relative consonance of the neuroformational, vital, and control dynamics of the personality and its conflicts. In my view, each of these integrating myths, symbols, archtypes, or images appears as a concentrated, always-limited expression of our managing-transcendent life. These images include both focal and nonfocal facets. Often they are explained as only symbols of individuation, as pointers to the process of what I see as the limited integration of such focal and nonfocal elements of pretranscendent human existence.

Often such educational traditions foster a subtle prevalence of what is practical and vitally pleasant over the higher facet of this intrasphere. This manifests itself in the tendency to control—in service of pretranscendent wellness— what announces itself as a pointer to fuller transcendence. They try to make transcendent symbols and ideals the servants of our self-actualization, individuation, and feelings of comfort, possession, and aesthetic pleasure. Subtle autarkic control of spiritual unfolding is the result. A slightly noticeable, partly transcendent, self-centeredness begins to dominate life. It may give rise to theories and projects of sophisticated self-disclosure. Its dominating tendency expresses itself in a spiritual manipulation of relatively transcendent dreams, images, myths, meditations, bodily exercises, and symbols. The formative imagination enhances experiences that in a refined, often aesthetic and poetic way, exalt one's higher sublime self-actualization.

Formative Imagination
in the Functional-Transcendent Dimension

The transcendent imagery and image manipulation that I find typical of this phase should not be confused with the vitalistic image formation we have earlier disclosed in the initial infant phase of formation. Vitalistically oriented people may see these two types of phasic imagery as somehow the same. Such a falsification is rooted in the assumption, which I reject, that all dimensions are mere elaborations of the vital. In their view, transcendent phases represent nothing but a mutation of pretranscendent vital dynamics. This prescientific assumption tends to look for confirmation in ostensible yet shallow resemblances between the two kinds of imagery. I want to point out briefly some basic divergences between image formation in, respectively, the vital and the managerial-transcendent phases of formation.

One deceptive resemblance is the nonfocal quality of both vitalistic and functional-transcendent image formation. There is a basic difference between the two kinds of nonfocal imaginings. Vitalistic image formation is infra*focal* and infra*vocal,* while functional-transcendent image formation is relatively trans*focal* and relatively trans*vocal.* This means that both forms of imagination are not at will available to focal conceptualization and verbalization. This resemblance in availability does not take away my far more basic distinction between the infra- and the transfocal regions of consciousness elaborated again in this book in my formation anthropology of consciousness, so different from all other theories of consciousness.

The vitalistic process of image formation is dominated, moreover, by prefunctional and pretranscendent pulsions. It is not open to any verification by a critical awareness of the wisdom of formation traditions. Reason, as well as the appraisals implicit in language, and the affirmative and nonaffirmative power of the will are not yet available in the early infantile period of the vital phase. The infant's pulsions and the images to which they give rise cannot be reformed by these not yet sufficiently unfolded formation powers. One observes only a prelingual, vitalistic formation of the infant's impulsive existence. This infantile life is rife with fantasies of impulse gratification, of blind absorption of the as yet undifferentiated field of life, and of corresponding larger-than-life images. How different this fantasy life is from imagery coformed by the functional-transcendent dimension of this later phase of adulthood.

Transcendent Image Formation

The functional-transcendent personality can be appraised either as the end point or as the most important crossover point on our formation journey. If we consider it the ideal end point, the managerial pole will subordinate to itself what was only meant to be a beginning passage from domination by management to initial transcendence. Functional-transcendent image formation will be equally restricted. It will limit itself to the imaginative enhancement of our controlling-transcendent personality, as if this were the final stage of our life's journey.

Fully transcendent image formation should be a means to grow beyond our still mainly controlling stance in life, of entering into the simplicity of our second childhood. What began as the self-actualizing–transcendent dimension must gradually turn into the self-abandoned–transcendent dimension. In accordance with my newly invented distinction, this transcendent phase should then be followed by a transcendent-functional instead of the former functional-transcendent phase of formation. Then, as I see it, new formation dynamics will begin to emerge in which true childlike transcendence prevails as an end phase of personality unfolding. Its dynamics will affect our image formation. Unlike vitalistic image formation, transcendent formation is not body centered. Neither is it bound to quasi-spiritual, self-actualizing, or aesthetic achievement only. Transcendent image formation, if allowed free rein, serves the upward movement of the transcendence dynamic. It facilitates the emergence of childlike forms of presence to the mystery that complements and transforms our sociohistorical, vital, functional, and functional-transcendent forms of life.

Transcendence dynamics, if consonant, do not suppress but foster the indispensable, consonant unfolding of all lower dimensions. We always need these to imbibe and assess information about our world. This information feeds back into our new transcendent center of insight and decision. Such information makes it possible for us to incarnate our transcendent inspirations and aspirations effectively into all spheres of everyday existence.

I have observed how the form dynamics of this newly emerging phase initiate us, through transcendent image formation, in a transcendent view of life. We are given a first "cataphatic" or earth-inspired appreciation of the mystery as appearing in the sense-perceptible forms of our field. The term "cataphatic" has been used by many masters of the life of transcendent transformation. In the way I use this term, it refers to our appreciative apprehension of the transcendent mystery in and through sense appearances and images. In accordance with my view of epiphany, the mystery pervades our sense-perceptible field. It makes all forms light up as pointers to itself, to the "more than" that in my vision grounds and embraces our field of life as well as our personal call within it. As a result, our personal-communal field in its sensible concreteness becomes epiphanic for us, filling the senses of the new transcendent child with love and wonder. Its concrete appearances begin to reveal a certain transparency. What I conceive as the cataphatic transparency of the world of sense and image is the source and fruit of transcendent image formation, which itself too is a gift of the mystery.

Transcendent image formation implies a new mode of appreciative apprehension. The veiled depth to which this sensual cataphatic apprehension points is translingual and transconceptual. Transcendent knowledge cannot be attained by functional conceptualization and verbalization alone. Words and concepts can give only limited mental form to certain partial aspects of what reveals itself to transcendent experience as somehow unfathomable. We need a higher capacity of global apprehension that transcends the conceptually comprehensible facets of the mystery of the whole and Holy shining forth uniquely in each sensible form.

We are not immediately ready for the "apophatic" gift of highest reason or imageless transcendent intuition. Therefore, the first subdimension of the transcendent dimension of the life form is initiated by transcendent cataphatic image formation. Unlike conceptualization and precise focal verbalization, transcendent images point the new child to the mysterious whole and Holy in and behind all things.

Differences between Transcendent and Vitalistic-Functionalistic Image Formation

In my opinion, transcendent image formation differs from vitalistic and functionalistic image formation. They differ in their connotations. Vitalistic sense images are accompanied by bodily pleasures, strivings, and feelings during and after early infancy. Functional images can be either functionalistic or functional-transcendent. Images that are functionalistic are animated, in my observation, by the felt satisfaction that comes from our having actualized our functional potencies and ambitions. Functional-transcendent images are motivated by an unacknowledged need for self-pleasing self-esteem on this level. It easily degenerates into a subtle mode of spiritual narcissism or self-pleasuring aestheticism.

The transcendent images of second childhood are inspired by love for the transcendent mystery in its concrete, sensible epiphanies within our world. This transformative love is pure gift. It finds its fulfillment in self-forgetful childlike abandonment to the transforming dynamic of the mystery in which the new transcendent child increasingly participates.

Unique Nature of Transcendent Image Formation

I conceive transcendent image formation as a means to connect people with the epiphanies of the mystery in their perceived field of life. It is a first means of transition to the explicitly transcendent dimension of life. In my theory transcendent images are symbols that represent the beginning transformation of both the intrasphere and the other spheres of our life and of the birth of the new child in us. The meaning of all spheres and dimensions of our life is transformed in and through our transformed intrasphere.

This image formation signals the actual passage from the realm of pre- or preparatory transcendence, often implicit, to that of transcendence proper and explicit. The unique function I attribute to transcendent image formation gave me the key to my explanation why many spiritual formation traditions teach their participants how to open up in the light of the mystery to the gift of this image formation and its attending active visualization. To support transcendent image formation, formatively meaningful sayings may be meditated upon. At privileged moments, the meditator may be lifted beyond these sayings to the translingual depth of transcendent experience beyond all forms, thoughts, and images.

Similarly, I conceive of transcendent poetry as a creation of the transcendent imagination. It touches us most deeply through its hidden melodies, its imaginative metaphors, and, above all, through the silent spaces between its words. It stirs the spirit most by what is not said but pointed to. I see transcendent poetry in the great traditions as the evocation of moods that suggest unspeakable epiphanies in and beyond poetic imagery and melody. Transcendent image formation gives rise to images that are symbols of the mystery, of its epiphanies, and of our venturing out into its sacred presence, not by our own power but by the power of the Most High.

The human potency for transcendent symbol formation inheres in the founding form of human life from its inception. Emerging gradually in the empirical human life form, it brings to a first light the deepest source of our human formation field and its horizons. This source is the omnipresent radical formation mystery. Transcendent symbol formation is thus rooted in our deepest mode of appreciative apprehension, which is initially prereflective, prelingual, and prediscursive until it breaks out gloriously in symbol and metaphor.

Call of the Mystery
to Our Functional-Transcendent Intrasphere

Human persons are called to rise above their functional-transcendent intrasphere. They are invited by the mystery to let go of its illusion of self-sufficiency. They are asked to engage in a bold adventure of abandonment of their pretranscendent self. A first intimation of this invitation is the gift of transcendent symbolic image formation. This gift represents our being empowered by the mystery to take a first step on the way to disclosing the indwelling mystery as an explicit, lasting presence.

Willful symbol formation cannot force the experience of this mysteriously indwelling yet transcending ground of our founding form of life. We can neither evade nor compel it; we can only allow it to enter our consciousness in its own good time. Our transcending ground is always already present in our life from its very beginning. But it usually does not manifest itself first in the phasic manifestations of our empirical life formation that I have described so far. Generally it manifests itself later in life. This mysterious ground is absolutely first, however, in terms of its mysterious potency in the depth of our intrasphere. The radical formation mystery moves us through our transcendence dynamic to give form to its unique call for our life within our field of distinctively human character and personality formation.

Limited Unmasking of the Gross Ego
by Some Psychological Traditions

Psychological functional-transcendent faith and formation traditions admit in some measure this meaning of transcendent image formation. Because this imaging is not merely functional but also relatively transcendent, some so-called transpersonal psychologies are able to put into perspective the more obvious symptoms of dominance of the functional self. They try to overcome gross symptoms of exclusive functional control by their concept of either a more sublime ego and superego or of a "higher self." They neither accept the gross ego nor the gross superego as an exclusive norm of life's formation.

Unfortunately, not all of these psychological traditions disclose sufficiently the far more subtle and intimate facets of the partly spiritualized functional self. What they fail to unmask is not the gross ego but a higher, more refined functional-spiritual control center, still linked secretly, however subtly, to the autarkic pride form of life. These subtle ties may be almost invisible, or they may look like pleasant innocent links to mature selfhood. No matter how thin the string, it still prevents the flight upwards, that is to say, unconditional childlike abandonment to the inviting mystery.

Functional-Traditional and Transcendent-Traditional

Unlike our functional-transcendent dimension, our full and focal transcendent dimension is the supreme realm of our existence. It tells us how far our life call can take hold of us at any moment in time. Nevertheless, it is a dimension, for it is, at any point in time, only a limited expression of what we are uniquely called to become in time and space. This dimension is also limited because of its dependency on the other lower dimensions for its full and effective embodiment within our field of presence and action. As the leading dimension, it affects all others; it is basically translingual and transconceptual. It is also transfunctional and classical traditional.

Here I make a distinction between functional-traditional and transcendent-traditional. None of us can shake off the hold tradition has on our life. We have only to look at the way people talk, dress, cook, eat, and recreate to catch the inescapable power of tradition. Most of these examples reveal fully the practical facets of tradition, for instance, the many ways people perform the same tasks everyday. In any tradition, both facets—the practical-traditional and the transcendent-traditional—remain necessary. Without them, tradition would lose its depth cohesiveness and effectiveness. In an intrasphere that is transformed, the transcendent-traditional prevails. The transcendent facets of tradition enable people to put their ways of functioning into harmony with the transcendent meaning of their life as persons.

We become overly pragmatic if we manage our life only in accordance with the practical facets of our traditions. We then see and appraise things only in the light of their managing customs and categories. We do not make our own the transcendent meanings they carry within them as their hidden sacred source, their epiphanic depth.

We must give first place to the transcendent dimension of our traditions. Our personal presence to traditions sheds fresh light on the store of our life experiences and on those of our community. The narratives of these experiences unveil to us deeper treasures of love and wisdom. At the same time, they affirm the worth of our practical labors and struggles. We hail the necessary schematization of truths in rites and customs and in the ideological and theological conceptualizations traditions offer us. If consonant, they keep alive the enduring treasures of wisdom and experience that make us distinctively human and transcendently childlike. They make these classic treasures available to our formational evolution spanning numerous historical stages.

Transcendent traditions are in many ways the driving forces that deepen and widen our true effectiveness. The functional facets of tradition inform us; the transcendent facets transform us. Remember that every renewal of a tradition has its origin in a renewed assimilation of its sources.

CHAPTER 21

Preliminary Steps to the Transition to Transcendence

I n the previous chapter I explained how in my personality theory the functional-transcendent phase precedes the phase of transcendence proper. In the next chapter I will describe the passage from this phase to a state of life in which transcendence is dominant. For now I want to consider the preliminary steps that partly precede and partly accompany our passage to the transcendent state.

What do I see as the dynamics that lead up to this change? In what way do they affect our self-perception? How do they alter the appraisal of our call? What processes do they initiate that make us ready for this passage? To answer the latter question I would say that in my research I have found that the passage to the transcendent state of life consists of four steps:

Step One: People in the functional-transcendent phase of life feel inspired by the mystery of formation to go beyond this phase. In cooperation with the mystery, they strive to purge this phase from any remnants of dominance by self-centeredness. Functional-transcendence has formed their current personality in such a way that their functional striving is still too dominant. Now one becomes more sensitive to the inspiration of the mystery to submit this pattern of dominance to purgation—a decision that triggers a crisis of transition

Step Two: People in this crisis may experience events that awaken them to ways of purgation that may free them from residues of autarkic strivings. I call these evocative events. They evoke awe by new disclosures of a person's unique-communal life call by the mystery. This awakening generates also new insights into the hidden treasures of classical faith and formation traditions.

Step Three: Awakened people appreciatively apprehend the nearness of the mystery that invites them graciously to give up their attempts to live a spiritual life in great part by their own power of formation. The experience of such nearness sustains them in these preliminary steps that promise to purify and reform their personality. They grow in appreciation and acceptance of each new showing of the love of the mystery for them.

Step Four: People touched this way become conscious of a change in their self-apprehension. This leads to a reformation of their identity; it becomes less autarkic, more mystery oriented than self-centered. Their first childhood, with its subsequent remnants of pretranscendent childishness, begins to be replaced by a second transcendent childhood.

I want to reflect upon each of these steps in more detail so that the pain and joy of the transition to transcendence does not catch us unaware.

Disclosing Remnants of Autarkic Functionalism

The functional-transcendent phase of our journey threatens to encapsulate us in the illusion that we, by our own spiritual power alone, can enter the transcendent state of life. This threat is amplified when we share in movements that foster a spirituality in which functional means and methods prevail. Examples would be a quietistic, fundamentalistic, existentialistic, gnostic, New Age, Jungian, Rogerian, Eriksonian, Maslowian, or Lacanian type of spirituality. All of these approaches may admit in one way or another that there is some mystery with which we should unite ourselves. This confession points to what I have identified as the transcendent aspect of a functional-transcendent spirituality.

Close appraisal of such movements discloses, however, that they still expect too much from human efforts. Tests, devotional systems, literalistic explanations, ethical perfectionism, plots and tricks, psychological procedures—all are overly emphasized. Among such movements there are some that deny the existence of a personal, objective (not reified) transcendent. This domineering functional aspect has to be purified before we can hope to be lifted by the mystery into a transcendent state of life.

In that state the mystery itself will complement our preliminary purgation by its own cleansing fire. The more the functional dominates, the more we shall be alienated from the true transcendent. The invitation to curb such residues of psychological and spiritual functionalism evokes in us a crisis of spiritual identity.

Scholastic and Contemporary Meaning
of Self-Actualization

Any remnant of autarkic self-actualization that remains in the spiritual life is due ultimately to our autarkic pride form. Pride exalts our illusion of what we by ourselves alone can accomplish, even in the realm of transformation. I relate the pride form consistently in my work to its contemporary expression in absolutized self-actualization. I make a distinction between the actualization of our potencies, as described by scholastic philosophers, and the way in which self-actualization is described by such psychologists as Carl Rogers, Abraham Maslow, and Carl Jung, to mention only a few.

In my earlier writings I used the term self-actualization or personality fulfillment in the scholastic sense. Later, I often discarded such terms when I discovered that their popular understanding was not based, as mine was, on a personal-communal life call by a mystery independent of our human efforts. Instead, their concept of self-actualization was linked to an inflated self-concept. It fostered an excessive pretranscendent self-esteem, self-centeredness, self-interest, and self-originated value clarification. Such self-preoccupation distances us from the transcendent and from others. It dims the messages the mystery may send to us through the spheres, dimensions, and regions of our formation field. It diminishes our intimacy with the depths of our consonant faith and formation traditions. Residues of self-absorption, self-indulgence, and self-sufficiency cling to the control aspect of our managerial-transcendent personality. As long as they contaminate our heart, the mystery cannot lift us into the union of transcendent love endowing us with the gift of a second childhood.

Another drawback of popular absolutized self-actualization is its preoccupation with a proliferation of poorly grounded "spiritualities" and "therapies." They do not teach us how to nourish our heart with the age-old wisdom of consonant formation traditions. These classical traditions, insofar as they are consonant and mutually confirmative over the centuries, point the way to true transcendence. They are based on the experience of numerous acknowledged masters of the spiritual life in a wide variety of times and cultures.

Field Events Inspiring Purgation
of Autarkic Strivings

In step two of this transition phase, we are faced with events in our field of life that make us question if we are on the right path. Certain happenings make us aware of how autarkic our striving after the spiritual life really is. They inspire us to try to free our spiritual lives from their secret self-centeredness.

Our formation field is overlaid with profane traditions. They tempt us to seek frantically for pleasures, powers, possessions, prestige, and popularity. We may become locked in the grip of self-aggrandizing traditions. Some of these are consumerism, careerism, activism, secularistic humanism, and so on. We want a transcendent life. But we are not willing to place it first on a scale of appreciations inspired by a spiritual wisdom nurtured by ancient, time-honored traditions. We may fear this wisdom because it may mean letting go of, as ultimate, an accumulation of earthly security, wealth, status, and success.

Threatening and disappointing events serve to remind us of our vulnerability and contingency. The transforming mystery uses these events to tell us how dominant the pragmatic aspect of our transcendent striving still is. We are reminded that the functional dimension is the servant, not the master, of transcendent transformation. It should be purified and submitted to the transcendence dynamic. Our self-actualizing strivings, if made absolute, fail to grant us peace. This reminds us that transcendent happiness cannot be attained unless we are willing to end the domination of clever and pragmatic controls in our ambitious spiritual projects.

Something similar may be said of evocative events in our life that remind us of death. It reveals, as nothing else can, the end of pragmatic performance and success. We face our death or witness the death of a person dear to us. At such moments, the controlling side of our functional-transcendent dimension seems to weaken its grip on our life. The transcendent side gains ascendency. This shift in ascendency offers us yet another chance to begin to purify the self-preoccupied facets of our passage to transcendence. It prepares us for our elevation into the transcendent phase of our formation.

Awakening to a Disclosure
of Our Unique Transcendent Call

I mentioned under step two that the events in our field of life have the power to awaken us. They disclose something of our life call.

A transcendence crisis poses the challenge of a turning point in our formation journey. Each disclosure of our call can reform our apprehension and appraisal of what we may be called to be. It teaches us that our transcendent identity is different from our pretranscendent identity. The basis of our transcendent character and personality is our unique-communal life call by the mystery. Faith in its life-embracing power enables us to maintain a relatively coherent sense of our true identity. With faith, hope, and love we look in awe at the hidden depth of our transcendent call, our founding life form.

This call is only intermittently and partially disclosed to us over a lifetime. Faith in our deepest identity helps us to go beyond our sense of being only a wounded and disjointed pretranscendent self. We no longer allow that part of us to define us totally. We begin to experience the woundedness of our pretranscendent "I." This experience makes us ready to acknowledge the deficiencies of a life dominated by autarkic self-actualization. We long to be lifted by the mystery into a new childhood, obediently and humbly open to the transcendent in itself and in all its epiphanies in our everyday existence.

I believe that this preliminary move toward transcendence, and even our elevation to the transcendent state itself, should take into account my basic fivefold field paradigm of formation science. Our unique-communal life call is disclosed by directives continually emanating from this lived paradigm. From this field an ever-new awareness of our call emerges.

Our call identity is always relational and interformational. Its disclosure is related to and interforms with spheres, dimensions, and regions of our field of life. Because of this interformation, our life call is not static but dynamic. I purposely call this mark of distinctive humanness our transcendence dynamic. It is as basic a concept in my formation science as is my field model.

Our preparation for transcendent transformation implies detachment from any fixation on a carefully planned, secure, and seemingly unchangeable identity. It is my contention that we must flow with the partial, precarious, and usually only probable disclosures of our life call. Once we accept this reality, we realize that we will never be able to halt the movement of our call. This appreciative abandonment makes us more ready to receive the inspirations of the mystery. Such inspirations advance our passage to a fully transcendent existence. In preparation for this transformation, we must learn to listen ever more receptively to the mystery manifesting itself in our field of life and its consonant faith and form traditions. We must do so without trying to manipulate any transcendent message to suit our anxious self-preoccupation.

Preparation by Nearness to the Mystery

The third preliminary step consists of a growing intimacy with the mystery of formation. The mystery becomes nearer to us and we to it. This happens in and with our ordinary experiences. We begin to appreciate in a new way the events, people, and things that appear in our everyday existence. Together they form a mysterious ambience inviting us more and more intimately to true transcendence.

The changes we experience first take place in our inner sphere of life. Therein resides an unacknowledged hidden awareness of our intimacy with the mystery. This transconscious gift is a treasure hidden in what I have identified and named as the transfocal region of our consciousness. The difference now is that we become aware, however vaguely, of this gift. We let awareness of it seep into what in my theory is the prefocal region of consciousness. If we create spaces of stillness, our focal awareness may be touched by moments of inner intimacy arising from our transfocal consciousness via our prefocal consciousness. It does not come from a suppressed oceanic or symbiotic childhood feeling that some other personality theories speak about.

Such moments of intimacy with the mystery may be prolonged as we become more attentive to the inter and outer spheres of our field. We discover that they, too, are epiphanic showings of the same mystery. When transcendent intraformation prevails, our field as a whole seems to be illumined by our presence to the mystery. All its spheres and dimensions appear to us as consecrated or transformed by this presence. A deeper sense of awe begins to diminish the pride-filled taken-for-grantedness of functional-transcendent self-actualization. Our striving for absolute control of our inner spirituality, of our outer surroundings, and of the wisdom of consonant formation traditions appears now to us as a sign that we were trying to master the mystery instead of allowing it to master us.

A new abiding with traditions inspires our symbolic imagination. The evocative power of traditional transcendent symbols deepens the intimacy experiences welling up from our released transfocal consciousness.

Not only do traditional symbols begin to speak in a new way to our heart. All appearances in our field may become evocative. As I wrote in my book *Formation of the Human Heart,* volume three in this series:

> Examples of the latter are the love of a spouse or friend, the genuine respect of a student, the smile of a child, the peace and spontaneity of a consonant person, the beauty of a sunset, the fragrance of a flower in early spring, the mellowness of a sip of wine, the smell and taste of freshly baked bread. Each can be experienced as a trace of the all-forming mystery, which discloses something while concealing much more. Each disclosure is but a glimpse of the ineffability of the great presence that fills the universe, a glimpse that is at the same time a moment of discovery and of closure. . . . Inner enlightenment, the song of the bird, the scent of a flower, the love of people who really care, are epiphanic intimations. Each of them grants a specific form to our predisposition to receive the universal mystery in our particularizing awareness. Such formative intimations should be experienced as feeble pointers to the ineffable they symbolize (pp. 209–10).

Such symbols sustain our abiding in inner spaces of stillness. They give form to an awed receptivity that will be deepened as the mystery itself takes over our transformation. Its way immensely surpasses any attempt to attain spiritual self-actualization. This preliminary experience of awe readies us for the intimation of ineffable truths. These may be experienced once we are lifted beyond the threshold of self-actualizing spirituality into the land of likeness to the mystery itself. The more receptive we become to the evocative power of transcendent symbols, the nearer we are to the moment of transformation. Spiritual abiding will change our appraisal of the meaning of our functional-transcendent phase. We no longer see it as an individualistic end point of our spiritual striving but as a rite of passage.

The inward movement of our heart makes us enter a new, less managerial realm of our spiritual existence. Still, between such moments of intimacy with the sacred, we may find ourselves often in the throes of a crisis pertaining once more to the direction of our life call.

Transcendent symbols have been familiar to us for a long time. Now they begin to strike us in a way previously unknown to us. The windows of our powers of apprehension and appreciation are cleansed. At the right time we may be gifted with the innocent eye of a new childhood. It discloses to us the transforming luminosity of the mystery itself in the next phase of our journey. Our ardent attentiveness paves the way for our elevation into the transcendent light of the mystery.

Attention to the Present

Another preparation for this transition is our growing awareness that the mystery is with us at every moment of our lives. We begin to recognize the opportunity hidden in each "now" of our fleeting existence. We escape idle regrets about past events, anxious musings that arise from our fantastic phantom "I." Such endless rehashing of past events is counterproductive. It makes us less present to the opportunity of the here and now or of the task at hand. Our introspection is complemented and purged by a transcendent self-presence that implies a new awareness of the mystery addressing us in our daily doings.

Similarly, attentiveness to the present liberates us from superfluous worries about the future that sap our energy. We should use this newly gained, precious energy to prepare for the future. Our tomorrows are really linked with what we are thinking and doing today in the light of the mystery and our own consonant traditions. Formation in this kind of attentiveness prepares us for the presence of the mystery in each here-and-now moment. Then we can respond to its invitation to the next phase of transcendent participation.

Gift of Anticipation

In my fourth proposed preliminary step I try to summarize the process. Toward the end of the preparatory stage, the mystery may gift us with an anticipation of the transcendent state of life. Such inspiring anticipation functions as a herald of the elevation the mystery may grant us in its own good time. It instills in us a hope-filled receptivity, lived in humble abandonment to the sovereign will of the mystery.

No disposition is more desirable as a fruit of our detachment; no disposition prepares us better for the gift of the transcendent state of life than the gift of anticipation. It enriches us with a new sense of hope and spiritual potency. Awe-filled anticipation strengthens our resolve to discard the remnants of the domination of the self-oriented facet of our personality. It enables us to surmise new, probable disclosures of our personal-communal call. Such disclosures are now related to the hoped-for passage to the transcendent state.

Out of this hope arises a summons to give up control of our life by mastery alone. We are invited to replace self-centeredness with mystery centeredness. We are asked not to search for spirituality as the happy ending of a project of self-actualization but as a gift that cannot be compelled by our endeavors only. We cannot expect it; we can only hope for it. Tossing the anchor of our life into the bottomless harbor of hope, we find peace in a turbulent world. Our self-identification, now less linked with coercive dispositions for self-actualization, becomes more rooted in the mystery of our call. This call gains a depth that it may not have had for us earlier. It is experienced as a herald of an in-breaking, transcendent Other, a provisional showing of what is awaiting us in the state of transcendence.

In terms of my formation science, we become aware that the mystery is immediately present to us as the ground of our transcendent founding life form. We begin to contemplate this sacred ground of what we most deeply are. Our focal consciousness mediates this always already-present mystery, initially known only in our transfocal region of consciousness. The mystery itself will heighten and intensify this mediated knowledge once it lifts us in the state of transcendence.

Approaching the end of our preliminary phase, the mystery may already begin to grant us incidental moments of such intensified awareness, a foretaste of its future work of transformation. We experience the mystery more and more as a presence that we cannot master but that we should allow to master us. We sense that we will be drawn into a transcendent intimacy with the mystery once we enter the state of transcendence proper. We are being led to a path that will take us beyond the duality of a functional-transcendent life. We are moved toward a life of transcendence with functionality wedded to it, though in a subordinate manner. Our subsequent transcendent-functional life will be a union of likeness with the mystery without losing its own uniqueness.

The endpoint of this preliminary phase is a salutary disruption of our functional-transcendent existence. The disruption is a result of the mystery's gift of increasing dissatisfaction with the ambiguous, half-hearted type of quasi spirituality that is the disappointing outcome of functional control.

CHAPTER 22

Transcendent State of Life

The transcendence dynamic is at work in us continuously. It always invites us to advance. It takes time before we can hear this appeal constantly and respond to it accordingly. We wait and waver. Often we let our lower dynamics take over.

Our river of life may show wavelets of transcendence but not a steady flow. Transcendence is not yet a state of life for us. It does not yet transform all dimensions of our existence.

Bridge from the Functional-Transcendent
to the Transcendent State of Life

The last of the phases I discovered as preceding the state of transcendence I named the functional-transcendent phase. I saw it as a bridge between our pre-transcendent life and the state of transcendence. I discussed this connecting phase in the preceding chapter. Here I shall focus on the transition from the functional-transcendent to the transcendent state of life. I want to emphasize that the term "state" can be used in a pretranscendent context, too. In that case, it usually refers to a fixed and inflexible condition. The same cannot be said of the term "transcendent state," as I have introduced it. In my theory it does not exclude that we may at times stray from it. The dynamics of the lower dimensions may overtake us. We may fall back on a mainly pretranscendent outlook. The term "state" thus signifies only that such incidences become more and more the exception rather than the rule.

To live in the state of transcendence means that we increasingly give form to our life in the light of this highest plane of distinctive humanness. We regret it when we fall out of this state momentarily. Spontaneously, we try to restore it.

Neither does the term "state", as I use it here, carry in this context the connotation of "static." Sometimes I call it paradoxically, a state of dynamism. We are moved by faith, hope, and love into a transcendent involvement in our ever-changing field of life.

In this part of my theory, my term "transcendent" points to a "going beyond without leaving behind." While this new way of life is rich in moments of stillness and recollection, it does not imply retirement in transcendent isolation. One of the basic principles of my science is that we do not leave behind any consonant dimension of our existence. All are gradually taken up in our transcendent state; they are transformed in the light of our personal-communal destiny. What we leave behind is not these dimensions but our encapsulation in them, our imprisonment in the cage of a myopic, exclusively pretranscendent life.

Life dimensions are like swift-footed antelopes meant to roam freely with poised elegance in the wide-open spaces of nature. As long as these magnificent animals are kept behind the bars of a zoo, they cannot fully realize their destiny.

Similarly, the state of transcendence can be compared to a wide-open land of creative unfolding of all dimensions of our life. We release them gradually from their incarceration in any one of a number of pretranscendent boxes. We allow each dimension to be in its own right. Each has a role to play within our restored, original state of transcendent openness, often compared to a lost paradise. Even if we are called and empowered by the mystery to enter this paradise, we usually are not lifted there all at once. A period of transition from the functional-transcendent phase precedes our entrance into the blessed land of childlike transcendence.

Preparing for Transcendence

We may be ready to be led by the mystery beyond the stage of functional transcendence. The mystery calls us to enter the deeper regions of intimacy with itself and its manifestations in our life and world. In former stages the mystery called us to give form to a well-functioning pretranscendent "I." It inspired us to order our vital senses and passions by means of this lower "I." Through the same "I" it enabled us to make our pretranscendent life compatible with the consonant facets of the situations in which we found ourselves. Above all, the mystery empowered us to relate this lower "I" to our unique-communal life call, understood as different from projects of individual-collective self-actualization.

On the functional-transcendent level we felt fine. We were pleased with our accomplishments, proud of the power of our lower "I," enjoying our spiritual pursuits and their many consolations. Now the mystery of transformation brings us to the "so what" moment. So what if I have formed a firm pretranscendent "I." Is this all that I am? Is my whole being condensed in this lower "I"? Is there not more to me, more to my life? The mystery makes us experience that we long for more than what we are at present. It readies us to rise beyond the functional-transcendent phase of life.

In this process of preparation, we must be liberated from our merely lower self-esteem and pretentious individualistic values clarification. We cannot continue in our old ways if we want to respond to the invitation to go beyond. We are called to advance beyond our lower modes of communion with the mystery. We must break away from this former phase. If we fail to understand that the loving mystery of transformation itself is the source of this invitation, we may fall back on our former ways.

To move toward the state of transcendence is quite an undertaking. The mystery leaves us the freedom to opt for or against this arduous path, which starts out as a path of reformation. The option to take this road demands the courage of endurance. We must be ready to endure the suffering of reformation of our functional-transcendent phase of life by the mystery itself. It has to cleanse away the hidden remnants of subtle self-centeredness. A certain self-preoccupation still mars our spiritual life. Only appreciative, childlike abandonment to the mystery and its transcendent reformation can prepare us for the state of transcendence.

Abandonment to this radical cleansing and clearing means that we bear its suffering with patience. We put up with it as long as this is the will of the mystery for this stretch of our journey. We have no way to end this radical reformation by our own power alone. As long as we abide in this phase of total abandonment, we can only trust that the mystery will accomplish its transcendent conversion of our life in its own good time. It will clear away our inordinate functionalism by the burning and piercing light of its transforming love. Only then can the mystery begin the purgating formation of the new person. This purgation is deepened by an illuminating reformation of our newly formed dispositions. Past contaminations may still darken some of their splendor. Then, in the end, the transforming union with the mystery may be granted to us.

The Cave Trial

To describe what our minds and hearts have to go through, I want to use the imagery of voyaging through a long, dark cave. Out of the daylight of our functional-transcendent life, we are led by the mystery into this darkness. The entrance of a cave is still illumined somewhat by daylight. We are made aware at its shadowy entrance of how much our former spiritual phase of life is still marred by lingering attachments to self-perfection, power, status, and possession. As we allow the mystery to begin to throw off these shackles, we may be drawn deeper into the cave of radical reformation—first of the spiritual functionalism that has dominated our life. The further we are led into it, the darker it becomes. The light of the functional-transcendent phase no longer reaches us as it did when we dwelt in the shadows of the entrance. The stage of a painful purifying formation of new transcendent dispositions has arrived. This formation implies an urging of the past relatively consonant dispositions insofar as they are still mixed with impure addictions that interfere with the formation of the new transcendent ones.

Our functional mind, memory, and will, our imagination and anticipation, can no longer sustain us as they did in pretranscendent support of our former, transitional way of transcendence. The diminishment of their dominance enables the transcendence dynamic to make us ready for the hidden light in the core of our being, the pure light of our life call by the mystery.

This call is an invitation to open up in love to the intimate self-communications and empowerments of the mystery in its forming will and calling. Once we live as loving children in this light, it illumines for us all other dimensions of our life. Functional knowing will expand, but it will no longer dominate our days. Faith will complement it as a main source of inner illumination. At the same time, the wise and effective execution of our call implies a high development of our functional-vital powers in service of the wisdom of pure faith.

Guided further through the cave, we approach its exit. We catch a glimpse of the marvel of a glorious day. We begin to see the first play of light on the walls of the outlet of the cave. It symbolizes the dawning of our awareness of the source of our call or our founding life form. It could only now be disclosed to us in the light of a radically reformed faith. This gift of faith liberates us from the complacent pretensions of the lower "I." To perform this purge, the mystery led us into the darkness of the cave. Now the mystery can disclose to us that the mysterious caller at the beginning and the end of our existence is the Beloved with Whom we are called to be united in and through fidelity to our founding life form.

Threefold Path of Radical Formation

After much reflection, I concluded that the voyage through the cave traverses three stages. I name these the threefold path of radical functional-transcendent reformation, of radical transcendent formation, and of radical transcendent-functional transformation. The images with which I choose to symbolize my three phases are water, light, and fire.

For radical functional-transcendent reformation I use the symbol of the thunderous fall of a powerful stream of water. It relentlessly pulverizes the rocky deformations that make us lose sight of the deep, clear ground of our life call.

After the reformation of our rocky functional-transcendent hearts and matching characters, light has free play. The light of the all-forming mystery can now shine through the falling waters. It discloses to our awed gaze the hidden ground of the ravine of our heart. This light shows us how we are called uniquely to give transcendent form to our life in consonance with this deepest and most mysterious of calls by the Beloved.

The gifts of transcendent water and light make us ready for entrance into the land of transcendent-functional transformation through the fire of love ignited in us by our mysterious caller.

The threefold path thus aims at the disclosure of the deepest ground of our founding form or life call. This mysterious call reveals itself to us over a lifetime. The state of transcendence does not end this story of disclosure. To the contrary, it helps us to deepen its revelations.

Until our last breath we have to appraise the unpredictable disclosures of the mystery in and through the spheres and dimensions symbolized in my formation paradigm. Even after our voyage through the mysterious cave of radical functional-transcendent reformation, transcendent formation, and transcendent-functional transformation, new disclosures of the life call may confuse us. At such moments the functional-transcendent "I," even the vital "I," may try to take over again. Our basic state of transcendence disposes us to enter anew the same cycle, only now it has the character of a restoration of what was temporarily lost, a repentant reunion with the transcendent call and caller. Because the cave voyage has basically reformed and enlightened us, this restoration of a passing loss along the way will be shorter and less painful.

Entering the Cave

My metaphor of entering the shadowy entrance of the cave symbolizes for me the functional-transcendent reformation of the vital dimension of our life. To be sure, the vital dimension of our passions, senses, needs, and desires has been reformed during our pretranscendent journey. Much of it was done by ourselves in ordinary coformation with the mystery. We did not leave sufficient room, however, for the mystery to complement and deepen this reformation in extraordinary coformation. As a result, our vital energies did not consistently flow from and back to this endless sea of reforming and transforming love. We must go through the shadows of the cave so that the mystery of reformation can reform in depth our vital dimension. Without such a reformation, the way in which we live, vitally speaking, may be a hindrance to the unveiling of the deepest transcendent ground of our call to love. Hidden excessive attachments to vitalistic pleasures turn them into idols that obscure for us the "how much more" to which we are called. This does not mean that pleasure and fun are bad. They can be consonant showings of the mystery of loving formation. They point us to the source of all good things in life. Radical reformation of our vital dimension does not mean eradication of our passions, diminishment of our innate needs, or denial of our biophysical makeup. Transcendent reformation, as I outlined in the previous chapters on the vital dimension, means to radically reform its orientation.

As I have said repeatedly, the true root or foundation of our life is our basic life call or founding form. This gift is veiled by the pride form. Pride itself pretends to be the basic guide of our life. Arrogantly, it functions as our quasi-foundational life form. The weeds of pride poison the garden of our life. Pride imprisons us in anxious self-centeredness. Pride arrests the relaxed, humble pointing of our life call toward vibrant self-unfolding in the light of the mystery. Pride is entrenched in our fallen human condition.

During the functional-transcendent phase, our transcendent attunement grew, but traces of selfism still lingered on. Like termites, they hollowed out our orientation toward the mystery. As a result, our ignorance of transcendent formation was not yet fully remedied. Only a radical reformation of the way in which the pride form has contaminated our vital-functional life can reveal to us the attraction of things in their pristine origin and beauty without our being absorbed by them. In the functional-transcendent phase we are always tempted to turn the "little beyonds" of passing vital consolations into the "Great Beyonds" of full transcendence. Thus, the cave purgation was unavoidable if we wanted to continue our ascent to the liberating light of transcendence.

CHAPTER 23

Post-Transcendent Formation Phase

I showed how the mystery led us into the transcendent state of being through the cave of purgation. This is not the end of the journey. Transcendence lights up our call with new clarity. Now we are invited by the mystery to descend from the blessed heights of the undiluted experience of transcendence into the valley of faithfulness to everydayness. The mystery enables us to function effectively because of the brightness of our transcendent state. Our life is reversed from a functional-transcendent to a transcendent-functional abiding with all we do and endure.

This state is dynamic, not static. Usually we move upward. Yet, at times, we may find ourselves having to take a short and passing detour. We experience moments of falling back into functional-transcendent ways. It may happen when we are too involved in concerns of management and control. At the root of such failings are coercive dispositions, not yet fully eradicated. They re-emerge, evoked by our activism.

The solution to this problem should not be sought in an attempt to retire to an imaginary abode of transcendence unencumbered by the distractions of everydayness. We must resist entering the hazy gardens of quietism. Instead, we should abide with the marvel of consonant functioning in the light of the eternal. I introduced the concept of the post-transcendent period as one of growth in praise and in thanksgiving for our enhanced functional and vital effectiveness. We begin to enjoy in a new and deeper way thinking, talking, driving, writing, typing, walking, playing music, doing the dishes, making the beds, cleaning the kitchen, preparing a meal. We are able to give our best to what we do in and with the mystery that redeemed us from spiritual myopia. We may still lose at times our outward composure. Even our mind may get upset and disturbed, but the deepest point of our soul will remain in peace in the midst of it all.

Post-transcendent Life in the Marketplace
The transcendent journey of people living in the marketplace is different from that of people called to a solitary life in monasteries. That is why I have

tried to write several books on everyday spirituality in family, school, and public life. Many books on transcendence have been written by hermits or solitary gurus. Some writers lived as monks or nuns in Hindu ashrams or Buddhist monasteries. Others led a secluded life in Catholic, Eastern Orthodox, Episcopalian, or Protestant convents, such as Taizé. They wrote about the post-transcendent phase of formation on the basis of their own experiences and those of their directees—experiences colored by their solitary or monastic circumstances.

Laity and clergy today as well as members of active religious communities are exposed to a confusing acceleration of information, demands, needs, and controversies. The outer spheres of their field of action are loaded with seductive and coercive solicitations of vitalistic and functionalistic traditions. Their post-transcendent phase seems different from what they read about in these monastic writings. They experience the public life as a veritable geyser of distractions. A waterfall of diversions interferes with felt contemplative experience. Even a doctor of the Church, like Teresa of Avila, confesses candidly to her less than effective maintenance of the felt state of transcendent presence when her mission involved her in complex social situations. She tells us of an increase of imperfections during her tours through Spain to establish new convents, to seek support for them from church, town administrators, and generous donors. Still, she felt sure that God would forgive her for this interruption of her experience of intimacy with him in order to serve him in a more active way. She realized that distractions unavoidably accompany travels and campaigns.

How much more does this loss of touch with the transcendent apply to contemporary people! Our post-transcendent state of life should be marked by faith in the embracing love of the mystery, even if we do not feel the sensation of intimacy. The latter experience may have been ours when we entered the state of transcendence. When one exits a long and dark tunnel, one stands in ecstasy before the wide expanse of land and light that welcomes the errant traveler. At a distance, a sunlit city spreads before us. But when we enter the bustling town we find ourselves in its winding streets clogged with crowds and traffic. Driving through the maze of vehicles and passersby, we lose the exuberance we felt when we exited the tunnel.

Conditions for the Post-transcendent Life
in Contemporary Society

What are the conditions for living a post-transcendent life for ordinary people today? To disclose what these are, we must take into account the insights developed in former volumes of this series. I situated our transcendent journey within the parameters of my 1944 field paradigm. Let me apply these insights to the post-transcendent phases of our journey.

I hope my remarks will contribute to the spiritual awakening now taking place in numerous groups of people around the globe. The science of formation is a science of the living way to peace and joy as gifts of the mystery. To show how it can clarify the conditions of post-transcendent life, I must take a brief detour to relate the history of what I call informational and formational theology. By so doing, I hope to clarify how formation science can be related to formation theology without losing its basic distinction and relative independence from the discipline of theology as such. Analogously, Thomas Aquinas related his pre-Christian philosophy to his informational-speculative theology.

When we grasp these distinctions, we begin to understand how pretheological formation science can deal with certain universal elements of post-transcendent life formation. It does not yet have to articulate them in a Christian or any other theology of formation.

Most of us have only heard or read about the transcendent life in the context of a particular theology, be it academic or popularized, formative or informative. We may feel uneasy, confused, and resistant when we read or hear about these matters in a pretheological context. Our state of mind could be compared to that of a new seminarian interested in learning about an intimate life with Jesus in a pastoral context. Instead, he is told to take two years of philosophy. If the staff does not explain the necessity of this pretheological phase, the seminarian may be disappointed. He may wonder why he has to take this course of study prior to that in systematic informational theology. As he soon learns, without this preparation in rational understanding, his ability to grasp the theology curriculum would be limited, to say the least.

Formational Theology and Informational Theology

My experience with Christians and adherents of other faith traditions hiding with me during the occupation of Holland at the time of the Second World War, and especially during the Hunger Winter, compelled me to initiate the following distinction. I sensed in myself and others the influence of two basically different types of theology.

The war had lifted me out of the seminary after finishing the third year of my theological studies. Without preparation, I was plunged in the midst of Dutch men and women struggling for survival, physically, psychologically, and spiritually. The excellent theology courses at the seminary had enriched my mind with profound information about my faith tradition. I soon found out that teaching this treasure of learned information by itself was not sufficient to help people cope transcendently with their anxieties, hunger, hate, rage, envy, frustration, and guilt.

I had to fall back on what I had read, learned, and reflected upon in a pre-seminary year of spiritual instruction and direction, on my readings, prayers, and meditations. This year, the novitiate, preceded the entrance of candidates in seminaries of religious communities. The staff of the novitiate did not concentrate on professional informational theology nor on its praiseworthy attempts to outline new doctrinal formulations and their attending controversies. The novitiate began with and returned to the foundationals of our faith tradition. These were already an integral part of authoritative church doctrine. The main emphasis during this year, however, was on how to give form to the basic faith doctrine in our daily inner and outer life in the light of classical formation traditions. The staff focused on our religious and spiritual living, on our transcendent life formation.

Curiously, once I entered the seminary itself I found no systematic courses in spiritual formation listed in the curriculum. What was there were mainly philosophical and informational theological courses. Providentially, my personal interest in formation had made me an avid student of each issue of the highly regarded French journal *La Vie Spirituelle* (The Spiritual Life). I studied any spiritual master and any book on spirituality in Dutch, French, German, or English I could find. I say "providentially" because I soon realized in my hiding place that these were sources whose formational wisdom could be adapted in my responses to the people who confided in me about their despair, anger, and guilt, their fearful facing of deportation, death, or famine. Elementary doctrinal information was necessary for them, too, but extensive informational-rational theology of a professional academic nature seemed less directly relevant to their distress at this moment. My interest in information-experiential theology was deepened by a soul friend whom I knew since I was thirteen years old, in the boarding school we both attended. This friend was granted the full journey to transcendence up to transforming union when he died at the early age of twenty-two as a first-year student of theology. His life and words were for me an introduction to my formative theology and formation science, which I began to develop two and a half years after his death.

Informational and Formational Theology

The war experience made me introduce a distinction between informational and formation theology. I came to the conclusion that both basic types of theology are necessary to maintain in a balanced and wise way any religious faith and formation tradition.

Rational informational theology researches and teaches systematically what can inform the human mind as to the content of the faith tradition. This type of theology can be innovative, intellectually daring, and creatively controversial. It can propose to the legitimate authorities of a faith tradition new, probable ways of intellectual interpretation of the faith. Such proposals may or may not be assimilated in its authoritative doctrine.

This type of theology applies its intellectual methodology also to the basics of spirituality. Logically, historically, theoretically, and systematically, it clarifies their relationship to doctrine. Its methodology is not sufficient, however, for the critical appraisal of many detailed empirical-experiential conditions and dynamics of the transcendent formation of people in their concrete fields of life. In that area, informational theology has to be complemented by the other basic type of theology I call formation theology.

Formation theology is about the empirical-experiential implementation of basic doctrinal and moral propositions into one's character and personality formation and into one's life situation in the light of classical formation traditions that are consonant with foundational doctrine. This theology examines the transcendent forms groups and individuals give to their life of faith in the concrete, everyday unfolding of their character and personality and in their interaction with other formation traditions in their societies.

For example, two saints and doctors of the Church, Catherine of Siena and Teresa of Avila, spoke or wrote profoundly about spiritual formation, especially in the post-transcendent phase of life. None of their counsels or treatises touched in depth upon the controversies that dominated the informational theologies of their day. They were called to be doctors of the Church primarily in the realm of formational-experiential, not informational theology.

This short introduction to the distinction in question readies us for the detour I want to make into some aspects of the history of both informational theology and formation theology. This will help us to examine the conditions that are relevant to the post-transcendent formation phase.

Formationally Relevant Aspects of Theologies

In the thirteenth century, Thomas Aquinas devised a pretheological philosophy. He brought together the intellectual coformants of a systematic knowledge of, among other topics, transcendent human nature. While devising this philosophy, he had to put into brackets, as it were, the Christian revelation.

Synthesizing the best information he could find about human nature as human in the philosophies available to him, he composed in due course his own philosophy that from the start was compatible, but by no means identical, with the Christian revelation. Later, he articulated this philosophy in his informational-speculative theology.

What Aquinas did for speculative-practical informational theology, I have tried to do for empirical-experiential formation theology. I complemented pre-Christian philosophy with a pre-Christian empirical-experiential science of transcendent life formation. As Aquinas drew critically and creatively on the philosophies of the time available to him, so I began to draw in 1944 on the empirical-experiential aspects of formational wisdom traditions. Only secondarily and critically did I take notice of the formationally relevant data and insights of sciences and disciplines available to me at this moment of history. I made them serve the wisdom of classical traditions. I also took into account, in the light of all of the great traditions, empirical formation events and experiences in my own life and that of others, past and present.

As a coherent system, formation science is new. Many of the coformants, however, that make up this living way of transcendent formation have been tried and tested for thousands of years. More recently, empirical-experiential disciplines have also researched certain pretranscendent aspects of the journey.

Thomas Aquinas considered in a critical way the contributions of philosophers preceding him before articulating their relevant findings in his speculative informational Christian theology. Similarly, I appraise critically the relevant contributions of empirical-experiential disciplines from the viewpoint of consonant transcendent formation. Only after that step can they be adapted responsibly and uniquely to any religious or ideological formation tradition. This method applies especially to my consideration of the post-transcendent phase of life.

My vision can become a reality only if I continue to stand on the shoulders of masters and researchers of the numerous formation traditions whose cumulative wisdom can never be dismissed. They lived in vastly different historical periods and cultures. Many of them generated basic insights into the conditions and dynamics of consonant transcendent formation. I found that a number of their insights were similar or mutually complementary to my own. Besides being a constant inspiration, they also play an important part in my own spiritual growth.

Historical Unfolding of the Post-transcendent Life

Let me now return to my reflections on the post-transcendent life. At present, such reflections represent a survival measure for the human spirit. Civilization, as we know it, is increasingly power-based, bureaucratically organized, and functional-economical. Progress in modern society depends on pragmatic perceptiveness, ingenuity, accomplishment, or clever politicking.

People of old held more openly to beliefs in a formation mystery. They expressed these sentiments in a variety of forms of worship. With the growth of modern civilization came an overriding esteem for the development of functional skills and achievements. The transcendent knowledge of higher reason, the wisdom of the heart, the perceptiveness of our senses as transformed by the human spirit, the treasures of classical traditions became less and less appreciated. The result was a lack of balance in human existence. A onesided functionalistic bent caused life to lose its spark, its harmony and consonance with the mystery. Exclusive concentration on informational sciences and theologies can dry up the human heart and the power of symbolic imagination. On the other hand, exclusive concentration on the formation approach would be as problematic. Such a onesided approach could weaken the rational, logical, systematizing, informational coformant of these disciplines and through them of life itself.

As I have recurrently stressed in this volume, the problem of Western culture is its functional preoccupation. We need personally and as a people to pay more attention to the transcendent-functional phase of the human journey. We need to know the conditions of the post-transcendent formation of those who participate in the public life of a functionalistic society.

Transcendent peace and effectiveness depend on our tuning in to all spheres of our field of life. The radiating center of this field is the mystery, which is at the heart of our daily actions and interactions. This field itself involves our being faithful to our inner personal-communal life call. It suggests reasonable compatibility with the people around us, with our environmental life situation as well as with our wider global and cosmic surroundings.

Neuroformational Anger, Fear, and Attention Dispositions

Transcendent perceptiveness, wisdom, and consonance are the sentinels of a transcendent-functional life. Even if we live by these virtues, we may be surprised by sudden eruptions of incompatible feelings. Reflecting on my concept of the neuroform, I realize that this form may still harbor unacknowledged dispositions of anger and fear. Bouts of anxious functionalism and uncontrolled vitalism may at times get the best of us. We may experience pretranscendently and automatically feelings of alienation, threat, or paranoia when interacting with others.

To cope with this danger, we have to become gently and prayerfully aware of the direction our power of attention tends to take. Is our neuroform secretly directing our attention to dissonant projects that diminish our presence to the sacred? What if we have no immediate control over such neuroformational coercive dispositions?

We may feel painfully reminded of the anonymous directions our power of attention is inclined to take. For example, we may find ourselves inclined to be on the outlook for any irritating behavior of others toward us. Our deformational imagination magnifies these little insect bites. They may appear to us as mean as the attacks of barking dogs. If such a distortion of reality remains constant, dissonance results. We experience less available energy, insight, and joyful appreciation (see Adrian van Kaam and Susan Muto, *The Power of Appreciation: A New Approach to Personal and Relational Healing* [New York: Crossroad, 1993]).

The transcendent state of life does not liberate us at once, as if by magic, from such deep-rooted tendencies. It grants us new light and strength, which ought to assist us in the gradual disclosure of the hidden sources of such deformational attentiveness.

On the pretranscendent level of life, we may have been conditioned to respond with paranoia, irritation, or oversensitivity to any threat of dissonance. Now, in response to our ongoing post-transcendent transformation, we may gradually evolve more instantaneous perceptions of consonance, epiphanic love, and compassion. A more appreciative understanding of people and of what happens to and around us may result. The transcendent light granted to us by the mystery is like a laser beam that can cut the link between the coercive dispositions of our neuroform and our paranoid pretranscendent dispositions. The latter may still slumber in us as potential seeds of disturbance and dissonance. The freeing grace, symbolized by this beam, restores us to the way of full realization of the transcendent gifts the mystery granted us when we emerged from the cave of purgation.

The gift of transcendence helps us in the post-transcendent phase to remedy the pretranscendent coercions associated with our neuroform. Insofar as the neuroform has become coercive, it tends to make us regress to deformational pretranscendent dispositions. As we enter the phase of transcendence, the mystery grants us new light and power, which protects us against paranoid dissonant individualism. When the transcendent state takes charge of our life, it liberates us slowly but surely from our coercive neuroformational dispositions. The neuroform is then disposed by the mystery to generate spontaneously appreciation, charity, clarity, and loving attentiveness—all sources of transcendent consonance.

If we follow the way of epiphanic appreciation, it will keep us in touch with the mystery and show us how to live more in transcendent than pretranscendent attention. The mystery will teach and inspire us to rise above coercive dispositions and their residues in our neuroform. It will enable us to abide here and now in a deeper joy that goes beyond pretranscendent understanding. Joy of spirit keeps on glowing in the center of our being, even in the midst of misunderstanding, disappointment, pain, and suffering.

Remnants of Lingual and Other Form Traditions

As I indicated in volume five, *Traditional Formation,* human life forms are not endowed with a full repertoire of automatic neuroformational reactions. Animals are dominated by inflexible dispositions or instincts directing them through their ready-made fields of life. By this I mean that they automatically evoke in animals appropriate corresponding vital reactions. Humans lack such instincts, but go far beyond them. Unlike animals, we share together with others the wise directives of age-old form traditions. We can place these in dialogue with our higher intelligence and creative imagination, both of which are lacking in animal life.

Because of this dependency on tradition, children cannot start the human formation journey on their own. For a number of years they have to rely on forms of effective human living taken over from their family traditions. This long period calls for a remarkable formational plasticity. It opens children to the assimilation of complex directive patterns of speaking and living sedimented in formation traditions as appropriated by their family or guardians.

The fluid interformation of form traditions, flexible intelligence, and imagination enable us to survive and prosper without the fixed directives we observe in animal behavior. This long nurturing period lets us learn complex language systems that carry the wisdom and experience of traditions developed by generations over centuries or even millennia. Our flexibility is such that we can appropriate already as children a veritable treasure of lingual directives, provided we are constantly exposed to them, be they in English, Dutch, Danish, Swahili, Greek, Russian, or any other tongue. The state of transcendence does not destroy such lingual traces in our nervous system. Thus the post-transcendent phase is characterized by different features in people of different language backgrounds.

Pretranscendent reactions can be deeply rooted in our vital makeup. As young children, we develop what I identify as pretranscendent *"I"-mechanisms*. We use these automatically to protect ourselves against any real or imagined threat or demand emanating from the situation in which we find ourselves. Our senses convey these challenges to our lower *"I"-mechanisms* through our neuroform. Once triggered, they evoke vital feelings and coercive emotions that may amplify and intensify our need for self-protection, our sense of alarm and suspicion, our marshaling of defenses. Growth in the post-transcendent phase depends on freeing ourselves from the last vestiges of dominance of our pretranscendent "I" and its defensiveness.

Reviewing the Journey

As I have shown, our pretranscendent attentiveness is directed by our lower "I." I hypothesized that this "I" develops a set of dispositions which it relates to the neuroform. Such secondary neuroformational dispositions can be flexible and subservient to our transcendent will and life call, or they can be coercive. If such is the case, they can control independently and automatically dispositions of our pretranscendent "I" as well as its subsequent acts and attitudes.

Central among coercive dispositions are those of paranoid, egocentric self-protection, defensive vigilance, relentless striving for power and control, and inordinate vitalistic pleasure seeking. These dispositions use the powers of the lower "I" and of lower functional reason coercively to advance pretranscendent designs. They compel us to rationalize the use of any means that foster the aims of our coercive neuroformational dispositions. For example, we may select and guard dissonant aspects of our pyramid of formation traditions and our individualistic interpretations of them.

When the mystery lifts us into the phase of transcendence and further into the phase of post-transcendent formation, we find ourselves at a new place. During our journey through the cave of purgation, we were liberated already from many coercive patterns of life. We were the recipients of transcendent light and strength. We were empowered to disclose the infrafocal, depreciative, coercive dispositions still operative in our neuroform and lower "I." The mystery enables us to find and eradicate these coercions. Gradually, it replaces them with appreciative flexible dispositions. These expand and deepen the flow of our transcendent journey in consonance with formation events in our life. We appreciate them as epiphanic expressions of the mystery, as opportunities for formation of self and others.

Influence of Neuroformational Dispositions on Transcendence

Through prolonged observation and reflection, I came to the conclusion that coercive neuroformational dispositions can still influence our vital dimension and pretranscendent "I" in spite of our transcendent state. The post-transcendent phase challenges us to disclose these hidden land mines in our field of life. Once we pinpoint them, we have to detonate their explosive power. Daily we grow in competence in this search-and-dismantle mission. Additional understanding of the neuroform and its function will help us in this regard. Such insight benefits not only people in the post-transcendent phase of life; it can also help those in preparatory formation phases. From the experience of those advanced on the path, they can learn of the general direction it takes.

The neuroform is the base of our vital dimension. We should learn to use it as a flexible instrument for the expression of our life call. The challenge is to "play it" consonantly. Its music should be in tune with the directives of the radical mystery, as well as of its servant, the cosmic mystery. Both give form to our life in intimate collaboration.

Transcendent maturity is marked by an awe-filled sensitivity and perceptiveness. Awe opens us to the showings of the mystery in all the spheres and dimensions of our field of presence and action. The input of our field of life can only reach our mind and heart through the neuroform. This form can manage countless visual and auditory messages at any one moment. It works around the clock, utilizing all the enigmatic coformants that comprise its amazingly complex structure. These enable the neuroform to make millions of concurrent computations instantly. This vast performance takes place primarily in the infrafocal region of our consciousness. Only a minimal part of its operation is available to our prefocal, and far less than that to our focal, region of consciousness.

Our pretranscendent sphere of life can be used by us as an instrument or tool to embody effectively the inspirations of our transcendent state. Transcendent effectiveness demands that we learn how to turn our neuroform and its controls into obedient servants of our life call. The mystery discloses this call not only inwardly but also in and through the consonant demands of the spheres, dimensions, regions, ranges, and ranks of our field of life. Sensual impressions containing possible directives for our life enter our neuroform. There they are selected, collected, discarded, arranged, and rearranged into a serviceable constellation of stimuli consonant or dissonant with our transcendent life direction.

The radical mystery gave form to its servant, the cosmic mystery. It enabled this cosmic power to develop our immensely refined neuroform during millennia of formative evolutions and through numerous generations of human forms of life. How could we not feel awe and gratitude in the face of this undeserved gift? The mystery of forming love granted us a remarkable intermediate instrument of field management. Under the command of the radical mystery, it is meant to assist us in improving life for ourselves and others as well as for the earth and cosmos entrusted to our care.

Deformative Style of Neuroformational Suffering

Unfortunately, our autarkic pride form threw this vital compass off its assigned course. Humans suffer from a deep-rooted original deviation, already manifest at the start of our pretranscendent life. It is the ultimate source of paranoid fears, excessive pleasure seeking, and anxious, overprotective, depreciative dispositions. These are the breeding ground of deformative pretranscendent pains and stresses. They diminish the powers of our immune system. They make us more vulnerable to sickness and depression. Our neuroform may have been wrongly disposed early in life. As a result, it records mainly events that evoke depreciation and dissonance. The transcendent state teaches us that every formation event should be appreciated as an opportunity for growth in peace, joy, and loving appreciation in the midst of the purifying suffering which formation entails.

The post-transcendent phase of life shows us how we may have given form to depreciative dispositions. Some of them may have survived the cave of purgation. How to break out of these last dormant traps, during the post-transcendent phase, will be disclosed to us by the mystery when we live in fidelity to its inspirations.

Potency of Praise

Let me now focus on the abyss I observed between beneficial purgative suffering that is profoundly formative—if we accept it appreciatively—and the wrong kind of suffering that is always deformative. Deformative suffering is the poisonous fruit of coercive depreciative and dissonant dispositions. It defeats our call to peace and joy.

I have often seen that even beneficial suffering can be accompanied by the deformative coercive suffering of dissonant and depreciative dispositions. These cloud the picture. They tempt people to reject beneficial suffering altogether rather than only suffering that is coercive and deformational.

One great task of the post-transcendent phase is to transform such coercive neuroformational dispositions for deformational suffering. They defeat our potency for giving joyous praise to the mystery from the depth of our vital being in the midst of formative suffering. Our transcendent state is the potency for continuous spiritual joy, serenity, vibrant courage, wisdom, and perceptiveness in the thick of overwhelming odds, displeasures, and dissatisfactions.

We should allow the mystery of transformation to activate in us to the full the gift of our potency-to-praise. Post-transcendent formation teaches us how to overcome interruptions of this activation. It discloses the remnants of faulty dispositions of our neuroform, which can be the hidden source of such interruptions. It lays bare the links with the pride form that are at work in us from the beginning.

Coercive depreciative dispositions make it difficult for us to appreciate our field of life at all times as a friendly place. By contrast, the mystery makes it possible for us to let every event in that space serve our transcendence joyously. Once we rise above our coercive dispositions, all of our field will be bathed in a new light. No event will be experienced any more as merely an irritating, excruciating, or indifferent coincidence. We enjoy to the full the faith that the mystery arranges everything for us so that it can deepen our love, peace, and appreciative abandonment. There are no coincidences, only providences.

Transcendent-Functional Phase

I introduced my notion that our post-transcendent phase of life is transcendent-functional instead of functional-transcendent. I related to it another concept of mine, that of the neuroform as formed in part by will and mind selection. Our functional mind may have been disposed to be coercively selective. It trained our neuroform to pick from incoming stimuli only those that fed into its coercive, inflexible, neuroformational dispositions. These are at odds with the always changing disclosures of our life call. They rupture repeatedly our consonance with changing people, events, and things.

For example, the neuroform of the paranoid, autarkic "I" zeroes in automatically on possible signs of depreciation and dissonance and fastens itself to them exclusively. It selects and presents them as the only relevant messages among the millions inundating its system at every moment. Such an exclusively negative selection stunts transcendent love. Deceptively, the functionalistic "I" imagines that it lives by sharp vision, clever judgment, and admirable self-protection. The transcendent-functional phase summons us to discover and destroy these illusions that represent the last outposts of the dominance of functionalism over our life.

I found that this change in our neuroformation can only happen through a change in both our focal and prefocal regions of dispositional attentiveness. They have to be inspired by epiphanic love. Such love has about it the miraculous quality of deepening beneficial suffering. At certain moments, it may fill our hearts with a peace and joy that surpasses any pretranscendent understanding.

Much more will be said about this topic when I complement my pretheological approach with my formation theology in volume eight of this series.

CHAPTER 24

Specific Challenges
of the Post-Transcendent Life

In the former chapter I discussed my observations of pretranscendent attachments and how they may still affect our post-transcendent life. I also looked at the concept of coercive dispositions, admittedly in a more general than in a more specific way. That is why in this chapter I want to focus on specific dispositions related to our post-transcendent life, such as those of peace, joy, compatibility, and compassion. My reflection will set the stage for a discussion of how to deal with remnants of the past I often see emerge in people while transformation is occurring.

Dispositions of Attention and Direction

I see as many dispositions in human persons as there are people who live them. One of the central dispositions in all people, however, is that of attention. Different people may direct their attention to different things. A novelist may be attentive to the characters of people she meets at a party. A social psychologist's attention may be drawn by the interaction between members of a group. A gourmet may savor food and drink, with less attention to conversation.

Different types of interest point to different life-directive dispositions. These give rise in turn to corresponding kinds of attention. Such "attention dispositions" play a foundational role in our character and personality formation. They make us select what goes into our sense perceptions, imaginations, memories, thoughts, and anticipations. Attention dispositions to this or that person, event, thing, idea, image, or tradition may have been inserted already at an early age into our neuroform. What happens then?

Coercive Dispositions

Before entering fully into the transcendent stage of life, we may have developed certain dispositions of direction and attention that were and still are deformational. These may have become neuroformational, not in a flexible way but in a coercive manner.

For example, we may have disposed ourselves to strive after individual safety and security at any price. Or we may have focused mainly on sensual gratification. Perhaps perfect control of life and world was the main focus of our striving and attention, to say nothing of the dispositions for popularity, power, status, and possession.

Such dispositions, if coercive, generate endless struggles for security, fame, fortune, and education that steal our peace and joy. They diminish our capacity for loving compatibility, compassion, and courage. Expecting too much from these coercive strivings, we plant in our heart a tree of illusions. Its fruits are bitter. They fill us with worry, suspicion, and irritation. True or imagined opposition to those of our ambitions that have become coercive nourishes in us a hidden hostility. When others outdo us, we feel devoured by envy. Threats to our excessive security dispositions lead to anxious withdrawal. Discrimination fills our heart with creeping resentment. Some of these or other past coercions may still survive in secret corners of our neuroform in spite of the post-transcendent blessings we have received.

Disillusion in the fulfillment of such dispositions opened us to the path of a more transcendent life. A crisis of disappointment compelled us to appraise our unhappy state. For example, we may have amassed lots of money or collected honors, degrees, and awards. Perhaps we advanced spectacularly in our careers. It was wonderful to succeed, until the bitterness of disappointment soured our taste for life. At such down moments we may have felt drawn to look inside ourselves.

We found that we were not growing in dispositions of love or empathy with others, of compassion or compatibility. Still, for a time, we felt on top of things in the world around us. Our outer appearance was that of the self-made man or woman, seemingly at ease and proudly secure. But an anxious question gnawed at our heart, Are we really content inside?

What prevents peace and joy from taking root in our hearts? The cause cannot be traced to missing things we would like to have. Things by themselves do not make us unhappy; our coercive strivings for them do. That is what makes us hoard things and hurry time. That is what keeps us from savoring the surprises of life the mystery inspires us to enjoy.

Compulsive striving carries the hidden fear of collapse and failure. We envy those who pass us by on the ladder of success. It makes us feel upset when someone criticizes us or puts us down. If our projects fail over time, we become cynical. When tedious work does not pay off in the results for which we strive, we feel bored. We lose interest.

Briefly, coercive strivings defeat our chances for happiness. Our journey is not relaxed, joyous, peaceful, wise, and effective. We feel falsely that fulfillment of our coercive dispositions is an absolute must if we want to be happy.

The mystery led us through the cave of purgation. In its darkness it readied us for growth in the joy of transcendence. It showed us the futility of embellishing or pacifying our life by our own efforts alone. It made us aware of our attempts to make situations fit coercive longings instead of flowing with them as formation opportunities.

Before entering the cave of purgation, we had reached the functional-transcendent phase of our journey. There our self-centeredness did not wholly disappear. It became refined and "spiritualized" in subtle and sometimes insidious ways. Many transcendent thoughts and feelings were genuine, but others were a camouflage for self-enhancement.

In the cave of purgation the mystery of transformation weaned our senses and spirit away from coercive attachments. In principle, it liberated us from the dominion of pretranscendent coercion. It let a new light shine in our heart. The eyes of our transformed heart could now see the remnants of many of our pre-transcendent attachments. We were set on the path of implementation of a new state of life.

Traditions and the Post-transcendent Phase

Why is the post-transcendent phase more difficult for people today than it was for those who lived in monoformational, homogeneous civilizations? To answer this question I have to return to my discoveries concerning the influence of traditional formation.

Form traditions affect our lives in all their spheres and dimensions. I began to see more clearly how we—in a pluritraditional society—are exposed not to one but to many traditions. A number of these play on our coercive self-centered longings. We may assimilate them in what I conceived as our inner pyramid of traditions. It became obvious to me in my reflections that self-centered traditions strengthen the hold neuroformational residues may still have over us, even in our enlightened post-transcendent phase of life.

What can we do to rise above such residues? With the new light and strength granted to us in the cave of purgation, it will be possible to uproot even these sediments. In due time, the mystery will grant us the transcendent competence to disclose and then transform our coercive reactions to people, events, and things.

Transcendent illumination will show us that, in spite of these remnants, we have more than enough about which to be joyful. It is true that the coercive patterns in our neuroform make us lose, from time to time, our poise and peace. This happens to us in spite of our usual state of transcendence. We cannot blame the inter and outer spheres of our life for the persistence of this condition. The mystery lifted us past the cave of purgation into the lush land of transcendent attentiveness. It grants us the joyous resilience that makes us grow patiently in transcendent competence and comportment. Slowly we will rise beyond depreciative feelings that will emerge from the remnants of our neuroform-in-transformation. They are like the wisps of the last smoke and smells of the embers of a dying fire.

We will feel ourselves being filled with epiphanic love. This is the love evoked in us by the epiphany or "experienced appearance" of the mystery in the people, events, and things of our everyday life. The gift of epiphanic love will enable us to detect gradually the remnants of depreciative dispositions of attention in our neuroform. It will graciously facilitate their transformation into transcendent dispositions of epiphanic appreciation.

This phase of transcendent epiphanic love advances our post-transcendent journey strikingly. We advance more rapidly than we ever could have without this blessing. The gift of continuous epiphanic presence comes from the same mystery that keeps disclosing to us our unique-communal life call both inwardly and in and through our life situation. Therefore, our enlightenment is, in principle, consonant with the everyday life we are called to live in family and marketplace. The gift of epiphanic love infuses us with transcendent appreciation of our present condition. We should only change it when the mystery lets us experience that such a move would be wise and reasonable in the light of new disclosures of our call.

Spiritual Direction in the Post-transcendent Phase

Once we thoroughly understand how to disclose and rise above the coercive residues of the pretranscendent stage, it is not always necessary to have a private formation director constantly at our side. In the post-transcendent phase, often the mystery itself may become our main director. Other directors will be there mainly to help us through emergencies and crises of life direction. Yet, even in our post-transcendent phase, we ought never to make a startling change without consulting wise directors known for their balance, learning, and experience in matters of this phase of the journey.

As transcending persons, we will soon discover that the mystery puts us in situations that offer opportunities for growth. Because of our transcendent state, the mystery lives in and with us in a special way. It knows better than we or anyone else what coercive dispositions we need to disclose and change. Being wise, powerful, and omnipresent, the mystery makes us experience our life situations in ways that foster the inner work we should be doing daily.

When we live the transcendent epiphanic life of the will to love, we will constantly deepen the peace, wisdom, and effectiveness granted to persons who reach the end of the cave of purgation. Then we enjoy the simplicity and openness of a second childhood and enter gladly into the kingdom of peace and compassion.

In the post-transcendence phase, we may remember the immense energy it took to try to reform the inter and outer spheres of our field of presence and action. In that past pretranscendent phase of life, we expected wrongly that complete control of our situation would make us loving, serene, and happy. We know now that wise control can ameliorate some practical difficulties but that no control in and by itself alone could make us totally happy or loving. Real joy is a gift of the mystery, not a feat of control. It is a transcendent surprise that survives in the midst of suffering. It is not the pleasure of excitement but the joy of the conviction that everything is an epiphanous expression of the love of the mystery. We need to recall that this gift was granted to us when the mystery lifted our life into the state of transcendence.

Looking back in wonder, we realize how often our former life was wounded by turmoil, downheartedness, and fear. Instead of flowing with life, we pushed against it in a desperate attempt to control our destiny. We cannot push a river. Neither can we dominate the unpredictable stream of life.

Transcendent Peace and Joy

Before entering the cave of purgation, we felt only spare drops of peace, love, and joy. They were not enough to stop the bickering and stubbornness, the pretending and protesting, that made our lives less appreciative and attractive. We were the greedy victims not only of the pride form but also of popularized, selfish traditions of human development. Like whirlwinds, they swirled around us. They strengthened the dispositions that arose from the poisonous well of our pride form. Like clouds of blinding fog, they obscured our vision of the call.

The mystery invites us to hide in the shelter of its presence from the seductions of selfish traditions. It calls us to find safety under its tent of love, under the shadow of its wings. This phase makes us see in awe how the transparent tent of the sacred covers all the earth, all of cosmos, history, and humanity, and within them each of us as a twinkling pearl, an original likeness of the mystery.

Before being purged by the cave experience, we dwelt in the illusion that selfish thoughts were clever directives to a happy and effective life. But no one ever entered the land of lasting joy by following selfish longings. These are not beacons to a paradise of peace. Looking back at our former life, we realize that we experienced flashes of pleasure and satisfaction but no enduring peace.

In the wasteland of the selfish life, we told ourselves, "If I can just become a good athlete, a popular fellow, have a great career, become an attractive well-to-do man or woman, I will be at peace and at ease." The light of transcendence shows us now the shallowness of such dreams, for what after all is athletic glory, popularity, money, cleverness, or charm if we are not really at ease inside?

Self-centered traditions tried to convince us that, "If I could go back to school and get a degree, then I would be really happy." What if we got the degree? It gave us moments of satisfaction and a sense of fulfilling great expectations of what would now happen to us. Then we suffered the "after-graduation blues." We discovered that we were not really happier or more honored than the rest of the population.

We realize that it is, of course, good to grow in pretranscendent knowledge, to earn degrees if that is in tune with our life call. Degrees can be used as instruments in service of the fulfillment of our call. Now the mystery shows us how misleading it was to ever expect them alone to bring us enduring peace, love, and joy.

Prior to being led to the state of transcendence, we may have told ourselves coercively, "If I could only find the person who could really appreciate and love me, my life would be at peace and filled with joy." We may have thought that we had found that person. We felt filled with gratification and satisfaction. We mistook our feelings for the peace and joy the masters of formation express. Soon the excitement faded. We did not know how to love transcendently. The relationship went downhill or, to say the least, the honeymoon was over. We decided that he or she was not the person for whom we were looking after all.

As we grow in the transcendent dimension, we shall find out that it is more important to be the right person—in consonance with our unique-communal life call—than to find the right person. Only if we are the right person may the mystery enable us to find the right person.

Coercive depreciative dispositions are misleading. They make us less able to take competent and effective action in situations the mystery entrusts to our care. Such dispositions are generated by the pride form and reinforced by selfish formation traditions. They are deepened, too, by a neuroformational pattern of scars and wounds in our prideful "I," which easily takes offense. Its self-centeredness makes it most vulnerable and oversensitive to real or imagined slights.

Defensive Self-Encapsulation

We realize now in this final phase how defensive self-encapsulation made us more eager to apprehend and depreciate what is different in other people than to seek and appreciate what we and they may have in common. The transcendent life teaches us that each person carries the epiphanous dignity of a unique life call. We do not know that call. The person may not yet live up to it. But the call is always there, granting each human being a unique transcendent identity. This truth helps us to understand and prompts us to love each person as he or she is called to be. We feel no longer so easily threatened by people or by the changing conditions in our situation. We are no longer trapped in coercive ways of apprehending and appraising life defensively.

In the post-transcendent phase, we grow in the persuasion that no one or no situation should be felt as a threat or a danger. We see things with the clearer perception of transcendent attention, apprehension, and appraisal. No longer is our energy sapped by worries or anxieties about the problems life brings to us. If we can do something about them we will do it as competently as we can, no matter how small the steps we can take. We are no longer attached to the pre-transcendent results of what we try to accomplish.

Embraced by the mystery, we refuse to create more worries for ourselves. Even if we cannot do anything about a problem, we do not drain our formation energy by worrying about it needlessly. For us, it is simply a part of the present disclosure of the transcendent call of our life.

In gentle love we welcome the epiphanous appearances of unsolvable questions. Worry, anxiety, or other coercive dispositions are superfluous on the path of pure transcendence.

Coercive worrying, if not caught in time, can still interfere with the flowing effectiveness and joyousness that mark this phase of life. Every time we give in to such anxiety, we retard our journey along the post-transcendent path. We lose our spark and energy when we hassle ourselves emotionally any time the inter and outer spheres of our field of action do not conform with the remnants of coercive dispositions and projects momentarily revived by our neuroform. The post-transcendent phase of new childhood is the time to be joyous and loving, to appreciate each moment of life as a gift of the mystery, no matter the adverse inter and outer conditions we may still have to endure.

Before we descended into the cave of purification, we developed a coercive self-consciousness. We loaded this consciousness with robotlike reaction patterns. We used them to protect the survival of our prideful, strident "I." This process probably started in childhood during our skirmishes with parental control. Well meaning but misdirected parents may have aggravated in us the build up of a coercive neuroform. They may have been more strict and controlling than necessary, sometimes even abusive.

Their behavior made us feel as if we should have the power to control people, events, and things to gain and maintain happiness. Eventually, our pretranscendent "I" became oversensitive to any person, event, or thing that even remotely threatened our excessive control dispositions. This radar sharp warning system protects the coercive need in us to control the conditions emanating from all the spheres and dimensions of our field of life.

Now we have been lifted into the post-transcendent phase of life. We have been granted the power to use our neuroform more wisely. We have been enlightened by the mystery about the coercive dispositions that diminished our freedom. Our neuroform may still be disposed to put us on anxious guard against any real or imagined slight or threat. Over a lifetime, excessive overprotectiveness has become like a second nature.

The transcendent dimension inspires us to flow in loving consonance with the people, events, and things that try to interfere with the mystery's mission for our life. As I have said, remnants of the coercive dispositions of our neuroform may still interfere. They warn us automatically against loving people, no strings attached. They depict them as threats to our power, prestige, and projects. If we want to be loved and loving in and with the mystery, we cannot allow our neuroform to keep interfering with the aspirations and inspirations central to transcendent formation.

To maintain the transcendent joy and peace of this post-transcendent phase, we have to remember first and foremost who we are. We are not our apparent form; neither are we our pretranscendent "I" or our self-image. We are a unique-communal call, a marvelous epiphanic expression of the mystery. We are a call that is in the process of being disclosed to us over a lifetime. The transcendent state was the beginning of the most sublime disclosure. Our post-transcendent phase is the process of a further deepening and widening of this highest disclosure and of its implementation in all of our life. It goes without saying that we have to be increasingly attentive to the successive conditions we meet in daily life. We are called to appraise them in the light of our transcendent life direction.

Appreciative Abandonment

The post-transcendent path seems simple, but to realize its possibilities takes constant inner work. The basic disposition for this to occur is appreciative abandonment of our will to anything the mystery allows or designs for us here and now. Relaxed abandonment will calm our neuroform. It will then be easier for us to enlist it as a flexible ally in the task of implementing our call. Our neuroform is meant to be the servant of our unique mission in life. It can contribute to our seeing clearly and wisely. It can evolve competent, effective ways to interact with people, events, and things in our surroundings.

Before reaching the transcendent state, we may have spent time and energy protesting and pouting about the here-and-now situation. Now, in appreciative abandonment, we try to assess our field of implementation in faithfulness to the probable disclosures of our life call. If we fail to do so, we shall become less perceptive. We shall be at the mercy of the neuroform as it was programmed during the pretranscendent stage of our life.

The basic directive of the post-transcendent life is, thus, to live in loving consonance with the transcendent mystery in itself and in all its epiphanies. This fundamental directive reminds us of the ability granted to us in the cave of purgation to believe in the hidden splendor of the unique life call within ourselves and others.

Transcendent love means loving people, events, things just because the mystery allowed them to emerge in our field as part of our here and now life. The people that are with us may think and feel differently than we do, but all of us are alike in being called to be a unique-communal expression of the same mystery.

Our pretranscendent life may have been influenced by the functionalistic and capitalistic traditions in our society. So was the life of our family. In this climate, love was dispensed mainly when it was earned or deserved. This condition gave rise to the disposition that we must first earn or deserve love before we can receive it and that others, too, should be loved by us only if they have done something to earn or deserve our attention. No wonder that so many well-intentioned attempts to love end up in separation and other kinds of alienation. We have been taught to place pretranscendent conditions on our love: "If you really loved me, you would. . . ." Then we insert one of our coercive dispositions to complete the sentence.

This barter-and-exchange love is not transcendent love. It does not lead to consonance but dissonance. Transcendent love means accepting and respecting a person as one whose deepest identity is hidden in the mystery of all formation. His or her face may be the face of a wounded mystery, disfigured not in itself but in its manifold expressions in failing and suffering humanity—all unfolding forms of human life are on a hidden journey toward transcendence.

When we let coercive dispositions interfere, we may find ourselves once again encapsulated in pretranscendent life. We must accept what happens then as also a learning experience. It can teach us how to return to the path of transcendence in new appreciation of its peace and beauty as well as of its being a source of calm effectiveness in the midst of the everyday turmoil of the world. We also learn from this experience which coercive dispositions are still embedded in our neuroform, how we can spot the first sign of their awakening and nip them in the bud.

The key to coping with coercive dispositions is instant appreciative abandonment to the mystery of transformation in the here and now. We abandon ourselves to each present challenge as part of our unfolding life call with its corresponding disclosure of formation opportunities.

When coercive dispositions are triggered, we cannot clearly appraise our call within the situation. Our neuroform sends a flood of depreciative information to our powers of attention. Overwhelmed by anxious depreciation, our attention focuses on signs of danger, threat, alienation, and separation. Our appraisal of the challenge is usually warped because we magnify the dissonances between us and others. We suppress the awareness of consonances between our life call and theirs. This interferes with the flow of transcendent, epiphanic love, which the mystery asks us to radiate into the world. Not only when we give offense but also when we take offense, we scatter the light of peace and love that the mystery granted us in order to illumine and pacify the world.

Moments of Inner Vacation and Recollection

In our pretranscendent life, we cherished vacation trips to other places. Some of these spots, far away from our daily surroundings, calmed us down.

One reason why this happened had to do with the absence of real or imagined threats to our illusion-filled coercive dispositions. For a while, our anxious suspicions and depreciations were not triggered continuously. We felt less tormented.

Lifted now into the post-transcendent life, we should take also repeated inner vacations or periods of recollection that distance us from reemerging coercive dispositions. Our life should be permeated by vacation moments of quiet meditations anytime our coercive dispositions reach the point of being triggered by the challenges of the daily struggle in which we find ourselves.

CHAPTER 25

Preservation of the Path

To preserve the gifts of purgation we must maintain vigilance where remnants of past coercions are concerned. They disrupt the peace to which we have been invited. First among these gifts is a living faith in the mystery, an abiding in its presence. Such abiding makes our hearts intuit things that are beyond our human senses and measuring minds.

The mystery at once reveals and conceals itself. It shines forth in our call of life; it plays in veiled ways in and around the events that comprise our formative field. The enlightened heart adores the hidden splendor of the Eternal in all that unfolds.

In early life we did not learn how to love transcendently. Our likes and dislikes were controlled by selfish desires, anxious plans, and excessive ambitions. In the cave we were purged of these obstacles and called forth to full awakening, at least in a beginning way. We were graced with a deeper capacity of transcendent faith and love. What makes us fail at times in spite of the transformation occurring in our hearts are the coercive remnants left behind like rusting battle gear after a war.

To rise above these coercions, we must imbibe the wisdom of the ages. The science of the spirit I have been developing for over fifty years presents us with a practical condensation of literally thousands of years of accumulated counsels for living. Treasures have been stored up for us in consonant traditions. They are like lights set to guide us when we are faced with leftover coercive dispositions that block our path. Such residues bubble up from the murky caverns of our life when we are confronted with people, events, and things that resist or threaten us.

The wisdom of the ages helps us to preserve a peaceful heart in spite of the pain we may have to undergo. The life of the spirit entails beneficial suffering, contradiction, and at times rejection. The difference is that our suffering is seen as formative; it is no longer contaminated by deformative coercions pushing us up and down like an escalator out of control, running incessantly between the floors of selfish gratification and gross disappointment. Purgation by the mystery made dramatic changes in our life. The directives of preservation protect this transformation in the midst of suffering.

Preservation directives enable us to hold onto faith and love, peace and joy—to all the gifts infused by the mystery. In the past we believed erroneously that suffering would disappear if only we could compel people, events, and things to fulfill our expectations. Coercive dispositions and the desires they generated increased faster than our ability to satisfy them. Discontent may have been delayed, but it was not wiped out. Suffering without transcendent meaning is harder to bear than suffering on the post-transcendent path.

One way in which a hidden coercion betrays itself is that we feel out of sorts if it is not satisfied. In this way the mystery gently warns us that we may be in danger of losing the path of peace opened up for us so graciously.

Even if a coercive disposition brought us pleasure in the past, our new state of wisdom makes us see it as short-lived. How often was satisfaction followed by feelings of let down, vague guiltiness, and dissatisfaction? The new light in which we live shows us that we were secretly afraid of threats to what we had achieved. We worried about changes that would grind away the power we gained by our own efforts and manipulations. Often we compared what had become ours with things we had before or with what others accomplished. What they had, or what we ourselves once enjoyed, looked more gratifying. We felt the turmoil of discontent, envy, and disappointment. We became embroiled in feverish planning to get more or do better. All this commotion kept us out of tune with the disclosures of our life call in each event. When we let remnants of the past impede our path today, we pay a price in peace tomorrow.

Liberation from Coercion

A coercive disposition should be liberated from its one-way-only compulsion. We have to realize that what a disposition suggests as *the* only way is merely a possible way to shape our thoughts and actions. Alternative options can be presented to us by other free dispositions. They preserve and foster our freedom and flexibility by reminding us that there are many avenues to consonant living.

A coercive disposition may have begun innocently enough. It started out from an appreciation of an apt way to respond to a specific situation. For example, as a police officer, one may develop a disposition to assert him or herself when having to restrain people who threaten the safety of others. A well-trained officer has to keep this disposition ready to hand when similar situations arise. The disposition of forceful self-assertion, however, would no longer be at an officer's command, if his or her life as a whole—in all situations—would be mainly guided by the disposition to assert oneself forcefully.

As I have observed, coercive dispositions tend to be entrenched in our neuroform. Initially, they are available only to our infrafocal, not to our focal or prefocal, consciousness. Therefore, neuroformational coercive dispositions may still be operational in our life without our knowing it. This can happen even if we live transcendently on the focal and prefocal levels of a purgated existence.

Coercive dispositions should be transformed into appreciative, free, and pliable ones. They should serve our call flexibly as it discloses itself in changing situations.

While no longer being enslaved to one or the other character disposition, we may still favor it over others. To the degree that we favored it onesidedly in the past, it may have been or may yet become coercive. Once purgated from its compulsion, it may still be favored by us, but no longer blindly. We may turn it into a preferential option and appraise ongoingly if it is consonant with the situation at hand and with the disclosure of our life call.

Say a period of free time suddenly becomes available to a well-rounded personality like Mary. Over the years she has developed dispositions of appreciation for sports, socializing, watching television, and gardening. She is free to choose any one of these activities when she wants to recreate, for none of them happens to be coercive for her. It so happens that her favored disposition is for gardening. She will probably opt to spend more free time in her garden, weather permitting, than to look at television. She enjoys seeing things grow. They are for her gifts of the mystery.

Evidently, on the post-transcendent path, one can still enjoy many past actions and experiences, provided the dispositions associated with them are not coercive. We have to change them into favored, not exclusive, dispositions of appreciation. At the same time, we have to turn them always into servants of our transcendent call.

As we become aware of how our appraisal power works, we will be able to distinguish between the neuroform itself and its service of either free or coercive dispositions. In the past, whether we knew it or not, we may have trained our neuroform to execute coercive dispositions. At present, we may sense sudden moments of a rude interruption of faith and love, of peace and joy, on our new path of life. This shift may signify that our neuroform is operating on the basis of its past coercive training. Though the mystery has liberated us from such coercions, it is up to us to implement our new found freedom. We must release our neuroform from the residues any past coercive training either we or others forced upon it.

Neuroform and Pretranscendent "I"

Our pretranscendent "I" played a crucial role in the past operation of our neuroform. At that time, this "managing I" was mainly in touch with the lower directives of the sociohistorical, vital, and functional dimensions of our life. From them it selected which of numerous possible dispositions should be routinely implemented in everyday life by the neuroform. It instructed this inner selective agent to generate corresponding attentions, feelings, and experiences about what was happening in our field of life.

Our pretranscendent "I" can be compared to the master controller of a computer system. It programs our neuroform. It tells it what attentions, feelings, images, and thoughts it should produce if triggered by certain selected events in our field of presence and action.

For example, people of one specific religious formation tradition may remember past generations who suffered at the hands of fanatic adherents of another religious tradition. They may program their neuroform to react automatically with hostility or depreciation any time any person, act, or symbol of the hated tradition shows up in their surroundings. Adherents of the opposed tradition may program their neuroform in a similar, though opposite, fashion. The result may be a war of formation traditions, especially when the mutual hate programming happens to coincide with territorial claims and contestations between cultural spheres of influence.

The elevation to the post-transcendent path does not necessarily undo all remnants of pretranscendent conditioning of our neuroform. This sociohistorical programming may stretch over generations. It can be so deeply rooted, even in post-transcendent persons, that in times of heated conflicts between their own and other formation traditions they lose peace and composure, the blessed balance of prudent judgment. Only by regaining it can they be the peacemakers they are called to be by the mystery of universal love.

If and when we are lifted into the transcendent life, we should be watchful when the pretranscendent programming of our formation tradition intrudes into the profound peace and appreciation associated with this path. Times of cruel clashes may offer the toughest test of our fidelity to the transcendent and its gifts. Fanatical adherents of our own formation tradition may detest and persecute us for what they see as a betrayal of the holy battle, as cowardice, or as wimpish evasion. And yet we can only protect the gifts of the mystery by extending to others the same equanimity, empathy, love-will, and appreciation the mystery of universal love wants to express to us and through us to all human beings. The mystery wants us to do so without betraying through inaction the basics of our consonant faith and formation traditions.

Our lower "I," left to its own devices, will not easily come under the control of our higher transcendent "I." It often determines on its own, informed only by the lower dimensions, what we should be aware of. In our pretranscendent past, we may have attended only to what our isolated lower "I" allowed us to see, hear, or read. Often the lower "I" was busy reacting to people, events, and things on the lower three dimensions of life. Our basic attention was focused on what we were anxiously striving after or what we feared. This evoked in us tense feelings of urgency. At unexpected moments these may still erupt into even our post-transcendent life of consonant peace.

Most of our lower dispositions represent the urgent demands and claims we developed under the dominance of merely the pretranscendent dimensions of life. This tendency started already in childhood. Insofar as residues of such dispositions still slumber in our neuroform, they may rise up and block the next phase of our journey. Until we let the mystery transform these inappropriate dispositions, they may at times turn off the lights and for a moment make us lose our way.

Implementation of Preservation Directives

The directives of preservation I shall outline at the end of this chapter keep us on the right path. They make us more attentive to the intrusions of past coercions. Though they do not work at once, in due course the mystery will grant us this gift and the patience we need to attain it.

We may read about and begin to understand the directives I was able to disclose over the years through constant observation and through reflection on the masters of many classical religious and generally human formation traditions. But this is not enough. In spite of our intellectual understanding, some hidden remnants of coercions in our core form will at first continue their usual control in a mechanical way. In the beginning, they will catch us before we can even think about applying the guidelines I know will help us. Try to see each of these incidences as a marvelous formation opportunity! It teaches us how susceptible we still are to our former neuroformational conditioning. The past training of our neuroform makes us automatically irritable if someone crosses us. We become anxious; we may even fly off the handle if someone triggers our old security directives, which have turned into coercive dispositions.

When this happens, it offers us yet another opportunity to reflect. Reflection, in turn, fosters the growth of dispositions of attention to these coercions and their subservient neuroformational routines. We begin to catch ourselves in the moments when we unguardedly let our neuroform run on. We realize on such occasions the power of the gifts the mystery endowed us with after the darkness of the cave. We are able to transform our coercions progressively into servant dispositions of the call increasingly disclosed to us.

Attention and Freedom from Coercion

This new disposition of relaxed attentiveness to signs of coercion alerts us to any dissonant feelings that might be related to compulsive dispositions. Our mastery of these peace-preservation directives enables us to zero in on the appreciative directives and dispositions we have neglected. We pay closer attention to the thoughts and images that triggered dissonant moods and feelings in the first place. These emotions, too, are connected with our neuroformational system. To transform them into servants of the mystery is a crucial part of the ongoing higher asceticism of the post-transcendent path of life. We realize more and more that our thoughts and images precede and guide the forms we give to our life and to its field.

Once we direct the attention dispositions of our rational mind to reflect on any experience of coercive dissonance, we can interpret it in the light of related preservation directives. Repeating this procedure, while strengthening our rational attention dispositions, helps us to diminish gradually the moments when former coercions take over. At times, it may still require many hours to dispel dissonant emotions. At least we will find that the time span of dissonance is gradually reduced. There will come a time that we experience obstructions of our peace of life only for a brief while. We may still be aware of the onslaught of dissonant emotions, but we are bound to them less and less; we let go of them faster and faster.

This process implies thus a transformation of the life of attention. It cannot happen all at once. When someone or something automatically evokes feelings of dissonance, we start up with excitement, fear, or irritation. In the same instant, the pertinent directives of peace preservation flash into our attention. They activate our growing disposition to preserve the gift of peace. The transforming mystery of love has endowed us increasingly with insight into the neuroformational process. Attentiveness to the process creates a pause. This pause interrupts the unfolding of our coercive depreciative spin. Spontaneously, it sets up a barrier against the mechanical pressing of the past into the present. We experience an increasing freedom from the past. Our new path, in the light of the love of the mystery, is restored to its serenity. Our consonant interformation with the epiphanic appearances of this mystery in our field of presence thus deepens immensely.

The victory of the mystery over the remnants of our past gives us hope. Silenced are these resistant residues. No longer do they trigger destructive reactions. Replacing them increasingly are new wise responses. We flow joyously with the challenging will of the mystery in each event of our life.

In the beginning of this struggle we had to pay strict attention to each and every directive that might help us to transform our past routines. Now our attention can begin to relax a little, to become less focal, so as to become more trans- and prefocal, more spontaneous and implicit. This frees our focal attention for the tasks at hand. We no longer have to focus directly on what caused us to lose our composure in a challenging situation. Former coercive feelings of dissonance and depreciation are no longer triggered. How grateful we are that the mystery has made us the gentle master of our anxious mind in this crowning phase of our journey.

You will not at once enjoy this kind of freedom, but be consoled. As soon as you begin to put into effect the directives of peace preservation, you will find a lessening of the coercive interruptions that blocked your post-transcendent path. You will begin to welcome every challenge the mystery allows in your life as a transformation opportunity. You will come to appreciate even your repeated failures as learning stations along the way. Awe becomes a lasting disposition of your heart. You realize that the love-will of the mystery in its all-embracing universal totality is as incomprehensible as are its diversified expressions and countless effects in cosmos, humanity, and history.

Every event in our life, no matter how imperfect or minute it seems to us, is a good and perfect expression of the mystery's love-will for our pilgrimage on earth. To live in this faith brings with it peace and joy. These are the precious fruits of our graced embrace of the will of the mystery as ultimately benevolent. Even when we have come this far, we may still experience the upsurge of a coercive emotion. Welcome it as an opportunity to work with the mystery for the sake of transformation. Each time you do so, you are preparing yourself for the next occasion to catch the coercion before it catches you.

Studying Preservation Directives

At the end of this chapter, read carefully the list of directives of peace preservation. Implant them deeply in your heart and in your character dispositions of attention. The mystery wants to use these directives to advance the transformation of your life into its own image.

What I present there—in accordance with my science of formation—is not a question of only intellectual information. Do not study these directives as if they were interesting bits of information. If you approach them mainly intellectually, you cannot use them as dynamic tools that keep your post-transcendent path open to the inspirations of the mystery. These directives are intended to give you a deeper understanding of the event-to-event disclosure of the effective love-will of the mystery for us. They seek to enable you to bear with sufferings and upheavals, to accept them graciously, while meeting the challenge to change and grow. In the midst of suffering, you may be blessed with the love, peace, joy, wisdom, and effectiveness that are the gifts of the mystery for the post-transcendent life.

Directives of Peace Preservation

Liberation from Coercive Dispositions

1. The mystery wants to free you from hidden remnants of coercive dispositions that challenge the peace of the post-transcendent (transcendent-immanent) life to which it elevated you undeservedly.

2. The mystery inspires you to disclose how coercive dispositions have conditioned your neuroform to compel your attention, thoughts, perceptions,

feelings, symbols, and other images automatically in a direction that interrupts the peace and joy of your post-transcendent (transcendent-immanent) path of life.

3. The mystery inspires you to welcome the opportunities that your everyday event-to-event experience offers you. On such occasions you become aware of the intrusion of past coercions. You are given the space you need to transform them, thus liberating your life from these robotlike emotional intrusions.

Being Present to Each Event

4. The mystery reminds you that its effective will for your life contains everything you need to be at peace with each event. You welcome each daily event as an expression of its loving call to you, as the gift of an opportunity for transformation. One condition for this peace is that you do not let your coercive dispositions generate demands, thoughts, images, memories, and anticipations that are at odds with your post-transcendent (transcendent-immanent) path of life.

5. The mystery delegates to you full responsibility for the preservation of its gifts of peace and joy and for the faithful pursuit of its call to you. You are responsible for the formation of consonant dispositions and their routinization in your neuroform. The dispositioning of your life is the ground of effective presence and action in your formation field. It also affects the reactions and responses of the people you encounter in that field.

6. The mystery wants you to share joyously in its loving appreciation of your unique-communal life call, in its unceasing forgiveness of your coercions and failures. It loves to see you grow in the faith that all obstacles can be a part of your progress on the post-transcendent way if you turn them into stepping stones.

Interformation with Others

7. The mystery calls you in unique-communal ways. The post-transcendent light makes you aware that your path, no matter how unique, is never isolated from the paths of others. You are called to live and move in formation fields that you share with others. Your formation is affected by the mystery's formation of others; the mystery, in turn, makes your formation affect them.

8. The mystery enters into your field of interformation. It wants you to foster in yourself and others loving candor, consonance, compatibility, courage, care, and compassion. The gift of the transcendent path is not given to you

alone. It fills you with a responsibility to radiate the mystery's benevolence to all whom you meet, to offer them in some way a share in the joy and peace you have received. At the same time you welcome gratefully what the mystery offers you through others continuously.

9. The mystery guiding you on this path does not want the communal aspect of its call to you to detract from the unique aspect of its calling of you and others. You should be interforming in love without getting totally caught up emotionally in other paths of life. You should not get so overinvolved that you lose the equanimity, peace, joy, and contemplative presence with which the mystery endowed your post-transcendent path.

10. The mystery inspires you to abstain from interventions in the lives of others when past coercions intrude into your post-transcendent path. They deprive you of the peace, joy, love, wisdom, and effectiveness that flow from the love-will of the mystery for you and from your love-will for the mystery. At such coercive moments, your interventions will be flawed and deformative instead of formative. They will be disconcerting to people around you. They are caught off guard by this strange and sudden loss of the usual composure the mystery granted you. If possible, you should postpone any intervention until you regain inner consonance.

Dimensional Roots of Presence

11. The mystery on this path is continuously calming your vital excitement, your restless functionalistic meandering. These dimensions are no longer the main roots of your thoughts, feelings, attentions, and actions. The post-transcendent dimension should be the foundation of your at-oneness with the mystery and its epiphanies in your field of life. Other dimensions are only at the disposal of this deeper presence granted to you undeservedly. You should be aware of any attempt by these other dimensions to regain their past dominance over your life.

12. The mystery on this path keeps you aware of the dimensions you are using in service of its post-transcendent calling. It inspires you to be open to all of them, to transform them in the light of your growing transcendent perceptiveness, love, and inner peace.

Trusting that you have taken these preservation directives to heart, I intend in the following chapter to take a closer look at some of them and the problems surrounding their implementation.

CHAPTER 26

Release from Coercion

Lest you give in to excessive anxiety on the way of the transcendent-functional phase of formation, I want to assure you that there is no reason to feel discouraged. If and when you are still surprised by a sudden upsurge of coercive thoughts, images, feelings, and patterns of behavior, take heart. These coercions stem from dispositions that are compulsive and hence deformative. They shape the routines of our neuroform. Whether these are coercive or flexible, they are executed initially automatically once we have set their course.

Unlike dispositions that are flexible and free, coercive ones with their fixed neuroformational routines direct our attention in an exclusively rigid fashion. Accordingly, our neuroform triggers dissonant reactions in us when our field of life does not fit its routinized coercive directives of the past. At that moment, remnants of deformative dispositions and the feelings they evoke interfere with our new transcendent-immanent life of love, peace, and joy.

Such interruption betrays itself in the warped emotionality of our reaction to a threatening demand, person, group, event, symbol, or situation. Our neuroform runs the whole gamut of dissonant feelings: resentment, paranoid guilt or fear, oversensitivity, worry, anxiety, envy, jealousy, dissonant sensual cravings, anxious plotting, discouragement, or despondency. Let me now review in this and the following chapter the meaning of some of the directives I gave you for peace preservation.

* * *

My first directive of peace preservation reads: *The mystery wants to free us from hidden remnants of coercive dispositions that challenge the peace of the post-transcendent (transcendent-immanent) life to which it elevated us undeservedly.*

How Coercive Dispositions Deform Our Life
How do coercions interfere with our peace and joy? Why do we always pay a price in lost serenity, even if we are lifted to the path of transcendent-immanent formation?

A frustrated coercion stirs up a rush of dissonant emotions; it ferments agitation in our heart. Such disturbances affect the spheres and dimensions of our field of life. They narrow our attention span. They fixate us on appearances in our field that evoke neuroformational coercions.

What if a remnant of a past form of coercive perfectionism recaptures our life? At once, our attention seems focused irresistibly on only one thing. Let us say we are in rigorous pursuit of what we have set up as ideals of impeccable social performance. Our neuroform makes us look at only one aspect of life anxiously: is there anything we do less perfectly than our coercive ideals tell us? If we spot an imperfection, we feel overwhelmed by depreciative emotions. Irritation, frustration, self-reproach, unreasonable guilt, resentment of others who seem to do better or whom we imagine as the cause of our own failure, all arise and disrupt our peace.

Such a coercion not only diminishes consonance with the mystery; it also affects our spontaneous interaction with others. To return to our example, morbid fear of imperfection clouds our appraisal of others. Are they less perfect than they ought to be according to our compulsive standards of perfection? Is their behavior a threat to our perfectionism? Those we inwardly condemn sense some distance growing between us and them. This, too, diminishes the peaceful flow of care and concern between us.

Past coercive dispositions hinder our progress, even if they signal a good outcome. What hinders our ascent is not the disposition as such but its binding and blinding of our heart and mind. Its tyranny makes us lose the gracious dance of consonance with the mystery. We are no longer light as a feather, playful as newly reborn children. We do not let the mystery guide us flexibly from free disposition to free disposition. No longer can we freely choose the disposition that responds best to the here and now intimations of the mystery in our field of life.

Pretranscendent Satisfaction
and Transcendent-Immanent Joy

Often the mystery inspires us to enjoy freely some of the same things that delighted us in the past, albeit then in a compulsive way. Now we enjoy them in a deeper, freer, pliable fashion. They no longer take away our initiative, our flexibility, our flow with life, our consonance with others, with the mystery, and with all of reality to which the mystery grants precious form constantly. We savor the blessing of detached attachment.

What would have happened had we not been granted the gift of transcendent-immanence or had we not gone along with this gift? We would have become more and more involved in endless battles between our coercive desires and the invitations of the mystery that are in conflict with them. Our field of life with its appeals, needs, and possibilities is always in fluctuation. Its mysterious, new demands cannot always gratify past dispositions, some of which were arbitrarily fixed in our neuroform during the dominance of the pre-transcendent phase of life.

Our past pretranscendent level could never fill us with enduring peace and joy. No matter how hard we tried, labored, and gained in power, possession, prestige, functionalistic and vitalistic spirituality, it was never enough to lift us beyond the limits of our lower desires and the constant threat of their disap-pointments. This was our painful predicament before we were raised by the mystery to the realm of transcendent-immanence and immanent-transcen-dence.

When we look back on our pretranscendent life, when it was still dominated by lower-level strivings and desires, we see that even when we were able to satisfy many of these, it was never enough. There was always one or the other desire or perfectionistic ideal not fully satisfied. That was what kept preying on our mind. It spoiled our contentment. Enlightened as we now are, we know that each coercive disposition carries in the end its own disappointment.

In the past, these dispositions controlled our neuroform at least in part. They had trained this system of our brain to manipulate automatically the inter and outer spheres of our life. We programmed our computer brain to press people, events, and things into our peculiar set of inordinate attachments. We believed that this would assure us the peace and joy for which we yearned. Such a onesided focus of attention made it difficult for us to tune in to other thoughts, needs, and feelings. We became insensitive to the deeper meanings of people, events, and things. Their transcendent-immanent message escaped us. To flow lovingly and wisely with our field of life as a whole, we must be open to the deeper music that the mystery infuses in the treasures with which it sur-rounds us.

To dwell in the light of the mystery, to radiate its healing presence, we must be able to apprehend and appraise both the pretranscendent and transcendent coformants of our field. It is only now in the transcendent-immanent phase that we more fully realize that giving in to our coercive attachments costs us too much in diminished perceptiveness, appreciation, wisdom, effectiveness, peace, and joy. Only now do we see that the beguiling fascination of inordinate attachments diminishes true peace and joy.

Once again, when the remnants of the coercions of our neuroform take us by surprise, no matter how advanced our ascent may be, we should learn to spot the first signs of their acting up. Only then can we nip this invasion in the bud, so to speak, and begin to replace them gradually with a wide variety of person-ally appreciated dispositions. The mystery of guiding love wants us to choose from among these dispositions the ones that are consonant with our ever changing field of life. The mystery grants us these changes as opportunity after opportunity for transformation. We must flow with its forming inspiration as expressed inwardly and in the consonant demands of our situation. We shall no longer suffer the letdowns of the past when one or the other coercive disposition could not be satisfied. We simply move to a personally appreciated disposition or choose an outlook inspired by the mystery.

Equanimity or Evenmoodedness

As we look back, we realize that when one or the other of our past coercions was satisfied, we felt, at least temporarily, some pleasure. We were relieved from the pressure of desire. Often we lost interest when what we hungered for was finally ours. Now, however, when one of our freely appreciated dispositions is not fulfilled, the transcendent-immanent path leaves us in peaceful equanimity or evenmoodedness. Equanimity is an effective coformant of our transcendent-immanent peace. Equanimity enables us to say to ourselves, it was only one of many free and flexible appreciations to which we gave form in the light of the mystery and of the consonant traditions in our own form-tradition pyramid. We are blessed now with a reasonable detachment from each of them. We are no longer heartbroken if a preferred disposition is not fulfilled.

Nothing is lost, for many pretranscendent appreciative dispositions, purged of their coercions, may still be satisfied. We welcome each fulfillment gratefully as an extra gift. Each of these lower satisfactions adds a relative feeling of bliss to the basic joy of transcendent-immanent appreciation granted to us by the mystery. How much more at peace we are at present. Our pretranscendent functionalistic "I" and mind have been transformed into pleasing servants of our transcendent life call.

No longer does our neuroform frantically have to guard our anxious attachments to what in the past used to relieve our coercive dispositions. We find ourselves less upset by relative disappointments. Our true, lasting joy is rooted in the mystery in which we share by transformation.

Conversion of Dispositions

The moment we discover that any remnant of a past coercive attachment threatens to create excessive dissonance, we work with the mystery to facilitate its transformation. Gradually we turn this coercive disposition into one of many available, freely appreciated dispositions.

In my formation science, I call this operation the *process of disposition conversion.* You will sometimes discover that the remnants of certain coercions cannot serve your new transcendent-immanent way of being. Let them gently and gradually drop out of the hierarchy of your core dispositions. This will make it easier for you to first of all detect and purge their residues in your neuroform. The mystery will reward you with a deepening facility to be peaceful, joyous, and loving under most circumstances. Keep working at it. Coercive remnants, no matter how small, always remain sources of dissonance. At any moment they can interrupt your peace.

Either a coercive or a free disposition determines, each in its own particular way, how our neuroform will be conditioned. Our either compulsively or freely conditioned neuroform directs in turn the orientation of our attention, affection, thought, and imagination. It gives rise to either coercive or spontaneous reactions, to either depreciative or appreciative feelings. Giving up or reforming a coercive disposition means simply that we reform, with the help of the mystery, the neuroformational part of our brain that leaves us dissonant, restless, mentally churning, and tense if the urge that prompts the coercion is not satisfied.

The apparent form we give to our daily life may or may not be different when we strive to reform coercive dispositions in the direction of freely appreciated, flexible ones. We favor them, but we no longer allow them to hold us captive. Our outer appearance and action may look the same. What is changed are the anxious, reality-distorting feelings of coercion and urgency. This inner emotional reversal is not always followed by a shift in our outer form of life.

As we have already seen, transcendent life by no means obliterates all the small enjoyments of the fulfillment of our consonant dispositions that are pre-transcendent. Immanent transcendence only demands that such fulfillment be congenial with the present disclosures of our life call. It forbids us to remain inordinately and coercively attached to such past satisfactions. In the measure of our freedom from coercions, our appreciations, dispositions, and actions will be marked by consonance, wisdom, and gracious effectiveness.

Some coercive dispositions and actions are more detrimental to our peace and joy than others. For example, the satisfaction of a coercive disposition to gain more success than others in one's family may promise less fulfillment than would the satisfaction of one's anxious striving to be a widely admired musician. Still, both coercions fill us with an underlying, tense awareness of possible threats to our success. Both keep our attention captive. Both diminish to some degree our ability to notice, enjoy, and appreciate the goodness, truth, and beauty also in people, events, and things that are not directly connected with our anxious preoccupation.

To gain the appreciation of our family or to be applauded for our gifts, it is not necessary at all that we strive coercively after such aspirations. As transcendent-immanent persons, we can enjoy and appreciate the kind attention and admiration of others without making them ultimate. The transcendent-immanent path has set us free to pursue joy, to savor wholeheartedly the good things life grants us as surprises of the mystery.

Personal Responsibility for Coercive Dispositions

Transcendent-immanent experience now lets us sense that it was never the inter and outer spheres of our life that forced upon us coercive dispositions and actions. It was our own coercive conditioning of our neuroform that had to be redeemed by the mystery of transformation. In the cave of purgation, the mystery lets us experience how we destroyed or lessened real peace and joy. It disclosed to us how futile our desperate attempt was to manipulate the inter and outer spheres of our life. We wanted them so badly to conform to the urgency patterns of our coercive dispositions, feelings, directives, and actions. The mystery liberated us. It lifted us into the blessed land of transcendent-immanent appreciation, wisdom, peace, and joy. Now it inspires us to overcome the last remnants of our past obsessive concerns.

We are called to a consonant life of transcendent-immanent inspiration, aspiration, and appreciation. Fidelity to this call will inspire new favored dispositions; they will transform in turn coercive ones, if they happen to be basically compatible with our life call. Our new appreciations will set them free. Inspired dispositions will turn these past coercions into appreciative dispositions that are in tune with our new phase of life.

* * *

My second directive of peace preservation is: *The mystery inspires us to disclose how coercive dispositions have conditioned our neuroform to compel our attention, thoughts, perceptions, feelings, symbols, and other images automatically in a direction that interrupts the peace and joy of our post-transcendent (transcendent-immanent) path of life.*

Even if we are now directed to the transcendent-immanent path, we do not always see people, events, and things as they really are. Unacknowledged remnants of our coercions may still distort our perception. Fortunately, transcendent-immanent apprehension and appraisal make us perceive people, events, and things in a new way. We experience them as manifestations or epiphanies of the mystery. Such manifestations are either invitational or challenging expressions of its presence.

Often the mystery will invite us to abandon ourselves receptively and silently to its forming will. For example, a striking sculpture, poem, or painting is experienced as an invitation to flow graciously with a manifestation of epiphanic beauty.

At other times, the manifestation of the mystery is an expression of its challenging will, inspiring courageous zeal. Illness, for instance, is experienced as allowed by the mystery. It is a consequence of its formational laws of nature. It is also a challenge to our wonderful powers of courageously coping with sickness in cooperation with health providers, researchers, and wellness teachers. Illness is an invitation, moreover, to turn it into an opportunity for transformation in the light of the mystery. In cases like this, we abandon ourselves in inventive and active form giving and form receiving to the challenging will of the mystery. The epiphanies of this challenge become sources of transcendent zeal and courageous creativity. They are the birthplace of innovative athletics, art, science, scholarship, and daring social action.

Automatic Vital Preappraisal

The transcendent-immanent path disposes us to appreciate things as epiphanies. Transcendent-immanent appreciation will condition our neuroform in consonance with this new liberated vision. It does so through the managing functional "I" as subordinated now to our transcendent "I." Our vital managing "I" embeds the directives we give to it in our autonomic vital nervous system. There it guides our preliminary sensate apprehension and appraisal.

The neuroform provides us with a constantly working neuroformational network of vital assistance. This network serves the implementation of the probable disclosures of our unique-communal life call. Its newly routinized appraisal direction is in tune with our transcendent-immanent direction. It screens automatically the millions of electrochemical impulses that our neuroform receives at every second.

This infrafocal screening takes place in the light of our transcendent-immanent dispositions. They direct our subservient managing "I." This lower "I" in turn conditions and supervises our liberated cerebral screening center or neuroform.

In milliseconds of time, this neurological network automatically screens the endless streams of incoming impulses. It highlights for our focal and prefocal regions of consciousness what is in tune and out of tune with our chosen dispositions and attitudes. Our conditioning managing "I" relays what I call the preappraisal of the neuroform to our prefocal and focal region of consciousness.

Once the preappraisal message has entered prefocal and focal consciousness, it will be subject to our sociohistorical, vital, functional-transcendent, and transcendent-immanent powers of appraisal. If the dispositions that conditioned the preliminary appraisal of the neuroform are not coercive, the higher "I," without excessive tension and crisis, can reject the message. It can choose another disposition or attitude that gave form to its own different conditioning of the automatic appraisal power of the neuroform. The whole process starts over again. New data are sent to our prefocal and focal regions of attention. Still, we have to be on guard for coercive dispositions that limit our mental and emotional flexibility. They are a source of small-mindedness and even at times of fanaticism.

A redeemed, pliable mind can switch back and forth with lightening speed between numerous freely appraised and chosen dispositions with their corresponding neuroformational conditionings. At such graced moments, our past coercive dispositions no longer determine what we experience in our field of life. They no longer suppress any information that is at odds with our coercions. No longer is our consciousness pointed in one direction only. The mystery has stopped the internal tyrannizing of our attention. We are no longer the victims of an illusory version of our field of life and of the people, events, and things within it. Our fears and desires cease to be programmed and preset in our neuroform. We go beyond or transcend the onesided feedback that continually molded our perceptions of life and world when our pretranscendent coercive dispositions were dominant. The mystery has set us free from such coercive programming. Now we can perceive how the forming mystery arranges our daily field of presence and action in ways that uncover for us form potencies hidden within our unique-communal call that from the beginning were meant to release us from coercion and direct our lives in consonance, peace, and joy. We have entered the benevolent land of our new transcendent childhood, the land of likeness to the mystery.

CHAPTER 27

How to Follow Some Directives
of Peace Preservation

While I cannot comment on all the directives of peace preservation I have set before you, I will consider a few more to set the stage for your own reflections on the others.

My third directive was: *The mystery inspires us to welcome the opportunities that our everyday event-to-event experience offers us. On such occasions we become aware of the intrusion of past coercions. We are given the space we need to transform them, thus liberating our lives from robotlike emotional intrusions.*

How do we recognize such opportunities for transformation? It is easy if we pay attention to the coercive desires and expectations that arise in our life. We recall how they used to blind us to formation opportunities. In the post-transcendent phase, we keep tuning in to our stream of thoughts and feelings. We do not deny the reemergence of these compelling dispositions and attitudes. We admit that they make us worried, anxious, irritable, lustful, or resentful. We accept every dissonant feeling gratefully as an opportunity to disclose the hidden pitfalls in our neuroformational life. We ask the mystery to make us profit from such teachable moments. We feel grateful for the deepening of the peace and joy granted to us for this final stretch of our journey.

To be sure, we may still feel tense or excited by the phantoms of the past. Yet, in the light of transcendence, we become aware of the roots of these sudden implosions. They remind us of the roller coaster of alternating moments of satisfaction, on the one hand, and the longer periods of lack of joy and serenity, on the other, when the pretranscendent dimension dominated most of our days.

In the pretranscendent past, we continuously tried to find people who would not upset us, who would not trigger our compulsive or hysterical emotions. Now the mystery of transformation makes us see that people to whom we feel no spontaneous attraction may help us unwittingly. By triggering the hidden remnants of our past dispositions, they compel us to acknowledge their presence. We feel no longer coerced to exclude such irritating persons from our formation story. We can now appreciate that they, too, have a role to play in the melodrama of our daily overconcerns. They, too, are a manifestation of the allowing and challenging will of the mystery. This transforming love-will sustains us on the path of consonance, no matter what people say and do.

We begin to experience that we no longer feel separated from so many people. Such boundaries of the past detracted from the wholeness of our life. Steadily we experience the deepening of the joyous consonance that holds our life together in a new and surprising fashion. The transcendent-immanent life keeps us aware that everyone and everything in our field of life is a channel of the mystery of transformation. It enables us to accept and appreciate both transcendently and immanently what was unacceptable to us when our life was mainly pretranscendent. In the past our obsessive attachment to success in everything made us suffer excessively when we failed. Downhearted, we superimposed on the problem of failure a refusal to cope courageously with the consequences of our defeat.

My fourth, fifth, and sixth directives of peace preservation help us to be present attentively to each event that comes our way. My fourth directive reads: *The mystery reminds us that its effective will for our life contains everything we need to be at peace with each event. We welcome each daily event as an expression of its loving call to us, as the gift of an opportunity for transformation. One condition for this peace is that we do not let our coercive dispositions generate demands, images, memories, and anticipations that are at odds with our post-transcendent (transcendent-immanent) path of life.*

The maintenance of our new gift of serenity demands that we do not let the compelling dispositions of yesterday force us to dwell in the dead past or to focus obsessively in a not-yet-here tomorrow.

The mystery enables us to appraise each field event in a newly illumined way. This new appraisal gradually transforms and enriches our character or core form of life. As I argued earlier, our character or heart is, among other things, a constellation of consonant dispositions or virtues or of dissonant dispositions or vices. Some of these are coercive. Instead of expanding our heart, they contract it. The gift of new appraisal gradually transforms our dissonant dispositions. These transformed dispositions of the heart reform in turn the preappraisal dispositions of our neuroform.

In the past, we often lost our line of thought in ceaseless inward and outward chatter. We babbled on about what we did in the past or what we hoped to do in the future or what such and such did or said in the present. The transcendent-immanent path invites us to many more moments of abiding in silence, stillness, and inwardness. It does not encourage us to dwell unnecessarily on elements of the past or future that stir our self-centered search for excessive security, pleasure, and satisfaction. It inspires us to still the constant churning of mind and heart, to calm down the spinning of our anxious brain, the torrents of idle words; instead, it makes us fully present to each here-and-now event.

The mystery lets us sense that a constant, anxious preoccupation with the future distracts us from its subtle disclosures of our life call in the present. It gently readies us to do effectively what has to be done at this moment in consonance with the messages of the spheres, dimensions, and traditions I symbolized in my basic 1944 interformation paradigm. Along with the transcendence dynamic, it is the foundation of my formation science. Instead of allowing events to hassle us, we appraise them from the viewpoint of our calming awareness of the call in the transcendent-immanent intrasphere of our life. We flow more and more in consonance with the slowly streaming river of immanent transformation. We are surprised by our new disposition to accept and appreciate instantly and affectively whatever happens in our life.

The challenging love-will of the mystery inspires us to change effectively what can be changed for the better in ourselves and in our field. It invests us with the power to follow that inspiration more competently than in the past. Our enlightened, peace-filled attentiveness is increasingly liberated from the affective turmoil of obsessive and hysterical dispositions. Our presence is more clear, spacious, perceptive, pliable, and powerful.

The full resources of our redeemed neuroform now become available to us. Its selective, preappraising, pliable power can be bent in any direction the mystery inspires through the successive disclosures of our life call, through our faith and formation traditions, and through the present events of our field of life. In the former phase of functional transcendence, we tried to conquer the transcendent by our functional plans and exercises. We decided, for instance, that we would discipline ourselves in such a way that we would accept with a smile any unpleasant thing that might happen to us.

A boisterous boy threw a ball that broke our just-installed new window. At once we lost our smile and our equanimity. We got mad at the boy, the ball, the window, and the stifling humidity invading our air-conditioned room. We felt resentment at the expenditure of the time and energy it took to get a new window installed. We discovered that our powers of only functional transcendence could not prevent our explosive dispositions from dissolving our equanimity.

Now in the transcendent-immanent phase of formation, we apprehend and appraise the field event of the shattered window as a part of the here and now of things allowed (not condoned) by the mystery and transformed by it into a formation opportunity. No longer are we compelled to make the situation more unpleasant by getting uptight. We overcome the obsessive inner demand to have all our windows clean and whole and never to be burdened by any accident.

This good and reasonable desire is still for us one of our many favored appreciations. We would still like it to be this way, but it is no longer an obsession. When a window is smashed now, we simply accept it as a challenge to take appropriate action. What pretranscendently had been unacceptable to us has now become acceptable. We realize that the mystery did not cause the window to be broken. Once that happened, however, it empowered us to make the best of it, to make it serve our ascent.

Although we have lost the beauty of an unbroken window, the mystery teaches us that we do not have to lose our peace, joy, and consonance. Neither do we have to explode in ways that trigger the compulsive and hysterical form potencies of people around us and cause them distress, tension, irritation, anger, and veiled or open hostility.

Firm and gentle consonance is the end—and it is also the means—by which we live effectively and competently in the field of life entrusted to our care. Consonance means to be fully tuned in to the providential treasures of each present event in our life. In the measure that our life is consonant, we will accept in love and appreciation whatever happens to us; we set out to make the best of it.

When pretranscendent obsessions dominated our past, we often lost our peace and joy. Our powers of attention and appraisal were controlled by obsessive desires for what we did not possess or by the anxious wish to hold on to what we did have but what seemed to be no longer in tune with the present disclosures of our call of life.

The transcendent-immanent meaning of the here and now events of life was beautifully exemplified for me by the story of Etty Hillesum, who died in a concentration camp. She was a modern Jewish woman, a scholar in linguistics, who lived in Amsterdam during the Nazi terror. She kept a diary and wrote letters that are a testimonial to heroic fidelity to the here-and-now message of the mystery.

Sensitivity to the needs of the moment made her volunteer as a "social worker" for the Dutch transition concentration camp at Westerbork, which warehoused prisoners from Holland until there would be room for them in Auschwitz. She volunteered to work there despite the fact that her post in the Jewish Council in Amsterdam exempted her temporarily from internment. Her heroic presence to the mystery kept her radiant in the midst of mud and misery, sickness, wretchedness, noise and fear. She was present with her lovingly disposed heart to the remorseless rhythm of deportation after deportation to Auschwitz. She saw thousands of horrified women, men, and children stuffed into cattle trains. No matter what happened, she was there to console and encourage them by her empathic presence, expressed by caring words and unsparing service.

Survivors still remember her "shining personality." Buoyed up by the mystery in her life, she wrote again and again, "Despite everything, life is full of beauty and meaning." Sensitivity to the mystery and to suffering people here and now, to victims of the holocaust, made her spurn attempts by friends to hide her in a safe place during the period in which escape would still have been possible before her own deportation to Auschwitz. Throughout this period and to the end, Elly maintained her joyous disposition. A friend described her departure on the cattle train toward certain death in Auschwitz in this way: "Talking gaily, smiling, a kind word for everyone she met on the way, full of sparkling humor, perhaps just a touch of sadness, but every inch the Etty you all know so well . . ." (see Etty Hillesum, *Letters from Westerbork* [New York: Pantheon Books, 1986] xvi).

This woman of valiant, joyous presence to the here-and-now events of her field of life threw a postcard out of the moving death train that said, "We left the camp singing . . ." (p. 146). The peace and joy of her transcendent presence light up when she wrote the following at Westerbork on August 18, 1943:

> You have made me so rich, O God, please let me share out your beauty with open hands. My life has become an uninterrupted dialogue with You, O God, one great dialogue. Sometimes when I stand in some corner of the camp, my feet planted on Your earth, my eyes raised toward Your heaven, tears sometimes run down my face, tears of deep emotion and gratitude. At night too, when I lie in my bed and rest in You, O God, tears of gratitude run down my face, and that is my prayer. I have been terribly tired for several days, but that, too, will pass. Things come and go in a deeper rhythm, and people must be taught to listen: it is the most important thing we have to learn in this life. I am not challenging you, O God, my life is one great dialogue with You. I may never become the great artist I would really like to be, but I am already secure in You, God. Sometimes I try my hand at turning out small profundities and uncertain short stories, but I always end up with just one single word: God. And that says everything and there is no need for anything more. And all my creative powers are translated into inner dialogues with You. The beat of my heart has grown deeper, more active, and yet more peaceful, and it is as if I were all the time storing up inner riches. (p. 116)

She appreciates every event as an opportunity to rise to a "life . . . full of beauty and meaning" (p. xi). She feels that the mystery wants her to be present, as the "thinking heart of the barracks," to every event transpiring in this gruesome place. Although only a short time from death, Etty could appreciate and take care of the here and now.

Life continually exposes us to the painful losses of pretranscendent pleasures and satisfactions; it also offers us as many opportunities for transformation, for real peace and joy. But do we let ourselves appreciate and enjoy these offerings? Or do we misuse our precious power of attention to focus worrisomely on threats to our vital pleasures and functional satisfactions?

Etty fully and effectively responded to the horrible events she had to witness. She did all she could as a member of the Jewish Council in Amsterdam to diminish the suffering of people. As a volunteer "social worker" in the Dutch concentration camp of transition, she alleviated the needs of desperate families and their children. At the same time, she remained fully immanent in the here and now, gratefully enjoying whatever these last weeks of life might still offer her.

Although death and cremation in Auschwitz were only a short time away, she did not let thoughts of the future terrify her. She remained fully present to every event of suffering in the camp. She brought others relief as well as she could. At the same time she profited from her own gift of transcendent attentiveness to all what was valuable here and now. It made her appreciate every moment of life left to her.

We can always find people, events, and things that threaten the fulfillment of our coercive dispositions. We can choose to focus on these threats to the exclusion of anything else. Or we can direct our power of attention to what we are called to do by the situation in which we find ourselves, appreciating it as the splendor of imprisonment in a providential segment of time and space. Daily, the mystery of ongoing transformation grants us more than enough gifts and graces, formation opportunities and challenges, to keep us joyous and peace-filled in the midst of the stresses with which we have to cope.

My fifth peace preservation directive reads: *The mystery delegates to us full responsibility for the preservation of its gifts of peace and joy and for the faithful pursuit of its call to us. We are responsible for the formation of consonant dispositions and their routinization in our neuroform. The dispositioning of our life is the ground of effective presence and action in our formation field. It also affects the reactions and responses of the people we encounter in that field.*

The reemergence of remnants of past illusionary coercive dispositions reminds us of our periods of prolonged distress in the past. We felt overly distressed when our feelings told us that people, events, and things were not fulfilling the compelling disposition patterns we had programmed into our neuroform. How ready we were at such times to deny that our own dispositions were the cause of our unhappiness, worry, and fear. Instead, we made somebody or something else in the outer spheres of our field accountable for our downheartedness. We would think: "John makes me mad," or "Connie drives me up the wall." But what really happened was that what they said or did was not in tune with the compelling directive patterns of our illusionary coercive dispositions—and it was the frustration of these dispositions that made us feel so distressed.

We are blessed now with the enlightenment that goes with the gift of the transcendent-immanent phase of formation. That light makes us see that we ourselves are responsible for letting the remnants of our illusions ruin our day. No longer do we blame anything outside of our intrasphere for the feelings of distress that try to overwhelm us and to steal our newly won peace. We can smile now about our past evasion of responsibility for our feelings.

We see more clearly than ever the link between our obsessive dispositions and our distress. We realize that we are personally responsible for the formation of consonant dispositions and their routinization in our neuroform. We understand also on a far deeper level that we are responsible for our cooperation with the transforming mystery in the disclosure and implementation of our life call.

How we dispose our life is the ground of our effective presence and action in our formation field. Our senses receive from the people, events, and things in our field all kinds of impressions. Our minds work these sensory impressions through. They coform our reactions and responses to that field. Our field of life is not only a *factual* field; it is also an *appraised* field. Our appraisal of our field of life is due in part to our sensory impressions. The fascinating thing is that we are in some measure responsible for the feedback people give us. Their reactions and responses are influenced by the way we approach them. If we are truly loving, peace-filled, and joyous, many will gradually be touched by the quality of our presence. Unwittingly, they may mirror our dispositions and give us back what we gave to them. A loving, joyous person will create a loving, joyous world around her or himself.

My sixth directive of peace preservation reads: *The mystery wants us to share joyously in its loving appreciation of our unique-communal life call, in its unceasing forgiveness of our coercions and failures. It loves to see us grow in the faith that all obstacles can be a part of our progress on the post-transcendent-immanent way if we turn them into stepping stones.*

Loving appreciation of our life call implies that we accept what this call implies here and now. Such loving acceptance does not mean to go along with unjust situations. It often means acceptance of the call to do something about, for instance, social injustice or discrimination. On the post-transcendent–immanent path, we are committed to what our unique-communal life call directs us to do, but we are no longer inordinately attached to the success of our actions. If failures, opposition, mean rumors, and envious slander against us succeed in reawakening remnants of our past obsessive dispositions, we are now inspired to look at such obstacles as opportunities allowed by the mystery for our transformation. We realize that opponents more than friends often enable us indirectly and implicitly to become more aware of remnants that still need to be reformed in our emotional life.

We grow in the faith that all obstacles in ourselves and in the outer and inter spheres of our life are a part of our formation journey. We find peace and joy in the very experience that every obstacle, including that of our own failures, is a necessary part of our post-transcendent–immanent unfolding. What we have to do is to be present to any event in an accepting, appreciative, and, above all, pliable, attentive way. The remnants of the past will gradually melt away. The main thing we have to do is to persist in relaxed attentiveness to what transpires in our mind and heart without excessive introspection. Thus, we accept our shortcomings joyously. They ought to be celebrated as pointers or stepping stones. They tell us where we still fail the transcendent-immanent life given to us.

As I said earlier, the praxis of transcendent transformation goes beyond the empirical-scientific mode. It implies a faith experience that may be monistic, theistic, or theistic-epiphanic. A more refined treatment of such praxis must either restrict itself to one of these three visions of the transforming mystery or treat each of them at length separately. Such treatment, no matter how interesting and helpful, would fall outside the purpose of the seven pretheological volumes of this series. Only in my forthcoming volume eight will I restrict myself to one specific formation tradition, that being the Christian, since I am most familiar with it. I shall show there the possibility of articulations of formation science within such a tradition and lay the groundwork for a systematic Christian formation theology. The afterword at the end of my next volume, the seventh in this series, *Transcendence Therapy,* will serve as a bridge between my pretheological formation science and my formation theology. I recommend that readers consult it for clarification as to the full extent of my project. The following afterword marks the end of this sixth volume.

Afterword

As readers may realize by now, I paid attention, in this volume on transcendent formation, mostly to personal formation. I distinguished between lower development and higher transcendent-immanent unfolding. Anything that unfolds in time will necessarily show both surface developmental stages and deeper formation phases.

The laws of developmental stages deepen when they are complemented by those of the unfolding of our transcendent-immanent human spirit, freedom, reason, heart, and corresponding character. The more people grow in their transcendent-immanent nature, the more their developmental stages will be complemented and transformed by such deeper formation phases.

The same is true of anything human beings as transcendent-immanent creatures initiate and develop. In this regard, a story is more convincing than an abstract treatise.

To exemplify what I mean, I would like to bend back upon the story of the phasic unfolding of the new science of formation I myself initiated along with my now-fifty-year-old creative crafting of a formation theology. I am still bringing the latter effort to full completion. The reason I want to present this story is not so much to explain what formation theology and formation science are but to highlight from experience the phases of their unfolding.

Seminal Phase

The first seeds (1935) for this new discipline, then called formative spirituality (*vormings spiritualiteit*), were the fruits of a profound soul friendship between myself and Marinus Scholtes (1919–1941). Rinus was a fellow student at the junior seminary. He was an unusually graced and gifted young man. In due course he was elevated by the mystery during his novitiate to the state of transforming union or mystical marriage. His three spiritual directors in, respectively, the junior seminary, the novitiate, and the senior seminary, asserted this remarkable event to be true. Rinus died of tuberculosis in 1941 in my presence at the age of twenty-two. We had journeyed together on the road to spiritual life formation, often discussing for hours on end the merits and limits of mainly informational religious instruction. We had started in 1933 a spiritual formation group, a prototype of the present Epiphany Association. It consisted of lay friends with whom we kept in touch during our holidays at home in the Hague, where our parents lived in neighboring parishes.

Rinus left various letters and notebooks about his spiritual ascent. They are filled with ideas of spiritual character and personality formation in the light of the Spirit. Soon these testimonials will be translated into English. They were among the first seeds that influenced my then presystematic flashes of insight into formation theology and formation science. Three years later, after my friend's holy death, I developed the first ideas for a systematic theology of empirical Christian character and personality formation.

I gave my fledgling undertaking various new names, most notably "formative or epiphanic spirituality." These terms were meant as a preparation for the art and discipline of transcendent-immanent character and personality formation, which I had been in the process of formulating since 1944. At that time, I conceived the beginnings of a more systematic theology of formation and its sustaining pretheological formation science. The aim of formation theology itself was to study the formation of transcendent-immanent human and Christian character and personality. By contrast, its supporting pretheological formation science was called the science of foundational human formation.

What I named formation theology preceded my initiation of pretheological formation science. The latter did for formation theology on the empirical-experiential-formational level what Aquinas's pretheological philosophy did for informational theology on the speculative-practical level.

In this seminal phase, the spiritual needs of Christians and non-Christians hiding with me during the Dutch Hunger Winter 1944-45 inspired me to initiate first an epiphanic theology of Christian formation for Christian believers and, subsequently, a human science of transcendent-immanent formation, especially for those among us of non-Christian persuasions. They came to me, a theology student, for spiritual counsel and encouragement in their anxiety, fear, and desperation during the infamous Dutch Hunger Winter of the last year of the Second World War (1944–45).

Post-War Phase
In this second interim formation phase of the new discipline, the Dutch Life Schools played an important role. Their program for the transcendent character formation of young adults had been initiated—also during the war—by Ms. Maria Schouwenaars, a Belgian school supervisor, whose first students were young working women. I added to this program in Gemert, Holland, a male division. These schools gave me an opportunity to test my epiphanic theology and pretheology in a catechetical fashion, with everyday working people. I taught many of them in factories and mills during their working hours.

In this same phase, Monsignor Giovanni Batista Montini, of the Vatican Secretariat of State, later Pope Paul VI, asked my provincial superior to release me from my duties as a seminary professor. He wanted me to develop in detail my personality theory and theology in service of the fast-expanding life school project.

These European phases of the work were followed by four other interim American phases. Three of these took place at Duquesne University from 1954 to 1994. The fourth and crowning phase constitutes the establishment and current unfolding of the international Epiphany Association, successor to the 1935 association founded by myself and Rinus Scholtes. How did all this come to be?

Monsignor Montini had expressed to Ms. Schouwenaars the Vatican's hope that this epiphanic theological and pretheological approach could be initiated in a Catholic university as an exemplar for other Christian centers of learning the world over. By providential coincidence, President Vernon Gallagher of Duquesne University invited two Dutch Spiritans, both involved in the life schools, to join his faculty at Duquesne. They were a theology professor, Fr. Bert van Croonenburg, and I, myself, a professor of philosophical anthropology. Both of us taught at the same Dutch seminary and worked side by side with the Dutch Life Schools.

Pre-Institute Phase at Duquesne
Father van Croonenburg was assigned to the theology department, and later he shifted to philosophy. I was asked by the president to prepare myself in three American universities for the introduction of something innovative, namely, psychology as a distinctively human science. We both kept promoting on the side, through nationwide talks and publications, my formative spirituality, a combination of formation theology and formation science.

In the meantime, I waited patiently until I would be able to implement my vision in a relatively independent institute. In 1963 I received permission to start the Institute of Man, first as a subdivision of the psychology department (hence its temporary name). Three years later I was allowed to begin an institute independent of the psychology department. In due time its name was changed to the "Institute of Formative Spirituality," the IFS, to match the original Dutch expression. Joining me as a teacher in the program and as the institute's first executive director under me as director was the theologian and philosopher Father Bert van Croonenburg.

History of the IFS
First Phase—1963-1980—Under My Directorship. This period witnessed an influx of students (laity, clergy, and religious) from the United States and abroad, as well as an expansion of the faculty and the hiring of a new assistant and later executive director and director, Susan Muto, Ph.D. She made a major

contribution to this early history not only by her administrative and editing skills for our three journals (*Humanitas, Envoy,* and the *Review of Existential Psychology and Psychiatry*—she as managing editor, I as editor) but also as a full-time professor in the field of spiritual literature taught in the light of my formation theology. I oversaw and encouraged her continuation of my theology through her six-semester core course cycle in the writings of the masters of the Christian formation tradition. She taught the works of these masters not primarily in a historical-informational way, but empirically, experientially, and formatively.

Dr. Muto's cycle proved basic for the program as a whole. Pretheological formation science would, of course, be as incomplete without its formation theology as pretheological Thomistic philosophy by itself would be incomplete without its informational theology. Similarly, "foundational human formation" on which I focused for my academic lectures was "foundational" not only for my pretheological formation science but also in relation to the formation theology it serves. The "science of foundational human formation" (SFHF), or simply formation science, should not be denied its other potential use, namely, as a servant source of my theology of Christian character and personality formation. To disconnect formation science from the fullness of the project, as I originally envisioned it, would be to misunderstand and misrepresent the intention of this new approach. Obviously a onesidedly developed formation science could become a threat to the integrity of religious or ideological formation traditions. It should be balanced by their respective formation theologies. My own Christian formation theology aims to elevate the theologically relevant concepts and constructs of the science and discipline of formation in the light of the Judeo-Christian Revelation. This goes far beyond only adding to a curriculum a few courses in informational spiritual reading and in the history of spirituality. Such an addition cannot prevent the secret dominance of a pretheological formation science in the minds of the students.

Therefore, I asked Dr. Muto to develop as the main basic underpinning of the program a formational-theological, six-semester course cycle in the masters to be taken by all the students. This was the key to guarantee the orthodoxy of the program over against psychologism and philosophism as well as cultic and New Age spiritualities. It provided one of the necessary conditions for its implicit compatibility with at least the natural human bases of my formation theology.

The result of this planning was the evolution from 1969 to 1979 of what the Middle States Accreditation Association praised as a three-year doctoral-style master's program. It led, on their strong recommendation, to the establishment in 1979 of the Ph.D. program in Formative Spirituality at Duquesne University.

For another reason 1979 was a fruitful year for my new discipline. It marked the cofounding by Dr. Muto and myself of the Epiphany Association. Its aim was to function as an independent international research, publication, archival, consultation, and educational association for the unfolding of formation theology. It readied us for the final phase that would secure the full continuation of many more of the crucial aspects of the epiphanic formation theology and pretheological formation science started in 1944. Certain inspirational aspects of this work, as we would learn, could not be fully implemented at any university. They required the establishment of an independent meditation, research, teaching, education, and publication base. This independent base of operations became more necessary in view of the rising economic costs of running any regular academic graduate program.

As the cofounders of Epiphany, we foresaw that the interim institute phase of formative spirituality was destined to be phased out. This would happen, coincidentally, at the time that its attention to formation theology, as taught implicitly in the cycle of the masters of formation, began to wane. This phase-out started in 1994, the same year the Epiphany programs and publications were expanding, nationally and internationally.

Second Phase—1980–1988—Under the Directorship of Susan Muto, Ph.D. This period of the institute saw the inauguration and expansion of a three-year Ph.D. program in formative spirituality, the start of the two-year master's program in formative leadership and ministry, the one-year master's program in ongoing formation, and the summer program. The journal *Humanitas* was phased out and a new journal, *Studies in Formative Spirituality,* was begun. Under the Muto directorship, the IFS enjoyed the highest increase in its American and international student population. Its six-semester cycle in spiritual classics in the light of my formation theology was dominant. God's blessing, ecclesial trust, and support were increasing along with student enrollment.

Third Phase—1988–1991—Under the Directorship of Father Richard Byrne, O.C.S.O., Ph.D. This brief, three-year period marked the first stage of transition leading to the closure of this interim university phase of my project. Demographic changes in religious congregations and the churches led to a drop in student enrollment. I sincerely believe that the refusal to continue the basic six-semester cycle in the classics as one of the main sources of a uniquely inspirational formation theology made some church authorities reluctant to send students. New course offerings by a younger faculty were only minimally effective in recruiting students, resulting in more budgetary deficits.

Following the death of then-director Byrne, I was asked by the president of the university to serve as interim director of the IFS during the academic year 1991–1992 in the hope of restoring the confidence so carefully cultivated in the previous twenty-five years. I was working on the fifth volume in this series. At the same time, I was searching for a new full-time IFS director. To recover the basis of the program, I resumed with Dr. Muto the coteaching of the core courses in pretheological formation science as well as the then neglected implicit formation theology of the masters. My intent was to bring the institute back to its former level of excellence and trustworthiness but, as time would prove, Holy Providence had other plans.

Fourth Phase—1992–1994—Under the Directorship of Father Clyde Bonar, Ph.D. Plans made by me in the previous year for the continuation of the institute, especially in regard to the restoration of its underpinning in the implicit and explicit theology of the masters, came perhaps too late. Some religious circles expressed concern that the inspirational, formational, theological base of the program was no longer central during the tumultuous three years between 1988 and 1991. What was intended to be a transition phase to renewal and survival marked the final phasing out of the institute at the university after almost six years of declining enrollment and increasing debt. There is not much more I can say of these years. During six years of decline, the archives were partially destroyed or left in disarray. Fortunately, this is not so for the archives of the first twenty-five years, which are now kept in the library of the Epiphany Association.

The Duquesne period of formation theology and formation science proved to be yet another interim phase. It was clear that I did not have the space and time to complete the crowning crucial integration of my formation theology with my formation science. This phase is now taking place under the auspices of the Epiphany Association while integrating all the fruits of the pretheological science of formation. The interim institute phases, like the preceding European periods, had been effective in their own limited way. The students graduating from its master's and doctoral programs, especially during the first twenty-five years, numbered upward of seven hundred, with at least another one hundred taking sabbatical or part-time courses. The religious affiliation of its students was, to name a few denominations, Roman Catholic, Byzantine, Presbyterian, Methodist, Baptist, Lutheran, Mennonite, and Episcopalian. The number of foreign countries represented by its students ranged around the globe. As far as publication is concerned, to cite as the main example of our progress, Dr. Muto and I either alone or together have written about fifty books to date and published over three hundred articles. We founded and edited four journals: *Humanitas, Envoy* (renamed *Inspiration*), *Studies in Formative Spirituality* (renamed for its final year of publication *The Journal of Spiritual Formation*), and in the earliest years, *The Review of Existential Psychology and Psychiatry,* so-named by the Association of American Psychiatrists and Psychologists interested in philosophical and religious issues.

The present phase and the crowning point of the original project, begun by me in 1944, continues under the auspices of the Epiphany Association, which is committed to the research, development, and promulgation worldwide of formation theology and formation science. Here we aim to bring to completion the original epiphanic ideas and theories started in Holland. We do that through, for example, our twice-yearly Epiphany Lay Formation Academy (ELFA) and the publication of our new journal, *Epiphany International.* Other programs are in the offing to serve diocesan lay ministers and postgraduate students (laity, clergy, and religious) locally, nationally, and internationally.

The history here cited illustrates what I mean when I claim that phasic formation pertains not only to persons but also to institutions. This thinking can even be applied to newly created disciplines in their phases of growth, decline, and restoration of their original inspiration.

The phasic history of formation theology and its servant science has demonstrated how the rise and fall of pretheological formation science depends on the rise and fall of formation theology. Each formation theology develops in the light of a faith tradition to which the formation theologian adheres, to name a few, the Jewish, Christian, Islamic, Hindu, or Buddhist. Since my own formation theology is Christian, it makes sense that the forthcoming eighth volume in this series will represent the crowning phase of my work. Formation theology and its servant science of formation has come a long way since 1944. I trust that this work will enjoy its finest hour through the research, teaching, programming, and publication efforts expanding at our Epiphany Center.

With this volume in mind, I would like to say that the next one, volume seven, will examine the meaning and methods utilized in my approach to transcendence or transtherapy. Needless to say, this new kind of therapy is rooted in my formation science. It does not replace standard therapies and counseling practices. On the contrary, if desirable, it refers people to existing therapies that specialize in their particular pretranscendent problems and their symptoms.

Transtherapy is a complementary treatment. It rounds off other therapies and counseling efforts. It crowns their achievements by helping counselees to integrate them experientially in their chosen traditional consonant character form. Transtherapy assists counselees in the disclosure and healing of any old or new dissonant split in their character. New ruptures of personality may have accompanied unwittingly an otherwise successful pretranscendent standard therapy. Similar personality gaps may have been caused by the indiscriminate application of pretranscendent self-help literature and lectures.

The volume on transtherapy will, by its very nature, prepare the reader for my eighth volume, *Christian Formation,* where I shall continue to examine, among other things, the grounds of transtherapeutic healing against the background of one's specific faith and formation tradition.

Bibliography

Books

Adams-Webber, J. R. *Personal Construct Theory: Concepts and Applications.* New York: Wiley, 1979.

Adler, A. *Superiority and Social Interest.* Ed. H. L. Ansbacher and R. Ansbacher. Evanston, Ill.: Northwestern University Press, 1964.

Adorno, T. W., E. Frenkel-Brunswik, D. J. Levinson, and R. N. Sanford. *The Authoritarian Personality.* New York: Harper, 1950.

Aguilera, D. C., J. M. Messick, and M. A. Ferrell. *Crisis Intervention: Theory and Methodology.* St. Louis: C. V. Mosby, 1970.

Aquinas, Thomas. *Treatise on Happiness.* Trans. John A. Oesterle. Notre Dame, Ind.: University of Notre Dame Press, 1983.

Ainsworth, M. D. S. *Infancy in Uganda: Infant Care and the Growth of Love.* Baltimore: Johns Hopkins Press, 1967.

Alcoholics Anonymous. New York: Alcoholics Anonymous World Services, 1976.

Allport, G. *Theories of Personality and the Concept of Structure.* New York: Wiley, 1955.

———. *Personality: A Psychological Interpretation.* New York: Holt, 1937.

———. *Personality.* New York: Holt, 1937.

———. *Patterns and Growth in Personality.* New York: Holt, 1961.

———. *Becoming.* New Haven, Conn.: Yale University Press, 1976.

Angyal, A. *Foundations for a Science of Personality.* New York: Commonwealth Fund, 1941.

Aries, P. *Centuries of Childhood: A Social History of Family Life.* New York: Knopf, 1962.

Aristotle. *Poetics.* In *The Basic Works of Aristotle*, ed. R. McKeon. New York: Random House, 1941.

Assagioli, R. A. *The Act of Will.* New York: Viking, 1973.

———. *Psychosynthesis.* Esalen, 1973.

Bach, G. R. *Young Children's Aggressive Play Phantasies.* Psychological Monographs 59, No. 272. Washington, D.C.: American Psychological Association, 1945.

———, and P. Wyden. *The Intimate Enemy.* New York: Morrow, 1968.

Bandler, R., and J. Grindler. *Frogs into Princes: Neuro-Linguistic Programming.* Moab, Ut.: Real People, 1979.

Bandura, A. "Modeling Theory." In *Psychology of Learning: Systems, Models, and Theories,* ed. W. S. Sahakian. Chicago: Markham, 1970.

———, and R. H. Walters. *Social Learning and Personality Development.* New York: Holt, Rinehart & Winston, 1963.

Becker, Ernest. *Escape from Evil.* New York and London: Free Press, 1973.

———. *The Denial of Death.* New York and London: Free Press, 1973.

Bender, L. *Child Psychiatric Techniques.* Springfield, Ill.: Thomas, 1952.

Benson, H. *The Relaxation Response.* New York: Avon, 1976.

Bergson, H. *Creative Evolution.* New York: Random House, 1944.

———. *The Two Sources of Morality and Religion.* New York: Henry Holt, 1935.

Bernard of Clairvaux: Selected Works in Classics of Western Spirituality. Trans. G. R. Evans. New York: Paulist Press, 1987.

Berne, E. *Beyond Games and Scripts.* New York: Grove Press, 1976.

Bettelheim, Bruno. *Freud and Man's Soul.* New York: Alfred A. Knopf, 1982.

Blanton, S. *The Healing Power of Poetry.* New York: Crowell, 1960.

Bloom, Allan. *The Closing of the American Mind.* New York: Simon & Schuster, 1987.

Boehme, Jacob. *Personal Christianity.* London: Constable & Co.

———. *Attachment and Loss,* Vol. I. *Attachment.* New York: Basic Books, 1969.

Buber, M. *The Way of Man.* Chicago: Wilcox and Follett, 1951.

———. *I and Thou.* Trans. R. G. Smith. New York: Macmillan, 1958.

Bucke, R. M. *Cosmic Consciousness: A Study in the Evolution of the Human Mind.* New York: Dutton, 1923.

Capra, F. *The Tao of Physics.* Boulder, Colo.: Shambhala Publications, 1975.

Cassirer, E. *The Philosophy of Symbolic Forms.* Vol. I. New Haven, Conn.: Yale University Press, 1944.

———. *The Philosophy of Symbolic Forms.* Vol. II. New Haven, Conn.: Yale University Press, 1953.

Catherine of Siena: The Dialogue in Classics of Western Spirituality. Trans. Suzanne Noffke, O.P. New York: Paulist Press, 1980.

Cautela, J. R. "Covert Condition." In *The Psychology of Private Events: Perspectives on Covert Response Systems,* ed. A. Jacobs and L. B. Sachs. New York: Academic Press, 1971.

Champion, R. A. *Learning and Activation.* New York: Wiley, 1969.

Chomsky, N. *Aspects of the Theory of Syntax.* Cambridge, Mass.: M.I.T. Press, 1965.

Coles, R. *Children of Crisis.* New York: Little, Brown, 1964.

———. *Eric H. Erikson: The Growth of His Work.* Boston: Little, Brown, 1970.

The Collected Works of St. John of the Cross. Trans. Kieran Kavanaugh, O.C.D., and Otilio Rodriguez, O.C.D. Washington, D.C.: ICS Publications, 1991.

Dell C. *A Primer for Movement Description.* New York: Dance Notation Bureau, 1970.

DeSilva, L. A. *The Problem of Self in Buddhism and Christianity.* London: The Macmillan Press Ltd., 1979.

Desoille, R. *The Directed Daydream.* Monograph No. 8. New York: The Psychosynthesis Research Foundation, 1965.

Dinkmeyer, D., and R. Dreikurs. *Encouraging Children to Learn.* Englewood Cliffs, N.J.: Prentice-Hall, 1963.

———, and L. Losoncy. *The Encouragement Book: On Becoming a Positive Person.* Englewood Cliffs, N.J.: Prentice-Hall, 1980.

Dossey, Larry, M.D. *Recovering the Soul.* New York: Bantam Books, 1989.

Douvan, E. and J. Adelson. *The Adolescent Experience.* New York: John Wiley, 1966.

Dreikurs, R., and V. Soltz. *Children: The Challenge.* New York: Duell, Sloan and Pearle, 1967.

———. *Psychology in the Classroom.* New York: Harper & Row, 1968.

Elgin, D. *Voluntary Simplicity.* New York: 1980.

Elkind, D. *Children and Adolescents: Interpretive Essays on Jean Piaget.* New York: Oxford University Press, 1970.

Ellenberger, H. F. *The Discovery of the Unconscious.* New York: Basic Books, 1970.

Ellis, A. *Reason and Emotion in Psychotherapy.* New York: Lyle Stuart, 1962.

Erikson, E. H. *Child and Society.* New York: Norton, 1950.

———. *Identity, Youth and Crisis.* New York: Norton, 1950.

———. *Childhood and Society.* 2nd ed. New York: Norton, 1963.

Ferreira, A. J. *Prenatal Environment.* Springfield, Ill.: Charles C. Thomas, 1969.

———. *A Theory of Cognitive Dissonance.* Evanston, Ill.: Row, Peterson, 1957.

Fingarette, H. *The Self in Transformation.* New York: Harper & Row, 1963.

———. *Confucianism: The Secular as Sacred.* New York: Harper and Row, 1979.

Fisher, S., and S. Cleveland. *Body Image and Personality.* 2nd rev. ed. New York: Dover, 1968.

Flavell, J. H. *The Development Psychology of Jean Piaget.* Princeton, N.J.: Van Nostrand, 1963.

——. *The Psychology of Sleep.* New York: Scribner's, 1966.

Fletcher, R. *Instinct in Man.* New York: International Universities Press, 1957.

Focillon, H. *The Life of Forms in Art.* New York: Wittenborn, Schultz, 1948.

Fowler, J. W. *Stages of Faith.* New York: Harper and Row, 1981.

——. *Persuasion and Healing.* Baltimore: Johns Hopkins Press, 1961.

Frankl, V. *Doctor and the Soul.* New York: Knopf, 1965.

Fransella, F. *Personal Change and Reconstruction.* London: Academic Press, 1972.

Friedman, M., Rosenman, R. *Type A Behavior and Your Heart.* Greenwich, Conn.: Fawcett, 1975.

Fromm, Erich. *Man for Himself: An Inquiry into the Psychology of Ethics.* New York: Holt, Rinehart & Winston, 1947.

——. Man for Himself: An Inquiry into the Psychology of Ethics. New York: Rinehart, 1947.

——. *Psychoanalysis and Religion.* New Haven, Conn.: Yale University Press, 1950.

——. *To Have or To Be?* New York: Harper and Row, 1976.

Gazda, G., et al. *Human Relations Development.* Boston: Allyn and Bacon, 1973.

Gesell, A., and H. Thompson. *The Psychology of Early Growth.* New York: Macmillan, 1938.

——, and F. L. Ilg. *Infant and Child in the Culture of Today.* New York: Harper & Row, 1943.

——, et al. *The Child from Five to Ten.* New York: Harper, 1946.

——, F. L. Ilg, and L. B. Ames. *Youth: The Years from Ten to Sixteen.* New York: Harper, 1956.

——, F. L. Ilg, and L. B. Ames. *The Child from Five to Ten.* Harper & Row: 1977.

Goffman, E. *Behavior in Public Places.* New York: Free Press, 1963.

——. *Frame Analysis: An Essay on the Organization of Experience.* Cambridge, Mass.: Harvard University Press, 1974.

Goldstein, K. *Human Nature in the Light of Psychopathology.* Cambridge: Harvard University Pres, 1940.

Goldstein, A. P., R. P. Sprafkin, N. J. Gershaw, and P. Klein. *Skillstreaming the Adolescent: A Structured Learning Approach to Teaching Prosocial Skills.* Urbana, Ill.: Research Press, 1980.

——, P. J. Monti, T. Sardino, and D. Green. *Police Crisis Intervention.* New York: Pergamon, 1977.

Goleman, D. *The Varieties of the Meditative Experience.* New York: Dutton, 1977.

Hillesum, Etty. *Letters from Westerbork*. New York: Pantheon Books, 1986.

Goodman, N. *Languages of Art: An Approach to a Theory of Symbols*. Indianapolis, Ind.: Hackett Publishing, 1976.

Greenstone, J. L., and S. Leviton. *The Crisis Intervener's Handbook*. Vol. I. Dallas: Crisis Management Workshops, 1979.

————, and S. Leviton. *The Crisis Intervener's Handbook*. Vol. II. Dallas: Rothschild Publishing House, 1980.

Griffiths, Ruth. *A Study of the Imagination in Early Childhood*. London: Routledge & Kegan Paul, Ltd. 1949.

Grolnick, S., and L. Barkin, eds. *Between Reality and Fantasy: Transitional Objects and Phenomena*. New York: Aronson, 1978.

Hall, E. T. *The Hidden Dimension*. Garden City, N.Y.: Doubleday, 1966.

Haring, N. G., and E. L. Phillips. *Education of Emotionally Disturbed Children*. New York: McGraw-Hill, 1962.

Hartmann, H. Ego Psychology and the Problem of Adaptation. New York: International Universities Press, 1958.

Havighurst, R. J. *Human Development and Education*. 3rd ed. New York: McKay, 1972.

Heisenberg, W. *Physics and Philosophy*. New York: Harper, 1958.

Henry, J. *Culture Against Man*. New York: Random House, 1963.

Hilgard, E. R. *Divided Consciousness*. New York: Wiley, 1977.

Horney, Karen. *Self Analysis*. New York: Norton, 1942.

————. *Neurosis and Human Growth*. New York: Norton, 1966.

Husserl, Edmund. *The Crisis of European Sciences and Transcendental Phenomenology*. Evanston, Ind.: 1970.

Inhelder, B., and J. Piaget. *The Growth of Logical Thinking from Childhood to Adolescence*. New York: Basic Books, 1958.

Jackins, H. *The Human Side of Human Beings*. Seattle, Wash.: Rational Island Publishers, 1965.

————. *The Human Situation*. Seattle, Wash.: Rational Island Publishers, 1973.

Jacob, S. W., and C. A. Francone. *Structure and Function in Man*. Philadelphia: W. B. Saunders, 1974.

Jacobson, E. *Progressive Relaxation*. Chicago: University of Chicago Press, 1938.

————. *The Self and the Object World*. New York: International Universities Press, 1964.

————. *Depression: Comparative Studies of Normal, Neurotic and Psychotic Conditions*. New York: International Universities Press, 1971.

Jaensch, E. R. *Eidetic Imagery*. New York: Harcourt, 1930.

Janov, A. *The Feeling Child*. New York: Simon and Schuster, 1973.

Johnson, R. C., and P. Dokecki, O. H. Mowrer, eds. *Conscience, Contract and Social Reality.* New York: Holt, Rinehart, Winston, 1972.

Jones, E. E. *Ingratiation: A Social Psychological Analysis.* New York: Appleton, 1964.

Jourard, S. *The Transparent Self: Self-Disclosure and Well-Being.* New York: Van Nostrand, 1971.

Jung, C. G. *Modern Man in Search of a Soul.* New York: Harcourt, 1933.

Kant, Emmanuel. *Critique of Pure Reason.* Trans. Norman Kemp Smith. New York: St. Martin's, 1965.

Kelley, H., and J. Thibaut. *Interpersonal Relations: A Theory of Interdependence.* New York: Wiley, 1978.

Kelly, G. A. *The Psychology of Personal Constructs.* New York: Norton, 1955 (2 vols).

———. *A Theory of Personality.* New York: Norton, 1963.

Keyes, R. *We, the Lonely People: Searching for Community.* New York: Harper & Row, 1973.

Kohlberg, L. "Continuities and Discontinuities in Childhood and Adult Moral Development Revsited." In *Lifespan Developmental Psychology: Personality and Socialization,* ed. P. B. Baltes and K. W. Schaie. New York: Academic Press, 1973.

Kohut, H. *The Analysis of Self.* New York: International Universities Press, 1971.

Kornfield, J. *Living Buddhist Masters.* Santa Cruz, Calif: Unity Press, 1977.

Kranz, S., ed. *The H Persuasion: How Persons Have Permanently Changed from Homosexuality through the Study of Aesthetic Realism with Eli Siegel.* New York: Definition Press, 1971.

Kuhn, T. S. *The Structure of Scientific Revolutions.* 2nd ed. Chicago: University of Chicago Press, 1970.

Nicholson, L., and L. Torbet. *How to Fight Fair with Your Kids and Win!* New York: Harcourt, 1980.

Laing, R. D., and A. Esterson. *Sanity, Madness and the Family.* New York: Basic Books, 1964.

———. *The Divided Self.* New York: Penguin Books, 1965.

———. *The Politics of Experience.* New York: Ballantine, 1967.

———. *The Politics of the Family and Other Essays.* New York: Pantheon, 1969.

———. *The Self and Others.* New York: Pelican Books, 1971.

Leary, T. *Interpersonal Diagnosis of Personality.* New York: Ronald Press, 1957.

Leedy, J. J., ed. *Poetry the Healer.* Philadelphia: Lippincott, 1973.

Lenneberg, E. H., ed. *New Directions in the Study of Language.* Cambridge, Mass.: M.I.T. Press, 1964.

———. *The Biological Foundations of Language.* New York: John Wiley, 1966.

———. "The Natural History of Language." Pp. 219–52 in *The Genesis of Language: A Psycholinguistic Approach,* ed. F. Smith and G. A. Miller. Cambridge, Mass.: M.I.T. Press, 1966.

Levine, S. *A Gradual Awakening.* New York: Anchor, 1979.

Lewin, K. *A Dynamic Theory of Personality.* New York: McGraw-Hill, 1935.

Lindemann, H. *Relieve Tension the Autogenic Way.* New York: Wyden, 1973.

Lorenz, K. *On Aggression.* New York: Harcourt Brace Jovanovich, 1966.

Losoncy, L. *Turning People On: How to Be an Encouraging Person.* Englewood Cliffs, N.J.: Prentice-Hall, 1977.

Luthe, W. "Physiological and Psychodynamic Effects of Autogenic Training." In *Topical Problems of Psychotherapy,* ed. B. Stokvis. New York: S. Jarger, 1960.

Maltz, Maxwell. *Psycho-Cybernetics.* Englewood Cliffs, N.J.: Prentice Hall, 1960.

Marcuse, H. *Eros and Civilization.* New York: Vintage Books, 1962.

Maslow, A. H. *Motivation and Personality.* New York: Harper & Row, 1954

———. *Toward a Psychology of Being.* New York: D. Van Nostrand Co., 1968.

———. *Toward a Psychology of Being.* 2nd ed. New York: Van Nostrand, 1968.

———. *Religions, Values, and Peak Experiences.* New York: Viking, 1970.

———. *Religions, Values, and Peak Experiences.* New York: Penguin, 1970.

———. *The Farther Reaches of Human Nature.* New York: Viking, 1972.

———. *The Plateau Experience. Journal of Transpersonal Psychology* 4 (1972).

May, Rollo. *Man's Search for Himself.* New York: W. W. Norton, 1953.

———. *Love and Will.* New York: W. W. Norton, 1969.

———. *The Meaning of Anxiety.* New York: Norton, 1977.

———. *The Courage to Create.* New York: Bantam, 1980.

———. *Freedom and Destiny.* New York: W. W. Norton, 1981.

———. *The Discovery of Being.* New York: W. W. Norton, 1983.

McGee, R. *Crisis Intervention in the Community.* Baltimore, Md.: University Park Press, 1974.

McHugh, P. *Defining the Situation: The Organization of Meaning in Social Interaction.* Indianapolis, Ind.: Bobbs-Merrill, 1968.

McNiell, J. *A History of the Cure of Souls.* New York: Harper & Row, 1951.

Mead, G. H. *Mind, Self and Society: From the Standpoint of a Social Behaviorist.* Ed. C. W. Morris. Chicago: University of Chicago Press, 1934.

Meerloo, J. A. M. "The Universal Language of Rhythm." In *Poetry Therapy,* ed. J. J. Leedy. Philadelphia: Lippincott, 1969.

Merton, Thomas. *The Ascent to Truth.* New York: Viking Press, 1959.

————. *The Wisdom of the Desert: Sayings from the Desert Fathers of the Fourth Century*. London: Sheldon Press, 1974.

Missildine, W. Hugh, M.D. *Your Inner Child of the Past*. New York: Simon & Schuster, 1963.

Moreno, J. L. *Who Shall Survive? A New Approach to the Problem of Human Interrelations*. Washington, D.C.: Nervous and Mental Disease Publication, 1934.

Morgan, C. O. "Disability Through Imagery Experience." In *Imagery: Its Many Dimensions*, ed. J. Shorr, et al. Proceedings of the First Annual Conference of the American Association for the Study of Mental Imagery. New York: Plenum, 1979.

Morita, S., and K. Mizutani. *Sei No Yokubo (The Desire to Live Fully)*. Tokyo: Hakuyosha, 1956.

Mott, Michel. *The Seven Mountains of Thomas Merton*. Boston: Houghton Mifflin, 1984.

Mowrer, O. H. *Learning Theory and the Symbolic Process*. New York: Wiley, 1960.

————. *The Crisis in Psychiatry and Religion*. Princeton, N.J.: Van Nostrand, 1961.

————, ed. *Morality and Mental Health: A Book of Readings*. Chicago: Rand McNally, 1967.

————, A. J. Vattano, G. Baxley, and M. Mowrer. *Integrity Groups: The Loss and Recovery of Community*. Urbana, Ill.: Integrity Groups, 1975.

Muto, S. A. *Approaching the Sacred: An Introduction to Spiritual Reading*. Denville, N.J.: Dimension Boosk, 1973.

————. *John of the Cross for Today: The Ascent*. Notre Dame, Ind.: Ave Maria Press, 1991.

————. *John of the Cross for Today: The Dark Night*. Notre Dame, Ind.: Ave Maria Press, 1994.

————. *The Journey Homeward: On the Road of Spiritual Reading*. Denville, N.J.: Dimension Books, 1977.

————. *Pathways of Spiritual Living*. New York: Doubleday; reprinted, Petersham, Mass.: St. Bede's Publications, 1988.

————. *A Practical Guide to Spiritual Reading*. Petersham, Mass.: St. Bede's Publications, 1994.

————. *Renewed at Each Awakening: The Formative Power of Sacred Words*. Denville, N.J.: Dimension Books, 1979.

————. *Steps Along the Way: The Path of Spiritual Reading*. Denville, N.J.: Dimension Books, 1976b.

O'Connell, R. J. *Saint Augustine's Confessions: The Odyssey of Soul*. Boston: Harvard University Press, 1969.

————. *Super-Natural Highs*. Chicago: North American Graphics, 1979.

Otto, R. *The Idea of the Holy.* London: Oxford University Press, 1978.

Pedersen, P. B. "The Field of Intercultural Counseling." In *Counseling Across Cultures,* ed. P. Pedersen, W. Lonner and J. Draguns. Honolulu: University Press of Hawaii, 1976.

———. *Basic Intercultural Counseling Skills.* Honolulu: DISC, 1979.

Peers, E. A. *Handbook to the "Life and Times of St. Theresa and St. John of the Cross."* London: Burns, Oates, & Washburn, 1951.

Peterson, D. "The Insecure Child: Oversocialized or Under-Socialized?" In *Morality and Mental Health,* ed. O. H. Mowrer. Chicago: Rand McNally, 1967.

Phillips, E. L. *The Social Skills Basis of Psychopathology: Alternatives to Abnormal Psychology and Psychiatry.* New York: Grune & Stratton, 1978.

———, and D. N. Wiener. *Discipline, Achievement and Mental Health.* 2nd ed. Englewood Cliffs, N.J.: Prentice-Hall, 1972.

Piaget, Jean. *The Child's Conception of the World.* Trans. Joan and Andrew Tomlinson. New York: Harcourt Brace and Company, 1929.

———. *The Moral Judgment of the Child.* New York: Free Press, 1948.

———. *The Construction of Reality in the Child.* Trans. M. Cook. New York: Basic Books, 1954.

———. *Play, Dreams and Imitation in Childhood.* New York: Norton, 1962.

———, and B. Inhelder. *The Psychology of the Child.* New York: Basic Books, 1969.

Pine, F., and A. Bergman. *The Psychological Birth of the Human Infant: Symbiosis and Individuation.* New York: Basic Books, 1975.

Polanyi, Michael. *Personal Knowledge.* Chicago: University of Chicago Press, 1962.

Prescott, F. C. *The Poetic Mind.* New York: Macmillan, 1922. (Reissued, Ithaca: Cornell University Press, 1959.)

Ravanette, A. T. "Personal Construct Theory: An Approach to the Psychological Investigation of Children and Young People." In *New Perspectives in Personal Construct Theory,* ed. D. Bannister. New York: Academic Press, 1977.

Reich, W. *Character Analysis.* New York: Farrar, Straus, 1971.

Reynolds, D. K. *Naikan Therapy: Meditation for Self-Development in Japan.* Submitted for publication (n.d.).

———. *Quiet Therapies.* Honolulu: University Press of Hawaii, 1980.

Riesman, D. *The Lonely Crowd.* Garden City, N.Y.: Doubleday, 1950.

Rogers, C. R. *Client-Centered Therapy.* Boston: Houghton Mifflin, 1951.

———. *On Becoming a Person.* Boston: Houghton Mifflin, 1961.

———. *On Personal Power.* New York: Delacorte, 1977.

Rohlen, T. *For Harmony and Strength.* Berkeley: University of California Press, 1976.

Rokeach, Milton. *The Nature of Human Values.* New York: Free Press, 1973.

Ruitenbeek, H. M., ed. *Varieties of Personality Theory.* New York: Dutton, 1964.

Satprem. *Sri Aurobindo, Or the Adventure of Consciousness.* New York: Harper & Row, 1968.

Schilder, P. *Mind: Perception and Thought in Their Constructive Aspects.* New York: Columbia University Press, 1942.

————. *The Image and Appearance of the Human Body.* New York: International Universities Press, 1950.

Schloss, G. A. *Psychopoetry.* New York: Grosset & Dunlap, 1976.

Schultz, J. *Das Autogene Training.* Stuttgart: Thieme Verlag, 1932.

————, and W. Luthe. "Autogenic Training." In *Proceedings of the Third International Congress of Psychiatry. Montreal, 1961.* Toronto: University of Toronto Press, 1962.

Schutz, W. C. *Elements of Encounter: A Bodymind Approach.* Big Sur, Calif: Joy Press, 1973.

————. *Profound Simplicity.* New York: Bantam, 1979.

Sheikh, A. A. and P. Richardson, L. M. Moleski. "Psychosomatics and Mental Imagery." In *The Potential of Fantasy and Imagination,* ed. A. A. Sheikh and J. T. Shaffer. New York: Brandon House, 1979.

Shorr, J. E. *Go See the Movie in Your Head.* New York: Popular Library, 1977b.

Shostrom, E. L. *Man, the Manipulator.* Nashville: Abingdon, 1967.

Siegel, E. *Is Beauty the Making One of Opposites?* New York: Terrain Gallery, 1955.

————. *The Aesthetic Method in Self-Conflict, Accompanied by Psychiatry, Economics, Aesthetics.* New York: Definition Press, 1976.

Sorokin, Pitirim A. *The Ways and Power of Love.* South Bend, Ind.: Gateway, 1967.

Spencer-Brown, G. *Laws of Form.* New York: Bantam, 1973.

Spranger, E. *Kultur und Erziehung.* Leipzig: Quelle & Meyer, 1923.

Steiner, C. *Scripts People Live.* New York: Grove Press, 1974.

Streng, F. J. *Emptiness: A Study in Religious Meaning.* Nasvhille/New York: Abingdon Press, 1967.

Sullivan, H. S. *The Interpersonal Theory of Psychiatry.* New York: Norton, 1953.

Suzuki T., and R. Suzuki. "A Follow-Up of Neurotics Treated by Morita Therapy." VI World Congress of Psychiatry, Honolulu, 1977.

Teresa of Avila: The Interior Castle in The Classics of Western Spirituality.

Trans. Kieran Kavanaugh, O.C.D. and Otilio Rodriguez, O.C.D. New York: Paulist Press, 1979.

Twelve Steps and Twelve Traditions. New York: Alcoholics Anonymous World Services, The AA Grapevine, 1952.

Underhill, Evelyn. *Mysticism.* New York: Dutton, 1961.

————. *Practical Mysticism.* New York: Dutton, 1943.

Vaihinger, H. *The Philosophy of "As If."* New York: Harcourt, 1925.

van Griethuysen, T. et al. *Aesthetic Realism: We Have Been There: Six Artists on the Siegel Theory of Opposites.* New York: Definition Press, 1969.

van Kaam, A. *The Art of Existential Counseling.* Denville, N.J.: Dimension Books, 1966.

————. and K. Healy. *The Demon and the Dove: Personality Growth through Literature.* Pittsburgh, Penn.: Duquesne University Press, 1967.

————. *The Dynamics of Spiritual Self-Direction.* Pittsburgh, Penn.: Epiphany Association, 1992.

————. *Existential Foundations of Psychology.* Denville, N.J.: Dimension Books, 1969.

————. *Foundations for Personality Study: An Adrian van Kaam Reader.* Denville, N.J.: Dimension Books, 1983.

————. *In Search of Spiritual Identity.* Denville, N.J.: Dimension Books, 1975.

————. *Living Creatively.* Denville, N.J.: Dimension Books, 1978.

————. *The Music of Eternity.* Notre Dame, Ind.: Ave Maria Press, 1990.

————. *On Being Yourself.* Denville, N.J.: Dimension Books, 1975.

————, and Susan Muto. *The Power of Appreciation.* New York: Crossroad, 1993.

————. *Religion and Personality.* Denville, N.J.: Dimension Books, 1980.

————. *The Transcendent Self: Formative Spirituality of the Middle, Early and Later Years of Life.* Pittsburgh, Penn.: Epiphany Association, 1991.

von Hildebrand, Dietrich. *Transformation in Christ.* New York: Image, 1962.

Watzlawick P., J. Weakland, and R. Fisch. *Change: Principles of Problem Formation and Problem Resolution.* New York: Norton, 1974.

Weir, R. H. *Language in the Crib.* The Hague: Mouton, 1962.

Werner H., and B. Kaplan. *Symbol Formation.* New York: Wiley, 1963.

Wolff, R. P., M. Barrington, and H. Mancuse. *A Critique of Pure Tolerance.* Boston: Beacon Press, 1969.

Wooldridge, Dean E. *The Machinery of the Brain.* New York: McGraw-Hill, 1963.

Zaslow, R. W. *Resistances to Growth and Attachment.* San Jose, Calif.: San Jose State University Press, 1970.

Articles, Theses, Dissertations, Monographs

Agnew, U. "Originality and Spirituality: The Art of Discovering and Becoming Oneself." Master's Thesis. Duquesne University, 1974.

Alexander, F. "Buddhistic Training as an Artificial Catatonia (The Biological Meaning of Psychic Occurrences.)" *Psychoanalytic Review* 18 (1931): 129-45.

Allan, J. "The Identification and Treatment of 'Difficult Babies': Early Signs of Disruption in the Parent-Infant Attachment Bond." *The Canadian Nurse* (1976): 11-17.

Allport, G. W. "Eidetic Imagery." *British Journal of Psychology* 15 (1924): 99-120.

Arbuthnot, J. "Modification of Moral Judgment Through Role Playing." *Developmental Psychology* 11 (1975): 319-24.

Atherton, W., et al. "We Have Changed from Homosexuality." *New York Times*, May 3, 1979, p. B-12.

Blanchard, W. H. "Ecstacy Without Agony is Baloney." *Psychology Today* 3/8 (1970): 8-11.

Bowlby, J. "Separation Anxiety." *International Journal of Psychoanalysis* 41 (1961): 89-113.

———. "The Making and Breaking of Affectional Bonds." *Journal of Psychiatry* 130 (1977): 201-10.

Carter-Haar, B. "Identity and Personal Freedom." *Synthesis* 2 (1975): 56-91.

W. W. Co-Founder. "The Society of Alcoholics Anonymous." *American Journal of Psychology* 106 (1949): 370-75, 1949.

Deikman, A. "Deautomatization and the Mystic Experience." *Psychiatry* 29 (1966): 324-38.

———. "Comments on the GAP Report on Mysticism." *Journal of Nervous and Mental Disease* 165 (1977): 213-17.

Dupont, H. "Meeting the Emotional-Social Needs of Students in a Mainstreamed Environment." *Counseling and Human Development* 10 (1978): 1-12.

Festinger, L. A. "A Theory of Social Comparison Processes." *Human Relations* 7 (1954): 117-40.

Fink, P. J. "Art as a Language." *Journal of Albert Einstein Medical Center* 15 (1967): 143-50.

Frank, J. D. "Some Psychological Determinants of the Level of Aspiration." *American Journal of Psychology* 47 (1935):285-93.

Friedenberg, W. P., J. S. Gillis. "An Experimental Study of the Effectiveness of Attitude Change Techniques for Enhancing Self-Esteem." *Journal of Clinical Psychology* 33 (1977): 1120-24.

Gratton, C. "Some Aspects of the Lived Experience of Interpersonal Trust." *Humanitas* 9 (1973): 273-96.

Karle, W., A. Switzer, S. Gold, and J. Binder. "A New Model for Continuing Affective Education." *Canadian Journal of University Continuing Education* 5/1 (1978): 35-39.

Kitsuse, J. I. "Moral Treatment and Reformation of Inmates in Japanese Prisons." *Psychologia* 8 (1965): 9-23.

Krippner, S., and D. Brown. "Altered States of Consciousness and Mystical-Religious Experiences." *Journal of the Academy of Religion Psych. Research* 2 (1979): 93-110.

LaCrosse, R. E., F. Litman, D. M. Ogilvie, and B. L. White. "The Preschool Project: Experience and the Development of Human Competence in the First Six Years of Life." Monograph No. 9. Harvard University Publications Office.

Levick, M. F. "The Goals of the Art Therapist as Compared to Those of the Art Teacher." *Journal of Albert Einstein Medical Center* 15 (1967): 157-70.

Nidich, S., W. Seeman, and T. Dreshin. "Influence of Transcendental Meditation: A Replication." *Journal of Counsel. Psychology* 20 (1973): 565-66.

O'Connell, W. "The Demystification of Sister Saint Nobody." *Journal of Individual Psychology* 35 (1979): 79-94.

Ogawa, B. K. *Morita Psychotherapy and Christianity.* Ph.D. Dissertation. San Francisco Theological Seminary, 1979.

Perry, M. A. "Didactic Instructions for and Modeling of Empathy." Ph.D. Dissertation. Syracuse University, 1970.

Preston, M. G., and J. A. Bayton. "Differential Effect of a Social Variable Upon Three Levels of Aspiration." *Journal of Exp. Psychology* 29 (1941): 351-69.

Rolls, L. J. "The Interrelation Between Guilt and Anxiety in the Freudian and Mowrerian Hypotheses." Ph.D. Dissertation. University of Ottawa, 1968.

Sharpe, M. J. "Life Form and its Transforming Influence Upon the Person." Master's Thesis. Duquesne University, 1971.

Sperry, R. "Neurology and the Mind-Brain Problem." *American Scientist* 40 (1951): 291-312.

Sprafkin, R. P. "The Rebirth of Moral Treatment." *Professional Psychology* 8/2 (1977): 161-69.

Staub, E. "The Use of Role Playing and Induction in Children's Learning of Helping and Sharing Behavior." *Child Development* 42 (1971): 805-16.

Tournier, P. "Relationships-The Third Dimension of Medicine." *Contact* Christian Medical Commission, World Council of Churches, Geneva, Switzerland 47 (1978): 1-8.

Turin, A. C., J. Nirenberg, and M. Mattingly. "Effects of Comprehensive Relaxation Training (CRT) on Mood. A Preliminary Report on Relaxation Training Plus Caffeine Cessation." *The Behavior Therapist* 2 (July/August 1979): 20–21.

van Kaam, Adrian. "Dynamics of Hope and Despondency in the Parents of Handicapped Children." *Humanitas* 13 (1977): 307-17.

———. "Structures and Systems of Personality." *The New Catholic Encyclopedia.* Washington, D.C.: The Catholic University of America, 1966.

———. "Human Potentialities from the Viewpoint of Existential Psychology." In *Explorations in Human Potentialities,* ed. Herbert A. Otto, Ill.: Charles C. Thomas, Inc., 1966.

———, ed. *Creative Formation of Life and World.* Washington, D.C.: University Press of America, 1982.

———. "Formative Spirituality." In *Dictionary of Pastoral Care and Counseling.* Nashville, Tenn.: Abingdon Press, 1990.

———. "Provisional Glossary of the Science of Foundational Life Formation." *Studies in Formative Spirituality* 1/1 (1980): 137-255; 1/2 (1980): 287-304; 1/3 (1980): 449-79; 2/1 (1981): 117-43.

Index